TOEFL iBT® Codebreaker
Reading Basic

About TOEFL iBT®

The TOEFL iBT®(Internet-based test) consists of four sections: Reading, Listening, Speaking, and Writing. The test is administered in testing centers around the world. It takes about three hours to complete the test and note-taking is allowed throughout. Test takers' scores are made available online approximately 10 days after the test.

THE FORMAT OF THE TOEFL iBT®

Section / Point	Reading	Listening	Speaking	Writing
Questions	3~4 passages • 10 questions each 30~40 questions in total	3~4 lectures • 6 questions each 2~3 conversations • 5 questions each 28~39 questions in total	1 independent task 3 integrated tasks (read/listen/speak, listen/speak) 4 tasks in total	1 integrated task (read/listen/write) 1 independent task 2 tasks in total
Time Limit (Minutes)	54~72	41~57	17	50
Score (Points)	0~30	0~30	0~30	0~30
Tips	• allows note-taking • provides pictures in some passages • passages (academic topics)	• allows note-taking • pronunciation (Multi-English) • lectures (academic topics) conversations (campus life)	• allows note-taking • speak into a microphone connected to a headset • preference/choice (general topics) passages/lectures /conversations (academic topics, campus situation topics)	• allows note-taking • only typing is allowed • passages/lectures (academic topics) preference/agree & disagree (general topics)

* Break Time: 10-minute break after the Listening Section

TOEFL iBT® Reading Section

There are three to four passages in the Reading Section (54~72 min.). For each passage, there are ten questions taken from ten specialized TOEFL® reading question types.

The Format of the Reading Section

Task	Task Description	Question Type
Main Idea	Identify the main topic.	What is the main idea of the passage?
Vocabulary	Recognize the meaning of a word or phrase from the context.	The word _____ in paragraph _____ is closest in meaning to
Reference	Find out what a pronoun or other reference refers to.	The word _____ in the passage refers to
Fact and Negative Fact	Select facts or negative facts from the passage.	According to paragraph _____, _____… All of the following are true EXCEPT (that)
Sentence Simplification	Choose the sentence which best restates and summarizes the information.	Which of the sentences below best expresses the essential information in the highlighted sentence in the passage? *Incorrect* choices change the meaning in important ways or leave out essential information.
Inference	Draw a conclusion based on information in the passage.	What can be inferred about…?
Rhetorical Purpose	Recognize the author's methods, attitude, and purpose.	Why does the author mention _____ in paragraph _____?
Insertion	Put a given sentence into the correct place in the passage.	Look at the four squares [■] that indicate where the following sentence could be added to the passage. Where would the sentence best fit?
Prose Summary	Choose three answer choices out of six to complete a summary of the passage.	**Directions:** An introductory sentence for a brief summary of the passage is provided below. Complete the summary by selecting the THREE answer choices that express the most important ideas in the passage. Some sentences do not belong in the summary because they express ideas that are not presented in the passage or are minor ideas in the passage.
Category Chart	Classify the given answer choices in the proper category in the chart.	**Directions:** Select the appropriate phrases from the answer choices and match them to the category to which they relate. TWO of the answer choices will NOT be used.

TIPS for the Reading Section: Read various subjects frequently to increase your background knowledge. It is essential to improve your vocabulary and be able to figure out the meaning of vocabulary from the context. Practicing note-taking skills is important to help you get the gist of and analyze the passage in a short time. Building up the ability to skim and scan passages for main ideas and supporting details is also needed.

PRIMARY FEATURES
of TOEFL iBT® Codebreaker Reading

A three-level test prep series designed to develop reading skills for test takers who want to improve their preliminary scores on the TOEFL iBT®! TOEFL iBT® Codebreaker Reading provides:

- A step-by-step learning process to strengthen primary reading skills
- Plenty of themes that cover every academic area
- Appropriate level of difficulty in dealing with each step of the units
- Essential test taking strategies with a sufficient number of practice questions
- A variety of vocabulary activities including vocabulary tests in the units
- Important tips for test takers to improve note-taking skills
- Summary activities for developing passage comprehension skills
- A number of tests including progress tests 1 & 2 and an actual test
- A QR code for every passage(Student Book) and MP3 files(www.ybmbooks.com)
- A reading time checkup based on WPM(words per minute) to train test takers in speed reading

FORMAT
of TOEFL iBT® Codebreaker Reading

01
PART STRATEGY

TOEFL iBT® Codebreaker reading questions fall into three categories: Basic Information Questions, Inference Questions, and Reading to Learn Questions. Core reading skills and strategies related to the questions in each category are presented with carefully designed exercises.

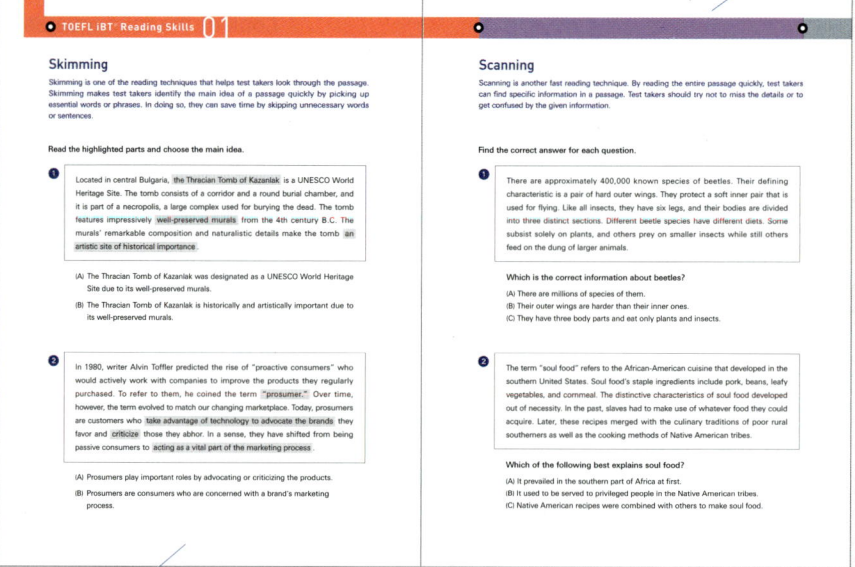

Provides core skills and strategies related to essential question types in each part

Offers adequate drills and exercises for enhancing comprehension of primary strategies

Introduces a specific question type and useful strategies for approaching it

Provides QR codes

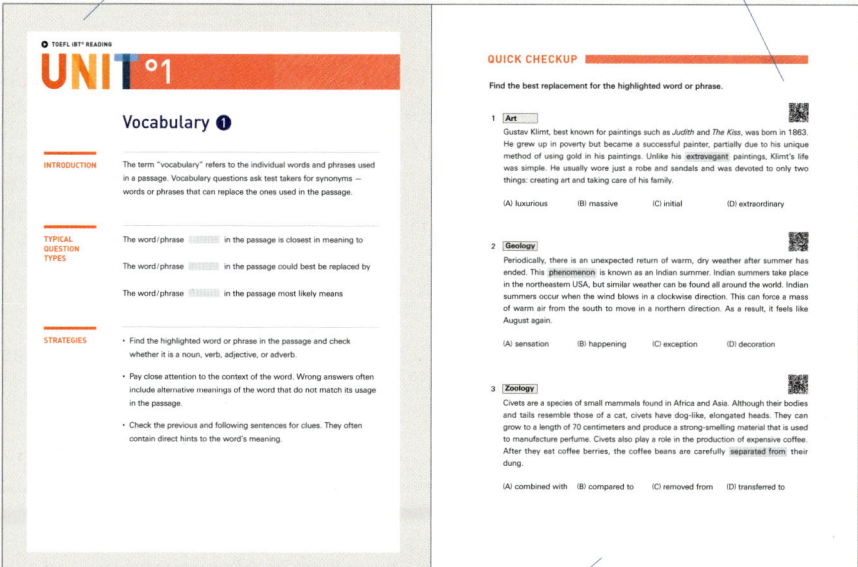

Offers short passages and questions for warming up

02
OUTLINE

At the outset of each unit, the Outline section introduces test takers to the question type and strategies for approaching it. This is followed by Quick Checkup, which offers test takers additional help to understand each question type.

Offers essential words and collocations with their definitions

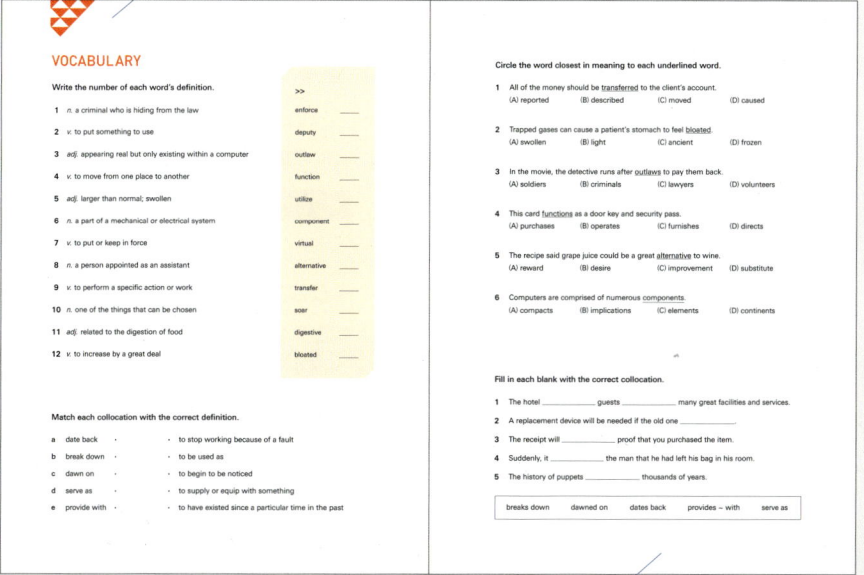

Provides vocabulary checkup exercises

03
VOCABULARY

The Vocabulary section offers a list of key words and collocations with their definitions ahead of the passages. Alongside these are some initial vocabulary questions, with vocabulary checkup exercises offered on the next page.

04
STEPS 01-03

Steps 01-03 offer a range of exercises designed to boost test takers' reading skills and question solving abilities. Classified according to difficulty level, each step contains activities intended to enforce reading comprehension skills.

05
UNIT TEST & VOCABULARY TEST

Final unit tests are provided to enhance test takers' familiarity with TOEFL iBT® reading question types. Each unit test focuses on the question type presented in that unit so that they can practice it more than other question types. In addition, vocabulary tests are provided to reinforce their vocabulary acquisition.

Offers a variety of TOEFL® reading questions

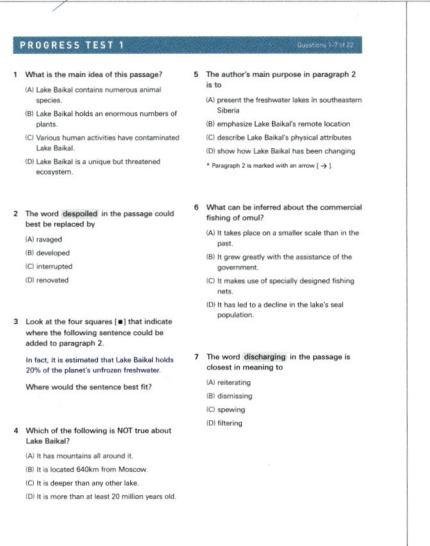

Gives longer thematic passages than the Unit Test passages

06

PROGRESS TESTS 1 & 2

After finishing several units, a Progress Test is provided as an interim evaluation.

Offers a variety of TOEFL® reading questions

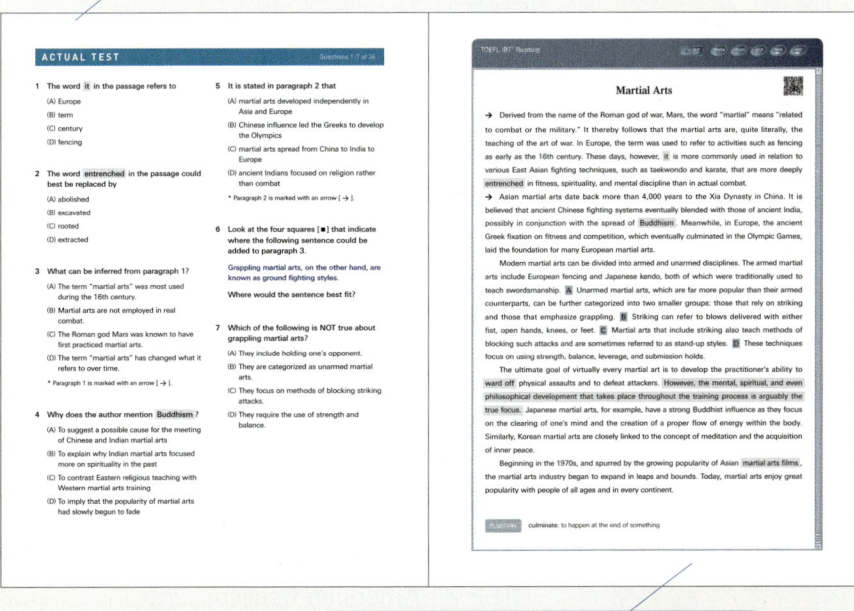

Provides the longest thematic passages in the book

07

ACTUAL TEST

An Actual Test is provided at the end of the book as a final checkup. This gives test takers an essential experience of real test conditions and checks their ability to correctly answer the question types that they have learned throughout the book.

* Provides a QR code for every passage in the book
* Offers free MP3 files (www.ybmbooks.com)

CONTENTS

Basic — TOEFL iBT® Reading

PART 1 — Basic Information Questions

TOEFL iBT® Reading Skills 01 — 12

UNIT 1 | Vocabulary 1 14
Quick Checkup
STEP 1 | American Sheriffs
STEP 2 | 3D Printing
STEP 3 | Bitcoins
Unit Test | An Apple a Day

UNIT 2 | Vocabulary 2 28
Quick Checkup
STEP 1 | Lacrosse
STEP 2 | Pressure
STEP 3 | Moss
Unit Test | The Interstellar Medium

UNIT 3 | Reference 42
Quick Checkup
STEP 1 | Emily Dickinson
STEP 2 | Pectin
STEP 3 | The Liberty Bell
Unit Test | Limestone Caves

UNIT 4 | Fact and Negative Fact 56
Quick Checkup
STEP 1 | The Thracian Tomb of Kazanlak
STEP 2 | Electricity
STEP 3 | Norovirus
Unit Test | Heinrich Schliemann

UNIT 5 | Sentence Simplification 70
Quick Checkup
STEP 1 | The Galapagos Tortoise
STEP 2 | American Realism
STEP 3 | Saturn
Unit Test | Effective Demand and Supply

Progress Test 1 86

PART 2 — Inference Questions

TOEFL iBT® Reading Skills 02 — 96

UNIT 6 | Inference 98
Quick Checkup
STEP 1 | Litmus
STEP 2 | Monet at Giverny
STEP 3 | Toothpaste
Unit Test | Plant-Animal Symbiosis

UNIT 7 | Rhetorical Purpose 112
Quick Checkup
STEP 1 | Canned Food
STEP 2 | Motion Capture
STEP 3 | Human Skin
Unit Test | Radio Astronomy

UNIT 8 | Insertion 126
Quick Checkup
STEP 1 | Axolotls
STEP 2 | The Irish Potato Famine
STEP 3 | Allergies
Unit Test | Monsoons

PART 3 — Reading to Learn Questions

TOEFL iBT® Reading Skills 03 — 142

UNIT 9 | Prose Summary 144
Quick Checkup
STEP 1 | Musicals and Operas
STEP 2 | Michelangelo
STEP 3 | The Archaeological Park and Ruins of Quirigua
Unit Test | Endocrine Disruptors

UNIT 10 | Category Chart 158
Quick Checkup
STEP 1 | MLB
STEP 2 | Lice and Mites
STEP 3 | German Militarism
Unit Test | Pierre-Simon Laplace

Progress Test 2 174
Actual Test 184

[TOEFL iBT® CODEBREAKER READING]

PART 1

Basic Information Questions

The part for Basic Information Questions involves effectively scanning the text for key facts and important information. To correctly answer the questions, test takers should be able to understand the general topic or main idea, supporting details, vocabulary in context, and pronoun references.

TOEFL iBT® Reading Skills 01

UNIT 1 | Vocabulary 1

UNIT 2 | Vocabulary 2

UNIT 3 | Reference

UNIT 4 | Fact and Negative Fact

UNIT 5 | Sentence Simplification

TOEFL iBT® Reading Skills 01

Skimming

Skimming is one of the reading techniques that helps test takers look through the passage. Skimming makes test takers identify the main idea of a passage quickly by picking up essential words or phrases. In doing so, they can save time by skipping unnecessary words or sentences.

Read the highlighted parts and choose the main idea.

Located in central Bulgaria, the Thracian Tomb of Kazanlak is a UNESCO World Heritage Site. The tomb consists of a corridor and a round burial chamber, and it is part of a necropolis, a large complex used for burying the dead. The tomb features impressively well-preserved murals from the 4th century B.C. The murals' remarkable composition and naturalistic details make the tomb an artistic site of historical importance.

(A) The Thracian Tomb of Kazanlak was designated as a UNESCO World Heritage Site due to its well-preserved murals.

(B) The Thracian Tomb of Kazanlak is historically and artistically important due to its well-preserved murals.

In 1980, writer Alvin Toffler predicted the rise of "proactive consumers" who would actively work with companies to improve the products they regularly purchased. To refer to them, he coined the term "prosumer." Over time, however, the term evolved to match our changing marketplace. Today, prosumers are customers who take advantage of technology to advocate the brands they favor and criticize those they abhor. In a sense, they have shifted from being passive consumers to acting as a vital part of the marketing process.

(A) Prosumers play important roles by advocating or criticizing the products.

(B) Prosumers are consumers who are concerned with a brand's marketing process.

Scanning

Scanning is another fast reading technique. By reading the entire passage quickly, test takers can find specific information in a passage. Test takers should try not to miss the details or to get confused by the given information.

Find the correct answer for each question.

There are approximately 400,000 known species of beetles. Their defining characteristic is a pair of hard outer wings. They protect a soft inner pair that is used for flying. Like all insects, they have six legs, and their bodies are divided into three distinct sections. Different beetle species have different diets. Some subsist solely on plants, and others prey on smaller insects while still others feed on the dung of larger animals.

Which is the correct information about beetles?

(A) There are millions of species of them.
(B) Their outer wings are harder than their inner ones.
(C) They have three body parts and eat only plants and insects.

The term "soul food" refers to the African-American cuisine that developed in the southern United States. Soul food's staple ingredients include pork, beans, leafy vegetables, and cornmeal. The distinctive characteristics of soul food developed out of necessity. In the past, slaves had to make use of whatever food they could acquire. Later, these recipes merged with the culinary traditions of poor rural southerners as well as the cooking methods of Native American tribes.

Which of the following best explains soul food?

(A) It prevailed in the southern part of Africa at first.
(B) It used to be served to privileged people in the Native American tribes.
(C) Native American recipes were combined with others to make soul food.

Reading Skills 1 13

UNIT °1

Vocabulary ❶

INTRODUCTION

The term "vocabulary" refers to the individual words and phrases used in a passage. Vocabulary questions ask test takers for synonyms — words or phrases that can replace the ones used in the passage.

TYPICAL QUESTION TYPES

The word/phrase _____ in the passage is closest in meaning to

The word/phrase _____ in the passage could best be replaced by

The word/phrase _____ in the passage most likely means

STRATEGIES

- Find the highlighted word or phrase in the passage and check whether it is a noun, verb, adjective, or adverb.

- Pay close attention to the context of the word. Wrong answers often include alternative meanings of the word that do not match its usage in the passage.

- Check the previous and following sentences for clues. They often contain direct hints to the word's meaning.

QUICK CHECKUP

Find the best replacement for the highlighted word or phrase.

1 Art

Gustav Klimt, best known for paintings such as *Judith* and *The Kiss*, was born in 1863. He grew up in poverty but became a successful painter, partially due to his unique method of using gold in his paintings. Unlike his extravagant paintings, Klimt's life was simple. He usually wore just a robe and sandals and was devoted to only two things: creating art and taking care of his family.

(A) luxurious   (B) massive   (C) initial   (D) extraordinary

2 Geology

Periodically, there is an unexpected return of warm, dry weather after summer has ended. This phenomenon is known as an Indian summer. Indian summers take place in the northeastern USA, but similar weather can be found all around the world. Indian summers occur when the wind blows in a clockwise direction. This can force a mass of warm air from the south to move in a northern direction. As a result, it feels like August again.

(A) sensation   (B) happening   (C) exception   (D) decoration

3 Zoology

Civets are a species of small mammals found in Africa and Asia. Although their bodies and tails resemble those of a cat, civets have dog-like, elongated heads. They can grow to a length of 70 centimeters and produce a strong-smelling material that is used to manufacture perfume. Civets also play a role in the production of expensive coffee. After they eat coffee berries, the coffee beans are carefully separated from their dung.

(A) combined with   (B) compared to   (C) removed from   (D) transferred to

VOCABULARY

Write the number of each word's definition.

1 *n.* a criminal who is hiding from the law

2 *v.* to put something to use

3 *adj.* appearing real but only existing within a computer

4 *v.* to move from one place to another

5 *adj.* larger than normal; swollen

6 *n.* a part of a mechanical or electrical system

7 *v.* to put or keep in force

8 *n.* a person appointed as an assistant

9 *v.* to perform a specific action or work

10 *n.* one of the things that can be chosen

11 *adj.* related to the digestion of food

12 *v.* to increase by a great deal

\>\>

enforce _____

deputy _____

outlaw _____

function _____

utilize _____

component _____

virtual _____

alternative _____

transfer _____

soar _____

digestive _____

bloated _____

Match each collocation with the correct definition.

a date back •   • to stop working because of a fault

b break down •   • to be used as

c dawn on •   • to begin to be noticed

d serve as •   • to supply or equip with something

e provide with •   • to have existed since a particular time in the past

Circle the word closest in meaning to each underlined word.

1. All of the money should be underlined{transferred} to the client's account.
   (A) reported   (B) described   (C) moved   (D) caused

2. Trapped gases can cause a patient's stomach to feel bloated.
   (A) swollen   (B) light   (C) ancient   (D) frozen

3. In the movie, the detective runs after outlaws to pay them back.
   (A) soldiers   (B) criminals   (C) lawyers   (D) volunteers

4. This card functions as a door key and security pass.
   (A) purchases   (B) operates   (C) furnishes   (D) directs

5. The recipe said grape juice could be a great alternative to wine.
   (A) reward   (B) desire   (C) improvement   (D) substitute

6. Computers are comprised of numerous components.
   (A) compacts   (B) implications   (C) elements   (D) continents

Fill in each blank with the correct collocation.

1. The hotel _____ guests _____ many great facilities and services.

2. A replacement device will be needed if the old one _____.

3. The receipt will _____ proof that you purchased the item.

4. Suddenly, it _____ the man that he had left his bag in his room.

5. The history of puppets _____ thousands of years.

| breaks down | dawned on | dates back | provides ~ with | serve as |

STEP 01

Timed Reading (WPM)
☐ 1'00" ☐ 1'30" ☐ 2'00"

History

American Sheriffs

Sheriffs are government officials who enforce the law. The history of sheriffs in the USA dates back about 200 years. Sheriffs were found in most of the states, and they were generally the highest law enforcement in the area.

Sheriffs had a big role in the country's westward expansion. In the 1800s, many Americans began to move west. However, because there was so much open space, it was difficult to keep everyone safe. Therefore, each community chose one of its members to be a sheriff.

Some sheriffs were responsible for protecting an enormous amount of territory. In this area, there were often one sheriff and many criminals. When in need of assistance, sheriffs could make other people their deputies. Together, they battled outlaws and often engaged in gunfights. In the history of America, sheriffs have been indispensable at eliminating criminals, just like today's police officers.

Note-Taking

American Sheriffs

What They Do	_____ the law
When Started	_____ about 200 yrs.
What They Did	1. helped the country's _____
	2. _____ an enormous _____ w/ their _____
	└ battled _____ & often had _____
	→ have been _____ at eliminating _____

Abbreviations & Symbols for Note-Taking: yrs. (years) w/: with &: and

1 The phrase had a big role in the passage could best be replaced by

   (A) refused to participate
   (B) asked for official approval
   (C) played an important part
   (D) offered helpful advice

2 The word enormous in the passage is closest in meaning to

   (A) anonymous
   (B) numerous
   (C) countable
   (D) immense

SUMMARY

Sheriffs are _____ who _____ the law. Sheriffs have a _____ history in the USA. Most of the states had them as _____ _____. The sheriffs participated in _____. Each sheriff was responsible for _____. Sheriffs made other people their _____ and battled _____. They have been _____ in the history of America like _____.

VOCAB

Match each word with the correct definition.

a official   •   • to take part in something

b expansion   •   • a person who is charged with certain duties

c territory   •   • help or support

d assistance   •   • the process of becoming bigger in size

e engage in   •   • any tract of land or region

STEP 02

Timed Reading (WPM)
☐ 1'00" ☐ 1'30" ☐ 2'00"

Technology

3D Printing

A 3D printer is a machine that is capable of creating nearly anything people want. The process of working the machine is simple: The user downloads a picture of an object, and the machine makes a copy.

A 3D printer functions much like normal ink printers, but, instead of ink, it uses materials such as plastic, wax, and even metal. Layer by layer, it produces actual objects with these materials. It may take many hours and thousands of layers, but the final result is an exact copy.

Surprisingly, 3D printing technology has been around since 1986. In its early phase, it was used solely for engineering and architecture. These days, however, 3D printers are utilized in a wide variety of industries. Some airplane components and plastic toys are manufactured with 3D printers. And doctors use 3D printing to recreate parts of patients' bodies, which allows them to practice before performing risky surgery. Even some food businesses are beginning to use 3D printing by using edible ingredients to create food products. Soon, 3D printing could allow astronauts in space to make any equipment parts they require. The 3D printers are considered a great move forward in science, and they seem to be changing people's lives significantly.

Note-Taking

MI = Main Idea   SD = Supporting Details

P1 MI   a _____ printer   SD   capable of _____ nearly anything

P2 MI   works like a _____ but uses different _____
    SD   - uses _____
         - produces actual objects _____ with these materials

P3 MI   is _____ in a wide variety of _____
    SD   • some _____ & plastic toys
         • _____ — practice before performing _____
         • _____ — use _____
         • astronauts — make _____

20 TOEFL iBT® Codebreaker

1   What is the main idea of the passage?

   (A) 3D printers are replacing normal ink printers.
   (B) There are many current and potential uses of 3D printers.
   (C) 3D printers were invented to help the space industry.
   (D) There are several kinds of materials that 3D printers can use.

2   The phrase capable of in the passage most likely means

   (A) available for
   (B) close to
   (C) able to be
   (D) comprised of

3   The word manufactured in the passage is closest in meaning to

   (A) produced
   (B) maintained
   (C) destroyed
   (D) captured

✱ VOCAB

Write the correct word for each definition.

a   a thin piece of material   _____

b   precise and correct   _____

c   dangerous; hazardous   _____

d   an element used to make something   _____

e   to have a need for   _____

exact
layer
require
risky
ingredient

Bitcoins

Bitcoins are a form of virtual currency. In other words, they are a type of money that does not exist in the actual world. However, they can be used to purchase actual products and services from real companies.

The bitcoin system was created in 2009 by an enigmatic person named Satoshi Nakamoto. In fact, no one is sure if Satoshi Nakamoto is an actual person or a group of people. Bitcoins are designed to serve as an alternative to national currencies, such as dollars and euros. They can be used to pay for things online instead of cash or credit cards. When bitcoins are transferred from a buyer to a seller, the transaction is recorded in a public database.

Governments are concerned that bitcoins can easily be stolen by hackers. It has dawned on them that they might be used for illegal purposes. For example, stolen goods could be purchased without the government's knowledge. Although more and more companies are beginning to accept bitcoins, the percentage of purchases made using bitcoins is minuscule compared to other online payment methods, such as credit cards. Instead, many bitcoin owners simply keep them as an investment since they believe their bitcoins will be more valuable in the future.

This may or may not be a wise approach. Currently, the value of bitcoins is fluctuating wildly, especially when compared to highly stable national currencies. Bitcoin investors are gambling on the hope that as this high-tech money becomes more widely accepted, its value will soar.

VOCAB

Find the correct word in the passage for each of the given definition.

a   something that is used as a medium of exchange: _____

b   mysterious and difficult to understand: _____

c   against the law or forbidden by law: _____

d   to change in an irregular way: _____

1 The word they in the passage refers to

(A) bitcoins (B) governments (C) hackers (D) stolen goods

2 The word minuscule in the passage could best be replaced by

(A) difficult (B) convenient (C) miraculous (D) insignificant

3 The word stable in the passage is closest in meaning to

(A) eligible (B) criminal (C) balanced (D) intelligent

4 All of the following are true about bitcoins EXCEPT:

(A) They only exist online.
(B) They were created in 2009.
(C) They are illegal in many countries.
(D) They can be worth a lot of money.

Note-Taking

MI = Main Idea   SD = Supporting Details

P1 MI _____
   SD _____
P2 MI _____
   SD _____
      _____
P3 MI _____
   SD _____
      _____
P4 MI _____
   SD _____

UNIT TEST

1. What is the main idea of the passage?

   (A) People in America disagree about the health benefits of apples.

   (B) Apples are a healthy food that should be eaten in the morning.

   (C) There are many beneficial chemicals that are found in apples.

   (D) Eating apples is an excellent way to get B vitamins.

2. The phrase a favorable source of in the passage could best be replaced by

   (A) the result of

   (B) a reason for

   (C) the cure for

   (D) a provider of

3. Why does the author mention a cup of coffee in the passage?

   (A) To emphasize how long energy from apples goes on

   (B) To show how drinking coffee can be hazardous

   (C) To offer an alternative to eating apples at night

   (D) To give an example of a good source of fructose

4. The word stimulates in the passage most likely means

   (A) disrupts

   (B) prescribes

   (C) encourages

   (D) simulates

5. Which of the sentences below best expresses the essential information in the highlighted sentence in the passage?

   (A) Only bright red fruits and flowers contain flavonoids.

   (B) The brightness of the colors of fruits and flowers comes from flavonoids.

   (C) Without flavonoids, fruits and flowers could not live.

   (D) Flavonoids give apples their sweet, flowery taste.

6. According to the passage, it is NOT true that

   (A) it is better to eat apples early in the day

   (B) a lot of fiber can be found in apples

   (C) coffee contain more fructose than apples

   (D) flavonoids can help you avoid diabetes

An Apple a Day

Apples are one of the healthiest foods you can eat every day. A traditional American proverb states: An apple a day keeps the doctor away. But it does not specifically say anything about the best time of day to eat apples. It is generally believed that eating an apple in the morning is good for people, but eating an apple in the evening is like eating poison.

There is actually a scientific reason behind this belief. One benefit of apples is that they are a favorable source of fructose, which is a natural form of sugar that gives you a big boost of energy. The energy you get from an apple is longer lasting than that provided by a cup of coffee. Clearly, this is something most people would rather experience in the morning than right before bedtime.

Apples also contain high levels of pectin, a kind of dietary fiber. Fiber stimulates bowel movements, which help maintain the health of your digestive system. But if you eat an apple shortly before going to bed, this can cause problems. While you are asleep, your bowels can fill up with gas, making you feel bloated and uncomfortable. You may also wake up several times to use the bathroom, which will prevent you from getting a good night's sleep.

Other health benefits of apples come from flavonoids, beta carotene, and B vitamins. Flavonoids are the material that gives flowers and fruits their bright colors, such as the deep red of apples. When eaten, flavonoids can decrease your risk of heart disease, diabetes, and other illnesses. Meanwhile, beta carotene helps prevent cancer, and B vitamins provide the body with a wide variety of important benefits. Apparently, starting your day with an apple really can keep the doctor away.

GLOSSARY
proverb: a well-known statement that offers good advice
bowel: the tubes through which food passes from the stomach to the anus
diabetes: a medical condition in which people have too much sugar in their blood

VOCABULARY TEST

Recall the essential words in the unit to reinforce your vocabulary acquisition. Write the meaning of each word in your language.

exact	method
digestive	soar
expansion	bowel
proverb	transfer
mammal	utilize
outlaw	enigmatic
poverty	component
bloated	official
alternative	risky
diabetes	elongated
ingredient	deputy
virtual	currency
function	require
devoted	resemble
fluctuate	territory

enforce	layer
assistance	illegal
engage in	break down
serve as	date back
provide with	dawn on

Complete each sentence with the correct word or collocation.

1 Klimt employed the unique _____ of using gold in his paintings.

2 3D printers are _____ in a wide variety of industries.

3 A bitcoin is a form of _____ currency.

4 Civets are mammals that have dog-like, _____ heads.

5 Dietary fiber stimulates our _____ movements.

6 Currently, the value of bitcoins _____ widely.

7 Doctors use 3D printing to practice before performing _____ surgery.

8 Your stomach can fill up with gas, making you feel _____.

9 Some sheriffs were responsible for protecting an enormous amount of _____.

10 It has _____ governments that the money might be used for illegal purposes.

| utilized | method | elongated | fluctuates | bowel |
| bloated | territory | dawned on | risky | virtual |

UNIT °2

Vocabulary 2

INTRODUCTION

Vocabulary questions ask about a test taker's knowledge of the words appearing in a passage. The test taker is supposed to choose the word or phrase that has the closest meaning with the highlighted vocabulary. These questions also challenge the test taker to find the meanings of unfamiliar words through context, prefixes, suffixes, and roots.

TYPICAL QUESTION TYPES

The word/phrase _____ in the passage is closest in meaning to

The word/phrase _____ in the passage could best be replaced by

The word/phrase _____ in the passage most likely means

STRATEGIES

- Check the words for familiar prefixes or suffixes. These can provide helpful hints about some words' meanings.

- Find context clues in the sentences. The sentences positioned before and after the highlighted words and phrases will give helpful information.

- Read the sentences with the highlighted words and phrases carefully and decide whether they are positive or negative. This will allow you to eliminate the choices that do not match the sentence's tones.

QUICK CHECKUP

Find the best replacement for the highlighted word or phrase.

1 Custom

Vappu is a traditional Finnish holiday held to welcome the coming of spring. It begins on the last day of April and continues until the first day of May. In modern times, it is celebrated primarily by university students. Wearing white student caps, they gather together to eat fried cakes and to drink special lemonade. The next day, they go to the park and have lavish picnics featuring white tablecloths, silver candle holders, and expensive food.

(A) solely (B) mainly (C) pleasantly (D) temporarily

2 Culture

People with hearing disabilities often communicate through sign language. Many people believe that there is a global common sign language, but that is not the case. Like spoken language, sign language is different all around the world. In fact, more than 100 varieties are known to exist. Another common misconception is that sign languages consist only of hand gestures. In reality, they are a combination of hand gestures, body movements, and facial expressions.

(A) false belief (B) helpful advice (C) strict rule (D) wise approach

3 History

The history of ice cream can be traced back for centuries. Originally, it was made by mixing honey with snow. The Chinese later used frozen milk. The explorer Marco Polo eventually brought this recipe to Italy. When King Henry II of France married an Italian noblewoman in the 16th century, she introduced ice cream to France. Rather than being the ubiquitous treat it is today, however, it was eaten only by royalty then.

(A) marvelous (B) unqualified (C) exclusive (D) widespread

VOCABULARY

Write the number of each word's definition.

1 *v.* to move slowly and without purpose

2 *v.* to contain large amounts of something

3 *v.* to dry up and to die

4 *v.* to go up

5 *v.* to begin doing or using something new

6 *adj.* containing large amounts of matter in a small space

7 *v.* to change something into a different form

8 *v.* to go beyond an amount in quantity, degree, rate, etc.

9 *n.* the act of breathing out

10 *v.* to make a guess based on limited information

11 *adj.* moderately or slightly wet

12 *adj.* originating from a local region

>>

indigenous _____

adopt _____

ascend _____

exhalation _____

abound _____

moist _____

convert _____

wither _____

estimate _____

exceed _____

drift _____

dense _____

Match each collocation with the correct definition.

a spread out •   • a range of different things

b a variety of •   • having large distances between one another

c evolve into •   • to get used to or to adjust to

d carry away •   • to take something and to bring it somewhere else

e adapt to •   • to gradually develop into something different

30 TOEFL iBT® Codebreaker

Circle the word closest in meaning to each underlined word.

1. We watched the hot-air balloon <u>ascending</u> in the sky.
   (A) drowning   (B) descending   (C) rising   (D) exploding

2. The bathroom walls were <u>moist</u> after he took a shower.
   (A) visible   (B) warm   (C) damp   (D) cracked

3. The <u>indigenous</u> people do not trust visitors.
   (A) unfriendly   (B) powerful   (C) ancient   (D) local

4. Travelers often use airport banks to <u>convert</u> their money to the local currency.
   (A) sell   (B) change   (C) loan   (D) borrow

5. Herds of hungry animals <u>drifted</u> through the countryside to find food.
   (A) originated   (B) contacted   (C) wandered   (D) discovered

6. The total price of the products seems to <u>exceed</u> 2,000 U.S. dollars.
   (A) surpass   (B) format   (C) insert   (D) extract

Fill in each blank with the correct collocation.

1. There are few towns in the desert, and they are _____.

2. Small pieces of food were _____ by ants.

3. The stray cat did not _____ its new home, so it ran away.

4. There are _____ cultures existing side by side on the island.

5. The small shop eventually _____ a worldwide business.

| evolved into | a variety of | adapt to | carried away | spread out |

STEP 01

Timed Reading (WPM)
☐ 1'00" ☐ 1'30" ☐ 2'00"

Sports

Lacrosse

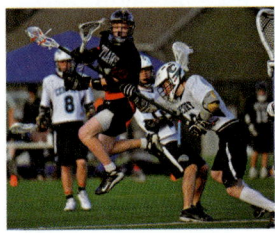

Although baseball is **unambiguously** considered America's national sport, another American sport has been around much longer. Originally known as stickball, it was first played by indigenous tribes in North America in the 17th century. Later, it was adopted by European settlers, who gave it the French name "lacrosse."

In Native American lacrosse, there were hundreds of players on a field that was miles long. However, it changed into the modern version of the game over time. Today, a standard lacrosse field measures 110 yards long and 60 yards wide. Each team has just 10 players, including a goalkeeper, who carry long sticks with a loose net on one end. The ball is carried in the net and passed from player to player. A team scores by **hurling** the ball into the opposing team's goal. Even though it is not as popular as baseball or basketball, lacrosse is one of the fastest-growing sports in North America.

Lacrosse

In the Past	Today
- known as _____	- called lacrosse
- _____ — miles long	- field is 110 yards long & _____
- hundreds of players	- _____ on each team
- played by _____ in North America	- one of the _____ sports in North America

32 TOEFL iBT® Codebreaker

1. The word unambiguously in the passage most likely means

   (A) notably
   (B) virtually
   (C) obviously
   (D) continuously

2. The word hurling in the passage is closest in meaning to

   (A) pitching
   (B) blocking
   (C) winning
   (D) suspending

SUMMARY

_____ has been around much longer than _____. Native Americans first played it in _____. When Europeans began to play it, they _____ In the past, the field was _____, and there were _____. Today, the field is much smaller, and there are just _____ on _____. Players _____ and _____ a ball as they try to _____ it into the other team's goal. Lacrosse is one of the _____ in North America.

VOCAB

Match each word with the correct definition.

a   tribe   •   • not firmly held or fixed in place

b   settlers   •   • being in competition with one another

c   modern   •   • people who go to live in a new country or region

d   loose   •   • a group of people with a common ancestor, culture, etc.

e   opposing   •   • relating to the present time

Pressure

Scuba diving allows people to spend long periods deep underwater. The human body, however, does not adapt to such depths. The primary cause for concern is pressure. Air exerts approximately 14.7 pounds per square inch of pressure. This is referred to as one atmosphere (ATA) of pressure. Underwater, the air continues to exert 1 ATA of pressure. But for every 10 meters divers descend, an additional ATA of pressure is experienced, causing the air inside their bodies to compress.

As the divers ascend, the air expands, potentially causing their eardrums or lungs to burst. To prevent this, divers must return to the surface gradually to allow the excess air to naturally be discharged from their bodies. Increased pressure also increases the rate at which body tissues absorb nitrogen gas. During a slow ascent, it is released through exhalation. But if divers ascend too rapidly, the nitrogen expands before it can be released and forms tiny bubbles in tissues and blood. This can lead to decompression sickness, a painful condition commonly referred to as the bends, which can cause strokes or paralysis. These dangers, however, can be avoided if divers carefully map out their descents and calculate exactly how deep they can go and how long they can safely stay there.

Note-Taking

MI = Main Idea   SD = Supporting Details

P1 MI _____ when scuba diving — the primary cause for _____
   SD causes the _____ inside the body to _____

P2 MI _____ pressure in water & its effects
   SD • causes _____ within the _____ to compress during _____
        → _____ or lungs _____ — divers must return _____
      • increases the _____ at which _____ absorb _____
        → can lead to _____ — the bends
        : can be _____ if divers carefully map out their _____

1 The word exerts in the passage could best be replaced by

   (A) twists
   (B) applies
   (C) professes
   (D) lengthens

2 The word discharged in the passage most likely means

   (A) depicted
   (B) located
   (C) chased
   (D) released

3 The word it in the passage refers to

   (A) pressure
   (B) rate
   (C) nitrogen gas
   (D) ascent

VOCAB

Write the correct word for each definition.

a	to suddenly break and open	_____
b	a gradual reduction in atmospheric pressure	_____
c	the rupture of a blood vessel in the brain	_____
d	the loss of the ability to move and feel in one's body	_____
e	to determine by reasoning or practical experience	_____

stroke
calculate
burst
paralysis
decompression

STEP 03

Timed Reading (WPM)
☐ 2'00" ☐ 2'30" ☐ 3'00"

Botany

Moss

During the early stages of the Earth's development, there was no life on the land. However, the oceans abounded with plants and animals. Algae were the first form of plant life that was able to live outside the water. More than 500 million years ago, these algae evolved into moss.

Although early moss could live on land, it still needed lots of water. In addition, there was little dirt on the Earth at the time. Therefore, it grew mostly on rocks that were in moist places. And instead of long roots that could seek water in the soil, it grew rhizoids, which are like short roots that can cling to hard surfaces. Like most plants, this moss used photosynthesis to convert sunlight into food. And to reproduce, it generated spores similar to tiny seeds, which were carried away by the wind.

After about 100 million years, some of this moss evolved into more advanced plants. However, simple moss can still be found all around the world. It has not changed much from its early ancestors. It grows in dark, cool, wet places, such as on rocks and on the sides of trees like it used to. During times of drought, it turns brown and seems to wither and die. It can remain this way for weeks. But as soon as heavy rains return, it turns green and comes back to life. It may not be tall like trees or pretty like flowers, but moss is more resilient than it looks.

⚙ VOCAB

Find the correct word in the passage for each of the given definition.

a the way that green plants make food by using sunlight: _____

b to produce offspring: _____

c superior or more highly developed: _____

d early types of animals and plants: _____

1. What is the main idea of the passage?

   (A) The very first animals to live on land survived by eating moss.
   (B) Both moss and algae are able to live on the land and in the water.
   (C) Without moss, other kinds of plants could not get enough water.
   (D) Moss is a simple form of plant life that has existed for a long time.

2. Why does the author mention roots in the passage?

   (A) To show how moss gets water
   (B) To contrast them with rhizoids
   (C) To explain why moss evolved
   (D) To introduce photosynthesis

3. The word cling in the passage could best be replaced by

   (A) copy   (B) grip   (C) erode   (D) resemble

4. The word resilient in the passage most likely means

   (A) prevalent   (B) fragrant   (C) restless   (D) persistent

Note-Taking

MI = Main Idea   SD = Supporting Details

P1 MI _____
   SD _____
P2 MI _____
   SD _____
P3 MI _____
   SD _____

UNIT TEST

1. What is the main idea of the passage?

   (A) The material that exists between the stars creates a new star.

   (B) The number of stars is decreasing rapidly due to the interstellar medium.

   (C) Our galaxy consists mostly of gas and dust, which are called interstellar clouds.

   (D) The universe is getting denser every day because of the harmful interstellar medium.

2. The word scattered in the passage most likely means

   (A) disappeared

   (B) scratched

   (C) dispersed

   (D) calculated

3. The word grain in the passage is closest in meaning to

   (A) detail

   (B) organization

   (C) electron

   (D) particle

4. What is the author's main purpose in paragraph 2?

   (A) To emphasize the size of the interstellar medium

   (B) To contrast the interstellar medium and the Milky Way

   (C) To describe where the interstellar medium is found

   (D) To explain what the interstellar medium consists of

   * Paragraph 2 is marked with an arrow [→].

5. The word it in the passage refers to

   (A) interstellar space

   (B) gravity

   (C) the ball

   (D) the interstellar medium

6. According to paragraph 3, interstellar clouds

   (A) hold star systems together

   (B) are where stars are formed

   (C) can destroy the interstellar medium

   (D) do not exist in the Milky Way

   * Paragraph 3 is marked with an arrow [→].

The Interstellar Medium

It is impossible to fully comprehend just how immense the universe is. It is estimated that the number of galaxies in the universe exceeds 100 billion. Within each of these galaxies, there are hundreds of billions of stars. Our own galaxy, the Milky Way, is home to between 200 and 400 billion stars. Most of these stars are part of a star system, meaning that they are held together by gravity. Vast spaces exist between these star systems, but these spaces are not empty.

→ The interstellar medium is the name for everything that exists in these spaces between star systems. It is estimated that the interstellar medium is made up of 99% gas and 1% dust. The gas found in the interstellar medium has a very low density, so the gas molecules are spread out over wide distances. As for the dust, it comes from a variety of sources, including carbon, ice, and a range of metals. Like the gas in the interstellar medium, most of this dust is widely scattered. For every million cubic meters of space, there is no more than a single grain of dust.

→ It is important to note, however, that the interstellar medium does not just drift aimlessly in interstellar space. In fact, it plays one of the most important roles in the universe. In certain places, the matter of the interstellar medium begins to gather together to create formations known as interstellar clouds. Within the largest and densest of these clouds, something very special happens. Gravity pulls the matter together into a ball, which then begins to heat up. In fact, it gets so hot that nuclear reactions occur, and the ball of matter starts to shine brightly. Deep within interstellar space, the interstellar medium has caused a new star to be born.

GLOSSARY vast: extremely big

VOCABULARY TEST

Recall the essential words in the unit to reinforce your vocabulary acquisition. Write the meaning of each word in your language.

dense	exceed
ascend	moist
convert	decompression
calculate	drift
stroke	loose
opposing	vast
burst	settlers
reproduce	adopt
comprehend	gesture
aimlessly	exhalation
paralysis	ancestor
estimate	indigenous
advanced	wither
abound	photosynthesis
disability	tribe

lavish	loyalty
modern	combination
trace back	adapt to
spread out	carry away
a variety of	evolve into

Complete each sentence with the correct word or collocation.

1 People with hearing _____ often communicate through sign language.

2 Interstellar medium does not just _____ in interstellar space.

3 A team scores by hurling the ball into the _____ team's goal.

4 Long ago, the oceans _____ with plants and animals, unlike the land.

5 People have _____ picnics in the park during Vappu.

6 Scuba divers should _____ exactly how deep they can go.

7 Most plants use _____ to convert sunlight into food.

8 Sign languages are a _____ of hand gestures and body movements.

9 Dust in the interstellar medium comes from _____ sources.

10 The sport called stickball was later _____ by European settlers.

abounded	calculate	lavish	combination	photosynthesis
a variety of	adopted	drift	opposing	disabilities

UNIT 03

Reference

INTRODUCTION

The purpose of reference questions is to check the test taker's ability to recognize what is being referred to by a given word. This word is usually a pronoun, such as *he*, *she*, *it*, or *they*. However, other words are sometimes used, including *which*, *this*, and *these*. The test taker should take a good look at the nouns before and after the pronoun.

TYPICAL QUESTION TYPES

The word/phrase ▢ in the passage refers to

The word/phrase ▢ in paragraph ___ refers to

STRATEGIES

- Identify the word's role in the passage and decide if it is referring to a person, place, or thing.

- Find all of the nouns in the same sentence as the word as well as those in the previous sentence.

- Eliminate the nouns that do not fit the general category the word is referring to.

QUICK CHECKUP

Find the word that the highlighted pronoun refers to.

1 Biology

Laughter is a type of behavior that only humans exhibit. Researchers believe it evolved as a method of strengthening social bonds and perhaps began as a way of showing relief after danger had been avoided. It also signals trust by showing that a person is comfortable with his or her companions. Laughter itself is a combination of involuntary sounds and physical gestures. When people laugh, their facial muscles contract, and it becomes difficult for them to breathe, which leads to the familiar "ha-ha" sounds.

(A) gestures (B) people (C) facial muscles (D) sounds

2 Entomology

There are approximately 400,000 known species of beetles. Their defining characteristic is a pair of hard outer wings. They protect the soft inner wings that are used for flying. Like all insects, they have six legs, and their bodies are divided into three distinct sections. Different beetle species have different diets. Some subsist solely on plants, others prey on smaller insects, and still others feed on the dung of larger animals.

(A) beetles (B) outer wings (C) inner wings (D) insects

3 Economy

In 1980, writer Alvin Toffler predicted the rise of "proactive consumers" who would actively work with companies to improve the products they regularly purchased. To refer to them, he coined the term "prosumer." Over time, however, the term evolved to match the changing marketplace. Today, prosumers are customers who take advantage of technology to advocate the brands they favor and to criticize those they abhor. In a sense, they have shifted from being passive consumers to acting as a vital part of the marketing process.

(A) prosumers (B) consumers (C) companies (D) brands

VOCABULARY

Write the number of each word's definition.

1 *adj.* strange but harmless

2 *adj.* shaped like a cone

3 *v.* to become stuck together

4 *adj.* capable of dissolving in liquid

5 *n.* a negative feature or quality

6 *n.* a small crack

7 *adj.* happening as the result of something else

8 *v.* to move in a downward direction

9 *adj.* located in or related to the countryside

10 *v.* to order someone to come somewhere

11 *v.* to formally remember a person or event from the past

12 *v.* to meet with or to contend against

>>

eccentric _____

rural _____

drawback _____

bind _____

resultant _____

summon _____

commemorate _____

conical _____

descend _____

encounter _____

fracture _____

soluble _____

Match each collocation with the correct definition.

a link up • • a small amount of

b melt down • • to convert a solid to a liquid, usually by heat

c break out • • to unexpectedly begin

d a handful of • • to connect to something else

e be attributed to • • to be regarded as resulting from a cause

Circle the word closest in meaning to each underlined word.

1 The only drawback of the plan is its high cost.
   (A) disadvantage   (B) supporter   (C) element   (D) foundation

2 Jane always thought her brother was eccentric in some ways.
   (A) attractive   (B) peculiar   (C) extra   (D) ascending

3 After the fierce storm, everyone was shocked at the resultant damage.
   (A) physical   (B) consequent   (C) expected   (D) severe

4 People came to commemorate the anniversary of the company's founding.
   (A) congregate   (B) negotiate   (C) decorate   (D) celebrate

5 The blood cells bind together and form a solid mass.
   (A) connect   (B) flow   (C) enlarge   (D) react

6 The boss summoned the workers into his office one by one.
   (A) escorted   (B) praised   (C) gathered   (D) interviewed

Fill in each blank with the correct collocation.

1 A fight _____ between two men in the crowded stadium.

2 Hundreds were invited to the event, but only _____ people came.

3 You can take either trail as they _____ after a few kilometers.

4 The actress's great popularity can _____ her positive attitude.

5 The old gold coins were _____ to make jewelry.

| be attributed to | broke out | a handful of | melted down | link up |

Emily Dickinson

Emily Dickinson was born in Massachusetts in 1830. Although her wealthy family was active in the community, she was a shy and reclusive child. After getting an education, she returned to her hometown, where she became known as a local eccentric. Dressing almost exclusively in white, she rarely left her home. Some of her time was spent maintaining a number of close friendships through enthusiastic letter writing, but most of it was devoted to the writing poetry.

She penned nearly 2,000 poems during her life, only a handful of which were published before she passed away in 1886. After her death, Dickinson's younger sister discovered hundreds of the writer's poems. She gave some of them to a family friend, Mabel Loomis Todd, who had them published in 1890. However, it was not until 1955 that a complete collection of Dickinson's poems became available. Today, she is considered one of the greatest poets of her time.

GLOSSARY pen: to write something such as a letter, a book, etc.

Note-Taking

Emily Dickinson

Dickinson's Youth
- shy & _____
- known as a _____
- letter writing & _____

Dickinson's Works
- wrote 2,000 poems, but few were _____
- published after her _____
- a _____ of her works published in 1955

1   The word it in the passage refers to

   (A) time
   (B) poetry
   (C) friendship
   (D) letter writing

2   The word She in the passage refers to

   (A) Emily Dickinson
   (B) Dickinson's younger sister
   (C) a family friend
   (D) one of the greatest poets

SUMMARY

Born in 1830, _____ was a shy and _____ child. In her hometown, she spent most of her time exchanging _____ with _____ and writing _____. She wrote nearly _____, but _____ were published. After she _____ in 1886, her _____ found _____. Some were _____ in 1890, but the _____ was not _____ until _____. She is now thought to be one of the greatest _____ of her time.

✦ VOCAB

Match each word with the correct definition.

a   reclusive   •   •   showing great excitement or interest

b   exclusively   •   •   of involving only a specific thing

c   enthusiastic   •   •   the gathered works of a single writer, painter, etc.

d   devote to   •   •   shut off or apart from the world

e   collection   •   •   to give an amount of time to something

Pectin

In many rural communities, people gather the season's excess fruit, such as apples, oranges, and peaches, and convert it into jams. The first step to making jam is to cook a mixture of fruit and sugar until it acquires the thick consistency of a gel. This time-consuming process has many drawbacks: It boils away a significant portion of the fruit's juices, can adversely affect the jam's flavor, and removes much of the fruit's natural vitamin content. This is why most people use pectin when making jam.

Pectin is a natural fiber found in fruit. The highest concentrations of pectin are found in apples and berries. Chemically, it is a type of carbohydrate that holds the individual cells of the fruit together. When pectin is heated with sugar in acidic environments, the large molecules of pectin bind together and trap liquid within their mesh-like structures. As a result, it can act as a natural thickening agent and dramatically reduce the required cooking time of jam while maintaining the distinctive flavor of the fruit. It has the added benefit of preserving the vivid color of the fruit, so it makes the resultant jam more appealing to the eye as well.

Note-Taking

MI = Main Idea   SD = Supporting Details

P1 MI the _____ to cooking a mixture of _____
    SD - _____ a portion of the _____
        - can adversely affect the _____
        - _____ the fruit's _____ content

P2 MI pectin — acts as a natural _____
    SD - _____ the required cooking _____
        - _____ the _____ of the fruit
        - _____ the _____ of the fruit

1   What is the main idea of the passage?

   (A) Pectin is a natural fiber that is found in fruit.
   (B) Pectin's properties are useful when making jam.
   (C) Pectin helps fruit keep its vitamins and flavor.
   (D) Pectin in fruit is used in cooking in various ways.

2   The word It in the passage refers to

   (A) cooking a mixture of fruit and sugar
   (B) using pectin when making jam
   (C) acquiring a thick consistency
   (D) gathering the season's fruit

3   The word their in the passage refers to

   (A) cells
   (B) environments
   (C) molecules
   (D) structures

VOCAB

Write the correct word for each definition.

a   a degree of density, firmness, etc.   _____
b   in an unfavorable and hostile manner   _____
c   to prevent something from escaping   _____
d   having a special and recognizable quality   _____
e   to keep something as it is   _____

trap
distinctive
consistency
preserve
adversely

STEP 03

Timed Reading (WPM) ☐ 2'00" ☐ 2'30" ☐ 3'00"

History

The Liberty Bell

The city of Philadelphia, located in the state of Pennsylvania, is home to a large metal bell known as the Liberty Bell. Although it is considered a symbol of the USA, it is actually older than the country itself.

In 1751, Pennsylvania was a colony of the British Empire. To celebrate the 50th anniversary of its constitution, the colony's government ordered the construction of a massive 2,000-pound bell cast from copper and tin. Hung from a rafter in the steeple of Independence Hall, the bell was rung to announce special occasions and to summon people to gather for important events. After war broke out between the British Empire and its American colonies, the bell was used to announce the outcome of key battles. In 1776, it was famously rung to gather citizens for the first reading of the Declaration of Independence. In 1777, as the British army advanced on the city, the bell was taken down and hidden in a nearby town amidst fears that it would be melted down to make ammunition. After the British were defeated, it was returned to its belfry.

The most famous characteristic of the Liberty Bell is the large crack in its side. No one is sure when the crack first appeared, but it expanded significantly in 1846 when the bell was rung to commemorate the birthday of George Washington. Since that time, it has not been rung. Today, the bell can be found in Philadelphia's Liberty Bell Center, where it remains a popular symbol of the nation.

GLOSSARY belfry: the top of the tower where the bells are

⚙ VOCAB

Find the correct word in the passage for each of the given definition.

a   an area controlled by a country and which is usually far away from it: _____

b   a document which states people's rights and duties: _____

c   a wooden piece that supports a roof: _____

d   the means of exploding a weapon: _____

1 The word its in the passage refers to

   (A) Pennsylvania   (B) the colony's government
   (C) the 50th anniversary   (D) the Liberty Bell

2 The word it in the passage refers to

   (A) the Liberty Bell   (B) the crack
   (C) the British army   (D) the birthday of George Washington

3 Which of the following is NOT true about the Liberty Bell?

   (A) It is made of copper and tin.
   (B) It is more than 250 years old.
   (C) It has not been rung since 1846.
   (D) It was stolen and hidden by the British.

4 What is mentioned about the crack in the Liberty Bell?

   (A) It has been repaired several times.
   (B) It is the reason the bell is no longer rung.
   (C) It happened due to the metals used to make the bell.
   (D) It was a part of the artist's original design.

Note-Taking

MI = Main Idea   SD = Supporting Details

P1 MI _____
    SD _____
P2 MI _____
    SD _____
        _____
        _____
        _____
P3 MI _____
    SD _____
        _____

UNIT TEST

1. The word which in the passage refers to

   (A) carbon dioxide

   (B) carbonic acid

   (C) hydrogen sulfide

   (D) the earth

2. The word its in the passage refers to

   (A) the ocean

   (B) the seafloor

   (C) limestone

   (D) calcium carbonate

3. It is indicated in paragraph 2 that calcium carbonate

   (A) makes water acidic

   (B) is found in limestone

   (C) eats away stalactites

   (D) contains water

   * Paragraph 2 is marked with an arrow [→].

4. The word it in the passage refers to

   (A) acidic water

   (B) the cave

   (C) the limestone

   (D) calcium carbonate

5. It is NOT stated in the passage that

   (A) most limestone formed on seafloors long ago

   (B) carbon dioxide can cause water to become acidic

   (C) stalactites and stalagmites are found in limestone caves

   (D) sulfuric acid and carbonic acid come from the same source

6. Directions: An introductory sentence for a brief summary of the passage is provided below. Complete the summary by selecting the THREE answer choices that express the most important ideas in the passage.

   Limestone caves are deep and long, and they feature distinctive formations.

   -
   -
   -

   Answer Choices

   (A) Carbon dioxide is found in the air.

   (B) Acidic water dissolves limestone and leaves behind holes.

   (C) Limestone contains high levels of calcium carbonate.

   (D) Limestone has numerous fractures on its surface.

   (E) Stalactites and icicles form in much the same way.

   (F) Calcium carbonate is left behind by running water, creating conical structures.

Limestone Caves

There are many types of caves, but limestone caves are among the deepest and longest in the world. They are also home to dramatic stalactites and stalagmites, which are conical rock formations that descend from their ceilings and rise from their floors much as icicles do in the winter. The usual sizes and features of limestone caves can be attributed to the manner in which the caves themselves are created.

→ The formation of limestone caves begins with slightly acidic water. This water acquires its acidity from one of two sources: carbon dioxide in the air, which creates carbonic acid, or hydrogen sulfide rising up from deep in the earth, which creates sulfuric acid. As this water moves through the ground, it often encounters limestone. Most limestone formed long ago on the seafloors of ancient oceans. Because of this, one of its main components is calcium carbonate, a mineral that is found in seashells and is easily dissolved by acidic water. Therefore, as the acidic water enters small fractures found in the limestone, it begins to break the rock down and carry it away, leaving behind a small cavity.

Over time, running water continues to enlarge the cavity until it becomes a cave. As the cave continues to expand, it may link up with other openings in the rock and eventually create an underground network of interconnected caves and tunnels. The water that dissolves the limestone acquires calcium carbonate in a soluble form. As the water moves through the cave, it leaves this calcium carbonate behind, which allows it to regain its solid form. Slowly building up, it creates the familiar formations that give limestone caves their otherworldly appearance. The largest limestone cave in the world is located in Vietnam and is at about 9 kilometers in length, 200 meters in width, and 150 meters in height.

GLOSSARY
icicle: a long, pointed piece of ice hanging down
dissolve: to become melted or liquefied

VOCABULARY TEST

Recall the essential words in the unit to reinforce your vocabulary acquisition. Write the meaning of each word in your language.

reclusive	consistency
bind	summon
rafter	advocate
enthusiastic	dissolve
resultant	colony
rural	eccentric
exclusively	collection
preserve	conical
soluble	commemorate
adversely	trap
constitution	icicle
descend	encounter
coin	subsist
bond	involuntary
abhor	drawback

distinctive	pen
ammunition	fracture
devote to	link up
melt down	be attributed to
a handful of	break out

Complete each sentence with the correct word or collocation.

1 Emily Dickinson's family was active in the community, but she was a _____ child.

2 Some beetles _____ solely on plants, and others prey on smaller insects.

3 In 1751, Pennsylvania was a _____ of the British Empire.

4 Stalactites form much as _____ do in the winter.

5 This time-consuming process can _____ affect the jam's flavor.

6 Prosumers take advantage of technology to _____ the brands they favor.

7 The water that _____ the limestone acquires calcium carbonate.

8 People feared that the bell would be _____ to make ammunition.

9 Emily Dickinson maintained close friendships through _____ letter writing.

10 Pectin has the added benefit of _____ the vivid color of the fruit.

| preserving | dissolves | advocate | reclusive | subsist |
| melted down | adversely | colony | enthusiastic | icicles |

TOEFL iBT® READING
UNIT 04

Fact and Negative Fact

INTRODUCTION

There are two types of questions related to the facts contained within a passage. The first category asks students to identify information that is included in the passage. The second category involves recognizing which information is not included in the passage.

TYPICAL QUESTION TYPES

According to paragraph _____,

It is stated in paragraph _____ that

It is NOT true that

It is NOT stated that

All of the following are true EXCEPT (that)

STRATEGIES

- Read the question carefully to make sure you understand whether you are looking for information that is or is *not* included in the passage.

- Scan the answer choices for key words and phrases.

- Keep in mind that "negative facts" can be either incorrect information or information that simply is not mentioned in the passage.

QUICK CHECKUP

Find the answer that is true according to the passage.

1 Culture

The term "soul food" refers to the African-American cuisine that developed in Southern America. Soul food's staple ingredients include pork, beans, leafy vegetables, and cornmeal. The distinctive characteristics of soul food developed out of necessity. In the past, slaves had to make use of whatever food they could acquire. Later, these recipes merged with the culinary traditions of poor rural southerners as well as the cooking methods of Native American tribes.

(A) Soul food was first created by Native American tribes.
(B) The original soul food recipes used any food available.

2 Social Science

People for the Ethical Treatment of Animals, known by the acronym PETA, is an American nonprofit organization that focuses on protecting the rights of animals and was founded in 1980. Although it is one of the largest animal rights groups in the world, PETA is better known for its tactics than for its size. Its confrontational campaigns against fur and animal testing have featured controversial ads designed to shock viewers and to draw attention to the group's causes.

(A) PETA uses extreme advertising to get attention.
(B) PETA is small but has effective campaign tactics.

3 Geology

On January 1, 2000, the World Meteorology Organization (WMO) put a new naming system into place for typhoons occurring in the Northwestern Pacific Ocean and South China Sea. It makes use of a list of 140 names contributed by different countries in the region. Rather than solely relying on women's names like it did in the past, the list also includes men's names, plants, animals, locations, mythical figures, and other words of local significance. Along with these names, the traditional numbering method continues to be used to identify typhoons.

(A) The WMO replaced a typhoon-naming system with a numbering system.
(B) Since 2000, a list of 140 names has been used to identify typhoons.

VOCABULARY

Write the number of each word's definition.

	>>	
1 v. to bring under conditions for effective use	depict	_____
2 v. to hold tightly	grasp	_____
3 adj. capable of being spread from person to person	harness	_____
4 adj. creating strong opinions and causing disagreement	respiratory	_____
5 n. having no result or effect	acute	_____
6 adj. extreme or severe	contagious	_____
7 n. the process of digging something out of the ground	abate	_____
8 adj. related to the lungs or the act of breathing	refrain	_____
9 v. to gradually lessen	controversial	_____
10 adj. having strong feelings of doubt about a claim	excavation	_____
11 v. to show something in a picture	futility	_____
12 v. to avoid doing something	skeptical	_____

Match each collocation with the correct definition.

a   be derived from   •   •   to take part in (an event, activity, etc.)

b   in leaps and bounds   •   •   to be legally forced to leave a place

c   be credited with   •   •   to be considered responsible for (a task, achievement, etc.)

d   participate in   •   •   to have come from something else

e   be evicted from   •   •   increasing or progressing very quickly

Circle the word closest in meaning to each underlined word.

1. Certain primate species grasp branches and swing from tree to tree.
   (A) comprehend (B) clutch (C) detect (D) lower

2. These murals depict the events that destroyed the ancient city.
   (A) illustrate (B) exaggerate (C) create (D) disguise

3. Solar panels are designed to harness the energy of the sun.
   (A) enhance (B) protect (C) analyze (D) utilize

4. The president waited for the applause to abate before speaking.
   (A) commence (B) continue (C) subside (D) magnify

5. Athletes suffering from sore muscles are advised to refrain from exercise.
   (A) abstain (B) relax (C) medicate (D) consult

6. A scientist claims she found a cure, but her colleagues are skeptical.
   (A) pliable (B) doubtful (C) violent (D) optimistic

Fill in each blank with the correct collocation.

1. The medicine _____ the fruit of a rare tropical tree.

2. A local man _____ discovering the ancient jungle village.

3. The outstanding athlete _____ several Olympic events.

4. After a slow start, her business began to expand _____.

5. Poor families can _____ their homes for failing to pay their rent.

| is derived from | in leaps and bounds | be evicted from |
| participated in | is credited with | |

The Thracian Tomb of Kazanlak

Located in central Bulgaria, the Thracian Tomb of Kazanlak is a UNESCO World Heritage Site. The tomb consists of a corridor and a round burial chamber, and it is part of a necropolis, a large complex used for burying the dead.

The tomb features impressively well-preserved murals from the 4th century B.C., which is the Hellenistic period, when the cultural influence of the ancient Greek empire could be seen in artwork across Europe and adjacent regions. The murals of the Thracian Tomb of Kazanlak depict a funeral feast. In the murals, a Thracian chieftain and his wife sit side by side, each grasping the other's wrist in what appears to be a touching farewell. Before them, a ceremonial procession of maids, servants and horses respectfully approaches.

Along with their well-preserved state, the murals' remarkable composition and naturalistic details make the tomb an artistic site of historical importance.

GLOSSARY   **chamber:** a room designed and equipped for a particular purpose

---

Note-Taking

The Thracian Tomb of Kazanlak

Where It Is	central _____
What It Consists of	a _____ & a round _____; part of a _____
Its Murals	are impressively _____
	were painted in the ____ century B.C. – _____ period
	depict a Thracian _____ & his wife at a _____
	have the remarkable _____ & _____

1 All of the following are true EXCEPT that

   (A) the tomb is considerably huge
   (B) some parts of the tomb are mangled
   (C) the burial chamber is circular
   (D) the tomb is thought to be culturally significant

2 It is stated that the murals

   (A) greatly influenced Greek culture
   (B) are placed in the burial chambers
   (C) show a man and woman at a festival
   (D) are considered to be composed excellently

SUMMARY

The _____ Tomb of Kazanlak is part of a _____ in central Bulgaria. It consists of a _____ and a round _____. The tomb contains _____ from the _____. The murals depict _____ with maids, servants and horses at a _____. The murals are _____ and are notable for their _____ and _____.

✦ VOCAB

Match each word with the correct definition.

a   adjacent   •   •   the chief of a clan

b   chieftain   •   •   lying near or close

c   procession   •   •   manner of being composed and placed

d   state   •   •   the condition that a person or a thing is in

e   composition   •   •   the act of moving along in order

Electricity

Electricity is a naturally occurring phenomenon that has been harnessed by humans, allowing the technology that powers modern civilization to advance in leaps and bounds.

Electricity begins with the electric charge found in subatomic particles known as protons, which carry a positive charge, and electrons, which carry a negative one. When a charge is transferred from one object to another, it is called an electric current. In order to control the movement of a current, an electric circuit can be constructed, consisting of three basic elements: a conductor, such as copper wire, a source of electricity, such as a battery, and a device that requires electricity, such as a light bulb.

→ The copper in the wire "conducts" the electric current, allowing it to move from the battery to the light bulb. How powerfully an electric current flows depends on two factors: the voltage of the current, which is the force that moves the charge, and the resistance of the conductor, which pushes against the flow. Metals are the most commonly used conductors, as they tend to have a lower resistance. Their protons are immobile, which means it is their electrons that carry the electric charge through the circuit.

Note-Taking

MI = Main Idea   SD = Supporting Details

P1 MI electricity
    SD a naturally occurring _____

P2 MI requires three elements to begin:
    SD • electric _____ – protons & _____
        • electric _____ – the transfer of a _____
        • electric _____ – consists of a _____, a _____ & a _____

P3 MI two factors that influence the power of electric _____
    SD • the _____ of the current: the _____ that moves the charge
        • the _____ of the conductor: _____ against the flow

1   The word their in the passage refers to

   (A) metals
   (B) conductors
   (C) protons
   (D) electrons

2   It is stated in paragraph 3 that

   (A) the voltage of a conductor should be low for a powerful current
   (B) a high voltage creates a high resistance of the material
   (C) electrons tend to move easily through metal conductors
   (D) a circuit cannot contain both electrons and protons
   * Paragraph 3 is marked with an arrow [→].

3   All of the following are true EXCEPT that

   (A) protons are subatomic particles
   (B) an electric current is the movement of a charge
   (C) the copper wire can act as a conductor
   (D) an electric charge requires a circuit

✪ VOCAB

Write the correct word for each definition.

a   an advanced state of human society   _____

b   an extremely small constituent   _____

c   a circular journey; a round   _____

d   the power to remain unaffected   _____

e   incapable of being moved   _____

| particle |
| circuit |
| civilization |
| immobile |
| resistance |

STEP 03

Biology

Norovirus

→ Norovirus is a type of RNA virus, consisting of a single species with a number of different variants. Its name is derived from the American city of Norwalk, where the first known outbreak of the virus occurred in 1968. Although it is colloquially referred to as "the stomach flu," it is unrelated to the influenza virus, which is a respiratory illness. Norovirus, on the other hand, causes acute gastroenteritis, an inflammation of the stomach and intestines.

Norovirus is highly contagious, and there are several ways in which a person can become infected. It can be transmitted from person to person, via contaminated food or by touching contaminated surfaces. Some of the most severe outbreaks of norovirus occur in isolated communities from which people cannot easily come and go. These include hospitals, prisons, school dormitories and, perhaps most infamously, cruise ships. The most common symptoms of norovirus include nausea, vomiting, diarrhea and stomach pain. These symptoms often lead to dangerous dehydration.

→ Despite the fact that there is no vaccine or effective treatment for norovirus, there are many preventative steps that can be taken. These include practicing proper hygiene, such as frequently washing one's hands, and cooking and washing food thoroughly before serving it. The illness itself usually lasts from just one to three days, but people suffering from norovirus continue to be contagious for several days after the symptoms have abated. They should therefore refrain from cooking, handling or serving food during this period.

GLOSSARY RNA: ribonucleic acid

VOCAB

Find the correct word in the passage for each of the given definition.

a   a painful redness or swelling on body parts: _____

b   to send from one place or person to another: _____

c   an abnormal loss of water from body: _____

d   a practice to keep oneself clean and healthy: _____

1. The word colloquially in the passage is closest in meaning to

   (A) temporarily
   (B) substantially
   (C) informally
   (D) infectiously

2. It is stated in paragraph 1 that

   (A) gastroenteritis can be caused by norovirus
   (B) RNA viruses can lead to respiratory illness
   (C) norovirus is unrelated to the stomach flu
   (D) the influenza virus is a form of gastroenteritis

   * Paragraph 1 is marked with an arrow [→].

3. The author's main purpose in paragraph 3 is to

   (A) show that norovirus is highly contagious
   (B) explain why there is no norovirus vaccine
   (C) compare norovirus to other illnesses
   (D) give advice on how to avoid norovirus

   * Paragraph 3 is marked with an arrow [→].

4. It is NOT true that

   (A) severe outbreaks of norovirus can occur on cruise ships
   (B) the treatment of norovirus involves hand washing
   (C) norovirus can be passed from one person to another
   (D) the symptoms of norovirus can cause dehydration

Note-Taking

MI = Main Idea   SD = Supporting Details

P1 MI _____
    SD _____
P2 MI _____
    SD _____
        _____
P3 MI _____
    SD _____

UNIT 4_ Fact and Negative Fact

UNIT TEST

1. What is the main idea of the passage?

   (A) Heinrich Schliemann proved that Troy was a myth.
   (B) Heinrich Schliemann figured out the location of Troy.
   (C) Heinrich Schliemann found the most important archaeological relics.
   (D) Homer's greatest poems were discovered by Heinrich Schliemann.

2. Why does the author mention the California Gold Rush in the passage?

   (A) To give an example of Schliemann's adventurous lifestyle
   (B) To indicate the first historical sites that Schliemann had been
   (C) To show how Schliemann searched the world for Troy
   (D) To explain how Schliemann became interested in mythology

3. The phrase ran afoul of in the passage is closest in meaning to

   (A) ran away to
   (B) conflicted with
   (C) escaped from
   (D) allied with

4. It is stated in paragraph 3 that

   (A) Hissarlik is a hill located west of the city of Rome
   (B) Turkey's government helped Schliemann finish his work
   (C) it took Schliemann about two years to find treasure beneath Hissarlik
   (D) Schliemann died while searching for the treasure of King Priam

   * Paragraph 3 is marked with an arrow [→].

5. All of the following are true EXCEPT

   (A) Schliemann thought Troy was beneath some remains of Rome
   (B) not everyone believed Schliemann found King Priam's treasure
   (C) Schliemann became an archaeologist when he was in his 40s
   (D) historians agreed that Homer's poems were fictional works

6. Directions: Select the appropriate phrases from the answer choices and match them to the category to which they relate. TWO of the answer choices will NOT be used.

Hissarlik	Troy
·	·
·	·
	·

   Answer Choices

   (A) Being described in Homer's poems
   (B) The site of a deadly shipwreck
   (C) A hill in western Turkey
   (D) Famous for its gold rush
   (E) A city that was controversial if it existed
   (F) Was once ruled by a King named Priam
   (G) The site of Roman ruins

Heinrich Schliemann

Heinrich Schliemann, a 19th-century German archaeologist, was a controversial figure considered by some to be a great pioneer in his field. He is best remembered as the man who discovered the location of ancient Troy, proving the existence of a city that many had believed to be nothing more than a myth.

Schliemann lived an adventurous life in his early years. He traveled the world, surviving a shipwreck and participating in the California Gold Rush. At the advanced age of 46, he decided to become an archaeologist. Interested in Greek mythology since childhood, he focused on finding the city of Troy, described in Homer's epic poems the *Iliad* and the *Odyssey*. At that time, there was a fierce debate among historians over whether these were historical accounts or works of fiction. Believing they were the former, Schliemann used Homer's works to guide him to the place where Troy once stood.

→ He eventually concluded that the remains of Troy could be found at Hissarlik, a hill in western Turkey, beneath the ruins of a Roman settlement. In 1871, he began a major excavation at the site. After more than two years of futility, Schliemann discovered a cache of silver and gold artifacts. He called these "Priam's Treasure," believing they once belonged to King Priam of Troy. His peers were skeptical, and Schliemann soon ran afoul of the Turkish government. He was evicted from the site, although he was later allowed to return. Schliemann continued his work until his death in 1890.

Today, many of Schliemann's claims are considered to be inaccurate and some of his excavation techniques, including the use of dynamite, have been sharply criticized. However, he is credited with having achieved the extraordinary feat of solving a centuries-old mystery and leading his fellow archaeologists to the site of a lost city.

GLOSSARY **cache:** a hiding place for weapons, food or treasures

VOCABULARY TEST

Recall the essential words in the unit to reinforce your vocabulary acquisition. Write the meaning of each word in your language.

particle	tactic
adjacent	civilization
contagious	abate
inflammation	hygiene
circuit	futility
skeptical	cache
state	harness
respiratory	procession
refrain	immobile
depict	composition
resistance	confrontational
chieftain	controversial
transmit	fierce
pioneer	dehydration
acute	staple

contribute	grasp
excavation	culinary
merge with	in leaps and bounds
be evicted from	be derived from
participate in	be credited with

Complete each sentence with the correct word or collocation.

1 PETA is better known for its _____ than for its size.

2 There was a _____ debate among historians.

3 A ceremonial _____ of maids, servants, and horses approaches.

4 Schliemann discovered a _____ of silver and gold artifacts.

5 The symptoms of norovirus often lead to dangerous _____.

6 Metals are commonly used as conductors, as they have a lower _____.

7 Electricity begins with the electric charge found in subatomic _____.

8 Soul food's _____ ingredients include pork, beans, and leafy vegetables.

9 In the murals, a Thracian _____ and his wife sit side by side.

10 The slaves' recipes _____ the culinary traditions of poor rural southerners.

| procession | fierce | dehydration | particles | resistance |
| staple | cache | tactics | chieftain | merged with |

TOEFL iBT® READING

UNIT °5

Sentence Simplification

INTRODUCTION

Sentence simplification usually involves changing the order of elements in a sentence and replacing some of the phrases with simpler synonyms while not leaving any important information out of the sentence. Incorrect answers change the meaning of a key phrase or clause or completely leave out important information.

TYPICAL QUESTION TYPE

Which of the sentences below best expresses the essential information in the highlighted sentence in the passage? *Incorrect* choices change the meaning in important ways or leave out essential information.

STRATEGIES

- Many highlighted sentences have more than one clause; focus on finding all of the highlighted sentence's subjects, verbs, and objects.

- Look for coordinating and subordinating conjunctions and note the relationship between the clauses (addition, contrast, choice, condition, sequence, etc.).

- Examine the answer choices. Look for clauses that are missing information that you have identified as important. Look for changes in verb voice or tense. Look for paraphrases that leave out important information.

QUICK CHECKUP

Find the answer that best expresses the essential information in the highlighted sentence.

1 **Art**

Calligraphy, the art of writing in ways that are pleasing to the eye, is a distinctive and long-practiced visual art. The English word "calligraphy" comes from the Greek roots *kallos* ("beauty") and *graphy* ("writing"). Calligraphy has been an important art since at least the 2nd century B.C. Calligraphers use very fine-tipped brushes, pens, and carving tools to write in a way that is both beautiful and harmonious though not always legible.

(A) The letters and words in calligraphy are easier to read when calligraphers use very nice brushes and tools.
(B) Calligraphers express letters and words in an artistic and interesting way though not everyone can always read them.
(C) Calligraphy involves using tools to create letters and words that look nice even if they are not easy to read.
(D) Some special writing tools are employed by calligraphers to make sure the letters are beautiful and easy to read.

2 **History**

Nelson Mandela was the first fully democratically elected president of South Africa and the nation's first black president. Mandela's presidency marked the end of apartheid in South Africa. Though imprisoned for more than 27 years for revolutionary activity, Mandela protested the systematic disenfranchisement of black South Africans while he was in jail. After being released from prison, he was elected president in 1994 and oversaw the beginning of racial reconciliation.

(A) Nelson Mandela protested for 27 years against the government that took away black South Africans' rights.
(B) During 27 years of imprisonment for fighting against the government, Nelson Mandela protested for black South Africans' rights.
(C) Nelson Mandela was in prison for 27 years for protesting the way that black South Africans' rights were being taken away.
(D) Nelson Mandela spent 27 years protesting the system that imprisoned many black Africans for fighting against the government in a peaceful way.

VOCABULARY

Write the number of each word's definition.

1   *n.* a very successful or inspiring person

2   *adj.* having more opportunities than others

3   *v.* to make a guess about a topic based on incomplete evidence

4   *v.* to press or squeeze something into a smaller size

5   *adj.* eating only or mostly plants

6   *v.* to be very successful

7   *adj.* very harmful or damaging

8   *v.* to be the cause of or the reason for

9   *v.* to be interesting, attractive, or charming

10 *n.* an animal that hunts and kills other animals for food

11 *adj.* intense and realistic

12 *v.* to limit or force someone or something

>>

herbivorous   _____

predator   _____

flourish   _____

gritty   _____

luminary   _____

privileged   _____

compress   _____

fascinate   _____

speculate   _____

determine   _____

constrain   _____

devastating   _____

Match each collocation with the correct definition.

a   in captivity   •   •   to hunt another animal for food

b   prey upon   •   •   to be prominent or easy to notice

c   in favor of   •   •   to break into many small pieces

d   be torn apart   •   •   arguing for, supporting, or choosing

e   stand out   •   •   being held in or kept in a cage

Circle the word closest in meaning to each underlined word.

1   The customer speculated about the source of the charge on the credit card.
    (A) scribbled   (B) described   (C) assumed   (D) pleaded

2   The empire flourished in 12th century B.C. thanks to its natural resources.
    (A) thrived   (B) flushed   (C) dissolved   (D) nourished

3   The conference included talks from several luminaries in the field of nanotechnology.
    (A) instruments   (B) experts   (C) disabilities (D) mammals

4   The woman had a very privileged childhood because her family was rich.
    (A) revealing   (B) advantaged   (C) expensive   (D) impoverished

5   There was a devastating earthquake in South America last weekend.
    (A) interfering   (B) exaggerating   (C) prosperous   (D) disastrous

6   Many people are fascinated by the stars that appear in the night sky.
    (A) scattered   (B) neglected   (C) attracted   (D) littered

Fill in each blank with the correct collocation.

1   Some wild animals are being bred _____ at the zoo.

2   The clock tower _____ during the civil war.

3   Many studies show that bullfrogs even _____ smaller frogs.

4   The intelligence of the professor _____ among his peers.

5   The jury ruled _____ the victim in the incendiary case.

| in captivity | was torn apart | stood out | in favor of | prey upon |

The Galapagos Tortoise

The Galapagos tortoise is the largest species of tortoise in the world and one of the longest living creatures on the Earth. Galapagos tortoises have been known to reach weights of 400 kilograms and to live for 170 years in captivity.

Galapagos tortoises are strictly herbivorous. They eat cacti, grasses, and berries and can spend 8 or 9 hours per day searching for food. Like all tortoises, the Galapagos tortoise moves very slowly and relies on its thick shell for protection. An adult Galapagos tortoise has no natural predators, but young tortoises are preyed upon by the Galapagos hawk, and the tortoise's eggs are routinely eaten by rats and wild pigs. The Galapagos tortoise is not currently considered endangered, but of the 10 islands in the Galapagos Archipelago that once were home to subspecies of the Galapagos tortoise, only 5 still have populations of living tortoises.

GLOSSARY
cactus: a thick fleshy plant that grows in hot and dry environments
Galapagos Archipelago: a group of islands about 400 miles west of South America

The Galapagos Tortoise

- the _____ species of _____
- reach _____ of 400 kilograms & _____ for _____ yrs.
- are _____, move _____, & have a thick _____ for _____
- young tortoises & eggs – _____ for some animals
- the _____ of living tortoises have decreased

1 Which of the sentences below best expresses the essential information in the first highlighted sentence in the passage?

(A) Galapagos tortoises have no enemies, but young tortoises frequently eat hawk eggs, which are also eaten by rats and wild pigs.

(B) Birds eat Galapagos tortoises, but their shells make the tortoises safe from other animals.

(C) Galapagos tortoises have no natural enemies, but some animals that are not originally from the islands, such as hawks, pigs, and rats, eat the tortoises.

(D) Birds frequently eat baby Galapagos tortoises, and other animals usually eat Galapagos tortoise eggs; however, fully grown tortoises are safe from other animals.

2 Which of the sentences below best expresses the essential information in the second highlighted sentence in the passage?

(A) Galapagos tortoises are endangered on 5 out of the 10 islands in the Galapagos Archipelago.

(B) Some subspecies have been threatened with death on some of the islands in the Galapagos Archipelago.

(C) Only 5 out of the 10 islands that have had subspecies of Galapagos tortoise living on them still have some groups of tortoises.

(D) Out of all of the islands in the Galapagos Archipelago, only 10 of them have groups of living tortoises.

SUMMARY

The _____ is the _____ tortoise in the world. Its weight is about _____, and its lifespan is _____. It is _____, moves _____, and has _____ to protect it. _____ are often eaten by other animals. About _____ of its _____ have died out.

⚙ VOCAB

Match each word with the correct definition.

a   creature   •   •   of one particular type

b   strictly   •   •   to need or depend on something

c   rely on   •   •   the number of a group of specific animals

d   protection   •   •   a living thing that is not a plant

e   population   •   •   a prevention from harmful elements

American Realism

American Realism was a movement in art, music, and literature that flourished in the United States at the beginning of the 20th century. In contrast to the high-minded idealism of the preceding century, this movement sought to portray the gritty reality of American life. Painters such as George Bellows, John French Sloan, and Edward Hopper captured scenes of working class city life: boxing matches, crowded bars, and nearly empty restaurants late at night. Musicians including W.C. Handy and Scott Joplin wrote fast-paced and chaotic pieces influenced as much by African-American musical forms such as the blues and jazz as by the frantic pace of city life in the 1910s.

Frequently, however, American Realism is remembered as a movement in literature encompassing such luminaries as Mark Twain, Henry James, F. Scott Fitzgerald, and Ernest Hemingway. Following the American Civil War, writers began to abandon the flowery prose and complicated plots of the 19th century novel in favor of simple language describing realistic characters and difficult moral choices. The subjects of these stories shifted from dramatized depictions of the lives of the wealthy and privileged elite to the very real struggles of regular people.

Note-Taking

_____ MI = Main Idea   SD = Supporting Details

- **P1** **MI** _____ — a movement that _____ in the _____
  - **SD** portrayed the _____ of American life
    - painters — showed scenes of _____ city life
    - musicians — wrote _____ & _____ pieces
- **P2** **MI** American Realism — remembered as a movement in _____
  - **SD** • writers — used simple language w/ _____ & difficult _____
    — wrote about real struggles of _____ ppl.

Abbreviations for Note-Taking: ppl. (people)

1. Which of the sentences below best expresses the essential information in the first highlighted sentence in the passage?

   (A) Jazz and Blues musicians, along with everyday life in the city, inspired early 20th century songwriters like W.C. Handy and Scott Joplin.

   (B) Blues and jazz were the two main influences on the music written by musicians like W.C. Handy and Scott Joplin in the 1910s.

   (C) W.C. Handy, Scott Joplin, and other composers were inspired by three things: the blues, jazz, and the quick pace of life in big cities.

   (D) In the 20th century, songwriters like Scott Joplin and W.C. Handy drew inspiration from the quickness of city life to write blues and jazz music.

2. Which of the sentences below best expresses the essential information in the second highlighted sentence in the passage?

   (A) American realist novels have complicated contents in contrast to pre-Civil War novels, which had simple language and realistic characters.

   (B) Before the American Civil War, books were written with more intricate stories and ornamental words while after the war, they became less complex and more realistic.

   (C) In the 19th century, novels were written with short sentences and common words, but, after the American Civil War, writers' word choices became more poetic and unrealistic.

   (D) Over the span of time beginning before the American Civil War and ending after it, American novels became more complex in their language and less complex in their characters and morals.

✲ VOCAB

Write the correct word for each definition.

a	going or coming before	_____
b	being in a state of disorder and confusion	_____
c	difficult to analyze, understand, or explain	_____
d	relating to beliefs about what is right or wrong	_____
e	a long and difficult attempt to achieve something	_____

preceding
moral
struggle
chaotic
complicated

Saturn

While all of the planets in the solar system are uniquely interesting to astronomers, few planets are as distinctive as Saturn. Like its neighbor Jupiter, Saturn is a so-called gas giant. Most of its mass comes from gaseous hydrogen and helium. These gases surround a layer of liquid metallic hydrogen. The hydrogen in this layer has been compressed into a liquid metal by the gravitational compression of Saturn's core.

Saturn is best known, however, for the beautiful rings of ice that surround it. Though other planets have ring systems, none is as extensive as that of Saturn. These rings extend 73,000 kilometers into space from an initial height of 7,000 kilometers above Saturn's surface. While astronomers are not sure how the rings were formed, there are several hypotheses: The rings could be the remains of a moon that was torn apart by Saturn's gravity, remnants of the cloud that Saturn originally formed from, or even the icy outer layer of one of Saturn's moons.

Though Saturn's rings have fascinated astronomers since the 17th century, Saturn began to gain fame in the 1940s for another reason: the uniqueness of its moon Titan. Of Saturn's 51 moons, Titan stands out to astronomers for two reasons: It is the only moon in the solar system to have an atmosphere, and it is the only object, other than Earth, to have stable bodies of liquid on its surface. These two facts have led astronomers to speculate about the possibility of life deep below Titan's icy surface.

VOCAB

Find the correct word in the passage for each of the given definition.

a   very wide and broad: _____

b   an idea that is a possible explanation: _____

c   a small part that is left over: _____

d   being not likely to change or to come to an end: _____

1. Which of the sentences below best expresses the essential information in the first highlighted sentence in the passage?

   (A) Saturn's rings were probably formed in the following way: gravity Caused a moon to break up into a cloud that mixed with ice torn from the moon's surface to form the rings.

   (B) Ice and other material formed a cloud which was compressed by gravity into the planet Saturn, its many moons, and the rings which surround the planet.

   (C) Saturn's rings were formed when the planet's gravity, the cloud of material that Saturn originally formed from, and a layer of ice caused a moon to be torn apart.

   (D) Saturn's rings might have formed by gravity which broke up a moon into pieces, matter left over from Saturn's formation, or the icy top layer of a moon.

2. Which of the sentences below best expresses the essential information in the second highlighted sentence in the passage?

   (A) Saturn's rings have been interesting to scientists for a long time, but Saturn's moon Titan is also intriguing.

   (B) Astronomers have been fascinated with Saturn's rings since the 1600s, but in the 1940s, astronomers began to pay more attention to the rings on Titan.

   (C) In the 1940s, astronomers became interested in Titan, which is one of Saturn's rings, because of it is most unique among the rings.

   (D) Though they have been studied since the 1600s, the moon Titan's unique characteristics have caused astronomers to pay more attention to Saturn's rings.

Note-Taking

MI = Main Idea   SD = Supporting Details

P1 MI _____
   SD _____
P2 MI _____
   SD _____
      _____
P3 MI _____
   SD _____

UNIT TEST

1. Which of the sentences below best expresses the essential information in the highlighted sentence in the passage?

   (A) Buyers are able to set a market to equilibrium by refusing to buy from sellers.

   (B) A market reaches equilibrium when buyers and sellers agree on the price of a good.

   (C) When sellers want to sell a good, they must negotiate with buyers until they agree on a price.

   (D) Buyers and sellers call a market equilibrium when they have goods that want to buy or sell.

2. What does the author imply about the Great Depression ?

   (A) Keynesian economic theory can explain the causes or effects of the crisis.

   (B) The crisis was caused by markets that were not at equilibrium.

   (C) High effective demand led to prices that were too high for most people to afford.

   (D) The crisis was caused mostly by poor notional demand in developed economies.

3. The word This in the passage refers to

   (A) a teacher's worries about falling wages

   (B) a teacher's demand for discretionary goods like a new television

   (C) spending more money on a good than a person can afford

   (D) spending less money on a good than a person wants to spend

4. What is the main idea of paragraph 3?

   (A) Demand for labor affects demand and supply for discretionary goods.

   (B) Keynesian economic theory helped governments respond to a financial crisis.

   (C) Effective demand explains how a lack of demand in one market can reduce demand in another market.

   (D) Effective supply and effective demand explain how the prices in markets for goods can reach equilibrium.

   * Paragraph 3 is marked with an arrow [→].

5. Directions: Select the appropriate phrases from the answer choices and match them to the category to which they relate. TWO of the answer choices will NOT be used.

   Classical Economics   Keynes' Theory
   •   •
   •   •
   •

   Answer Choices

   (A) Says the supply and demand determines the price

   (B) Assumes equilibrium determines the supply

   (C) Considers equilibrium is the natural state of a market

   (D) Argues effective demand outweighs notional demand

   (E) Focuses on the effective demand

   (F) Is blamed for the Great Depression

   (G) Insists lack of demand in one market forces demand in another market

Effective Demand and Supply

In classical economics, the price of a good is determined by the supply of it and the demand for it. If many people want to buy something, but few people are willing or able to sell it, the price of that thing will increase. If, on the other hand, few people want to buy something, but many people want or need to sell it, the price will decrease. When buyers and sellers have arrived at an agreement on what the price should be, the market for that item is said to have reached equilibrium. Classical economists believed that equilibrium was the natural state of a market and that if a market for one good suffered from excess demand, another market was suffering from excess supply.

However, the Great Depression in 1930s shook the foundations of many economies around the world, and the classical economic theory was blamed for it. The governmental responses to this crisis led to a renewed interest in Keynesian economic theory and one of its central ideas: effective versus notional demand.

→ Keynes argued that it is possible for demand in one market to be constrained by lack of demand in another market. If, for example, the demand for teachers is low, then the pay for teachers will also be low. This will cause the teachers' wages to fall. As teachers' wages fall, their demand for discretionary goods will also fall. A teacher may want to spend a lot of money on a new television(notional demand), but actually spend very little(effective demand) because she is worried about her falling wages. This can have a devastating effect on an economy — as demand for labor drops, laborers' demand for goods also drops. The dropping demand for goods causes suppliers to produce less, which further reduces the demand for labor and the cycle repeats. The Keynes' theory shows new economic paradigms in modern society, refuting the classical economics.

GLOSSARY
equilibrium: a balance between several different aspects
notional: existing only in theory or an idea, not in reality
discretionary: not fixed by rules and decided on each individual case

VOCABULARY TEST

Recall the essential words in the unit to reinforce your vocabulary acquisition. Write the meaning of each word in your language.

predator	flourish
population	moral
compress	racial
gritty	constrain
speculate	luminary
herbivorous	struggle
fascinate	determine
devastating	extensive
protection	reconciliation
preceding	hypothesis
remnant	discretionary
chaotic	notional
protest	legible
privileged	complicated
elect	creature

strictly	equilibrium
imprisoned	stable
rely on	prey upon
in favor of	in captivity
be torn apart	stand out

Complete each sentence with the correct word or collocation.

1. There are several _____ on how Saturn's rings were formed.

2. The price of a good is _____ by the supply of it and the demand for it.

3. The novels showed the very real _____ of regular people.

4. Nelson Mandela oversaw the beginning of racial _____.

5. The musicians wrote fast-paced and _____ pieces.

6. Young Galapagos tortoises are _____ by the Galapagos hawk.

7. As teachers' wages fall, their demand for _____ goods will also fall.

8. The politician was _____ for more than 27 years.

9. Unlike the _____ century, American Realism portrayed the gritty reality.

10. Demand in one market can be _____ by lack of demand in another market.

determined	preceding	hypotheses	preyed upon	reconciliation
imprisoned	chaotic	constrained	struggles	discretionary

[TOEFL iBT® CODEBREAKER READING]

PROGRESS TEST 1

PROGRESS TEST 1

1. What is the main idea of this passage?

   (A) Lake Baikal contains numerous animal species.
   (B) Lake Baikal holds an enormous numbers of plants.
   (C) Various human activities have contaminated Lake Baikal.
   (D) Lake Baikal is a unique but threatened ecosystem.

2. The word despoiled in the passage could best be replaced by

   (A) ravaged
   (B) developed
   (C) interrupted
   (D) renovated

3. Look at the four squares [■] that indicate where the following sentence could be added to paragraph 2.

   In fact, it is estimated that Lake Baikal holds 20% of the planet's unfrozen freshwater.

   Where would the sentence best fit?

4. Which of the following is NOT true about Lake Baikal?

   (A) It has mountains all around it.
   (B) It is located 640km from Moscow.
   (C) It is deeper than any other lake.
   (D) It is more than at least 20 million years old.

5. The author's main purpose in paragraph 2 is to

   (A) present the freshwater lakes in southeastern Siberia
   (B) emphasize Lake Baikal's remote location
   (C) describe Lake Baikal's physical attributes
   (D) show how Lake Baikal has been changing

   * Paragraph 2 is marked with an arrow [→].

6. What can be inferred about the commercial fishing of omul?

   (A) It takes place on a smaller scale than in the past.
   (B) It grew greatly with the assistance of the government.
   (C) It makes use of specially designed fishing nets.
   (D) It has led to a decline in the lake's seal population.

7. The word discharging in the passage is closest in meaning to

   (A) reiterating
   (B) dismissing
   (C) spewing
   (D) filtering

Lake Baikal

Sometimes referred to as the "Galapagos of Russia," Lake Baikal is one of the world's most unique geological formations. Due to its size, age, and geographic isolation, it is home to a vast array of unique flora and fauna, which makes it a site of significant scientific interest. Unfortunately, it exists under the constant threat of being despoiled by human activity.

→ **A** The lake is located in southeastern Siberia about 4,350 kilometers east of Moscow and is surrounded by mountains on all sides. **B** It is about 640 kilometers in length, and, with a depth of nearly 1,700 meters, it is the deepest lake in the world. **C** It may also be the Earth's oldest freshwater lake as it is believed to have formed between 20 and 25 million years ago. **D**

About 1,340 animal species live in and around the lake, with 745 of them being endemic to the region. Among these animals is the Baikal seal, the only seal species found exclusively in freshwater environments. The lake is also home to the omul, a species of whitefish considered to be a great delicacy in the region. The commercial fishing industry was active on the lake as fishermen sought it in great numbers. This led to a dangerous decline in the omul population, but the imposition of strict quotas has allowed the species to bounce back.

The lake has also escaped other serious environmental threats. A paper mill that was discharging waste directly into its waters went bankrupt in 2013, and an oil company planning to run a pipeline along the lake's shore was forced by the government to make use of an alternative route. Other disruptive human activity on Lake Baikal includes the continued development of the local tourism industry and plans to build a uranium plant, which many fear will lead to the storage of radioactive waste in the area.

Efforts continue to keep Lake Baikal safe and unsullied. Its great beauty and biological diversity have inspired many, both in Russia and abroad, to advocate on behalf of its conservation.

GLOSSARY
endemic: natural to or characteristic of a specific place or people
quota: a proportional part or share of a fixed total amount or quantity

8 The word *its* in the passage refers to

(A) the lake

(B) a paper mill

(C) waste

(D) an oil company

9 Which of the sentences below best expresses the essential information in the highlighted sentence in the passage? *Incorrect* choices change the meaning in important ways or leave out essential information.

(A) The lake's tourism industry has been disrupted by plans to build a uranium plant.

(B) People hope that money from tourism will help replace a radioactive storage site.

(C) Radioactive material stored near the lake will be processed by a uranium plant.

(D) The growing tourism industry and a planned uranium plant are threatening the lake.

10 It is NOT stated that

(A) freshwater seals are found in Lake Baikal

(B) Lake Baikal is the largest lake in the world

(C) omul is one of the species that live in Lake Baikal

(D) a kind of industrial facility may be built in the area around Lake Baikal

11 Directions: An introductory sentence for a brief summary of the passage is provided below. Complete the summary by selecting the THREE answer choices that express the most important ideas in the passage.

Lake Baikal, home to a wide range of unique creatures, faces threats from human development.

-
-
-

Answer Choices

(A) The lake has about 745 indigenous animal species.

(B) The lake is located in a mountainous area of southeastern Siberia.

(C) Some of the lake's animal species are endemic, and strict quotas have been imposed.

(D) The lake is the deepest and oldest freshwater lake in the world.

(E) Even though some human activities have endangered the lake, there are plans to conserve the area.

(F) The local tourism industry is working to protect the lake by building a uranium plant.

Lake Baikal

Sometimes referred to as the "Galapagos of Russia," Lake Baikal is one of the world's most unique geological formations. Due to its size, age, and geographic isolation, it is home to a vast array of unique flora and fauna, which makes it a site of significant scientific interest. Unfortunately, it exists under the constant threat of being despoiled by human activity.

→ A The lake is located in southeastern Siberia about 4,350 kilometers east of Moscow and is surrounded by mountains on all sides. B It is about 640 kilometers in length, and, with a depth of nearly 1,700 meters, it is the deepest lake in the world. C It may also be the Earth's oldest freshwater lake as it is believed to have formed between 20 and 25 million years ago. D

About 1,340 animal species live in and around the lake, with 745 of them being endemic to the region. Among these animals is the Baikal seal, the only seal species found exclusively in freshwater environments. The lake is also home to the omul, a species of whitefish considered to be a great delicacy in the region. The commercial fishing industry was active on the lake as fishermen sought it in great numbers. This led to a dangerous decline in the omul population, but the imposition of strict quotas has allowed the species to bounce back.

The lake has also escaped other serious environmental threats. A paper mill that was discharging waste directly into its waters went bankrupt in 2013, and an oil company planning to run a pipeline along the lake's shore was forced by the government to make use of an alternative route. Other disruptive human activity on Lake Baikal includes the continued development of the local tourism industry and plans to build a uranium plant, which many fear will lead to the storage of radioactive waste in the area.

Efforts continue to keep Lake Baikal safe and unsullied. Its great beauty and biological diversity have inspired many, both in Russia and abroad, to advocate on behalf of its conservation.

GLOSSARY
endemic: natural to or characteristic of a specific place or people
quota: a proportional part or share of a fixed total amount or quantity

PROGRESS TEST 1

12 The word salient in the passage most likely means

(A) solid

(B) prominent

(C) intervenient

(D) complicated

13 What is implied about animal cells in the passage?

(A) They are also eukaryotic.

(B) They usually have one vacuole.

(C) They do not contain cytoplasm.

(D) Vacuoles in them push their organelles toward the outside of the cell.

14 The phrase this tough structure in the passage refers to

(A) cell wall

(B) animal cell

(C) eukaryotic cell

(D) characteristic shape

15 Why does the author mention turgor pressure in the passage?

(A) To argue for the importance of the vacuole in the cell

(B) To give an example of square-shaped plant cells

(C) To explain how plant cells get their shape and strength

(D) To describe how a physical force interacts with plant cells

16 Look at the four squares [■] that indicate where the following sentence could be added to paragraph 1.

By maintaining turgidity, plant cells are able to control their internal pressure without the simple pumps that exist in many animal cells.

Where would it best fit?

17 According to the passage, which of the following is true of chloroplasts?

(A) They are found in every plant cell.

(B) They require water from the vacuole to live.

(C) They require sunlight to produce energy.

(D) They are the most common part of plant cells.

18 What does the passage imply about photosynthesis?

(A) It is only done in one type of plant cell.

(B) It occurs both in chloroplasts and in the vacuole.

(C) Smaller cells produce more energy through it.

(D) If plant cells had smaller vacuoles, they would be unable to conduct it.

Plant Cells

Though similar to animal cells in many ways, plant cells share a number of features that distinguish them from other eukaryotic cells. The most salient feature of any plant cell is its cell wall. **A** Though its rigidity is often overestimated, this tough structure helps to give plant cells their characteristic rectangular or cubic shapes through turgor pressure. **B** The movement of water between the cell's large central vacuole, which is like a storage space for the cell, and the cell's cytoplasm, the soup that fills up the interior of the cell, causes the cell membrane to expand until it reaches the cell wall and is unable to expand any further. **C** The vacuole itself is much bigger than vacuoles found in animal cells, and there tends to be only a single vacuole in any adult plant cell. **D** This single organelle can take up between 30% and 80% of the space in the interior of a plant cell. The size of the vacuole helps the best-known parts of plant cells do their jobs; due to its size, the vacuole pushes chloroplasts against the cell wall, where they are exposed to sunlight which they use to generate energy for the cell and its organelles.

→ Most of a plant's biological needs are handled by parenchyma cells. These cells produce energy through photosynthesis and continue to divide and grow throughout a plant's life. A second type of plant cell, collenchyma cells, has strong, thick cell walls that retain some plasticity. They can stretch and provide support for areas of the plant that are growing. In contrast, sclerenchyma cells are hard and tough. These cells have waterproof cell walls filled with lignin, a type of carbon molecule that gives wood its strength. Since water cannot enter these cells, they quickly die. Their value to the plant, however, continues long after they are dead. Sclerenchyma cells provide much of the structure of woody plants. All three of these types of cells are found in most parts of plants, and plant tissues may be composed of one or more of these types of cells working together.

GLOSSARY
turgor pressure: the pressure exerted on a plant cell wall by water passing into the cell
vacuole: a fluid-filled cavity in the cytoplasm of a cell

PROGRESS TEST 1

19 The word plasticity in the passage could best be replaced by

(A) thickness

(B) flexibility

(C) carbon

(D) viscosity

20 According to paragraph 2, which of the following is NOT a function of plant cells?

(A) producing energy

(B) fighting diseases

(C) giving shape to the plant

(D) making up plant tissues

* Paragraph 2 is marked with an arrow [→].

21 Which of the sentences below best expresses the essential information in the highlighted sentence in the passage? *Incorrect* choices change the meaning in important ways or leave out essential information.

(A) Sclerenchyma cells are waterproof thanks to the material called lignin, which is made of carbon molecules.

(B) Although all plant cells are rigid, sclerenchyma cells gain extra strength from the carbon lignin that makes them waterproof.

(C) A particular type of carbon called lignin fills the waterproof cell walls of sclerenchyma cells and makes them tough and woody.

(D) Collenchyma and sclerenchyma cells have waterproof cell walls that fill the inside of the cells with a tough type of carbon called lignin.

22 Directions: Select the appropriate phrases from the answer choices and match them to the category to which they relate. TWO of the answer choices will NOT be used.

Parenchyma Cells
-
-
-

Collenchyma Cells
-
-

Sclerenchyma Cells
-
-

Answer Choices

(A) Do not stop dividing

(B) Are found where the plant is growing

(C) Have only one vacuole

(D) Are dead in adult plants

(E) Are a plant's energy factories

(F) Are like a plant's bones

(G) Make up most of a plant's tissue

(H) Control a plant's biological needs

(I) Have strong and thick cell walls

Plant Cells

Though similar to animal cells in many ways, plant cells share a number of features that distinguish them from other eukaryotic cells. The most salient feature of any plant cell is its cell wall. [A] Though its rigidity is often overestimated, this tough structure helps to give plant cells their characteristic rectangular or cubic shapes through turgor pressure. [B] The movement of water between the cell's large central vacuole, which is like a storage space for the cell, and the cell's cytoplasm, the soup that fills up the interior of the cell, cause the cell membrane to expand until it reaches the cell wall and is unable to expand any further. [C] The vacuole itself is much bigger than vacuoles found in animal cells, and there tends to be only a single vacuole in any adult plant cell. [D] This single organelle can take up between 30% and 80% of the space in the interior of a plant cell. The size of the vacuole helps the best-known parts of plant cells do their jobs; due to its size, the vacuole pushes chloroplasts against the cell wall, where they are exposed to sunlight which they use to generate energy for the cell and its organelles.

→ Most of a plant's biological needs are handled by parenchyma cells. These cells produce energy through photosynthesis and continue to divide and grow throughout a plant's life. A second type of plant cell, collenchyma cells, has strong, thick cell walls that retain some plasticity. They can stretch and provide support for areas of the plant that are growing. In contrast, sclerenchyma cells are hard and tough. These cells have waterproof cell walls filled with lignin, a type of carbon molecule that gives wood its strength. Since water cannot enter these cells, they quickly die. Their value to the plant, however, continues long after they are dead. Sclerenchyma cells provide much of the structure of woody plants. All three of these types of cells are found in most parts of plants, and plant tissues may be composed of one or more of these types of cells working together.

GLOSSARY

turgor pressure: the pressure exerted on a plant cell wall by water passing into the cell
vacuole: a fluid-filled cavity in the cytoplasm of a cell

[TOEFL iBT® CODEBREAKER READING]

PART 2 / Inference Questions

The part for Inference Questions asks test takers to infer what is implied in a passage based on the given facts and information. They are also asked to find out why the author mentions a certain piece of information in the passage and understand the logical and consistent relationship between parts of something whole.

TOEFL iBT® Reading Skills 02

UNIT 6 | Inference

UNIT 7 | Rhetorical Purpose

UNIT 8 | Insertion

TOEFL iBT® Reading Skills 02

Understanding Sentence Structure

Sentences can be divided into grammatical parts. Each part has a specific role to play in communicating ideas clearly. Most sentences are made up of a subject, verb, object or complement.

Type 1	S + V	The boy runs (quickly).
Type 2	S + V + C	Some of my friends are Hispanics.
Type 3	S + V + O	The shell on the back protects the turtle.
Type 4	S + V + I.O. + D.O.	The novel gave the author a great fortune.
Type 5	S + V + O + O.C.	The detective persuaded the man to reveal the secret.

Find the subject (S), verb (V), complement (C), direct object (D.O.), indirect object (I.O.) or objective complement (O.C.) in each sentence and write which sentence type it is.

1   Mystras was a fortified city built in 1249 by a prince of Achaea. Type 2

2   Keynes' theory shows us new economic paradigms in modern society. Type ___

3   Major depressive disorder causes people to experience feelings of sadness. Type ___

4   Claude Monet spent much of his time in painting in the garden. Type ___

5   Peter Durand made a process using tin cans that he patented in 1810. Type ___

6   Mystras became a cultural center known for its scholars. Type ___

7   The gases surround a layer of liquid metallic hydrogen. Type ___

8   Motion capture technology allows animated characters to move like actual actors. Type ___

Understanding Transition Words

Transition words and phrases indicate relations from sentence to sentence or from paragraph to paragraph. They make sentences and paragraphs flow together smoothly by providing logical organization.

Transition Words and Phrases	
To add	in addition, moreover, furthermore, as well as, on top of that
To compare	similarly, as ~ as, likewise, by comparison, compared to
To contrast	on the other hand, on the contrary, in contrast, whereas
To prove	evidently, obviously, that is
To summarize	in brief, briefly, overall, in short, to sum up, to summarize
To conclude	therefore, consequently, thus, in conclusion, as a result
Cause and effect	because (of), since, due to, owing to, hence, for the reason that
Examples	for example, for instance, such as, namely, to illustrate
Sequence	first, next, afterward, subsequently, consequently, later
Emphasis	in fact, indeed, definitely, without doubt, certainly, absolutely
Time	at that time, during, for, in, until

Fill in each blank with the appropriate transition word or phrase.

1. Litmus has a number of uses. Botanists, _____, use it to test soil's acidity.
2. Claude Monet rented a farmhouse in the suburb. _____, he painted many artworks of the garden in the house.
3. When _____ winter monsoons, summer monsoons are more powerful.
4. _____ motion capture technology, the modern cinema had a revolutionary advancement.
5. The astronomers discovered quasars _____ masers.
6. The Romantic Movement dominated the art scene _____ the 19th century.

| because of | during | compared to | as well as | afterward | for example |

TOEFL iBT® READING

UNIT 06

Inference

INTRODUCTION

Inference questions involve information that is not directly stated in the passages. Instead, the test taker must analyze the facts that are present and use them to draw a logical conclusion. Along with clues found within the passages, the test taker must use common sense and logic to find the unwritten implications of the material. These questions may ask the test taker to make inferences based on specific details or entire paragraphs.

TYPICAL QUESTION TYPES

What can be inferred about ~?

It can be inferred from paragraph ____ that

What probably occurs after ~?

STRATEGIES

- Find the key words in the question and then scan the passage to locate them. This will help you determine where the important information is.

- Once you find the important information, look for clearly positive or negative words. This can make you eliminate choices that do not match the mood.

- Remember that the inferred information will not be mentioned directly. You must use logic to figure out what is being suggested.

QUICK CHECKUP

Choose the sentence that makes the correct inference.

1 **History**

Mystras was a fortified city built by a prince of Achaea in 1249. It was soon conquered by the Byzantines and made the capital of a new Byzantine province, the Despotate of Mystras. This was the height of the city's glory as Mystras became a cultural center known for its beautiful churches, large libraries, and great scholars. Later, the city was taken by the Turks and then by the Venetians. In 1832, it was abandoned and today exists only as ruins.

(A) Several cultures dominated the city of Mystras for centuries.
(B) The city of Mystras was destroyed in a battle with the Turks.

2 **Psychology**

Major depressive disorder is a serious medical condition that causes people to continually experience feelings of profound sadness and hopelessness. Sufferers also tend to have trouble sleeping and eating, which can have severe consequences in terms of their physical health. Unlike normal feelings of depression, major depressive disorder does not stem from a clear cause and is not likely to dissipate quickly. Generally, a full recovery requires treatment from a certified health professional.

(A) Major depressive disorder can last for an extended period of time.
(B) Major depressive disorder can be caused by physical illnesses.

3 **Zoology**

The kagu is a flightless bird found only on the island of New Caledonia. Unlike other birds that live on the forest floor and which rely on their dark colors to camouflage them from predators, the kagu is light gray with a bright orange beak and legs. The kagu's large, fully formed wings are another unusual feature for a flightless bird. Unfortunately, nonindigenous animals introduced to New Caledonia by humans have been preying on the kagu and have made it an endangered species.

(A) The kagu uses its large wings to defend itself.
(B) New Caledonia's kagu population is in decline.

VOCABULARY

Write the number of each word's definition.

>>

1 *n.* the opposite of something

2 *v.* to rub a surface to make it shine

3 *n.* loss of strength or health

4 *adj.* related to improving the appearance to be more appealing

5 *v.* to decide to avoid or not do something

6 *v.* to drag something hard across a surface

7 *v.* to take food or medicine

8 *v.* to undergo a reaction that changes sugar to alcohol

9 *v.* to inform someone of the direction he or she is facing

10 *adj.* representing ideas rather than resembling actual objects

11 *adj.* of wide extent or occurrence

12 *v.* to affect one another through actions or communication

reverse _____

ferment _____

forgo _____

orient _____

abstract _____

decay _____

cosmetic _____

scrape _____

polish _____

ingest _____

interact _____

prevalent _____

Match each collocation with the correct definition.

a be applied to   •   • working together with

b be made up of   •   • to be put into something

c be placed in   •   • to be put with a substance for a specific purpose

d in conjunction with   •   • to consist of

e be treated with   •   • to be spread on a surface

Circle the word closest in meaning to each underlined word.

1 The man always emphasized the importance of interacting.
 (A) affirming (B) devising (C) injecting (D) communicating

2 Those who choose to forgo the study sessions will do poorly on the exam.
 (A) forsake (B) combine (C) select (D) enhance

3 Some people say violence in films has become prevalent.
 (A) equivalent (B) refreshing (C) widespread (D) precise

4 The doctor told the kid to chew his food well before he ingests it.
 (A) terminates (B) swallows (C) remodels (D) sterilizes

5 When the decay of the walls of the house begins, you must replace them.
 (A) expansion (B) deterioration (C) reinforcement (D) construction

6 The underside of the car scraped along the pavement and caused sparks to fly.
 (A) defined (B) craved (C) dragged (D) trimmed

Fill in each blank with the correct collocation.

1 A thick layer of sunscreen should _____ your skin.

2 The school committee _____ students, parents, and teachers.

3 The wood must _____ chemicals to make it waterproof.

4 The company created the service _____ the government.

5 Illegal immigrants will _____ a holding cell until the police arrive.

| be treated with | be placed in | be applied to |
| in conjunction with | | is made up of |

STEP 01

Timed Reading (WPM) □1'00" □1'30" □2'00"

Chemistry

Litmus

Litmus, a dye made from organic sources, is most notably used by chemists to determine whether a solution is an acid or base. When exposed to an acid solution, blue litmus will turn red. The reverse will occur when red litmus is placed in a base solution.

Chemists generally make use of paper that has been treated with litmus. The litmus itself is made from lichens, small plantlike organisms that grow on rocks and trees. The lichens are crushed, mixed with ammonia and potash, and fermented. Finally, chalk is added, and the mixture is dried and made into a powder. It is believed that litmus was first used in the early 14th century. Today, litmus has a number of uses. Botanists, for example, use it to test soil's acidity to make sure it is suitable for plants while doctors use it to check the health of pregnant women.

GLOSSARY **potash:** a white powder that is from wood ashes

Note-Taking

Litmus

What It Is	a _____ made from _____ sources
What It Does	determine whether a solution is an _____ or _____
	an acid makes _____ litmus _____ / a _____ makes _____ litmus _____
How It Is Made	_____ – crushed, mixed, _____, dried → becomes a _____
How It Is Used	to test _____ or to check the health of _____ women

1 What probably occurs after litmus is made into a powder?

    (A) It is applied to paper for a chemical use.
    (B) It is fermented and used to treat plants.
    (C) It is dissolved in a liquid and turns blue or red.
    (D) It is added to chalk, which consists of other powders.

2 What can be inferred from the passage?

    (A) Litmus paper was invented by some chemists.
    (B) If a solution is neutral, litmus becomes transparent.
    (C) Blue and red lichens are used to make litmus.
    (D) Soils can have different levels of acidity.

SUMMARY

Litmus is used to tell if a solution is an _____ or a _____. It changes color from _____ to _____ and vice versa. _____ that has been treated with _____ is usually used. Litmus is made from _____. They are _____ and _____ with _____ and potash. After they are _____, _____ is added, and the entire mixture is turned into a _____. Litmus is used to test _____ and to check the _____ of _____ women.

VOCAB

Match each word with the correct definition.

a   dye   •   • left or being without cover or protection

b   organic   •   • a group of tiny plants that look like moss

c   solution   •   • a substance that is used to change something's color

d   exposed   •   • a liquid in which a solid substance has been dissolved

e   lichen   •   • pertaining to only to natural elements

STEP 02

Timed Reading (WPM)
☐ 1'00" ☐ 1'30" ☐ 2'00"

Art

Monet at Giverny

Claude Monet was a famous French painter best known as the founder of the Impressionist Movement. In 1883, looking to escape the city, he relocated to the small village of Giverny, where he and his family rented a farmhouse and two acres of surrounding land. Together, they created an elaborate garden that provided the painter with both the inspiration and subjects for some of his greatest work.

Monet spent much of his time painting in the garden while forgoing the traditional artist's studio in favor of working outdoors. As with his earlier Impressionist paintings, he focused on colors and the movement of light across his subjects, which included irises, dahlias, and weeping willow trees.

In 1893, Monet expanded his garden to include a Japanese water garden with a pond that contained beautiful water lilies. His paintings of these flowers are considered some of the greatest masterpieces of their time. Without a horizon to orient viewers, the paintings created rough representations of the water lilies against the reflections of the sky and clouds on the surface of the pond. The abstract nature of these works has been attributed to the influence of modern art, but some believe that Monet's worsening eyesight also played a role.

Note-Taking

MI = Main Idea   SD = Supporting Details

P1 MI _____ – relocated to _____ in 1883

SD created a _____ which offered the _____ & _____

P2 MI painted in the _____

SD focused on _____ & the movement of _____ across his subjects

P3 MI his masterpieces

SD paintings of _____ – created _____ representations of the _____

_____, the _____ of the sky & _____ on the surface of the _____

1 What can be inferred about Giverny?

   (A) It was Monet's hometown and was in a suburban area of France.
   (B) Monet liked the area because it was very near Paris.
   (C) Many of the villagers in Giverny had Japanese gardens.
   (D) It was in the countryside and had beautiful natural scenery.

2 The word elaborate in the passage is closest in meaning to

   (A) eligible
   (B) prodigious
   (C) vigorous
   (D) devastated

3 What can be inferred about Monet's water lily paintings?

   (A) They are still on display in the village of Giverny.
   (B) They are somewhat blurrier than other paintings.
   (C) They feature a wide variety of dark colors.
   (D) They were completed in the artist's studio.

VOCAB

Write the correct word for each definition.

a   a feeling of enthusiasm from something   _____

b   having slender hanging branches   _____

c   to have as contents   _____

d   a description of something   _____

e   an image that is seen in a mirror or water _____

| weeping |
| contain |
| reflection |
| representation |
| inspiration |

Toothpaste

Traditionally, toothpaste serves as the foundation of the standard oral hygiene regimen. When applied to the teeth with a toothbrush, it removes plaque and food particles, reduces halitosis, and helps prevent tooth decay and gum disease. It can also have the cosmetic effect of removing stains and whitening teeth.

Toothpaste is primarily made up of abrasives such as aluminum hydroxide and calcium carbonate. Rather than reacting on the chemical level, these particles work in conjunction with the mechanical motions of the toothbrush. Essentially, they scrape unwanted material from the teeth and provide a low level of polishing, which can give teeth a brighter appearance.

The main active ingredient of most commercial toothpastes is fluoride. This is a naturally occurring material known to strengthen bones and enamel, which is the outer covering of teeth. Fluoride is added to toothpaste to aid in the prevention of cavities and gingivitis, an oral disease that causes an inflammation of the gums. Although harmless if swallowed in small quantities, ingesting large amounts of fluoride can be a serious health risk. Other components of commercial toothpastes include surfactants, which cause the toothpaste to foam and to spread evenly through the mouth, and antibacterial agents, which are added mainly to reduce bad breath. Most toothpastes also contain either natural or artificial flavoring agents. Nowadays, there are many commercial toothpastes with a variety of pleasing tastes although these serve no practical purpose.

VOCAB

Find the correct word in the passage for each of the given definition.

a   a set of rules about food and exercise: _____

b   the scientific term for bad breath: _____

c   any material or substance used for grinding: _____

d   made by human skill: _____

1 Why does the author mention mechanical motions ?

   (A) To show how abrasives work
   (B) To explain how abrasives are made
   (C) To give advice on avoiding polishing effects
   (D) To warn about some harmful methods of brushing one's teeth

2 Which of the following is NOT true about fluoride?

   (A) It is not an artificial substance.
   (B) It has a whitening effect.
   (C) It makes bones and enamel stronger.
   (D) Swallowing too much of it can make a person ill.

3 What can be inferred about flavoring agents?

   (A) They are not included in most commercial toothpastes.
   (B) They are a health hazard to young children and the elderly.
   (C) They are added to make brushing one's teeth a more enjoyable experience.
   (D) They are activated by artificial chemicals that are found in toothpaste.

4 What can be inferred from the passage?

   (A) Natural toothpaste is better than artificial toothpaste.
   (B) Surfactants make toothpaste less effective.
   (C) Toothpaste foam can harm tooth enamel.
   (D) Intaking fluoride without caution can harm one's health.

Note-Taking

MI = Main Idea   SD = Supporting Details

P1 MI _____
    SD _____
P2 MI _____
    SD _____
P3 MI _____
    SD _____
        _____
        _____

UNIT TEST

1. What is the main idea of the passage?

   (A) Symbiosis occurs between two members of the same species.

   (B) Relationships between plants and animals take several different forms.

   (C) Animals benefit more than plants in most interspecies relationships.

   (D) Mutualism is the most common type of plant-animal symbiosis.

2. The word them in the passage refers to

   (A) flowers

   (B) honeybees

   (C) pollen and nectar

   (D) honeybees and their larvae

3. What can be inferred from paragraph 2?

   (A) Nectar prevents honeybees from harming flowers.

   (B) Honeybees work together to provide their larvae with food.

   (C) Some flower species harm insects such as honeybees.

   (D) Flowers need to share their pollen in order to reproduce.

   * Paragraph 2 is marked with an arrow [→].

4. What can be inferred about aphids?

   (A) They are preyed upon by some plants.

   (B) They help protect plants from parasites.

   (C) They damage plants by taking advantage of them.

   (D) They both receive and provide benefits by living on certain plants.

5. All of the following are true EXCEPT

   (A) it is possible for symbiosis to occur between two animal species

   (B) both bees and flowers benefit from their symbiotic relationship

   (C) trees with bird nests in their holes are protected from predator

   (D) Ophiocordyceps unilateralis is a parasite that preys on ants

6. Directions: Select the appropriate phrases from the answer choices and match them to the category to which they relate. ONE of the answer choices will NOT be used.

   Mutualism   Commensalism   Parasitism
   •   •   •
                •   •

   Answer Choices

   (A) Involves the relationship between honeybees and flowers

   (B) May help one species but hurt the other

   (C) Takes place when aphids suck on animals' brains

   (D) Can happen between some plants and aphids

   (E) May result in one species being harmed while the other is killed

   (F) Can have one species be unaffected

   (G) Happens when birds nest in tree holes

Plant-Animal Symbiosis

Symbiosis is said to occur when two different species regularly interact in a way that affects both species. This commonly occurs between two animal species, but symbiotic relationships can also exist between plant and animal species.

→ One of the most prevalent forms of symbiosis is mutualism, a relationship in which both species receive beneficial effects from their interactions. A classic example of mutualism can be seen with flowers and honeybees. Honeybees gather both pollen and nectar from flowers and use them as food for their larvae. As they do so, they inadvertently spread pollen from flower to flower, which allows them to reproduce. In this way, each species depends on the other for survival.

Commensalism is another type of symbiosis. In commensalism, one species benefits from the interaction while the second is neither helped nor harmed in any significant way. Some trees, for example, develop large holes in their trunks as they grow. These holes are used by many types of birds as places to build their nests. Therefore, the trees provide the birds with shelter and safety from predators without being significantly affected by the presence of the birds.

Finally, there is plant-animal symbiosis in which one species is helped and the other is harmed or even killed. Known as parasitism, it can be seen in the behavior of aphids, small insects that live on plants and suck the sap from them. Plant life, however, can also be parasitic. Fungal parasites can be found living in or on many types of mammals, insects, and fish. The most extreme of these is Ophiocordyceps unilateralis, a fungus that infects ants and eventually takes control of their brains. The fungus forces ants to walk to suitable places for the fungus to grow before killing the unfortunate insects.

GLOSSARY
pollen: a fine powdery substance produced by a flower or plant
sap: the juice or fluid of a plant

VOCABULARY TEST

Recall the essential words in the unit to reinforce your vocabulary acquisition. Write the meaning of each word in your language.

exposed		ferment	
dye		inspiration	
cosmetic		reverse	
interact		suck	
sap		orient	
ingest		pollen	
halitosis		decay	
contain		fortified	
abandon		lichen	
dissipate		representation	
artificial		prevalent	
regimen		scholar	
polish		camouflage	
organic		conquer	
solution		weeping	

forgo	abstract
scrape	reflection
abrasive	be placed in
in conjunction with	be made up of
be applied to	be treated with

Complete each sentence with the correct word or collocation.

1 When _____ to an acid solution, blue litmus will turn red.

2 Toothpaste is primarily _____ abrasives such as aluminum hydroxide.

3 Mystras became a cultural center known for its great _____.

4 One of the most _____ forms of symbiosis is mutualism.

5 Honeybees gather both _____ and nectar from flowers.

6 Most toothpastes _____ either natural or artificial flavoring agents.

7 Monet created a beautiful garden that provided him with the _____.

8 Mystras was soon _____ by the Byzantines.

9 Litmus is made from _____, small plantlike organisms that grow on rocks.

10 Major depressive disorder does not stem from a clear cause and is not likely to _____ quickly.

inspiration	conquered	scholars	pollen	contain
lichens	exposed	made up of	prevalent	dissipate

UNIT 07

Rhetorical Purpose

INTRODUCTION

Rhetorical purpose questions require the test taker to identify the reason an author includes particular information in a passage or emphasizes a specific point. They can also ask about the purpose of an entire paragraph.

TYPICAL QUESTION TYPES

The author's main purpose in paragraph _____ is to

Why does the author mention _____ in paragraph _____?

The author refers to _____ in the passage to indicate that

STRATEGIES

- Read the question carefully to determine if you are being asked about the purpose of a paragraph as a whole or about a single point or detail.

- For questions about details, try to identify the broad category that the information falls into. It could be comparing two things, giving an example, emphasizing a point, or showing that an idea is incorrect.

- For questions about the main point of a paragraph, focus on the opening and concluding sentences. If these do not contain enough clues, scan the body of the paragraph for key words.

QUICK CHECKUP

Choose the reason why the author mentioned the highlighted sentence.

1 Custom

In Judaism, a bar mitzvah is a ritual marking a boy's transition to adulthood. Bar mitzvahs are held when boys turn thirteen. **This is the age at which they are considered to be responsible for their own actions.** The ceremony itself requires months of preparation as the boy will be required to lead a prayer service, to read a section of the Torah, or to give a speech about the Torah. The ceremony is generally followed by an extravagant party, featuring food and beverages.

(A) To emphasize the importance of bar mitzvahs
(B) To give the reason for the timing of bar mitzvahs

2 Economy

The bandwagon effect is a term used to explain the behavior of investors who purchase stocks without doing research or consulting a stockbroker. Instead, they simply invest in stocks that many other people have already purchased. **While this may seem like irrational behavior, it can be a strategic way of utilizing the collective knowledge of the market.** However, this kind of behavior can result in bad investments since it tends to keep investors from making rational choices.

(A) To show a positive side of the bandwagon effect
(B) To illustrate the primary cause of the bandwagon effect

3 Art

During the 19th century, the Romantic Movement dominated the European art scene. Romantic music in particular thrived in Germany, where composers such as Beethoven, Mendelssohn, and Wagner created some of the greatest compositions in the history of Western classical music. **While these composers used traditional formats, such as sonatas and symphonies, they also made use of rich harmonies and new types of melodies.** Ultimately, their goal was to express strong feelings that would elicit emotional responses from their audiences.

(A) To explain the features of Romantic music
(B) To compare Romantic music with another musical style

VOCABULARY

Write the number of each word's definition.

1 *n.* something that must be done and that is very important

2 *v.* to make something dirty or harmful

3 *n.* a material used to keep something warm

4 *n.* something that replaces another thing

5 *n.* a person who actively supports something

6 *v.* to adjust the amount, degree or rate of something

7 *adj.* relating to heat

8 *n.* the quality of being resilient

9 *adj.* relating to space or the sky

10 *v.* to use logic to figure something out

11 *v.* to send out something

12 *v.* to recreate something exactly

>>

imperative   _____
deduce   _____
contaminate _____
replicate   _____
substitute   _____
elasticity   _____
insulation   _____
regulate   _____
emit   _____
celestial   _____
thermal   _____
proponent   _____

Match each collocation with the correct definition.

a flake off   •   • the greater number or part of

b in terms of   •   • to fall off a surface in flat pieces

c embark on   •   • to address as a topic

d the majority of   •   • as related to a specific subject

e be concerned with   •   • to begin something long and difficult

Circle the word closest in meaning to each underlined word.

1   The detective was able to deduce the criminal's identity.
    (A) announce   (B) retract   (C) impair   (D) infer

2   The artist tried to replicate the painting she saw in a museum.
    (A) purchase   (B) copyright   (C) analyze   (D) reproduce

3   The emissions from the factory are contaminating the river.
    (A) polluting   (B) solidifying   (C) flooding   (D) infiltrating

4   The device emits a beeping sound when its battery is low.
    (A) emanates   (B) records   (C) utilizes   (D) installs

5   According to the recipe, yogurt can be a(an) substitute for milk.
    (A) subtitle   (B) replacement   (C) elimination   (D) assistance

6   It is the heart's job to regulate the flow of blood in the body.
    (A) coagulate   (B) complicate   (C) coordinate   (D) aggregate

Fill in each blank with the correct collocation.

1   _____ salary, this is one of the best careers to pursue.

2   The polls showed that _____ voters support the president.

3   The paint is beginning to _____ this old house.

4   The survey questions _____ attitudes toward religion.

5   Before someone _____ a journey, certain preparations must be made.

| the majority of   flake off   are concerned with   in terms of   embarks on |

UNIT 7_ Rhetorical Purpose 115

STEP 01

Timed Reading (WPM)
☐ 1'00" ☐ 1'30" ☐ 2'00"

History

Canned Food

Throughout history, finding effective ways to preserve food for later use was considered an imperative for survival. Some cultures relied on salting while others practiced various methods of pickling. However, it was not until the late 18th century that the idea of storing food in airtight containers was conceived.

In 1810, a process using tin cans was patented by an Englishman named Peter Durand. Three years later, the first canning factory was established to mass-produce canned edible goods for sailors embarking on lengthy sea journeys. Much as they are today, the cans were filled with food, sealed, and then heated. Interestingly, the reason that canned food lasts longer without spoiling was not fully understood at this time. It was not until fifty years later that the scientist Louis Pasteur deduced that heat killed the bacteria that cause food to go bad while the airtight cans prevented further bacteria from contaminating the food.

GLOSSARY practice: to do or perform habitually

Note-Taking

The Timeline of Canned Food

Before 18th	relied on _____ & _____ to _____ food for later use
In 1810	used _____ — _____ by Peter Durand
In 1813	_____ the first _____
50 Years Later	found out _____ killed the _____ & the _____ prevented further _____

1   Why does the author mention salting and pickling in the passage?

   (A) To illustrate the problems caused by canning
   (B) To give examples of earlier preserving methods
   (C) To contrast two different types of food-canning methods
   (D) To explain why unpreserved food goes bad

2   The author refers to sailors in the passage to indicate that

   (A) canned food was exported around the world
   (B) there was a shortage of canning factory workers
   (C) some people did not trust food kept in cans
   (D) canned food was helpful on a long-term voyage

SUMMARY

In the past, food was _____ through _____. Then, people realized that food could be stored in _____. In _____, a process using _____ was _____. A _____ was _____ three years later. It mass-produced _____ goods that could be eaten by _____ on ships. About _____ later, Louis Pasteur figured out that _____ killed the _____ that cause food go bad and that _____ protected the food from other _____.

⚙ VOCAB

Match each word with the correct definition.

a   conceive   ·   · fit to be eaten as food

b   patent   ·   · to cover something to prevent from other materials

c   edible   ·   · to make or sell a new product

d   seal   ·   · to form a notion or idea

e   spoil   ·   · to go bad

STEP 02

Technology

Motion Capture

Motion capture technology is a type of visual recording system. Its basic function is to record the exact movements of a person or object. It can also be used to capture a person's subtle facial expressions. These movements and expressions can then be applied to a 3D virtual model on a computer and replicated with great accuracy.

→ A subject to be recorded with motion capture technology must first be covered with a large number of small markers. In the case of human subjects, a special motion capture bodysuit with built-in markers located near all of the body's major joints can be worn. To capture facial expressions, up to 300 tiny markers are applied directly to the skin of a person's face.

Although it has sports, gaming, military and medical applications, motion capture technology is most often employed by the film industry. In terms of special effects, it is commonly used as a substitute for traditional computer animation. Its primary advantage is that it provides animated characters with previously unachievable levels of realism and allows them to move and to express emotions just like actual actors. Because of this, it is considered by many to be a revolutionary advancement in modern cinema.

Note-Taking

MI = Main Idea   SD = Supporting Details

P1 MI _____ — a type of _____ sys.
    SD records the _____ of a prsn. or object
P2 MI what is needed for motion capture technology
    SD human — a _____ w/ built-in _____
P3 MI motion capture technology in the _____
    SD _____ — a _____ for TD _____

Abbreviations for Note-Taking: sys. (system), prsn. (person), TD (traditional)

1 The word subtle in the passage could best be replaced by

   (A) vivid
   (B) initial
   (C) delicate
   (D) conspicuous

2 The author's main purpose in paragraph 2 is to

   (A) contrast various forms of computer animation
   (B) show the high cost of motion capture technology
   (C) illustrate an advantage of motion capture technology
   (D) explain how the motion capture process is prepared

   * Paragraph 2 is marked with an arrow [→].

3 Why does the author mention actual actors in the passage?

   (A) To offer a solution to a technical difficulty
   (B) To stress how motion capture characters look real
   (C) To show who benefits from motion capture technology
   (D) To explain the origins of traditional computer animation

✲ VOCAB

Write the correct word for each definition.

a	the condition of being exact	_____	
b	the use of an idea or method	_____	
c	first in rank or importance	_____	
d	not being able to be attained by effort	_____	
e	very new and innovative	_____	

primary
accuracy
revolutionary
unachievable
application

STEP 03

Timed Reading (WPM)
☐ 2'00" ☐ 2'30" ☐ 3'00"

Biology

Human Skin

Skin is the human body's largest organ, averaging approximately 2 square meters in size and 3.6 kilograms in weight. Being made up of three main layers, it serves many valuable functions as the body's outer layer.

The waterproof outer layer, known as the epidermis, protects the body from bacterial infection. Unlike most other body tissue, the epidermis contains no blood vessels, drawing the bulk of its nourishment from oxygen in the air. The majority of epidermal cells, called keratinocytes, form in the middle of the epidermis and gradually move toward the surface. There, they die and eventually flake off, providing the body's front line of protection. The dermis is the next layer, located directly beneath the epidermis. Made up of connective tissue, it gives the skin its strength and elasticity. Hair follicles and sweat glands are also found in the dermis, as are numerous blood vessels and the nerve endings that give us our sense of touch and ability to sense outside temperatures. The skin's deepest layer is the hypodermis, also known as the subcutis. Made up primarily of fat that cushions the body from the impact of physical contact and provides vital insulation, it anchors the skin to the body's bones and muscles as well. The fat in this layer can also be used as fuel by the body when the available food supply is short.

Overall, the skin with three layers protects us from external threats, regulates our body temperature, allows our sense of touch to connect us to the outside world and acts as a vital insulation.

GLOSSARY follicle: a small hollow in the skin which hairs grow from

⚙ VOCAB

Find the correct word in the passage for each of the given definition.

a   the process of acquiring a disease: _____

b   something that sustains with food or nutriment: _____

c   to fix or fasten: _____

d   existing on the outside of something: _____

1 What can be inferred about keratinocytes?

(A) They are larger than average cells.
(B) They must be replaced continuously.
(C) They are found in most human organs.
(D) They protect our body from inner bacteria.

2 Why does the author mention our sense of touch in the passage?

(A) To explain why the skin has blood vessels
(B) To compare hair follicles with sweat glands
(C) To show where the dermis is located
(D) To present one of the roles of the dermis

3 Why does the author mention fuel in the passage?

(A) To offer one of the causes of fat
(B) To show how fat damages the skin
(C) To illustrate how fat accumulates on skin
(D) To introduce another function of fat

4 Which of the following is NOT true about the layers of human skin?

(A) The deepest layer is mostly made up of fat.
(B) The middle part of the skin has no blood vessels.
(C) The hypodermis is located below the dermis.
(D) It is the epidermis which keeps us from outer threats.

Note-Taking

MI = Main Idea   SD = Supporting Details

P1 MI ____
   SD ____
P2 MI ____
   SD ____
      ____
      ____
P3 MI ____
   SD ____

UNIT 7_ Rhetorical Purpose 121

UNIT TEST

1. What is the main idea of the passage?

   (A) Radio astronomy is a generally misunderstood scientific field.
   (B) Radio astronomy is important in figuring out celestial objects.
   (C) Radio astronomy has made important contributions to science.
   (D) The ultimate goal of radio astronomy is to find new planets.

2. What can be inferred about quasars, pulsars and masers?

   (A) They move through space.
   (B) They emit radio waves.
   (C) They are very large.
   (D) They caused the Big Bang.

3. The author's main purpose in paragraph 2 is to

   (A) describe a common source of radio waves
   (B) contrast radio astronomy and astronomy
   (C) explain how radio telescopes function
   (D) give a brief history of radio astronomy

   * Paragraph 2 is marked with an arrow [→].

4. The word they in the passage refers to

   (A) skies
   (B) astronomers
   (C) radio telescopes
   (D) radio wave sources

5. Why does the author mention an intelligent source in the passage?

   (A) To suggest that radio astronomy may one day detect alien life
   (B) To emphasize the complexity of radio astronomy technology
   (C) To show why radio astronomy is not well respected
   (D) To praise the creator of the Big Bang theory

6. Directions: An introductory sentence for a brief summary of the passage is provided below. Complete the summary by selecting the THREE answer choices that express the most important ideas in the passage.

   Radio astronomy is the study of objects in space that emit radio waves.

   -
   -
   -

   ### Answer Choices

   (A) It uses radio telescopes to detect radio waves and enables to study distant objects.
   (B) Karl Jansky was an American physicist.
   (C) It is considered a subfield of astronomy.
   (D) Many important discoveries have been made through radio astronomy.
   (E) It supports the Big Bang theory giving important evidence and raises the hope for extraterrestrials.
   (F) The world's largest radio telescope is located in Puerto Rico.

Radio Astronomy

A subfield of astronomy, the scientific study of planets and stars, radio astronomy is concerned with studying objects in space through the use of radio telescopes. These are used to detect and record radio signals being emitted from beyond our planet. The largest radio telescope, located at the Arecibo Observatory in Puerto Rico, is more than 300 meters in diameter.

→ Radio astronomy began in the 1930s when an American physicist named Karl Jansky observed that radio signals were being broadcast from parts of our galaxy. Since that time, radio astronomers have come to realize that space is full of radio waves, some of them coming from deep in space. They have also discovered a number of completely new celestial objects, such as quasars, pulsars and masers.

The radio telescopes used by astronomers are essentially large dish antennas that can be pointed in the direction of distant radio wave sources. Often they are used simply to scan the skies, gathering data that may allow scientists to eventually find new sources of radio wave signals. The sun is one of the most active radio wave emitters in our galaxy, but there are other far more powerful sources located billions of light years away. The brilliance of radio astronomy is that it allows scientists to "observe" these unknown objects, even though they cannot actually be seen.

One of the most important scientific achievements of radio astronomy was the detection of the "cosmic microwave background." Discovered in 1964, this thermal radiation is believed to be left over from the creation of the universe and provides proponents of the Big Bang theory with valuable evidence. And, of course, there is also the hope that radio telescopes will someday detect broadcasts from an intelligent source, proving that human beings are not alone in the universe.

GLOSSARY cosmic: of or pertaining to the part of space

VOCABULARY TEST

Recall the essential words in the unit to reinforce your vocabulary acquisition. Write the meaning of each word in your language.

edible	imperative
infection	elasticity
substitute	anchor
celestial	proponent
nourishment	animated
external	primary
cosmic	transition
patent	strategic
spoil	seal
contaminate	revolutionary
emit	elicit
regulate	follicle
deduce	application
brilliance	unachievable
accuracy	irrational

conceive	dominate
replicate	insulation
thermal	flake off
in terms of	the majority of
be concerned with	embark on

Complete each sentence with the correct word or collocation.

1 Made up of connective tissue, the dermis gives the skin its _____.

2 Canned food was used for sailors _____ lengthy sea journeys.

3 The Romantic Movement _____ the European art scene.

4 Radio telescopes detect radio signals being _____ from beyond our planet.

5 Motion capture technology also has sports, military and medical _____.

6 In Judaism, a bar mitzvah is a ritual marking a boy's _____ to adulthood.

7 The composers' goal was to _____ an emotional response from their audience.

8 It can be a _____ way of utilizing the collective knowledge of the market.

9 Finding effective ways to preserve food was considered an _____.

10 It provides animated characters with previously _____ levels of realism.

applications	embarking on	strategic	dominated	transition
elasticity	unachievable	elicit	emitted	imperative

UNIT 08

Insertion

INTRODUCTION

Insertion questions ask the test taker to find the proper location within the passage for a given sentence. In order to insert the sentence correctly, the test takers must comprehend how the passage flows both grammatically and logically.

TYPICAL QUESTION TYPE

Look at the four squares [■] that indicate where the following sentence could be added to the passage.

Moreover, they were even barred from buying land in their own country.

Where would the sentence best fit?

STRATEGIES

- Search the sentence and possible insertion points for linking words and phrases. These will give clues as to where the sentence belongs.

- Find the pronouns in the sentence and around the possible insertion points. Then, look for the nouns to which the pronouns refer.

- Carefully read the sentences on either side of the possible insertion points. If the two sentences cannot be separated, you can eliminate that choice.

QUICK CHECKUP

Check the square where the given sentence fits.

1 Social Science

> The definition of plagiarism in the art world is more ambiguous.

Taking the creative output of another and representing it as your own is known as plagiarism. [A] Plagiarism is widespread in many professional fields, most notably journalism and the arts. [B] Journalists are expected to consult previously written works on the topics they address; however, failure to clearly cite these sources is considered unethical. [C] Artists regularly borrow from one another and, in doing so, blur the line between inspiration and copyright infringement. [D]

2 History

> It is believed that this population shift was spurred by increased soil salinity, which sharply reduced crop production.

Sumer was one of the Mesopotamian region's earliest civilizations and was located in what is now Kuwait and southern Iraq. [A] Like ancient Greece, Sumer was originally made up of numerous city-states. [B] A dynastic period began around 2900 B.C., with a series of powerful dynasties uniting the region. [C] However, Sumer fell into decline approximately 800 years later as people began to move north. [D]

3 Culture

> It is traditionally used to dictate the orientation of buildings to ensure that they are in harmony with this energy.

Literally meaning "wind-water," feng shui is a Chinese philosophy that deals with the invisible energy holding the universe together. [A] This could be in relation to the stars, geographical features, or the points on a compass. [B] Although it is more than 3,000 years old, feng shui is still practiced today. [C] Some modern homes and offices are arranged with its principles in mind. [D]

VOCABULARY

Write the number of each word's definition.

1 v. to discover the presence of something

2 v. to supply crops with water

3 n. a severe shortage of food

4 n. an official public announcement of something

5 v. to have a feeling in mind

6 v. to cause or influence

7 adj. living or growing in water

8 v. to make something harmless or ineffective

9 adj. not capable of being affected by a disease

10 n. a feeling of harshness

11 v. to leave one country to permanently live in another

12 n. a tax imposed on imported or exported goods

>>

aquatic _____

famine _____

emigrate _____

severity _____

tariff _____

harbor _____

proclamation _____

immune _____

neutralize _____

detect _____

induce _____

irrigate _____

Match each collocation with the correct definition.

a be ruled by   •   • to have a wide range of

b take control   •   • to be under the control of

c take steps   •   • linked or related to

d vary in   •   • to have the power to dominate

e associated with   •   • to figure out a measure or solution

Circle the word closest in meaning to each underlined word.

1. The mathematician was able to <u>detect</u> an error in the equation.
   (A) analyze   (B) identify   (C) correct   (D) interpret

2. The woman wanted the <u>severity</u> of her life to end.
   (A) rigor   (B) variety   (C) embracement   (D) serendipity

3. This document is the <u>proclamation</u> of the new ruling government.
   (A) obstacle   (B) formation   (C) enforcement   (D) decree

4. After the war, thousands of people <u>emigrated</u> from the country to neighboring lands.
   (A) bordered   (B) relocated   (C) contrasted   (D) accumulated

5. The boy used to <u>harbor</u> a wish of being a musician.
   (A) entertain   (B) abandon   (C) lash   (D) medicate

6. This medicine will <u>neutralize</u> the effects of the poison.
   (A) categorize   (B) announce   (C) pollinate   (D) nullify

Fill in each blank with the correct collocation.

1. The party won the national election by a large margin and _____.

2. The bird's feathers _____ color from dark blue to vibrant red.

3. Obesity is usually _____ an unhealthy diet.

4. The executives started to _____ to overcome the company's crisis.

5. The colony _____ a distant kingdom for many years.

| associated with | take steps | took control | was ruled by | vary in |

STEP 01

Timed Reading (WPM)
☐ 1'00" ☐ 1'30" ☐ 2'00"

Zoology

Axolotls

The axolotl is a type of salamander indigenous to a pair of lakes in central Mexico. **1A** It grows to a length of about 30 centimeters. **1B** Unlike most other amphibians, which transform from aquatic larvae into land-dwelling adults through a process called metamorphosis, the axolotl spends its whole life in the water. **1C** Perhaps the most unusual trait of the axolotl is its regenerative powers as it is capable of growing back entire limbs. **1D**

2A Unfortunately, the axolotl has lost its natural habitats, which are two lakes. **2B** It is estimated that only about 1,000 still exist in the wild. **2C** Nevertheless, the axolotl is now commonly kept in captivity by people who raise this unique creature as a pet. **2D** It can also be found in laboratories, where it is studied by scientists hoping to learn the secret of its healing abilities.

Note-Taking

Axolotls

- **What They Are**: a type of _____ w/ a _____ of about 30 centimeters
- **Where They Live**: spend their whole lives in the _____
- **What They Have**: _____ powers — capable of growing back _____
- **Today**:
  - only about 1,000 _____ in the _____
  - kept in _____ by ppl. as _____
  - found in _____ where scientists learn about its _____ abilities

1. Look at the four squares [■] that indicate where the following sentence could be added to paragraph 1.

   Because of this, it possesses external gills, which resemble feathers.

   Where would the sentence best fit?

2. Look at the four squares [■] that indicate where the following sentence could be added to paragraph 2.

   One of its native lakes has been completely drained, and the other is heavily polluted.

   Where would the sentence best fit?

SUMMARY

The axolotl is a _____ found in central Mexico. It grows to a _____ of 30 centimeters. Most _____ change from _____ larvae into _____ adults. But the axolotl spends its entire life in the _____. It can also grow back lost _____. Sadly, it has lost its _____, and there are a few left in the _____. However, the axolotl is often kept as a _____. It is also studied by scientists interested in its _____.

VOCAB

Match each word with the correct definition.

a   amphibian   •   •   an arm or a leg

b   metamorphosis •   •   growing again after being lost, damaged, etc.

c   trait   •   •   a particular characteristic or quality

d   regenerative   •   •   an animal that can live both on land and in water

e   limb   •   •   an animal's change between life stages

The Irish Potato Famine

Beginning in 1845, Ireland suffered from a devastating famine that left a million people dead and caused a million more to emigrate from the country. The direct cause of the famine was a potato blight, but there were many social and political factors that contributed to the severity of the disaster.

1A Ireland in the mid-19th century was ruled by Great Britain, which was Protestant, and Irish Catholics faced systematic discrimination. 1B Forced to rent only small farm plots, they grew mostly potatoes, which require less space than grain. 1C By the time the blight arrived, half of the population depended on potatoes to survive. 1D

→ After the famine began, the British government abolished the Corn Law, which placed a high tariff on foreign corn, but this had little effect. Later, a new political party took control and only made halfhearted attempts to end the crisis. The head of the relief effort went so far as to offer the opinion that "God sent the calamity to teach the Irish a lesson."

3A The famine ended several years later. 3B However, the Irish continued to harbor feelings of bitterness and distrust toward the British. 3C Eventually, their efforts led to the proclamation of the Republic of Ireland in 1949. 3D

Note-Taking

MI = Main Idea   SD = Supporting Details

- **P1** MI: the outbreak of Irish _____ in 1845
  - SD: caused due to a potato _____ w/ social & _____ factors
- **P2** MI: _____ against Irish Catholics by Great Britain
  - SD: allowed only small _____ → mostly grew _____
- **P3** MI: British _____'s actions
  - SD: abolished the _____ & made _____ to end the crisis
- **P4** MI: the _____ of the Republic of Ireland
  - SD: the Irish: harbored feelings of _____ & _____ toward the British

1   Look at the four squares [■] that indicate where the following sentence could be added to paragraph 2.

    Moreover, they were even barred from buying land in their own country.

    Where would the sentence best fit?

2   The author's main purpose in paragraph 3 is to

    (A) illustrate the famine's effect on the British political system
    (B) compare the tariff on corn to the one imposed on potatoes
    (C) show how little the British government did to stop the famine
    (D) give an example of the poor farming practices of the Irish

    * Paragraph 3 is marked with an arrow [→].

3   Look at the four squares [■] that indicate where the following sentence could be added to paragraph 4.

    The Irish began a struggling to gain their independence from Great Britain.

    Where would the sentence best fit?

✦ VOCAB

Write the correct word for each definition.

a   a disease that kills plants   _____
b   systematic unfair treatment   _____
c   with little enthusiasm or effort   _____
d   a tragic disaster   _____
e   doubt and suspicion   _____

> distrust
> halfhearted
> discrimination
> calamity
> blight

STEP 03

Timed Reading (WPM)
☐ 2'00" ☐ 2'30" ☐ 3'00"

Biology

Allergies

Allergies are a common disorder caused by an improper reaction of the immune system to an otherwise harmless substance, known as an allergen. It is estimated that up to 30% of the world's population suffers from some type of allergy, and that number is believed to be growing.

2A The primary function of the body's immune system is to identify dangerous foreign materials and to take steps to neutralize them. 2B It does this by producing antibodies that lock onto the materials and destroy them before they can harm the body. 2C These antibodies release chemicals, including something called histamine, into the body. 2D

3A Once it does, however, it will continue to do so every time the allergen is detected. 3B Allergic reactions can vary in severity from mild to life threatening. 3C Natural airborne allergens normally cause mild symptoms while food allergies and insect stings can cause anaphylaxis, a serious reaction that induces rashes, throat swelling, and a drop in blood pressure. 3D

Although avoidance is the most effective method of dealing with allergies, there are also a variety of allergy medications. However, it is important to note that these products merely treat the symptoms of allergies and are not cures. For certain types of allergies, doctors may recommend allergen immunotherapy, a series of shots that expose the body to small doses of the allergen and eventually minimize the resultant reaction.

✿ VOCAB

Find the correct word in the passage for each of the given definition.

a   an illness which affects someone's body: _____

b   carried in the air: _____

c   an enlarged area: _____

d   a measured amount that is intended to be taken: _____

1. Which of the following is true about allergens?

   (A) They are produced by the body to deal with antibodies.
   (B) They are released when the body experiences anaphylaxis.
   (C) They are more severe than most common allergies.
   (D) They can be treated with allergen immunotherapy.

2. Look at the four squares [■] that indicate where the following sentence could be added to paragraph 2.

   It causes many common allergy symptoms, including runny noses, irritated eyes, and itchy skin.

   Where would the sentence best fit?

3. Look at the four squares [■] that indicate where the following sentence could be added to paragraph 3.

   No one is sure what causes the immune system to misidentify harmless allergens as serious threats.

   Where would the sentence best fit?

4. The word `minimize` in the passage is closest in meaning to

   (A) eradicate   (B) stabilize   (C) diminish   (D) isolate

Note-Taking

MI = Main Idea   SD = Supporting Details

P1	MI	
	SD	
P2	MI	
	SD	
P3	MI	
	SD	
P4	MI	
	SD	

UNIT TEST

1. What does the passage mainly discuss?

   (A) How global warming affects monsoon formation
   (B) The meteorological conditions that cause monsoons
   (C) The damage caused by and benefits of different monsoons
   (D) Why summer monsoons are more powerful than winter ones

2. The word shift in the passage is closest in meaning to

   (A) boost
   (B) thermal
   (C) decrease
   (D) deviation

3. Look at the four squares [■] that indicate where the following sentence could be added to paragraph 3.

   Once it reaches the land, the warmer temperatures heat up the air and cause it to rise, and the moisture then falls to the ground in the form of rain.

   Where would the sentence best fit?

4. Look at the four squares [■] that indicate where the following sentence could be added to paragraph 4.

   The corresponding changes in pressure cause the air over the land to move toward the warmer ocean areas.

   Where would the sentence best fit?

5. Why does the author mention hydroelectric power plants?

   (A) To suggest a solution to the problems caused by monsoons
   (B) To explain how monsoons are studied
   (C) To highlight a positive effect of monsoons
   (D) To illustrate the phenomenon of temperature change

6. Directions: Select the appropriate phrases from the answer choices and match them to the category to which they relate. TWO of the answer choices will NOT be used.

   Summer Monsoons
   •
   •
   •

   Winter Monsoons
   •
   •

   Answer Choices

   (A) Are the less powerful type
   (B) Are used to irrigate crops
   (C) Can sometimes cause droughts
   (D) Involve the wind blowing from a warm area to a cold one
   (E) Have a high pressure area over an ocean
   (F) Occur several times a year
   (G) Have moist air moving toward land

Monsoons

Traditionally associated with the Indian Ocean region, the term "monsoon" is now commonly applied to any annual shift in wind direction that leads to either an extended dry spell or a prolonged period of heavy rains. The term itself is derived from *mausem*, an Arabic word meaning "season."

There are two general types of this phenomenon: summer monsoons and winter monsoons. To understand the difference between the two, there are two important points to remember. The first is that monsoon winds always blow from cold regions to warmer ones, and the second is that land both heats up and cools down more quickly than water.

→ 3A Therefore, during the summer when the sun is strong, the air located above land masses is warmer than that which is above the ocean. 3B This causes a low pressure area over the land and a high pressure area over the water. 3C Moist ocean air rushes from the high pressure area to the low pressure one. 3D

→ During the winter, the opposite occurs. 4A In the absence of strong sunlight, the land loses its warmth more rapidly than the ocean does. 4B There, the air rises, and heavy precipitation occurs. 4C As a result, land areas undergo a dry season and occasionally experience droughts. 4D

In general, summer monsoons are more powerful than winter monsoons. Many people in tropical regions depend on the rains of summer monsoons to irrigate their crops and to power their hydroelectric power plants. However, the strong winds and heavy rains of unusually intense monsoons can also cause flooding and serious property damage.

GLOSSARY
dry spell: a short period with less rain than usual
undergo: to experience something
drought: an extended rainless period that causes crops to die

VOCABULARY TEST

Recall the essential words in the unit to reinforce your vocabulary acquisition. Write the meaning of each word in your language.

irrigate	tariff
dose	calamity
proclamation	famine
amphibian	consult
harbor	aquatic
swelling	severity
detect	airborne
immune	distrust
dynasty	metamorphosis
limb	emigrate
decline	neutralize
trait	undergo
dry spell	disorder
halfhearted	blight
unethical	regenerative

plagiarism	discrimination
induce	blur
drought	vary in
associated with	be ruled by
take steps	take control

Complete each sentence with the correct word or collocation.

1 Beginning in 1845, Ireland suffered from a devastating _____.

2 Failure to clearly cite one's sources is considered _____.

3 As a result, land areas _____ a dry season.

4 Allergies are caused by an improper reaction of the _____ system.

5 Ireland in the mid-19th century _____ Great Britain.

6 Axolotls are capable of growing back their entire _____.

7 Sumer fell into _____ approximately 800 years later.

8 _____ is widespread in art and journalism these days.

9 Most amphibians transform from _____ larvae into land-dwelling adults.

10 The body system _____ to neutralize dangerous foreign materials.

aquatic	was ruled by	famine	decline	plagiarism
limbs	unethical	takes steps	immune	undergo

[TOEFL iBT® CODEBREAKER READING]

PART 3 / Reading to Learn Questions

The part for Reading to Learn Questions asks test takers to understand how a passage is logically organized and complete a summary while recalling the main idea and primary details of the passage. They are also asked to identify essential points in a passage and put them where they belong in a category chart.

TOEFL iBT® Reading Skills 03

UNIT 9 | Prose Summary

UNIT 10 | Category Chart

TOEFL iBT® Reading Skills 03

Summarizing

Summarizing is the act of reducing a passage to its main idea and the most important supporting details. To do so, test takers should paraphrase the content into their own words without changing its meaning. They can start by identifying the topic sentence, which is usually located in or near the passage's introduction. They should look for the major points the writer uses to support the topic sentence. Lastly, they need to paraphrase the topic sentence and its supporting details and arrange them into a short paragraph.

Find the topic sentence and major points of the passage. Then complete the summary.

> Archaeologists remain unsure of how the mysterious city of Teotihuacan in Mexico was built. For one thing, nobody is sure who built the city of Teotihuacan, which is believed to date back to about 100 B.C. Although its name comes from the Aztec language and means "the place where the gods were created," it far precedes the Aztec empire. In addition, the people of Teotihuacan disappeared without a trace in the 8th century. It is uncertain why they abandoned the city or where they went.

- **Main Idea** _____ remains _____ to archaeologists.

- **Supporting Details**
  - Nobody knows who _____ the city.
  - It has an _____ name but far _____ the Aztec Empire.
  - It is uncertain why the _____ of Teotihuacan _____.

- **Summary** _____ in ancient Mexico _____ _____ to archaeologists. First, nobody knows _____ _____. Even though _____ _____, it far _____. Additionally, it is uncertain _____ _____ or where they went.

Categorizing

Categorizing is an important organizational skill. It involves taking the information presented in a passage and dividing it into two or more broad categories for clearer understanding. Once test takers notice that the passage is about two subjects, they should take note of things that are compared or contrasted.

Write the correct information for each category.

> The Bactrian camel can easily be identified by its two large humps. Its more common cousin, the dromedary camel, has only a single hump. Native to the Central Asia region, the Bactrian camel has dwindled to a population of about two million, the majority of which are domesticated. The dromedary camel is also largely domesticated. Its population of about fifteen million is mainly scattered across North Africa and parts of Southwest Asia.

- Bactrian Camel: _____, native to the _____, population of about _____

- Dromedary Camel: a single hump, population of about _____, scattered across _____ and parts of _____

Select the appropriate phrases from the answer choices.

> Women's figure skating competitions are divided into two sections, the short program and free skating. The short program must be completed within two minutes and fifty seconds and includes eight mandatory elements. Free skating lasts for up to four minutes, and skaters try to include as many difficult maneuvers as possible. Although the music used in the short program must conform to certain rhythms, free skating music does not have such limitations.

(A) Has certain musical limitations
(B) Contains as many complex moves as possible
(C) Has a time limit of just under three minutes
(D) Includes eight required components
(E) Can be four minutes in length

Short Programs
· · ·

Free Skating
· ·

Reading Skills 3 143

TOEFL iBT® READING
UNIT 09

Prose Summary

INTRODUCTION

The purpose of summary questions is to determine whether test takers are able to identify the most important points in a passage. A number of different facts and statements are presented, and the three key points that support the main idea of the passage must be selected.

TYPICAL QUESTION TYPE

Directions: An introductory sentence for a brief summary of the passage is provided below. Complete the summary by selecting the THREE answer choices that express the most important ideas in the passage. Some sentences do not belong in the summary because they express ideas that are not presented in the passage or are minor ideas in the passage.

An introductory sentence

-
-
-

Answer Choices

STRATEGIES

- Read the given introductory sentence carefully as it is a restatement of the passage's main idea or thesis. Understanding it fully will help you identify its supporting details.
- It is important to remember that you are not only looking for incorrect facts. You are also trying to eliminate unimportant details or information that is not included in the passage.
- The main supporting details from the passage will be paraphrased as answer choices. Therefore, look for synonyms of the passage's key words.

QUICK CHECKUP

Read each passage and choose the three major ideas in order to complete the summary.

1 Social Science

Smishing is criminal behavior that tricks individuals into revealing personal information. Smishing uses cell phone text messages which are designed to appear as though they were sent by a legitimate financial institution. However, they can be identified by the particular numbers appearing in place of the sender's phone number.

Smishing is a form of illegal activity.   ▪ _____ ▪ _____ ▪ _____

(A) Smishing is used to steal private data.
(B) Smishing requires special cell phones.
(C) Smishing messages often include certain particular numbers.
(D) Banks often use smishing to solve problems.
(E) Smishing uses text messages.

2 Culture

Established in 1917 by a provision in publisher Joseph Pulitzer's will, the Pulitzer Prize is an award honoring authors, journalists, and composers. It is given annually in 21 categories and is accompanied by $10,000 in cash. Winners are chosen by 102 judges divided into juries consisting of either five or seven members.

The Pulitzer Prize is an annual award.   ▪ _____ ▪ _____ ▪ _____

(A) The Pulitzer Prize was started by a journalist.
(B) The Pulitzer Prize is given to writers, journalists, and composers.
(C) A certain amount of money is given with the Pulitzer Prize.
(D) There are 21 Pulitzer Prize categories.
(E) Some Pulitzer Prize juries only have five members on them.

3 Astronomy

The world's largest astronomical observatory is located on Mauna Kea, a dormant volcano on the island of Hawaii. This location was chosen due to its dark skies, clean air, low humidity and high altitude, all of which contribute to an unusually clear view of the universe. The observatory has 13 functioning telescopes, including the world's largest infrared telescopes.

The largest observatory in the world is located in Hawaii.   ▪ _____ ▪ _____ ▪ _____

(A) The location of the observatory allows for good viewing.
(B) The volcano is named Mauna Kea.
(C) The observatory is on the inactive volcano.
(D) Hawaii is home to many observatories.
(E) There are 13 telescopes at the observatory.

VOCABULARY

Write the number of each word's definition.

1 v. to make a judgment about something

2 v. to include something as a part of a larger whole

3 v. to recognize or show the difference between two things

4 v. to gradually take in a substance

5 n. the protection and preservation of something

6 v. to construct or build

7 v. to emphasize something

8 n. widespread praise and respect

9 v. to cause something undesirable

10 n. a person who works for little or no money to learn a trade

11 n. the result of an action or decision

12 v. to copy something or its behavior, speech, etc.

>>

differentiate _____

accentuate _____

incorporate _____

apprentice _____

acclaim _____

conservation _____

erect _____

consequence _____

mimic _____

pose _____

assess _____

absorb _____

Match each collocation with the correct definition.

a be renowned as   •   • to be given an official title

b coincide with   •   • to occur at the same time as

c be engraved with •   • to be recommended to take a certain action

d be designated as •   • to be famous and respected as something

e be advised to   •   • to be carved with (words or symbols)

Circle the word closest in meaning to each underlined word.

1. Women wear cosmetics to <u>accentuate</u> their natural features.
   (A) eradicate (B) replicate (C) renounce (D) enhance

2. The mockingbird can <u>mimic</u> the songs of other birds.
   (A) imitate (B) recognize (C) deteriorate (D) analyze

3. Young children are unable to anticipate the <u>consequences</u> of their actions.
   (A) appearances (B) degrees (C) results (D) strategies

4. The scientists received international <u>acclaim</u> for their breakthrough.
   (A) excellence (B) commendation (C) funding (D) cooperation

5. His ideas were eventually <u>incorporated</u> into the manufacturing process.
   (A) integrated (B) outdated (C) patented (D) separated

6. The woman's task is to <u>assess</u> the antiques to determine if they are worth being preserved.
   (A) abandon (B) alleviate (C) estimate (D) access

Fill in each blank with the correct collocation.

1. The politician _____ an excellent debater.

2. The entire campus _____ a smoke-free area.

3. Unfortunately, the bad weather _____ the student's vacation period.

4. Every foreign visitor _____ register with the embassy.

5. The inside of the ring _____ the jeweler's initials.

| coincided with | is advised to | is designated as |
| is engraved with | is renowned as | |

STEP 01

Timed Reading (WPM)
☐ 1'00" ☐ 1'30" ☐ 2'00"

Culture

Musicals and Operas

The line that differentiates musicals from operas can sometimes be blurred, especially in modern theater, but there are some fairly clear distinctions that can be made between the two genres.

One of these is that the storyline of a musical generally progresses through action and dialogue, with songs serving as accessories that accentuate the established mood and emotions of the play. In operas, on the other hand, it is most often the songs themselves that tell the story. In other words, the text of the plot is incorporated directly into the music.

Other distinct features of musicals are that they can easily be translated into other languages and are likely to use dancing, along with singing and acting, as a form of expression. Singing, however, is undeniably the centerpiece of operas, which are traditionally performed in the language in which they were written.

Note-Taking

	Musicals	Operas
Storyline	• progress through _____ & _____ • songs – serve as _____	• use songs to _____ the story • the _____ of the plot – _____ directly
Performance	• use _____ as a form of _____	• use singing as the _____
Language	• are easily _____ into other languages	• are _____ in the language in which they were _____

1 The word blurred in the passage is closest in meaning to

(A) reluctant   (B) unprecedented   (C) versatile   (D) ambiguous

2 Directions: An introductory sentence for a brief summary of the passage is provided below. Complete the summary by selecting the THREE answer choices that express the most important ideas in the passage.

Despite their similarities, musicals and operas are two distinct genres.

-
-
-

Answer Choices

(A) Operas have a longer history than musicals.
(B) Musicals only have one storyline while operas have many.
(C) Operas are generally not translated into other languages.
(D) Musicals feature dancing along with singing and acting.
(E) Both operas and musicals are mostly played in auditoriums.
(F) Unlike operas, musicals rely on dialogue and action to move the story along.

SUMMARY

There are some _____ between _____ and _____. For example, musicals use music to _____ the established mood and _____ while operas use music to _____ the story. In addition, musicals can be performed in many _____, but operas are only _____ in their original language. Finally, _____, singing, and _____ are all featured in musicals, but it is music that is clearly the _____ of operas.

⚙ VOCAB

Match each word with the correct definition.

a   distinction   •   • in an unquestionable or obvious manner

b   accessory   •   • a clear difference between two things

c   translate   •   • to change one language into another

d   undeniably   •   • the main feature of something

e   centerpiece •   • something added to improve something else

Michelangelo

Michelangelo di Lodovico Buonarroti Simoni, best known simply as Michelangelo, was a 16th-century Italian Renaissance artist. Although primarily a sculptor, he excelled in a number of genres, including painting, architecture, and poetry, and is considered by many to be one of the greatest and most influential artists of all time.

Born in the Italian city of Caprese in 1475, Michelangelo became an apprentice to Domenico Ghirlandajo, a respected painter from nearby Florence, at the age of 12. It is said that Ghirlandajo soon grew jealous of his young apprentice's budding talent and sent him off to work with a sculptor instead. Michelangelo's sculpting abilities soon earned him acclaim.

Unlike many artists who only achieved their fame posthumously, Michelangelo was renowned as an artistic genius during his lifetime. Nicknamed *Il Divino* (the divine one) by his peers, he was so famous that two biographies about him were published while he was still alive. He sculpted both the *Pieta* and *David* before he was 30 years of age and went on to paint his masterpiece on the ceiling of the Sistine Chapel. Many other artists attempted to recreate the passion and harmony of Michelangelo's style, with their efforts eventually leading to a new major art movement called Mannerism.

Note-Taking

MI = Main Idea   SD = Supporting Details

P1 MI Michelangelo — Italian _____ artist
SD one of the _____ and _____ artists of all time
P2 MI became an _____ to Domenico Ghirlandajo
SD developed _____ which earned him acclaim
P3 MI _____ as an artistic _____ during his lifetime
SD • _____ the *Pieta* and *David* before he was 30
• _____ the _____ of the Sistine Chapel
• inspired many other artists and led to the art movement _____

1   The word budding in the passage could best be replaced by

    (A) enticing   (B) debilitating   (C) emerging   (D) annoying

2   It is NOT stated that Michelangelo

    (A) worked for a famous painter named Domenico Ghirlandajo
    (B) was considered a genius but was detested by his peers
    (C) had two books written about him during his lifetime
    (D) created two famous statues before he was 30 years old

3   Directions: An introductory sentence for a brief summary of the passage is provided below. Complete the summary by selecting the THREE answer choices that express the most important ideas in the passage.

    Michelangelo was one of history's greatest and most influential artists.

    -
    -
    -

    Answer Choices

    (A) He worked with both a sculptor and a painter as a youth.
    (B) He was born in a city near Florence in 1475.
    (C) His style inspired a new major art movement.
    (D) He enjoyed fame and acclaim during his life.
    (E) He often referred to himself as *Il Divino*.
    (F) The painter he apprenticed for was jealous of his talent.

✿ VOCAB

Write the correct word for each definition.

a	to do something extremely well	_____	
b	happening after one has died	_____	
c	someone in the same age or social group	_____	
d	an account of someone's life written by someone else	_____	
e	to make something in a different time exist	_____	

biography
posthumously
excel
recreate
peer

STEP 03

Timed Reading (WPM)
☐ 2'00" ☐ 2'30" ☐ 3'00"

Geography

The Archaeological Park and Ruins of Quirigua

Quirigua, located in what is now southeastern Guatemala, was an ancient Mayan city established nearly 2,000 years ago. Today, its ruins are preserved in a 34-hectare conservation zone known as the Archaeological Park and Ruins of Quirigua.

The city reached the height of its power at the start of the 8th century, when it became the royal and administrative center of the Mayan Empire, but it soon fell into a period of sharp decline for reasons that remain unclear. This decline, however, is believed to have coincided with the mysterious collapse of the entire Mayan civilization. Quirigua's ruins are now considered a significant source of information about the Maya.

Architecturally, Quirigua was centered on an enormous public space called the Great Plaza. This space was surrounded by a complex system of staircases, pyramids, and terraces. Quirigua's ruins feature 17 sandstone monuments, most of which date from the 8th century and are engraved with hieroglyphics. One of these monuments, known simply as Stela E, is thought to be the largest freestanding stone monument ever erected by the Maya. Some of the engravings on these monuments act as calendars marking important dates and recording natural events such as eclipses. Others describe ancient Mayan myths as well as notable political and social events of the time.

It is partly because of the valuable insights provided by these monuments, which have helped shape our understanding of Mayan civilization, that Quirigua has been designated as a UNESCO World Heritage Site.

✦ VOCAB

Find the correct word in the passage for each of the given definition.

a   organizing and supervising an organization or nation: _____

b   occurring suddenly and greatly: _____

c   a structure built to honor someone or something: _____

d   a picture that is a part of a writing system: _____

1. Why does the author mention the Great Plaza in the passage?

   (A) To emphasize the collapse of Mayan civilization
   (B) To give an example of a sandstone monument
   (C) To compare two different architectural styles
   (D) To explain how the city was arranged

2. What can be inferred about Mayan hieroglyphics?

   (A) They can be understood by modern archaeologists.
   (B) They can only be found in the ruins of Quirigua.
   (C) They are similar to hieroglyphics used by other civilizations.
   (D) They were only used throughout the 8th century.

3. Directions: An introductory sentence for a brief summary of the passage is provided below. Complete the summary by selecting the THREE answer choices that express the most important ideas in the passage.

   The ruins of Quirigua, an ancient Mayan city, are now an important archaeological site.

   -
   -
   -

   Answer Choices

   (A) The ruins are located in southeastern Guatemala.
   (B) The city was likely destroyed by a natural disaster.
   (C) The ruins are now a UNESCO World Heritage Site.
   (D) The ruins include numerous monuments mostly from the 8th century.
   (E) The monuments are engraved with myths, important dates, and notable events.
   (F) The city had the royal estate surrounded by pyramids, terraces, and stairs.

   Note-Taking

   MI = Main Idea   SD = Supporting Details

   P1 MI _____
       SD _____
   P2 MI _____
       SD _____
   P3 MI _____
       SD _____
   P4 MI _____
       SD _____

UNIT TEST

1. The word they in the passage refers to

   (A) health threats
   (B) endocrine disruptors
   (C) harmful effects
   (D) hormones

2. Why does the author mention the pituitary gland?

   (A) To illustrate a negative consequence of endocrine disruptors
   (B) To show how endocrine disruptors are distributed
   (C) To explain how the body regulates development
   (D) To give an example of an endocrine system component

3. The word detrimental in the passage is closest in meaning to

   (A) damaging   (B) decreasing
   (C) abnormal   (D) indisputable

4. Look at the four squares [■] that indicate where the following sentence could be added to paragraph 3.

   All of them can leak into the water supply and cause humans to eat contaminated food or to drink contaminated water.

   Where would the sentence best fit?

5. It is stated in paragraph 4 that

   (A) endocrine disruptors are more likely to be found in fatty foods
   (B) endocrine disruptors are also found in glass and ceramic receptacles
   (C) pesticides do not affect foods that have been wrapped in plastic
   (D) soft plastic poses less of a health risk than hard plastic

   * Paragraph 4 is marked with an arrow [→].

6. Directions: An introductory sentence for a brief summary of the passage is provided below. Complete the summary by selecting the THREE answer choices that express the most important ideas in the passage.

   Endocrine disruptors are chemicals that can have harmful effects on the body.

   -
   -
   -

   Answer Choices

   (A) Avoiding pesticides and fatty foods can reduce the risk of endocrine disruptor exposure.
   (B) Scientists are unsure why endocrine disruptors affect humans but not fish and amphibians.
   (C) Endocrine disruptors are sometimes artificial but can also be naturally occurring chemicals.
   (D) The endocrine system is a network of glands located throughout the body.
   (E) Endocrine disruptors can enter the body via the consumption of contaminated substances.
   (F) Endocrine disruptors adversely affect the system that produces and regulates hormones.

Endocrine Disruptors

One of modern society's gravest potential health threats comes from a class of chemicals known as endocrine disruptors. Some of these chemicals are artificial while others are naturally occurring. Their common denominator is that they all have harmful effects on the body's endocrine system, which controls the production and distribution of hormones.

The endocrine system is made up primarily of glands located throughout the body and includes the pituitary gland, the thyroid gland, and the reproductive glands. Among other things, it is responsible for growth and sexual development. Endocrine disruptors can affect this system in a number of ways, all of which have negative consequences. Some fool the endocrine system by mimicking hormones whereas others block hormones from performing their intended functions. There are also endocrine disruptors that either reduce or increase the production of certain hormones.

A Due to the nature of the endocrine system, endocrine disruptors pose the most serious risk to children, fetuses, and pregnant women. B Scientists are still assessing just how much of an impact these chemicals have on humans, but there is increasing evidence that they have had a detrimental effect on wildlife, most notably fish and amphibians. C Endocrine disruptors are most commonly found in pesticides, plastics, and detergents. D

→ To reduce their risk of exposure, people are advised to purchase organic fruit and vegetables and to limit their use of home pesticides. They should also avoid fatty foods, such as cheese and meat, as they absorb more of these chemicals. For this reason, fatty foods should not be wrapped in plastic. In fact, nothing intended for ingestion should be heated up in plastic containers, which should be replaced with glass or ceramic receptacles. Furthermore, soft plastic toys that might be chewed on should not be given to children.

GLOSSARY
common denominator: a trait that is shared by all of the members of a group
pesticide: a chemical which is used to prevent harmful insects
receptacle: an object which people use to put or keep things in

VOCABULARY TEST

Recall the essential words in the unit to reinforce your vocabulary acquisition. Write the meaning of each word in your language.

accentuate	translate
dormant	reveal
peer	incorporate
erect	monument
accessory	biography
sharp	distinction
posthumously	provision
trick	excel
centerpiece	assess
conservation	consequence
pose	administrative
recreate	undeniably
differentiate	mimic
absorb	pesticide
receptacle	apprentice

jury	acclaim
legitimate	hieroglyphic
be jealous of	be renowned as
be engraved with	coincide with
be designated as	be advised to

Complete each sentence with the correct word or collocation.

1 Michelangelo became an _____ to a respected painter.

2 The ruins are well-preserved in a _____ zone.

3 Singing is undeniably the _____ of operas.

4 Quirigua's ruins feature 17 sandstone _____.

5 Smishing is criminal behavior that tries to _____ individuals.

6 Musicals can easily be _____ into other languages.

7 Endocrine disruptors are most commonly found in home _____ and plastics.

8 Although primarily a sculptor, Michelangelo _____ in a number of genres.

9 Some endocrine disruptors fool the endocrine system by _____ hormones.

10 Quirigua has been _____ a UNESCO World Heritage Site.

| mimicking | apprentice | pesticides | translated | centerpiece |
| excelled | trick | conservation | designated as | monuments |

TOEFL iBT® READING

UNIT 10

Category Chart

INTRODUCTION

Category chart questions present several important details from the passage along with two or three broad categories. The test taker must demonstrate an understanding of the passage by identifying which category each detail belongs to.

TYPICAL QUESTION TYPE

Directions: Select the appropriate phrases from the answer choices and match them to the category to which they relate. TWO of the answer choices will NOT be used.

Answer Choices	Category 1	Category 2
(A)	•	•
(B)	•	•
(C)	•	•
(D)	•	
⋮		

STRATEGIES

- Start by reading the two categories and make sure you understand them as they pertain to the passage.

- Next, think of some key words related to each of the categories. Then, scan the answer choices for these words or their synonyms.

- Remember that two of the answer choices will not be used. Identifying these will make it easier to choose the correct category for the other details.

QUICK CHECKUP

Select the appropriate phrases from the answer choices and match them to the category to which they relate.

1 **Music**

The violin is often confused with its slightly larger cousin, the viola. Both possess four strings, but the violin has A, D, G, and C strings. On a viola, the C string is replaced by an E string. In addition, the handle of a viola bow has a curved corner while that of a violin bow has a corner with a right angle. Finally, a viola creates a deep, mellow sound and is traditionally used for harmonies while the higher-pitched violin is generally used for melodies.

Answer Choices
(A) Is played without a bow
(B) Has a C string
(C) Is a bit bigger than the other
(D) Has a fifth string
(E) Has a bow with a curved corner
(F) Is used to play the melody

Violin   Viola
  ·   ·

  ·   ·

2 **Botany**

Deciduous trees, such as oaks and maples, have broad leaves that fall off in autumn and regrow the following spring. They can be contrasted with coniferous trees, which have thin needles that grow year round. Coniferous trees also have cones, which they use in lieu of seeds as a means of reproduction. The large surfaces of deciduous leaves allow them to photosynthesize sunlight at higher rates. But coniferous needles have the advantage of being more resistant to insects and the elements.

*in lieu of: instead of

Answer Choices
(A) Are less vulnerable to insects
(B) Do not need sunlight to survive
(C) Include oaks and maples
(D) Reproduce via cones
(E) Have thinner branches
(F) Photosynthesize more effectively

Deciduous Trees   Coniferous Trees
       ·   ·

       ·   ·

VOCABULARY

Write the number of each word's definition.

1 v. to make someone or something suffer

2 n. a government run by a king or queen

3 adj. applying to two people or things

4 v. to continue to possess something

5 v. to exist in large numbers and to be harmful

6 v. to officially remove someone from a job

7 n. a field of study

8 n. the domestic affairs of a country

9 v. to exist or happen some time before

10 v. to find a way to avoid a problem or rule

11 n. an attempt to accomplish something

12 n. the formal act of admitting defeat

>>

retain   _____
infest   _____
predate   _____
surrender   _____
circumvent   _____
dismiss   _____
monarchy   _____
inflict   _____
endeavor   _____
discipline   _____
mutual   _____
interior   _____

Match each collocation with the correct definition.

a in earnest   •   • a symbol that makes scattered groups gather together

b be mistaken for   •   • to remove one thing and to put another in its place

c be divided into   •   • with increased effort in a serious way

d rallying point   •   • to be misunderstood as

e replace ~ with   •   • to be broken up into (smaller groups)

Circle the word closest in meaning to each underlined word.

1. The politician's popularity <u>predated</u> his ascension to power.
   (A) preceded (B) instigated (C) hastened (D) confounded

2. The manager <u>dismissed</u> some people due to incompetence.
   (A) deregulated (B) analyzed (C) terminated (D) promoted

3. Multiple <u>disciplines</u> will be affected by the professor's research.
   (A) punishments (B) fields (C) followers (D) graduates

4. The crushing defeat led to the army's eventual <u>surrender</u>.
   (A) submission (B) triumph (C) determination (D) unity

5. The organization's latest <u>endeavor</u> involves expanding internationally.
   (A) executive (B) reversal (C) morale (D) undertaking

6. Companies are finding ways to <u>circumvent</u> the restrictions.
   (A) bypass (B) fortify (C) negotiate (D) break

Fill in each blank with the correct collocation.

1. The layoff became a _____ for the workers to strike.

2. Sometimes cheetahs _____ jaguars or leopards.

3. The employees _____ six separate teams.

4. The rebel leader decided to _____ threats _____ negotiations.

5. After weeks of preparation, the project finally began _____.

are mistaken for	in earnest	are divided into
replace ~ with		rallying point

STEP 01

Timed Reading (WPM)
☐ 1'00" ☐ 1'30" ☐ 2'00"

Sports

MLB

Major League Baseball(MLB), the world's premier baseball league, was founded in 1876 and currently consists of 30 teams. These teams are further divided into two leagues, the National League and the American League.

Originally, MLB only included the National League, with the American League forming as an independent organization in 1901. The two leagues began competing two years later and formally merged in 1921. However, they retain some differences, the most notable of these being the American League's designated hitter rule, which allows a single player to bat in place of the pitcher.

At the season's conclusion, each league sends its top team to play in the World Series. As of 2013, the American League has claimed 63 championships to the National League's 46. The best players from the two leagues also meet in the All-Star Game midseason. The National League holds a 43 to 39 advantage in this contest.

	National League	American League
Differences	• started as the only _____ in MLB • formally _____ with the American League in _____	• formed as an _____ _____ in 1901 • has the _____ rule
Common Grounds	• sends its _____ to play in the _____ • sends the _____ to the _____ midseason	

162 TOEFL iBT® Codebreaker

1 The word merged in the passage could best be replaced by

(A) dissolved (B) negotiated (C) consolidated (D) differentiated

2 Directions: Select the appropriate phrases from the answer choices and match them to the category to which they relate. TWO of the answer choices will NOT be used.

Answer Choices

(A) Began as MLB's sole league
(B) Had won fewer World Series by 2013
(C) Was founded in 1901
(D) Makes pitchers bat for themselves
(E) Changed its rules in 1921
(F) Allows fewer players on each team
(G) Had been victorious in 39 All-Star Games by 2013

National League
·
·
·

American League
·
·

SUMMARY

MLB began _____ and has 30 teams _____ two leagues. It started with only the _____. The _____ formed in 1901, and the two leagues formally _____ in _____. They have some _____. Only the American League allows a player to _____. The two leagues' best teams play in the World Series at the _____. Their best players also meet in the All-Star Game _____.

✹ VOCAB

Match each word with the correct definition.

a league   ·   · worthy of noticing
b premier   ·   · a superior position
c notable   ·   · a group of teams that play a sport against one another
d claim   ·   · the most important or admired
e advantage ·   · to gain or win something

Lice and Mites

Tiny creatures that inspire revulsion due to their propensity to infest human beings, lice and mites are often mistaken for each other. However, their differences far outnumber their similarities.

Lice are parasitical insects found on virtually every species of mammal and bird. Being scavengers, they depend on their hosts as sources of food and feed on their skin, blood, and bodily secretions. They are generally gray in color, are about three millimeters in size, and have a lifespan of approximately 30 days. Mites, on the other hand, are actually arthropods, not insects. They are microscopic invertebrates that sometimes live as parasites, not only on animals but also on plants. However, many of the nearly 50,000 known species of mites tend to live freely in water or on land.

Lice lay their eggs, known as nits, directly on their host by using saliva to attach them to hair shafts. While lice cause itching and discomfort, they do not pose any serious health threats to humans. Mites, however, are responsible for many allergic diseases, including asthma and eczema. There is also a species of mite that burrows into human skin and lays eggs, which causes a condition known as scabies.

Note-Taking

MI = Main Idea   SD = Supporting Details

- **P1** MI _____ & _____
  - SD have more _____ than similarities
- **P2** MI the features of lice & mites
  - SD • lice: _____ insects — depend on their _____ as _____ of food
  - • mites: _____ which mostly live freely in _____ or on _____
- **P3** MI their harmful effects on humans
  - SD • lice: cause _____ & _____ ← lay their _____ on their hosts
  - • mites: cause _____ diseases — include _____, _____, & scabies

1   The word revulsion in the passage could best be replaced by

    (A) disgust   (B) curiosity   (C) confusion   (D) disagreement

2   What can be inferred about the saliva of lice?

    (A) It has no odor.
    (B) It is sticky.
    (C) Mites also have it.
    (D) It causes diseases.

3   Directions: Select the appropriate phrases from the answer choices and match them to the category to which they relate. TWO of the answer choices will NOT be used.

    Answer Choices
    (A) Are invertebrates
    (B) Feed on insects
    (C) May live on plants
    (D) Attach their eggs to hair
    (E) Are an endangered species
    (F) Live for about a month
    (G) Can cause scabies

    Lice
    ·
    ·

    Mites
    ·
    ·
    ·

✸ VOCAB

Write the correct word for each definition.

a   a natural tendency   _____

b   to be greater in number   _____

c   living in or on another living thing   _____

d   a substance discharged by a living thing   _____

e   to dig into something   _____

| outnumber |
| parasitical |
| burrow |
| propensity |
| secretion |

UNIT 10_ Category Chart

STEP 03

Timed Reading (WPM)
☐ 2'00" ☐ 2'30" ☐ 3'00"

History

German Militarism

When examining the various reasons behind the two world wars, one should notice that a sizable portion of the focus invariably falls on the deep-seated German attitude toward maintaining a strong and aggressive military.

The origin of German militarism predates the nation itself as it has roots in Napoleon's defeat of Prussia in 1806. As a condition of its surrender, Prussia was required to keep an army of no more than 42,000 soldiers. To circumvent this stipulation, the King of Prussia would train 42,000 soldiers for a year and then immediately dismiss them and replace them with a fresh group. By the time Germany unified in 1871, a significant portion of the male population had received military training. Japanese militarism, which relied on the nation's emperor as a rallying point, used Prussian militarism as a model, with a Prussian general serving as a military adviser from 1885 to 1888. German militarism survived the fall of the monarchy in 1918 and actually gained strength under Nazi rule. Rather than have an all-powerful emperor, the Nazis used the nation's wounded pride as the impetus for increased militarism by focusing on its defeat in World War I and the subsequent heavy punishment inflicted upon it. The common ground between German militarism and Japanese militarism is that both countries used racism as a driving force behind their military aggression.

Today, Germany still has a large military and one of the largest defense budgets in the world. However, modern public opinion has turned firmly against militarism, and German involvement in any sort of international military endeavor proceeds with great caution.

⚙ VOCAB

Find the correct word in the passage for each of the given definition.

a   a requirement stated as a part of an agreement: _____

b   to bring separate groups together: _____

c   hurt or insulted: _____

d   the force used to accomplish something: _____

1. The word subsequent in the passage is closest in meaning to

   (A) unfair   (B) increasing   (C) inferior   (D) ensuing

2. It is NOT stated that

   (A) Prussia had a limit on the size of its military
   (B) Germany defeated the Prussian army
   (C) Germany still has a large military today
   (D) a Prussian general advised the Japanese

3. Directions: Select the appropriate phrases from the answer choices and match them to the category to which they relate. TWO of the answer choices will NOT be used.

   Answer Choices
   (A) Began when Napoleon defeated Prussia
   (B) Ended shortly after World War I
   (C) Was powered by a prior defeat and punishment
   (D) Trained both men and women
   (E) Continued after the monarchy ended
   (F) Used the emperor as a symbol
   (G) Copied Prussian militarism

   German Militarism
   •
   •
   •

   Japanese Militarism
   •
   •

Note-Taking

MI = Main Idea   SD = Supporting Details

P1 MI _____
   SD _____
P2 MI _____
   SD _____
   _____
   _____
P3 MI _____
   SD _____

UNIT TEST

1. Which of the sentences below best expresses the essential information in the highlighted sentence in the passage?

   (A) Beginning in 1771, he gave up on statistics and astronomy to focus on the stability of the solar system.

   (B) It was in 1771 that he published his notes on the stability of the solar system and focused on statistics and astronomy.

   (C) He changed his focus from statistics to astronomy, particularly the stability of the solar system, in 1771.

   (D) In 1771, he began to concentrate on the stability of the solar system as well as other elements of astronomy and statistics.

2. The word contracted in the passage is closest in meaning to

   (A) compressed   (B) scattered
   (C) pulsated   (D) exploded

3. It is stated in paragraph 3 that

   (A) other scientists disagreed with the results of Laplace's research

   (B) *Mécanique Céleste* argued against the nebular hypothesis

   (C) *Exposition du Systéme du Monde* was written on the basis of *Mécanique Céleste*

   (D) Laplace eventually lost interest in celestial mechanics

   * Paragraph 3 is marked with an arrow [→].

4. The word It in the passage refers to

   (A) theory   (B) outcome
   (C) equal likelihood (D) calculation

5. The author's main purpose in paragraph 5 is to

   (A) compare Laplace to Napoleon
   (B) illustrate the problems Laplace faced
   (C) provide additional details about Laplace's life
   (D) explain the cause of Laplace's success

   * Paragraph 5 is marked with an arrow [→].

6. Directions: Select the appropriate phrases from the answer choices and match them to the category to which they relate. TWO of the answer choices will NOT be used.

   Exposition du Systéme du Monde
   •
   •
   •
   •

   Théorie Analytique des Probabilités
   •
   •
   •

   Answer Choices

   (A) Included the nebular hypothesis
   (B) Introduced a way to calculate large sums
   (C) Argued against politicians
   (D) Is considered a masterpiece of scientific literature
   (E) Was published in 1812
   (F) Is based on Laplace's earlier work
   (G) Discussed the equilibrium of the sun
   (H) Was released in 1796
   (I) Presented the correlation between outcomes and likelihoods of occurring

Pierre-Simon Laplace

The work of Pierre-Simon Laplace, a French mathematician and astronomer, had a strong influence on multiple disciplines and has lead many to consider him one of the greatest scientists of all time.

Laplace was born the son of a farmer in 1749, and his education was financed by his wealthy neighbors. In 1771, he began his work in earnest as he focused on statistics and astronomy, most notably the stability of the solar system. Building on the work of Isaac Newton, he came to the mathematical conclusion that any two planets and the sun must exist in a state of mutual equilibrium.

→ He later moved on to celestial mechanics as he sought, in his own words, to find "a complete solution of the great mechanical problem presented by the solar system." In 1796, his results were published in *Exposition du Systéme du Monde*, now considered to be one of scientific literature's masterpieces. Based on one of his previous publications, *Mécanique Céleste*, it is this book that introduced his well-known nebular hypothesis, which theorized that the solar system formed when a large cloud of interstellar gas contracted.

Next shifting to statistics and probabilities, Laplace published *Théorie Analytique des Probabilités* in 1812. It is perhaps best known for stating that, statistically speaking, every possible outcome has an equal likelihood of occurring. It also introduced generating functions, which can be used to assist in the calculation of long sums in probability equations. Laplace wrote in his conclusion, "One sees in this essay that the theory of probabilities is basically only common sense reduced to a calculus."

→ In his later years, Laplace became involved in politics, briefly served as Napoleon's minister of the interior in 1799, and was given the title of marquis during the Bourbon Restoration in 1817.

GLOSSARY
nebular: related to clouds of dust and gas in space
equation: a mathematical statement showing equality

VOCABULARY TEST

Recall the essential words in the unit to reinforce your vocabulary acquisition. Write the meaning of each word in your language.

propensity	mellow
notable	parasitical
secretion	premier
predate	dismiss
racism	endeavor
impetus	burrow
outnumber	claim
league	interior
surrender	discipline
inflict	nebular
equation	wounded
stipulation	curved
retain	unify
monarchy	mutual
infest	bow

coniferous	circumvent
advantage	be contrasted with
in lieu of	be mistaken for
in earnest	rallying point
replace ~ with	be divided into

Complete each sentence with the correct word or collocation.

1. The handle of a viola bow has a _____ corner.

2. The differences between the two creatures _____ their similarities.

3. Deciduous trees can be contrasted with _____ trees.

4. German involvement in international military _____ proceeds with great caution.

5. The viola has a deep, _____ sound and is traditionally used for harmonies.

6. There is a species of mite that _____ into human skin.

7. The 30 baseball teams in America _____ two leagues.

8. German militarism survived the fall of the _____ in 1918.

9. Some trees have cones, which they use _____ seeds.

10. Laplace served as Napoleon's minister of the _____ in 1799.

monarchy	mellow	endeavor	curved	are divided into
coniferous	burrows	interior	outnumber	in lieu of

[TOEFL iBT® CODEBREAKER READING]

PROGRESS TEST 2

PROGRESS TEST 2

1. Which of the following is mentioned as a distinctive feature of the Kurds and other ethnic groups?

   (A) their language
   (B) their culture
   (C) their genetics
   (D) their anthropological features

2. Look at the four squares [■] that indicate where the following sentence could be added to paragraph 1.

   Though its borders are not well defined, Kurdistan is commonly thought to extend from the Taurus Mountains in the west to the Zagros Mountains in the east.

   Where would the sentence best fit?

3. The word its in the passage refers to

   (A) Afghanistan
   (B) Azerbaijan
   (C) Kurdish culture
   (D) Persian culture

4. According to the passage, which of the following is true of *Hilperkê*?

   (A) It is practiced by the Kurds, Pashtuns, and Azerbaijanis.
   (B) It is both art and a way of remembering Kurdish history.
   (C) It has been practiced by the Kurdish people for 2,000 years.
   (D) It has been banned by Arab, Turkic, and Persian government.

5. The word persecuted in the passage is closest in meaning to

   (A) attacked
   (B) prosecuted
   (C) sustained
   (D) victimized

6. What can be inferred from paragraph 2 about the oppression of the Kurdish people?

   (A) The Kurds have been killed by the majorities in Syria and Iran.
   (B) Violence against the Kurds stopped around the time that the 20th century ended.
   (C) Some Kurds do not want an independent Kurdistan.
   (D) Discrimination against the Kurdish people is common in the countries in which Kurdistan is located.

   * Paragraph 2 is marked with an arrow [→].

7. The word autonomous in the passage could best be replaced by

   (A) independent
   (B) anonymous
   (C) unpopular
   (D) respected

The Kurds

Inhabiting a large area of mountainous land roughly due north of the Arabian Peninsula, the Kurdish people comprise a stateless ethnic group. [A] The homeland of the Kurds, frequently called "Kurdistan," stretches across four different countries — from Iran in the east through Iraq and Syria to Turkey in the West. [B] The origins of the Kurdish people are disputed. However, it is commonly believed that the Kurdish people moved into the Kurdistan region from Iran more than 2,000 years ago. [C] Linguistic, genetic, and anthropological evidence indicates that the Kurds share close ties to other Iranian ethnic groups, such as the Pashtuns of Afghanistan and the people of Azerbaijan. [D] Kurdish culture is distinct from the Arab, Turkic, and Persian cultures of its neighbors in several notable ways. For example, Kurds practice a form of singing and dancing called *Hilperkê*. Centuries of history can be recounted through the words and movements associated with these songs, and the dances serve as a form of recordkeeping.

→ Despite the linguistic and cultural ties that bind the Kurdish people together, they remain a people without a nation of their own. Minority Kurds have historically been persecuted by the majorities in the nations that contain and surround Kurdistan. In the 20th century, the Kurds endured massacres in Iraq, cultural suppression and genocide in Turkey, and discrimination in Iran and Syria. In Turkey alone, it is likely that more than 100,000 Kurds were killed since the end of the Ottoman Empire.

→ The 21st century, in contrast, has seen the prospects of an independent Kurdish state improve. The breakdown of the Iraqi government following the 2003 invasion of that country by American and coalition forces led to northern Iraq becoming an autonomous political entity called Iraqi Kurdistan. While not a completely separate country from Iraq, Iraqi Kurds are able to govern themselves in this region without interference from Baghdad. In 2012, the Syrian Civil War broke out. It provided Kurds in western Kurdistan with a similar opportunity; Kurdish militias took control of northeastern Syria in 2013. Whether these moves will lead to the establishment of an independent nation remains to be seen.

GLOSSARY
massacre: the killing of a large number of people at the same time
coalition: a group consisting of people from different political or social groups

8 Why does the author mention the Syrian Civil War in the passage?

(A) To describe one way in which the Kurds have been discriminated against

(B) To argue that the Kurds are a destabilizing force in the four countries in which Kurdistan is located

(C) To give an example of an event that may lead to the establishment of a Kurdish state

(D) To explain why the Kurds in Syria want to have a separate homeland

9 Which of the sentences below best expresses the essential information in the highlighted sentence in the passage? *Incorrect* choices change the meaning in important ways or leave out essential information.

(A) From 2013, Kurdish revolutionaries, with help from Iraqui Kurds, fought the Syrian government for control of northeastern Syria.

(B) Beginning in 2013, Kurdish fighters took control of Syrian Kurdistan and began to govern themselves like Iraqi Kurds in Iraqi Kurdistan have done.

(C) Syrian Kurds got the chance to govern themselves in 2013 although they had to fight very hard against the Syrian army.

(D) Since 2013, the Kurds in western Kurdistan have been fighting with the Syrian government for control of northeastern Syria.

10 According to the passage, which of the following is true of Kurdistan?

(A) It was divided in a bloody civil war.

(B) It is home to a large number of non-Kurdish people.

(C) It has suffered at the hands of people in surrounding nations.

(D) It was a single country during the Ottoman Empire period.

11 Directions: An introductory sentence for a brief summary of the passage is provided below. Complete the summary by selecting the THREE answer choices that express the most important ideas in the passage.

The Kurdish people are an ethnic minority in the four countries that control the Kurdish homeland.

-
-
-

Answer Choices

(A) Kurds have their own unique culture.

(B) The Kurds have taken steps toward establishing a sovereign, independent homeland.

(C) *Hilperkê* is a Kurdish form of dancing and singing.

(D) More than 100,000 Kurds were killed in Turkey.

(E) The U.S. Army and coalition forces helped northern Iraq be independent.

(F) For many years, Kurds have faced violence and discrimination in the countries where they live.

The Kurds

Inhabiting a large area of mountainous land roughly due north of the Arabian Peninsula, the Kurdish people comprise a stateless ethnic group. **A** The homeland of the Kurds, frequently called "Kurdistan," stretches across four different countries — from Iran in the east through Iraq and Syria to Turkey in the West. **B** The origins of the Kurdish people are disputed. However, it is commonly believed that the Kurdish people moved into the Kurdistan region from Iran more than 2,000 years ago. **C** Linguistic, genetic, and anthropological evidence indicates that the Kurds share close ties to other Iranian ethnic groups, such as the Pashtuns of Afghanistan and the people of Azerbaijan. **D** Kurdish culture is distinct from the Arab, Turkic, and Persian cultures of its neighbors in several notable ways. For example, Kurds practice a form of singing and dancing called *Hilperkê*. Centuries of history can be recounted through the words and movements associated with these songs, and the dances serve as a form of recordkeeping.

→ Despite the linguistic and cultural ties that bind the Kurdish people together, they remain a people without a nation of their own. Minority Kurds have historically been persecuted by the majorities in the nations that contain and surround Kurdistan. In the 20th century, the Kurds endured massacres in Iraq, cultural suppression and genocide in Turkey, and discrimination in Iran and Syria. In Turkey alone, it is likely that more than 100,000 Kurds were killed since the end of the Ottoman Empire.

→ The 21st century, in contrast, has seen the prospects of an independent Kurdish state improve. The breakdown of the Iraqi government following the 2003 invasion of that country by American and coalition forces led to northern Iraq becoming an autonomous political entity called Iraqi Kurdistan. While not a completely separate country from Iraq, Iraqi Kurds are able to govern themselves in this region without interference from Baghdad. In 2012, the Syrian Civil War broke out. It provided Kurds in western Kurdistan with a similar opportunity; Kurdish militias took control of northeastern Syria in 2013. Whether these moves will lead to the establishment of an independent nation remains to be seen.

GLOSSARY
massacre: the killing of a large number of people at the same time
coalition: a group consisting of people from different political or social groups

12 What is the main idea of the passage?

(A) Found in many cultures, shamanism is the practice of connecting our world to the spiritual world.

(B) Shamanism originated in Turkey but was spread across the world by people called shamans.

(C) Although called a religion, shamanism is actually a social phenomenon.

(D) In the past, it was the job of shamans to connect widespread cultures.

13 The word realm in the passage could best be replaced by

(A) mechanism

(B) territory

(C) phantom

(D) irritation

14 It is stated in paragraph 2 that

(A) shamans make rules in communities

(B) shamanism has some undesirable effects

(C) shamans from different cultures often interact

(D) shamanism around the world shares certain traits

* Paragraph 2 is marked with an arrow [→].

15 Which of the sentences below best expresses the essential information in the highlighted sentence in the passage? *Incorrect* choices change the meaning in important ways or leave out essential information.

(A) There is a direct connection between a shaman's consciousness and the way he or she generally behaves.

(B) Shamans use a number of techniques that change the state of their consciousness in order to connect to the other world.

(C) After connecting to the other world, a shaman alters reality through chanting and consuming special medicines.

(D) Chanting and drinking intoxicants allow a shaman to connect to the consciousness of others and to alter the way they perceive the world.

16 The word venerated in the passage most likely means

(A) shunned

(B) suspended

(C) renounced

(D) worshiped

17 The word those in the passage refers to

(A) gods

(B) efforts

(C) the Sami

(D) spirits

Shamanism

The term "shamanism" refers to the practice, found in a range of diverse cultures, of individuals, known as shamans, descending into a trance-like state in order to communicate or interact with some sort of spiritual realm. The term itself was first applied specifically to an ancient religion of the Turks and Mongols but has since transitioned into a more general usage.

→ Although varying widely in both intent and appearance, shamanistic behavior shares some globally common elements. A shaman's primary role is to serve as a bridge between the world of the living and the world of the dead. Generally, this is done either to protect the community from harm or to heal individuals suffering from various afflictions. To make this otherworldly connection, the shaman must enter an altered state of consciousness, which can be achieved in a variety of manners, from the ingestion of intoxicants to simple chanting.

[A] In Northern Europe, an ethnic group known as the Sami practiced shamanism up until the early 18th century. [B] They would conduct ceremonies that made use of drums and flutes to put them into a trance, under which they would travel there to negotiate with gods, spirits, and the ghosts of their ancestors. [C] Through their efforts, the well-being of their clan would be ensured. The Sami also venerated animal spirits, particularly those of bears. [D]

Although Sami shamanism has long since been replaced by Christianity, the Hmong, an ethnic group from China, continue to practice shamanism today. They believe a special god selects individuals to become their shamans. Known as txiv neeb, these shamans conduct special ceremonies, including the burning of joss paper and the ritual sacrifice of animals, to heal illnesses. These shamans can be male or female and tend to be highly respected within their communities.

Some may look down upon shamanism as a primitive religious practice of the past, but even in today's modern culture, many people continue to turn to it for healing, comfort, and a means of connecting with the dead.

GLOSSARY

trance: a state of mind in which someone has no conscious control
affliction: something that causes physical or mental suffering
intoxicant: anything, such as drinks or drugs, that makes someone drunk

18 Look at the four squares [■] that indicate where the following sentence could be added to paragraph 3.

Their shamans, known as noaides, acted as mediators with the underworld.

Where would the sentence best fit?

19 What can be inferred about txiv neeb?

(A) They are forbidden from getting married.

(B) They play roles that are constantly changing.

(C) They are no longer a part of Hmong culture.

(D) They hold positions that are desirable to attain.

20 The author mentions a primitive religious practice to indicate that

(A) shamanism generally did more harm than good

(B) other religions have replaced shamanism

(C) some people have a poor opinion of shamanism

(D) shamanism has changed greatly over time

21 The word it in the passage refers to

(A) shamanism

(B) past

(C) modern culture

(D) healing

22 Directions: Select the appropriate sentences from the answer choices and match them to the category to which they relate. TWO of the answer choices will NOT be used.

Sami Shamanism   Hmong Shamanism
·   ·
·   ·
·   ·
                  ·

Answer Choices

(A) Musical instruments were used to induce trances.

(B) People of both sexes could be shamans.

(C) There were competitions between shamans.

(D) They practiced shamanism in Northern Europe.

(E) They admired animal spirits.

(F) They sacrificed animals in ceremonies.

(G) It originated from Christianity.

(H) Shamans were known as txiv neeb.

(I) It is still practiced today.

Shamanism

The term "shamanism" refers to the practice, found in a range of diverse cultures, of individuals, known as shamans, descending into a trance-like state in order to communicate or interact with some sort of spiritual realm. The term itself was first applied specifically to an ancient religion of the Turks and Mongols but has since transitioned into a more general usage.

→ Although varying widely in both intent and appearance, shamanistic behavior shares some globally common elements. A shaman's primary role is to serve as a bridge between the world of the living and the world of the dead. Generally, this is done either to protect the community from harm or to heal individuals suffering from various afflictions. To make this otherworldly connection, the shaman must enter an altered state of consciousness, which can be achieved in a variety of manners, from the ingestion of intoxicants to simple chanting.

A In Northern Europe, an ethnic group known as the Sami practiced shamanism up until the early 18th century. B They would conduct ceremonies that made use of drums and flutes to put them into a trance, under which they would travel there to negotiate with gods, spirits, and the ghosts of their ancestors. C Through their efforts, the well-being of their clan would be ensured. The Sami also venerated animal spirits, particularly those of bears. D

Although Sami shamanism has long since been replaced by Christianity, the Hmong, an ethnic group from China, continue to practice shamanism today. They believe a special god selects individuals to become their shamans. Known as txiv neeb, these shamans conduct special ceremonies, including the burning of joss paper and the ritual sacrifice of animals, to heal illnesses. These shamans can be male or female and tend to be highly respected within their communities.

Some may look down upon shamanism as a primitive religious practice of the past, but even in today's modern culture, many people continue to turn to it for healing, comfort, and a means of connecting with the dead.

GLOSSARY

trance: a state of mind in which someone has no conscious control
affliction: something that causes physical or mental suffering
intoxicant: anything, such as drinks or drugs, that makes someone drunk

[TOEFL iBT® CODEBREAKER READING]

ACTUAL TEST

Reading Section Directions

In this section you will read three passages and answer reading comprehension questions about each passage. Most questions are worth one point, but the last question in each set is worth more than one point. The directions indicate how many points you may receive.

You will have 60 minutes to read all of the passages and answer the questions. Some passages include a word or phrase that is underlined in blue. Click on the word or phrase to see a definition or an explanation.

When you want to move on to the next question, click on **NEXT**. You can skip the questions and go back to them later as long as there is time remaining. If you want to return to previous questions, click on **BACK**. You can click on **REVIEW** at any time and the review screen will show you which questions you have answered and which you have not. From this review screen, you may go directly to any question you have already seen in the reading section.

You may now begin the Reading section.

Click on **CONTINUE** to go on.

ACTUAL TEST

1. The word it in the passage refers to

   (A) Europe
   (B) term
   (C) century
   (D) fencing

2. The word entrenched in the passage could best be replaced by

   (A) abolished
   (B) excavated
   (C) rooted
   (D) extracted

3. What can be inferred from paragraph 1?

   (A) The term "martial arts" was most used during the 16th century.
   (B) Martial arts are not employed in real combat.
   (C) The Roman god Mars was known to have first practiced martial arts.
   (D) The term "martial arts" has changed what it refers to over time.

   * Paragraph 1 is marked with an arrow [→].

4. Why does the author mention Buddhism ?

   (A) To suggest a possible cause for the meeting of Chinese and Indian martial arts
   (B) To explain why Indian martial arts focused more on spirituality in the past
   (C) To contrast Eastern religious teaching with Western martial arts training
   (D) To imply that the popularity of martial arts had slowly begun to fade

5. It is stated in paragraph 2 that

   (A) martial arts developed independently in Asia and Europe
   (B) Chinese influence led the Greeks to develop the Olympics
   (C) martial arts spread from China to India to Europe
   (D) ancient Indians focused on religion rather than combat

   * Paragraph 2 is marked with an arrow [→].

6. Look at the four squares [■] that indicate where the following sentence could be added to paragraph 3.

   Grappling martial arts, on the other hand, are known as ground fighting styles.

   Where would the sentence best fit?

7. Which of the following is NOT true about grappling martial arts?

   (A) They include holding one's opponent.
   (B) They are categorized as unarmed martial arts.
   (C) They focus on methods of blocking striking attacks.
   (D) They require the use of strength and balance.

Martial Arts

→ Derived from the name of the Roman god of war, Mars, the word "martial" means "related to combat or the military." It thereby follows that the martial arts are, quite literally, the teaching of the art of war. In Europe, the term was used to refer to activities such as fencing as early as the 16th century. These days, however, it is more commonly used in relation to various East Asian fighting techniques, such as taekwondo and karate, that are more deeply entrenched in fitness, spirituality, and mental discipline than in actual combat.

→ Asian martial arts date back more than 4,000 years to the Xia Dynasty in China. It is believed that ancient Chinese fighting systems eventually blended with those of ancient India, possibly in conjunction with the spread of Buddhism. Meanwhile, in Europe, the ancient Greek fixation on fitness and competition, which eventually culminated in the Olympic Games, laid the foundation for many European martial arts.

Modern martial arts can be divided into armed and unarmed disciplines. The armed martial arts include European fencing and Japanese kendo, both of which were traditionally used to teach swordsmanship. **A** Unarmed martial arts, which are far more popular than their armed counterparts, can be further categorized into two smaller groups: those that rely on striking and those that emphasize grappling. **B** Striking can refer to blows delivered with either fist, open hands, knees, or feet. **C** Martial arts that include striking also teach methods of blocking such attacks and are sometimes referred to as stand-up styles. **D** These techniques focus on using strength, balance, leverage, and submission holds.

The ultimate goal of virtually every martial art is to develop the practitioner's ability to ward off physical assaults and to defeat attackers. However, the mental, spiritual, and even philosophical development that takes place throughout the training process is arguably the true focus. Japanese martial arts, for example, have a strong Buddhist influence as they focus on the clearing of one's mind and the creation of a proper flow of energy within the body. Similarly, Korean martial arts are closely linked to the concept of meditation and the acquisition of inner peace.

Beginning in the 1970s, and spurred by the growing popularity of Asian martial arts films, the martial arts industry began to expand in leaps and bounds. Today, martial arts enjoy great popularity with people of all ages and in every continent.

GLOSSARY
culminate: to happen at the end of something

8 The phrase ward off in the passage most likely means

(A) imitate

(B) deflect

(C) disregard

(D) assign

9 Which of the sentences below best expresses the essential information in the highlighted sentence in the passage? *Incorrect* choices change the meaning in important ways or leave out essential information.

(A) By focusing on training and development, martial arts practitioners can improve their focus.

(B) It can be argued that personal mental development is the actual goal of martial arts.

(C) Many people argue about which martial arts are the best for spiritual and mental development.

(D) No one is sure which type of development is best for learning a martial art.

10 Why does the author mention martial arts films in the passage?

(A) To give a reason for the rising interest in martial arts

(B) To illustrate a common misconception about martial arts

(C) To suggest that few people actually practice martial arts

(D) To explain why martial arts changed dramatically in the 1970s

11 All of the following are true EXCEPT

(A) the word "martial" comes from the Roman god of war

(B) the ancient Greeks enjoyed exercise and physical contests

(C) fencing and kendo both teach sword fighting skills

(D) European martial arts were influenced by Buddhism

12 Directions: An introductory sentence for a brief summary of the passage is provided below. Complete the summary by selecting the THREE answer choices that express the most important ideas in the passage.

Martial arts are the teaching of the art of combat.

-
-
-

Answer Choices

(A) The first martial arts were dedicated to the Roman god of war.

(B) Martial arts include Japanese kendo and European fencing.

(C) Martial arts developed in ancient China, India, and Greece.

(D) Martial arts can be broken down into a variety of categories.

(E) In the 1970s, martial arts films became extremely popular.

(F) Physical defense and personal development are the focuses of martial arts.

Martial Arts

→ Derived from the name of the Roman god of war, Mars, the word "martial" means "related to combat or the military." It thereby follows that the martial arts are, quite literally, the teaching of the art of war. In Europe, the term was used to refer to activities such as fencing as early as the 16th century. These days, however, it is more commonly used in relation to various East Asian fighting techniques, such as taekwondo and karate, that are more deeply entrenched in fitness, spirituality, and mental discipline than in actual combat.

→ Asian martial arts date back more than 4,000 years to the Xia Dynasty in China. It is believed that ancient Chinese fighting systems eventually blended with those of ancient India, possibly in conjunction with the spread of Buddhism. Meanwhile, in Europe, the ancient Greek fixation on fitness and competition, which eventually culminated in the Olympic Games, laid the foundation for many European martial arts.

Modern martial arts can be divided into armed and unarmed disciplines. The armed martial arts include European fencing and Japanese kendo, both of which were traditionally used to teach swordsmanship. **A** Unarmed martial arts, which are far more popular than their armed counterparts, can be further categorized into two smaller groups: those that rely on striking and those that emphasize grappling. **B** Striking can refer to blows delivered with either fist, open hands, knees, or feet. **C** Martial arts that include striking also teach methods of blocking such attacks and are sometimes referred to as stand-up styles. **D** These techniques focus on using strength, balance, leverage, and submission holds.

The ultimate goal of virtually every martial art is to develop the practitioner's ability to ward off physical assaults and to defeat attackers. However, the mental, spiritual, and even philosophical development that takes place throughout the training process is arguably the true focus. Japanese martial arts, for example, have a strong Buddhist influence as they focus on the clearing of one's mind and the creation of a proper flow of energy within the body. Similarly, Korean martial arts are closely linked to the concept of meditation and the acquisition of inner peace.

Beginning in the 1970s, and spurred by the growing popularity of Asian martial arts films, the martial arts industry began to expand in leaps and bounds. Today, martial arts enjoy great popularity with people of all ages and in every continent.

GLOSSARY
culminate: to happen at the end of something

ACTUAL TEST

13 What is the main idea of this passage?

  (A) France has been the site of numerous art movements.
  (B) Two art movements occurred in the same rural region.
  (C) A pair of competing art schools founded a French town.
  (D) Barbizon is home to many schools of artists.

14 The word `it` in the passage refers to

  (A) lodge
  (B) forest
  (C) king
  (D) goal

15 Why does the author mention the `Wars of Religion` in the passage?

  (A) To suggest it was a consequence of the greed of King Francis I
  (B) To show why mostly Italian artists were invited to Fontainebleau
  (C) To give an example of the movement's artistic themes
  (D) To explain the gap between the first and second schools

16 The word `cessation` in the passage could best be replaced by

  (A) contact
  (B) expansion
  (C) termination
  (D) dissemination

17 Which of the sentences below best expresses the essential information in the highlighted sentence in the passage? *Incorrect* choices change the meaning in important ways or leave out essential information.

  (A) The school's French artists focused more on depth and contrast than the Flemish artists did.
  (B) The work of the second school resembled that of the first, but it had more depth and contrast.
  (C) French and Flemish art more closely resembled the work of the artists of the first school.
  (D) The artists of the first school taught the artists of the second school to use light to increase the depth of their composition.

18 Which of the following is NOT true about the second school of Fontainebleau?

  (A) It took place centuries after the first school.
  (B) It had a style much like that of the first school.
  (C) It had a greater focus on contrasting light and dark.
  (D) It consisted mostly of `Flemish` and `French` artists.

Two Schools of Art

In north-central France, the tiny village of Barbizon lies nestled at the edge of the vast forest of Fontainebleau. Despite this region's unassuming appearance, it has served as the center of two major art movements.

The first of these, known as the school of Fontainebleau, took place over two periods. The initial period commenced in 1531, and most of the artists involved were Italians, including Rosso Fiorentino and Francesco Primaticcio. They were invited by the French king, Francis I, to work on a hunting lodge located in the forest of Fontainebleau. It was the king's goal to gather great artists and architects to renovate it into an extravagant royal residence.

The Italians were Mannerists and were strongly influenced by the style of Michelangelo. Their work was characterized by the heavy use of stucco, and their paintings, featuring bright colors and strong lines, often contained elongated figures. From 1584 to 1594, work was abandoned due to the ongoing Wars of Religion. Upon cessation of the violence, a new group of artists was gathered to continue the renovation. This second school was led mainly by French and Flemish artists, and similar in style to the first school, their works featured a greater depth of composition and stronger contrast between light and shadow.

A The region's second art movement rose to prominence centuries later and existed from roughly 1830 to 1870. B The beginnings of the movement, later dubbed the Barbizon school, can be found in an 1824 exhibition of the paintings of John Constable in Paris. C Instead of following the period's rigid insistence on painting scenes of historical importance, they began to focus on nature, so they traveled outside the city to paint in the open air, with the forest of Fontainebleau a favored destination. D

During the European revolutions in 1848, many of these young painters, including Théodore Rousseau and Jean-François Millet, fled Paris altogether and gathered in the village of Barbizon. There, they continued to focus on painting landscapes but began to include human figures — primarily farmers and peasants — in much of their work. The Barbizon school influenced a number of young painters, including Monet and Renoir, who went on to form the next great art movement, Impressionism.

Today, Barbizon and Fontainebleau are popular tourist destinations. The village is home to many art galleries, but the focus is more on celebrating the region's storied past than on contemporary art.

GLOSSARY
stucco: a type of plaster used for covering walls and decorating ceilings
dub: to give something or someone a particular name

19 Look at the four squares [■] that indicate where the following sentence could be added to paragraph 4.

Constable's rural themes inspired many young Parisian painters to abandon Formalism, a popular style of art at the time.

Where would the sentence best fit?

20 What can be inferred about the European revolutions in 1848?

(A) They were caused by tension between France and Italy.
(B) They made painters want to live somewhere other than Paris.
(C) They had their origins in the Wars of Religion.
(D) They took place mostly in rural regions.

21 Which of the following is NOT true about the Barbizon school?

(A) It existed during the 19th century.
(B) It influenced Monet and Renoir.
(C) It focused on natural themes.
(D) It went against Impressionism.

22 The word storied in the passage is closest in meaning to

(A) ashamed
(B) exaggerated
(C) multilayered
(D) illustrious

23 Which of the following is NOT mentioned in the passage?

(A) Barbizon and the forest of Fontainebleau are in close proximity.
(B) Michelangelo influenced the artists of the first school of Fontainebleau.
(C) John Constable was a founding member of the Barbizon school.
(D) Impressionism followed the Barbizon school art movement.

24 Directions: Select the appropriate phrases from the answer choices and match them to the category to which they relate. TWO of the answer choices will NOT be used.

School of Fontainebleau
-
-
-
-

Barbizon School
-
-
-

Answer Choices

(A) Was inspired by John Constable
(B) Mainly painted the royals
(C) Included Italian Mannerists
(D) Led to the rise of Formalism
(E) Featured elongated bodies
(F) Tended to use stucco
(G) Painted outdoors
(H) Involved painters who worked for the French King
(I) Appeared in the 19th Century

Two Schools of Art

In north-central France, the tiny village of Barbizon lies nestled at the edge of the vast forest of Fontainebleau. Despite this region's unassuming appearance, it has served as the center of two major art movements.

The first of these, known as the school of Fontainebleau, took place over two periods. The initial period commenced in 1531, and most of the artists involved were Italians, including Rosso Fiorentino and Francesco Primaticcio. They were invited by the French king, Francis I, to work on a hunting lodge located in the forest of Fontainebleau. It was the king's goal to gather great artists and architects to renovate it into an extravagant royal residence.

The Italians were Mannerists and were strongly influenced by the style of Michelangelo. Their work was characterized by the heavy use of stucco, and their paintings, featuring bright colors and strong lines, often contained elongated figures. From 1584 to 1594, work was abandoned due to the ongoing Wars of Religion. Upon cessation of the violence, a new group of artists was gathered to continue the renovation. This second school was led mainly by French and Flemish artists, and similar in style to the first school, their works featured a greater depth of composition and stronger contrast between light and shadow.

A The region's second art movement rose to prominence centuries later and existed from roughly 1830 to 1870. B The beginnings of the movement, later dubbed the Barbizon school, can be found in an 1824 exhibition of the paintings of John Constable in Paris. C Instead of following the period's rigid insistence on painting scenes of historical importance, they began to focus on nature, so they traveled outside the city to paint in the open air, with the forest of Fontainebleau a favored destination. D

During the European revolutions in 1848, many of these young painters, including Théodore Rousseau and Jean-François Millet, fled Paris altogether and gathered in the village of Barbizon. There, they continued to focus on painting landscapes but began to include human figures — primarily farmers and peasants — in much of their work. The Barbizon school influenced a number of young painters, including Monet and Renoir, who went on to form the next great art movement, Impressionism.

Today, Barbizon and Fontainebleau are popular tourist destinations. The village is home to many art galleries, but the focus is more on celebrating the region's storied past than on contemporary art.

GLOSSARY
stucco: a type of plaster used for covering walls and decorating ceilings
dub: to give something or someone a particular name

ACTUAL TEST

25 The word his in the passage refers to

(A) Tycho Brahe
(B) Johannes Kepler
(C) Isaac Newton
(D) the emperor

26 According to paragraph 2,

(A) Newton initially disagreed with Kepler's ideas
(B) Brahe's work was the basis of Kepler's three laws
(C) Kepler abandoned mathematics after Brahe's death
(D) the Holy Roman Emperor introduced Kepler to Newton

* Paragraph 2 is marked with an arrow [→].

27 Which of the following is NOT true about Johannes Kepler?

(A) He worked for Tycho Brahe.
(B) He served as an imperial mathematician.
(C) He proposed the law of gravitation.
(D) He studied the motion of the planets.

28 What can be inferred about Isaac Newton?

(A) He proved one of Kepler's Law was inaccurate.
(B) He studied the work of Johannes Kepler.
(C) He was once a mentor to Tycho Brahe.
(D) He had a rivalry with Johannes Kepler.

29 Why does the author mention circles ?

(A) To illustrate the shape of most planets
(B) To explain why sunlight travels in a curve
(C) To show how the solar system expands
(D) To contrast their shape with that of ellipses

30 Look at the four squares [■] that indicate where the following sentence could be added to paragraph 3.

In the case of planetary orbital paths, one of these two focal points will necessarily be the sun itself.

Where would the sentence best fit?

31 The word it in the passage refers to

(A) line
(B) center
(C) sun
(D) planet

32 The word fluctuating in the passage could best be replaced by

(A) varying
(B) diminishing
(C) astonishing
(D) accelerating

Kepler's Laws

Johannes Kepler was a German mathematician who, during the late 16th and early 17th centuries, focused on discovering the mechanics behind the motion in the planets of the solar system. He worked closely with Tycho Brahe by acting as an assistant to the well-respected Danish astronomer, who, in turn, effectively served as Kepler's mentor.

→ After Brahe's death in 1601, Kepler stepped into his role as an imperial mathematician of the emperor of the Holy Roman Empire. He used the astronomer's painstakingly accrued data and detailed observations to develop three laws of planetary motion. These laws, considered to be Kepler's greatest contribution to the body of scientific knowledge, allowed Isaac Newton later to formulate his famous law of universal gravitation.

A Kepler's first law, known as the law of ellipses, explains that the paths followed by planets as they orbit the sun are elliptical, rather than circular, in shape. B Whereas circles are curves upon which every point is an equal distance from a single focal point, ellipses have two such focal points. C This law has since been proven to apply to other orbiting bodies as well. D

Generally referred to as the law of equal areas, the second law states that if an imaginary line were to be extended outward from the center of the sun to the center of an orbiting planet, it would pass through equal areas in equal periods of time as the planet moved. This is significant because the planets, as they move through space in their orbits around the sun, travel at fluctuating speeds. The shorter the distance between each planet and the sun, the faster its speed.

Finally, there is Kepler's third law, called the law of harmonies. Published in 1619, about ten years after the publication of his first two laws, it consists of an equation showing that the ratio of the squares of the periods of two given planets will always be equal to the ratio of the cubes of their average distance from the sun.

→ Although Kepler's reasoning behind these laws is no longer considered valid, the laws themselves are accurate and scientifically important. Kepler's three laws, along with Newton's subsequent theories, can be considered a catalyst of the 17th-century Scientific Revolution as well as a keystone in the foundation of both modern astronomy and modern physics.

GLOSSARY
ellipse: an oval shape similar to a circle but longer and flatter
focal point: the point where waves of lights or sound that are moving towards each other meet

ACTUAL TEST

33 Which of the sentences below best expresses the essential information in the highlighted sentence in the passage? *Incorrect* choices change the meaning in important ways or leave out essential information.

(A) Although his laws have been proven wrong, Kepler is still well respected.

(B) The reason Kepler's laws were forgotten is that they were not valid.

(C) Kepler's laws are still considered correct, but his reasoning is not.

(D) Kepler later abandoned his laws for a concept that was more accurate.

34 The word catalyst in the passage most likely means

(A) scientist
(B) catharsis
(C) trigger
(D) remainder

35 The author's main purpose in paragraph 6 is to

(A) emphasize the significance of Kepler's work
(B) explain why Kepler's reasoning was incorrect
(C) contrast the legacies of Kepler and Newton
(D) suggest that Kepler has been misunderstood

* Paragraph 6 is marked with an arrow [→].

36 Direction: An introductory sentence for a brief summary of the passage is provided below. Complete the summary by selecting the THREE answer choices that express the most important ideas in the passage.

Johannes Kepler was a highly influential German mathematician.

-
-
-

Answer Choices

(A) Kepler's work played an important role in the Scientific Revolution and influenced modern astronomy and modern physics.

(B) The law of equal areas explains that the planets orbit the sun at different speeds.

(C) Kepler proposed a third law ten years after his first two.

(D) Tycho Brahe mentored Kepler and was succeeded by him as an imperial mathematician.

(E) Kepler and Newton worked closely together, and they influenced each other.

(F) Kepler devised three laws of planetary motion, which are the law of ellipses, the law of equal areas, and the law of harmonies.

Kepler's Laws

Johannes Kepler was a German mathematician who, during the late 16th and early 17th centuries, focused on discovering the mechanics behind the motion in the planets of the solar system. He worked closely with Tycho Brahe by acting as an assistant to the well-respected Danish astronomer, who, in turn, effectively served as Kepler's mentor.

→ After Brahe's death in 1601, Kepler stepped into his role as an imperial mathematician of the emperor of the Holy Roman Empire. He used the astronomer's painstakingly accrued data and detailed observations to develop three laws of planetary motion. These laws, considered to be Kepler's greatest contribution to the body of scientific knowledge, allowed Isaac Newton later to formulate his famous law of universal gravitation.

A Kepler's first law, known as the law of ellipses, explains that the paths followed by planets as they orbit the sun are elliptical, rather than circular, in shape. B Whereas circles are curves upon which every point is an equal distance from a single focal point, ellipses have two such focal points. C This law has since been proven to apply to other orbiting bodies as well. D

Generally referred to as the law of equal areas, the second law states that if an imaginary line were to be extended outward from the center of the sun to the center of an orbiting planet, it would pass through equal areas in equal periods of time as the planet moved. This is significant because the planets, as they move through space in their orbits around the sun, travel at fluctuating speeds. The shorter the distance between each planet and the sun, the faster its speed.

Finally, there is Kepler's third law, called the law of harmonies. Published in 1619, about ten years after the publication of his first two laws, it consists of an equation showing that the ratio of the squares of the periods of two given planets will always be equal to the ratio of the cubes of their average distance from the sun.

→ Although Kepler's reasoning behind these laws is no longer considered valid, the laws themselves are accurate and scientifically important. Kepler's three laws, along with Newton's subsequent theories, can be considered a catalyst of the 17th-century Scientific Revolution as well as a keystone in the foundation of both modern astronomy and modern physics.

GLOSSARY
ellipse: an oval shape similar to a circle but longer and flatter
focal point: the point where waves of lights or sound that are moving towards each other meet

← THIS IS THE END OF THE TEST.

TOEFL iBT® Codebreaker
Reading Basic

PART 1
TOEFL iBT® Reading Skills 01

Skimming

Skimming은 수험자로 하여금 지문을 살펴볼 수 있게 도와주는 독해 기술 중 하나이다. 이러한 훑어보기 방식은 수험자가 중요한 단어들이나 어구들을 파악하여 재빨리 지문의 주제를 인지하게 한다. 그렇게 함으로써, 그들은 불필요한 단어들이나 문장들을 걸러내어 시간을 절약할 수 있다.

Read the highlighted parts and choose the main idea.
음영 처리된 부분을 읽고 주제를 고르시오.

1. (B)   2. (A)

1. 중부 불가리아 지역에 위치한 카잔루크의 트라키아인 무덤 은 유네스코 세계문화유산이다. 이 무덤은 복도와 둥근 묘실로 되어 있는데, 죽은 사람을 매장하기 위해 사용된 거대한 집합체인 공동묘지의 일부이다. 무덤은 기원전 4세기경부터 인상 깊게 잘 보존된 벽화들 로 장식되어 있다. 그 벽화의 뛰어난 구성과 자연적인 세부묘사는 무덤을 역사적 중요성을 가진 예술공간 으로 만든다.
   (A) 카잔루크의 트라키아인 무덤은 그것의 잘 보존된 벽화들 덕분에 유네스코 세계문화유산으로 지정되었다.
   (B) 카잔루크의 트라키아인 무덤은 그것의 잘 보존된 벽화들 덕분에 역사적으로, 그리고 예술적으로 중요하다.

   ● 음영 처리된 부분들은 주어진 지문의 핵심 내용을 나타내고 있다. 이를 조합하여 주제를 나타내면 (B)가 된다.

2. 1980년에 작가인 Alvin Toffler는 '주도적인 소비자들'의 증가를 예견했는데, 그들은 정기적으로 구입하는 제품들을 발전시키기 위해 적극적으로 회사들과 일을 하는 이들이다. 그들을 지칭하기 위해, 그는 '프로슈머' 라는 용어를 만들어냈다. 하지만 시간이 흘러, 그 용어는 변화하는 시장에 맞게 진보했다. 오늘날, 프로슈머는 자신들이 선호하는 상표를 변호하고 그들이 싫어하는 상표를 비판하기 위해 기술을 이용하는 소비자들을 뜻한다. 어느 정도, 그들은 수동적인 소비자에서 마케팅 과정의 중요한 일부의 역할을 하는 자들이 되었다.
   (A) 프로슈머는 제품을 변호하고 비판하면서 중요한 역할을 한다.
   (B) 프로슈머는 상표의 마케팅 과정에 관계되어 있는 소비자들이다.

   ● 음영 처리된 부분을 조합해 보면, 프로슈머는 상표를 변호하고 비판하기 위해 기술을 이용하는 소비자들로, 마케팅 과정의 중요한 역할을 한다. 따라서 답은 (A)이다.

Scanning

Scanning은 빠르게 독해하는 또 다른 기술이다. 전체 지문을 빠르게 읽음으로써, 수험자는 지문에 있는 주요 내용을 찾을 수 있다. 수험자는 세부내용을 놓치지 않거나 주어진 정보에 의해 혼동되지 않도록 노력해야 한다.

Find the correct answer for each question.
각 문제에 알맞은 답을 고르시오.

1. (B)   2. (C)

1. 딱정벌레는 대략 400,000 종류가 알려져 있다. 그들의 큰 특징은 한 쌍의 딱딱한 외부 날개이다. 그것들은 나는 데 쓰이는 부드러운 내부 날개를 보호한다. 다른 모든 곤충처럼, 그들은 여섯 개의 다리를 지니고 있고, 그들의 몸체는 세 부분으로 나뉘어 있다. 각각의 딱정벌레는 서로 다른 먹이를 먹는다. 어떤 딱정벌레들은 오로지 식물을 먹고 다른 딱정벌레들은 더 작은 곤충을 잡아 먹으며, 또 다른 딱정벌레들은 더 큰 동물들의 배설물을 먹고 산다.

   다음 중 딱정벌레에 대해 올바른 정보는 무엇인가?
   (A) 수백만 종류가 있다.
   (B) 그것들의 외부 날개는 내부 날개보다 딱딱하다.
   (C) 그들의 몸은 세 부분으로 되어 있고, 오로지 식물과 곤충만을 먹는다.

   ● 딱정벌레는 약 400,000 종이 있고 딱딱한 외부 날개와 부드러운 내부 날개를 가지고 있으며 식물, 더 작은 곤충, 더 큰 동물들의 배설물 등을 먹는다. 따라서 답은 (B)이다.

2. '소울푸드'라는 말은 미국 남부에서 발달된 아프리카 식의 미국 요리를 나타낸다. 소울푸드의 주재료에는 돼지고기, 콩, 잎 채소, 그리고 옥수수가루가 있다. 소울푸드의 독특한 특징은 필요성에 의해 발전했다. 과거에 노예들은 그들이 취할 수 있는 음식이면 어떤 것이라도 모두 이용해야 했다. 후에, 이러한 요리법은 미국 원주민의 요리법뿐만 아니라, 가난한 시골 남부인들의 음식 문화와 합쳐졌다.

   다음 중 소울푸드를 가장 잘 설명한 것은 무엇인가?
   (A) 처음에 아프리카의 남부 지역에서 만연했다.
   (B) 미국 원주민 부족들의 특권층에게 제공되었다.
   (C) 미국 원주민의 요리법이 다른 요리법들과 결합하여 소울푸드가 되었다.

   ● 소울푸드는 미국 남부에서 발달하였고, 미국 원주민들과 가난한 시골 남부인들의 음식 문화가 합쳐진 것이다. 따라서 답은 (C)이다.

UNIT 01
Vocabulary ❶

INTRODUCTION
'어휘'라는 용어는 지문 내에서 사용된 각각의 단어와 어구를 뜻한다. 수험자가 지문 내에서 쓰인 단어나 어구를 대체할 수 있는 동의어를 찾는 문제 형식이다.

TYPICAL QUESTION TYPES
지문에서 단어/어구 ▭ 와 의미가 가장 가까운 것은
지문에서 단어/어구 ▭ 을 대체하기에 가장 적합한 것은
지문에서 단어/어구 ▭ 와 가장 비슷한 의미는

STRATEGIES
- 지문에서 음영 처리된 단어나 어구를 찾아 그것이 명사인지, 동사인지, 형용사인지, 또는 부사인지 확인한다.
- 단어가 쓰인 곳의 문맥을 잘 살펴 보아야 한다. 오답들은 종종 여러 가지 뜻을 지닌 단어로, 지문에서의 쓰임과 다른 뜻을 지니고 있다.
- 정답에 대한 단서를 찾기 위해서는 전후 문장을 확인해 봐야 한다. 단어의 뜻을 암시하는 단서가 있을 수 있다.

QUICK CHECKUP   p. 15
정답 | 1. (A)   2. (B)   3. (C)

Find the best replacement for the highlighted word or phrase.
음영 처리된 단어나 어구를 가장 잘 대체할 수 있는 것을 찾으시오.

1. *유디트*와 *키스*와 같은 작품들로 가장 잘 알려진 Gustav Klimt는 1863년에 태어났다. 그는 가난하게 태어났지만 성공한 화가가 되었는데, 작품에 금을 사용하는 그의 독특한 방식이 부분적으로 이에 기인했다. 그의 화려한 작품들과는 달리, Klimt의 삶은 소박했다. 그는 보통 가운을 입고 샌들을 신었으며, 예술을 창조하고 가족을 돌보는 단 두 가지의 일에 전념했다.
   (A) 호화로운   (B) 거대한
   (C) 처음의   (D) 기이한

   ➤ extravagant는 '사치의, 호화로운'이라는 뜻으로 지문에서는 Klimt가 금을 써서 작품들이 화려해 보였다는 것을 의미한다. 따라서 (A) luxurious가 가장 가까운 의미를 가지고 있다.

2. 정기적으로, 여름이 끝나고 나면 따뜻하고 건조한 기후가 예상치 못하게 다시 찾아온다. 이 현상은 인디언 서머로 알려져 있다. 인디언 서머는 미국 북동부에서 일어나지만, 유사한 기후가 세계 곳곳에서 일어날 수 있다. 인디언 서머는 바람이 시계 방향으로 불 때 일어난다. 그것은 남쪽의 따뜻한 공기 덩어리가 북쪽 방향으로 움직이게 한다. 그 결과, 다시 8월처럼 느껴지는 것이다.
   (A) 느낌   (B) 현상
   (C) 예외   (D) 장식

   ➤ phenomenon은 '사건, 현상'이라는 뜻을 지닌 (B) happening과 대체될 수 있다.

3. 사향 고양이는 아프리카와 아시아에서 발견되는 작은 포유류의 한 종류이다. 그들의 몸체와 꼬리는 고양이를 닮았지만, 사향 고양이는 개와 닮은 길쭉한 머리를 지니고 있다. 그들은 70센티미터까지 자랄 수 있고, 향수를 제조할 때 쓰이는 강한 향의 물질을 배설한다. 또한 사향 고양이는 값비싼 커피 생산에도 기여하는데, 그들이 커피 열매를 먹고 나면, 그들의 배설물에서 커피 콩이 조심스럽게 분리된다.
   (A) 합쳐지다   (B) 비교되다
   (C) 빼내지다   (D) 옮겨지다

   ➤ be separated from은 '~에서 구분되다, 떼어지다'라는 뜻을 가지므로 (C) removed from이 알맞다.

VOCABULARY   pp. 16-17

Write the number of each word's definition.
각 단어의 뜻을 찾아 번호를 쓰시오.

enforce / 7 집행하다   deputy / 8 대행인
outlaw / 1 범법자   function / 9 기능하다
utilize / 2 활용하다   component / 6 부품
virtual / 3 가상의   alternative / 10 대안
transfer / 4 옮기다   soar / 12 치솟다
digestive / 11 소화의   bloated / 5 부은, 부푼

Match each collocation with the correct definition.
각 연어에 알맞은 뜻을 찾아 연결하시오.

a. date back – to have existed since a particular time in the past 역사가 ~까지 올라가다
b. break down – to stop working because of a fault 고장이 나다
c. dawn on – to begin to be noticed ~이 깨닫게 되다
d. serve as – to be used as ~로 쓰이다
e. provide with – to supply or equip with something ~을 제공하다

Circle the word closest in meaning to each underlined word.
각 밑줄 친 단어의 뜻과 가장 가까운 단어를 찾아 동그라미 하시오.

정답 | 1. (C)   2. (A)   3. (B)
       4. (B)   5. (D)   6. (C)

해석

1. 모든 돈은 고객의 계좌로 옮겨져야 한다.
   (A) 보고되어야   (B) 묘사되어야
   (C) 옮겨져야   (D) 야기되어야

2. 배출되지 않은 가스는 환자의 배가 부푼 것처럼 느껴지게 할 수 있다.
   (A) 부은   (B) 가벼운
   (C) 오래된 (D) 얼은

3. 영화에서, 그 탐정은 범법자들에게 복수하기 위해 그들을 쫓는다.
   (A) 군인들   (B) 범죄자들
   (C) 변호사들 (D) 자원봉사자들

4. 이 카드는 문을 여는 열쇠와 보안 패스의 기능을 한다.
   (A) 구입하다 (B) 작동하다
   (C) 비치하다 (D) 겨냥하다

5. 그 요리법에서는 포도 주스가 포도주의 훌륭한 대안이 될 수 있다고 되어 있었다.
   (A) 보상 (B) 욕구
   (C) 발전 (D) 대체물

6. 컴퓨터는 아주 많은 부품들로 구성되어 있다.
   (A) 콤팩트들 (B) 영향들
   (C) 요소들   (D) 대륙들

Fill in each blank with the correct collocation.
알맞은 연어를 골라 빈칸을 채우시오.

정답 | 1. provides ~ with   2. breaks down
     | 3. serve as   4. dawned on
     | 5. dates back

해석

1. 그 호텔은 많은 훌륭한 시설과 서비스를 투숙객들에게 제공한다.
2. 만약 구(舊)장비가 고장 나면, 대체 장비가 필요할 것이다.
3. 그 영수증은 물건을 구입했다는 증거로 쓰일 것이다.
4. 갑자기, 그 남자는 방에 가방을 두고 왔다는 것을 깨달았다.
5. 손 인형의 역사는 수천 년을 거슬러 올라간다.

STEP 1   pp.18-19

정답 | 1. (C)   2. (D)

미국 보안관

보안관은 법을 집행하는 정부 관료이다. 미국 보안관의 역사는 200년 전으로 거슬러 올라간다. 보안관은 대부분의 주에 있었고, 보통 그 지역의 가장 높은 법 집행관이었다.

보안관은 미국이 서쪽으로 확장하는 데 큰 역할을 했다. 1800년대, 많은 미국인들은 서쪽으로 이주하기 시작했다. 하지만 공용지가 너무 많았기 때문에, 모두를 안전하게 지키는 일은 어려웠다. 따라서 각 지역 단체는 구성원 중 한 명을 보안관으로 선택했다.

몇몇 보안관들은 광활한 넓이의 영토를 지키는 책임을 맡았다. 이러한 지역에서, 흔히 한 명의 보안관과 많은 범죄자들이 있었다. 도움이 필요할 때, 보안관은 다른 이들을 자신의 대행인으로 삼을 수 있었다. 그들은 함께 범법자들과 싸우고 종종 총격전을 벌였다. 미국 역사에서, 보안관들은 마치 오늘날의 경찰관들처럼 범죄자들을 없애는 데에 필수적이었다.

• Structure Zone

- 동사 begin은 to부정사를 목적어로 취한다. 이와 같은 동사에는 hope, decide, want, promise, plan, choose 등이 있다.

  ... many Americans **began to move** west.
  Each community **chose** one of its members **to be** a sheriff.

- 'It is/was + 형용사 + to부정사'의 형태에서, It은 가주어이고 to부정사는 진주어 역할을 한다. 이러한 구조를 취할 수 있는 형용사들로는 difficult, easy, hard, possible, good, dangerous, interesting, safe 등이 있다.

  It was difficult to keep everyone safe.

- 'when + 주어 + be 동사 + in'의 형태에서, 주어와 be 동사는 생략될 수 있다.

  When they are in need of assistance, sheriffs could make other people their deputies.
  → **When in** need of assistance, sheriffs could make other people their deputies.

1. 지문에서 어구 had a big role 을 대체하기에 가장 적합한 것은
   (A) 참여하기를 거부했다   (B) 공식적인 허가를 요청했다
   (C) 중요한 역할을 했다   (D) 도움이 되는 조언을 제공했다

   ➤ had a big role은 '큰 역할을 했다'라는 의미를 지니고 있다. 따라서 이를 대체하기에 가장 알맞은 어구는 (C) played an important part이다.

2. 지문에서 단어 enormous와 의미가 가장 가까운 것은
   (A) 익명의   (B) 수가 많은
   (C) 셀 수 있는 (D) 어마어마한

   ➤ enormous는 '거대한, 막대한'이라는 뜻을 가지고 있으며, 주로 양이나 크기를 지칭할 때 쓰인다. 보기 중 이를 대신할 수 있는 단어는 (D) immense이다.

• Note-Taking

American Sheriffs

What They Do   — enforce the law
When Started   — date back about 200 yrs.
What They Did —

1. helped the country's westward expansion
2. protected an enormous territory w/ their deputies
   - battled outlaws & often had gunfights
→ have been indispensable at eliminating criminals

SUMMARY
Sheriffs are government officials who enforce the law. Sheriffs have a 200 year history in the USA. Most of the states had them as the highest law enforcement. The sheriffs participated in the country's westward expansion. Each sheriff was responsible for protecting an enormous territory. Sheriffs made other people their deputies and battled outlaws. They have been indispensable in the history of America like today's police officers.

보안관들은 법을 집행하는 정부 관료이다. 미국 보안관의 역사는 200년이다. 대부분의 주에서 그들은 가장 높은 법 집행관이었다. 보안관들은 국가가 서쪽으로 확장하는 데 참여했다. 각각의 보안관은 거대한 지역을 지키는 일을 책임졌다. 보안관들은 다른 이들을 대행인으로 삼고 범법자들과 싸웠다. 그들은 오늘날의 경찰관들처럼 미국 역사에서 필수적인 존재였다.

VOCAB_ Match each word with the correct definition.
각 단어에 알맞은 뜻을 찾아 연결하시오.

a. official – a person who is charged with certain duties 관료
b. expansion – the process of becoming bigger in size 확장
c. territory – any tract of land or region 지역, 영토
d. assistance – help or support 도움
e. engage in – to take part in something ~에 참여하다

STEP 2 pp. 20-21

정답 | 1. (B) 2. (C) 3. (A)

3D 프린팅

3D 프린터는 사람들이 원하는 것이면 거의 무엇이든 창조해낼 수 있는 기계이다. 기계를 작동하는 절차는 간단하다. 사용자가 물체가 그려진 그림을 다운로드하고, 기계가 그것을 복사한다.

3D 프린터는 보통의 잉크 프린터와 아주 비슷한 기능을 하지만, 잉크 대신 플라스틱, 왁스, 또는 금속 같은 물질을 사용한다. 이와 같은 물질들로 프린터는 실제 존재하는 물체를 층층이 만들어낸다. 많은 시간이 걸리고, 몇 천 층을 쓸 수도 있지만, 최종적 결과물은 실제와 똑같은 복사물이다.

놀랍게도, 3D 프린팅 기술은 1986년부터 존재했다. 초창기에는, 공학과 건축 부분에서만 쓰였다. 하지만 오늘날, 3D 프린터는 다방면의 산업에서 활용된다. 몇몇 비행기 부품과 플라스틱 장난감은 3D 프린터로 생산된다. 그리고 의사들은 환자들의 신체 부분을 만들어내기 위해 3D 프린터를 쓰는데, 이런 식으로 그들은 위험한 수술을 집도하기 전에 예행 연습을 할 수 있다. 몇몇의 요식업에서도 3D 프린팅을 사용하기 시작했는데, 먹을 수 있는 재료를 사용해서 식품을 만들어낸다. 머지 않아, 3D 프린팅은 우주에서 우주비행사들이 원하는 어떠한 부품들도 만들어내게 할 수도 있다. 3D 프린터는 과학계에서 위대한 발전으로 여겨지고 있으며, 사람들의 삶을 현저히 바꿔놓을 것으로 보인다.

• **Structure Zone**

• 과거의 어느 시점으로부터 현재까지 진행되어 온 일을 표현할 때 'have + p.p. ~ since'의 현재분사형을 쓴다.
3D printing technology **has been** around **since** 1986.

• 관계대명사 which를 써서 선행사를 수식할 수 있다.
Doctors use 3D printing..., **which** allows them to practice before performing risky surgery.

1. 지문의 주제는 무엇인가?
   (A) 3D 프린터는 보통의 잉크 프린터를 대체하고 있다.
   (B) 3D 프린터는 현재와 미래에 쓰임이 많다.
   (C) 3D 프린터는 우주 산업을 돕기 위해 발명되었다.
   (D) 3D 프린터에 사용할 수 있는 물질들이 몇몇 있다.

   ● 주어진 지문은 3D 프린터가 무엇인지, 어떻게 기능하는지, 그리고 어떻게 활용되는지를 설명하고 있다. 따라서 지문의 주제로 알맞은 것은 (B)이다.

2. 지문에서 어구 capable of와 가장 비슷한 의미는
   (A) ~을 위한 시간이 있는 (B) ~와 가까운
   (C) ~하기 가능한 (D) ~로 구성된

   ● capable of는 '~할 수 있는'이라는 의미로, 보기에서 이와 가장 가까운 뜻을 가진 것은 (C) able to be이다.

3. 지문에서 단어 manufactured와 의미가 가장 가까운 것은
   (A) 생산된 (B) 유지된
   (C) 파괴된 (D) 포획된

   ● manufacture은 '만들다, 생산하다'라는 뜻을 가지고 있고, 지문에서는 과거분사형으로 쓰여 수동적인 의미를 지닌다. 이와 가장 가까운 의미를 지닌 것은 '생산된'이라는 뜻의 (A) produced이다.

• **Note-Taking**

P1 MI a 3D printer
   SD capable of creating nearly anything

P2 MI works like a normal ink printer but uses different materials
   SD - uses plastic, wax, or metal
       - produces actual objects layer by layer with these materials

P3 MI is utilized in a wide variety of industries
   SD • some airplane components & plastic toys
       • doctors – practice before performing surgery

- food businesses – use edible ingredients
- astronauts – make equipment parts

VOCAB_ Write the correct word for each definition.
각 뜻에 알맞은 단어를 찾아 적으시오.

a. layer 층, 겹
b. exact 정확한
c. risky 위험한
d. ingredient 재료
e. require 필요로 하다

STEP 3				pp. 22-23
정답	1. (A)	2. (D)	3. (C)	4. (C)

비트코인

비트코인은 가상 화폐의 유형이다. 즉, 그것은 실제로 존재하지 않는 돈이다. 하지만 실재하는 회사의 진짜 물건이나 서비스를 구입하는 데 쓰일 수 있다.

비트코인 시스템은 2009년에 Satoshi Nakamoto라는 수수께끼의 인물이 만들었다. 사실, Satoshi Nakamoto가 실제 존재하는 사람인지 또는 여러 명의 사람들인지는 아무도 모른다. 비트코인은 달러와 유로 같은 국제 통화를 대체하도록 제작되었다. 그것은 온라인 상에서 물건을 구입할 때 현금이나 신용카드 대신 쓰일 수 있다. 비트코인이 구매자에서 판매자로 옮겨갈 때, 그 거래는 공공의 데이터베이스에 기록된다.

각 정부는 비트코인이 해커들에 의해 쉽게 도난당할 것을 우려한다. 정부들은 그것들이 불법적인 목적으로 사용될 수 있다는 것을 깨달았다. 예를 들면, 장물이 정부가 모르는 새 구입될 수도 있다. 점점 더 많은 회사들이 비트코인을 받아들이고 있지만, 비트코인으로 구매하는 비율은 신용카드와 같은 다른 온라인 지불 방법에 비해 미미하다. 대신, 많은 비트코인 소유자들은 단순히 투자 목적으로 비트코인을 가지고 있는데, 그것이 미래에 더 가치 있을 것으로 믿기 때문이다.

이것은 현명한 접근 방식일 수도 아닐 수도 있다. 현재 비트코인의 가치는 대단히 변동이 심한데, 특히 매우 안정적인 국제 통화에 비해 그러하다. 비트코인 투자가들은 이 첨단기술의 화폐가 더 폭넓게 받아들여지면, 가치가 치솟을 것으로 희망하고 도박 중인 것이다.

- **Structure Zone**

'주격관계대명사 + be 동사'는 뒤에 분사가 올 때 생략될 수 있다.
The bitcoin system was created in 2009 by an enigmatic person **who is named** Satoshi Nakamoto.
→ The bitcoin system was created in 2009 by an enigmatic person **named** Satoshi Nakamoto.

1. 지문에서 단어 they가 가리키는 것은
   (A) 비트코인   (B) 정부들
   (C) 해커들   (D) 장물들

▶ 음영 처리된 they는 불법적인 목적으로 쓰일 수도 있는 존재를 지칭한다. 따라서 답은 (A) bitcoins이다.

2. 지문에서 단어 minuscule을 대체하기에 가장 적합한 것은
   (A) 어려운   (B) 편리한
   (C) 기적적인   (D) 하찮은

▶ minuscule은 '극소의'라는 의미이다. 따라서 이를 대체하기에 가장 알맞은 것은 '사소한, 하찮은'이라는 의미를 지닌 (D) insignificant이다.

3. 지문에서 단어 stable과 의미가 가장 가까운 것은
   (A) ~의 조건을 가진   (B) 범죄의
   (C) 안정된   (D) 지적인

▶ stable은 '안정된'이라는 의미로, 국제 통화들의 변동이 거의 없다는 것을 뜻한다. 따라서 이와 의미가 가장 가까운 것은 (C) balanced이다.

4. 비트코인에 대한 설명으로 옳지 않은 것은
   (A) 온라인 상에서만 존재한다.
   (B) 2009년에 만들어졌다.
   (C) 많은 국가에서 불법이다.
   (D) 큰 돈의 가치가 있다.

▶ 주어진 지문에 따르면, 2009년에 만들어진 비트코인은 온라인 상에서만 존재하며, 실제 돈으로 환산했을 때 가치가 커질 수 있다. 따라서 비트코인에 대해 옳지 않은 것은 (C)이다.

VOCAB_ Find the correct word in the passage for each of the given definition.
주어진 뜻에 알맞은 단어를 지문에서 찾으시오.

a. currency 통화, 화폐
b. enigmatic 수수께끼의
c. illegal 불법적인
d. fluctuate 변동을 거듭하다

- **Note-Taking** (Sample Answer)

P1 MI bitcoins
    SD a form of virtual currency

P2 MI created in 2009 by Satoshi Nakamoto
    SD - designed to serve as an alternative to national currencies
        - can be used instead of cash or credit cards online

P3 MI concerns on using bitcoins
    SD - can easily be stolen by hackers and used for illegal purposes
        - are used less than other online payment methods

P4 MI the current value of bitcoins
    SD fluctuating but expected to soar in value

• **More Info Zone**

비트코인 캐기

비트코인은 각국의 중앙은행이 화폐 발행을 독점하고 자의적인 통화정책을 펴는 것에 대한 반발로 고안된 것으로 알려져 있다. 컴퓨터가 제시하는 매우 난해한 수학 문제를 풀면 그 대가로 비트코인을 지급하는 작동방식으로, 프로그래밍 설계도가 공개되어 있어서 개발자라면 누구나 프로그래밍 업그레이드에 참여할 수 있다. 비트코인을 만드는 과정은 광산업에 빗대어 '캔다(mining)'라고 하며 이러한 방식으로 비트코인을 만드는 사람을 '마이너(miner)', 즉 '광부'라고 부른다. 광부가 아닌 사람은 돈을 주고 비트코인을 구입해 거래할 수 있게 되어 있다.

UNIT TEST   pp.24-25

정답 | 1. (B) 2. (D) 3. (A) 4. (C) 5. (B)
     6. (C)

하루에 사과 한 알

사과는 매일 섭취할 수 있는 가장 건강한 음식물 중 하나이다. 미국의 오래된 속담에는 '하루에 사과 한 알씩을 먹으면 병원에 갈 일이 없다'라는 말이 있다. 하지만 하루 중 언제 사과를 먹는 것이 가장 좋은지에 대해서는 명백히 나타나 있지 않다. 보통 아침에 먹는 사과는 사람들에게 유익하지만, 저녁에 먹는 사과는 독을 먹는 것이라고 여겨진다.

이러한 믿음에는 사실 과학적인 이유가 뒷받침된다. 사과의 장점 중 하나는 그들이 사람들에게 큰 에너지를 주는 자연적 당의 한 형태인 과당의 좋은 원천이라는 것이다. 사과로부터 얻는 에너지는 한 잔의 커피로부터 얻을 수 있는 것보다 더 효과가 길다. 분명, 이것은 많은 사람들이 잠자리에 들기 직전보다는 아침에 얻고 싶은 효과일 것이다.

또한 사과는 식이성 섬유의 한 종류인 높은 수준의 펙틴을 지니고 있다. 섬유질은 장의 움직임을 활성화해서 소화 계통의 건강을 유지하는 데 도움을 준다. 하지만 잠자리에 들기 직전에 사과를 먹으면 문제를 일으킬 수 있다. 당신이 잠들어 있을 때, 장이 가스로 차게 되어 속이 붓고 불편함을 느끼게 된다. 화장실에 가기 위해 여러 번 잠에서 깰 수도 있어 숙면을 방해할 수 있다.

사과가 주는 또 다른 이점에는 플라보노이드, 베타 카로틴, 그리고 비타민 B군이 있다. 플라보노이드는 사과의 진한 빨간색처럼 꽃과 과일이 선명한 색을 띠게 해 주는 물질이다. 플라보노이드를 섭취하면, 심장병, 당뇨병, 그리고 다른 질병의 위험이 낮아진다. 한편, 베타 카로틴은 암을 막아주고, 비타민 B군은 중요한 이점을 다양하게 우리 몸에 준다. 명백히, 사과를 먹으며 하루를 시작하는 것은 병원에 갈 일을 막아준다.

Glossary proverb 속담, 격언   bowel 장의, 창자의
              diabetes 당뇨병

• **Structure Zone**

- 'one of + the + 최상급' 뒤에 오는 명사는 복수로 쓴다.
  Apples are **one of the healthiest foods** you can eat every day.

- that의 쓰임
  - 접속사 that은 완전한 절을 이끌며 보어 역할을 한다.
    One benefit of apples is **that** they are a favorable source of fructose.
  - 관계대명사 that은 불완전한 절을 이끌며 앞에 나온 명사를 대신하여 중복을 피한다.
    The energy you get from an apple is longer lasting than **that**(the energy) provided by a cup of coffee.

- 동명사 형태와 to부정사 형태 모두 문장의 주어로 쓰일 수 있다.
  Starting(=**To start**) your day with an apple really can keep the doctor away.

1. 지문의 주제는 무엇인가?
   (A) 미국인들은 사과의 건강적 이점에 대해 서로 동의하지 않는다.
   (B) 사과는 아침에 섭취되어야 하는 건강한 음식물이다.
   (C) 사과에는 많은 이로운 물질이 있다.
   (D) 사과를 먹는 것은 비타민 B군을 얻는 좋은 방법이다.

   ➔ 주어진 지문은 하루 중 아침에 사과를 먹으면 좋은 이유에 대해 여러 가지 영양분을 예로 들며 설명하고 있다. 따라서 주제로 가장 알맞은 것은 (B)이다.

2. 지문에서 어구 a favorable source of 를 대체하기에 가장 적합한 것은
   (A) ~의 결과로   (B) ~의 이유로
   (C) ~을 치료하는   (D) ~의 제공처로

   ➔ 음영 처리된 a favorable source of는 '좋은 원천'이라는 뜻이다. 따라서 이를 대체하기에 가장 적절한 어구는 '~의 제공처로'라는 뜻의 (D) a provider of이다.

3. 왜 작가는 지문에서 a cup of coffee 를 언급하는가?
   (A) 사과로부터 얻는 에너지가 얼마나 오래가는지 강조하기 위해서
   (B) 커피를 마시는 것이 얼마나 위험한지 보여주기 위해서
   (C) 밤에 사과를 섭취하는 것의 대안을 제시하기 위해서
   (D) 과당을 얻기 좋은 원천의 예를 들기 위해서

   ➔ 지문을 보면 사과가 주는 에너지는 길게 지속되며, 그것이 커피 한 잔의 에너지보다 더 오래 지속된다는 것을 알 수 있다. 따라서 (A)가 답이 된다.

4. 지문에서 단어 stimulates 와 가장 비슷한 의미는
   (A) 방해하다   (B) 처방하다
   (C) 고무하다   (D) 가장하다

   ➔ stimulate는 '활성화시키다, 자극시키다'라는 의미를 가지고 있다. 따라서 보기 중 이를 대신할 수 있는 단어는 '고무하다, 장려하다'라는 뜻의 (C) encourages가 된다.

7

5. 아래 문장 중 지문에서 음영 처리된 문장의 핵심 정보를 가장 잘 나타낸 것은 어느 것인가?
   (A) 선명한 빨간색을 지닌 과일들과 꽃들만이 플라보노이드를 함유하고 있다.
   (B) 과일들과 꽃들의 선명한 색은 플라보노이드 때문이다.
   (C) 플라보노이드가 없으면, 과일들과 꽃들은 생존할 수 없다.
   (D) 사과의 달콤하고 꽃 향기가 나는 맛은 플라보노이드 때문이다.

   ● 음영 처리된 문장은 플라보노이드가 꽃들과 과일들의 선명한 색을 띄게 한다는 의미이다. 이를 가장 잘 나타낸 문장은 (B)이다.

6. 지문에 따르면, 사실이 아닌 것은
   (A) 아침 일찍 사과를 먹는 것이 더 좋다.
   (B) 다량의 섬유질이 사과에서 발견된다.
   (C) 사과보다 커피에 과당이 더 많다.
   (D) 플라보노이드는 당뇨병을 막는 데 도움을 준다.

   ● 사과보다 커피가 과당을 더 많이 함유하고 있다는 (C)는 사실이 아니다.

VOCABULARY TEST   pp. 26-27

Recall the essential words in the unit to reinforce your vocabulary acquisition. Write the meaning of each word in your language.
유닛에서 배운 주요 단어들을 떠올려 각 단어의 뜻을 쓰시오.

exact | 정확한
expansion | 확장
mammal | 포유류의
poverty | 가난, 빈곤
alternative | 대안
ingredient | 재료
function | 기능하다
fluctuate | 변동을 거듭하다
soar | 치솟다
transfer | 옮기다
enigmatic | 수수께끼의
official | 공식적인
elongated | 가늘고 긴
currency | 통화, 화폐
resemble | 닮다
enforce | 집행하다
engage in | ~에 참여하다
provide with | ~을 제공하다
illegal | 불법인
date back | 역사가 ~까지 올라가다
dawn on | ~이 깨닫게 되다

digestive | 소화의
proverb | 속담, 격언
outlaw | 범법자
bloated | 부은, 부푼
diabetes | 당뇨병
virtual | 가상의
devoted | 헌신적인
method | 방법
bowel | 장의, 창자의
utilize | 활용하다
component | 부품
risky | 위험한
deputy | 대행인
require | 필요로 하다
territory | 영토
assistance | 도움
serve as | ~로 쓰이다
layer | 층, 겹
break down | 고장 나다

Complete each sentence with the correct word or collocation.
문장에 알맞은 단어나 연어를 찾아 쓰시오.

정답 |
1. method
2. utilized
3. virtual
4. elongated
5. bowel
6. fluctuates
7. risky
8. bloated
9. territory
10. dawned on

해석 |
1. Klimt는 그의 작품들에 금을 쓰는 독특한 방법을 사용했다.
2. 3D 프린터는 다양한 산업에서 활용된다.
3. 비트코인은 가상 화폐의 한 종류이다.
4. 사향 고양이는 개와 닮은 길쭉한 머리를 지닌 포유동물이다.
5. 섬유질은 장의 움직임을 활성화한다.
6. 현재, 비트코인의 가치는 대단히 변동이 심하다.
7. 의사들은 위험한 수술 집도 전에 예행 연습을 하는 데 3D 프린터를 쓴다.
8. 당신의 장이 가스로 차게 되어 속이 부은 느낌이 들 수 있다.
9. 몇몇 보안관들은 광활한 넓이의 지역을 지키는 책임을 맡았다.
10. 정부들은 그 화폐가 불법적인 목적으로 사용될 수 있다는 것을 깨달았다.

UNIT 02
Vocabulary ❷

INTRODUCTION

어휘 문제는 지문에 나타난 단어에 대한 지식을 수험자에게 묻는 문제이다. 수험자는 음영 처리된 어휘에 가장 근접한 의미를 가진 단어나 어구를 찾아야 한다. 이 문제 유형은 또한 수험자에게 익숙하지 않은 단어의 의미를 맥락, 접두사, 접미사, 또는 어근을 통해 찾을 수 있게 한다.

TYPICAL QUESTION TYPES

지문에서 단어/어구 ▇▇ 와 의미가 가장 가까운 것은
지문에서 단어/어구 ▇▇ 을 대체하기에 가장 적합한 것은
지문에서 단어/어구 ▇▇ 와 가장 비슷한 의미는

STRATEGIES

• 익숙한 접두사나 접미사가 있는지 단어를 확인하라. 어떤 단어에서는 유용한 힌트를 제공하기도 한다.

- 문장 안에서 문맥의 단서를 찾아라. 강조 단어와 어구의 앞이나 뒤에 위치한 문장들은 유용한 정보를 제공할 것이다.
- 음영 처리된 단어와 어구가 포함된 문장을 주의하여 읽고 그 문장들이 긍정적인지 부정적인지를 판단하라. 이를 통해 문장의 어조와 부합되지 않는 선택지를 제거할 수 있다.

QUICK CHECKUP   p. 29

정답 | 1. (B)   2. (A)   3. (D)

Find the best replacement for the highlighted word or phrase.
음영 처리된 단어나 어구를 가장 잘 대체할 수 있는 것을 찾으시오.

1. 바푸는 다가오는 봄을 맞이하기 위해 열리는 전통적인 핀란드 휴일이다. 이는 4월의 마지막 날에 시작되어 5월의 첫째 날까지 계속된다. 현대에는 주로 대학생들에 의해 기념된다. 그들은 하얀 학생모자를 쓴 채 모여서 튀긴 케이크를 먹고 특별한 레모네이드를 마신다. 다음날, 그들은 공원에 가서 하얀 식탁보, 은 촛대, 그리고 비싼 음식으로 마련된 풍성한 피크닉을 즐긴다.
   (A) 오로지   (B) 주로
   (C) 유쾌하게   (D) 일시적으로

   ● primarily는 형용사 primary의 부사형으로 '주로, 본래'라는 뜻을 나타내므로 mainly로 대체될 수 있다.

2. 청각 장애가 있는 사람들은 보통 수화를 통해 의사소통을 한다. 많은 사람들은 세계적인 공통 수화가 있다고 믿고 있지만, 그것은 사실이 아니다. 음성 언어와 마찬가지로, 수화는 전세계적으로 다르다. 사실, 100개 이상의 다양한 종류가 존재한다고 알려져 있다. 또 다른 보편적 오해 하나는 수화가 단지 손 동작으로만 이루어진다는 것이다. 실제로 수화는 손 동작, 몸 동작, 그리고 얼굴의 표정이 결합된 것이다.
   (A) 잘못된 생각   (B) 유용한 조언
   (C) 엄격한 규칙   (D) 현명한 접근

   ● 접속사 mis-는 단어에 '잘못된, 틀린'이라는 의미를 주는 접두사이므로 '이해'라는 뜻의 conception에 붙어 '오해'라는 뜻으로 바뀌었다. 따라서 (A)의 false belief가 그 의미이다.

3. 아이스크림의 역사는 수세기를 거슬러 올라간다. 원래 이것은 꿀에 눈을 섞어서 만들었다. 나중에 중국인이 언 우유를 사용했다. 탐험가 Marco Polo는 마침내 이 조리법을 이탈리아로 가져왔다. 프랑스의 왕인 Henry 2세는 16세기에 이탈리아의 귀족 여인과 결혼하였는데, 그녀는 아이스크림을 프랑스에 소개했다. 하지만, 오늘날 이것이 흔한 간식인 것과 달리, 그 당시에는 단지 왕족들만이 먹었다.
   (A) 놀라운   (B) 자격이 없는
   (C) 독점적인   (D) 광범위한

   ● ubiquitous는 '흔한, 어디에서나 볼 수 있는'이라는 의미의 형용사이므로 '널리 퍼진'이라는 뜻의 widespread가 그 의미와 가장 비슷하다.

VOCABULARY   pp.30-31

Write the number of each word's definition.
각 단어의 뜻을 찾아 번호를 쓰시오.

indigenous / 12 토종의   adopt / 5 쓰다, 채용하다
ascend / 4 오르다   exhalation / 9 숨을 내쉼
abound / 2 풍부하다   moist / 11 습한
convert / 7 전환시키다   wither / 3 시들다
estimate / 10 추정하다   exceed / 8 초과하다
drift / 1 표류하다   dense / 6 조밀한

Match each collocation with the correct definition.
각 연어에 알맞은 뜻을 찾아 연결하시오.

a. spread out – having large distances between one another 넓게 퍼진
b. a variety of – a range of different things 다양한
c. evolve into – to gradually develop into something different ~로 진화하다
d. carry away – to take something and to bring it somewhere else ~을 가져가다
e. adapt to – to get used to or to adjust to ~에 적응하다

Circle the word closest in meaning to each underlined word.
각 밑줄 친 단어의 뜻과 가장 가까운 단어를 찾아 동그라미 하시오.

정답 | 1. (C)   2. (C)   3. (D)
      4. (B)   5. (C)   6. (A)

해석 |

1. 우리는 열기구가 하늘로 떠오르는 것을 보았다.
   (A) 익사하는   (B) 하강하는
   (C) 올라가는   (D) 폭발하는

2. 그가 샤워한 후에 욕실 벽이 축축해졌다.
   (A) 눈에 보이는   (B) 따뜻한
   (C) 축축한   (D) 갈라진

3. 원주민들은 방문객을 믿지 않는다.
   (A) 불친절한   (B) 강력한
   (C) 고대의   (D) 현지의

4. 여행객들은 그들의 돈을 현지 화폐로 바꾸기 위해 종종 공항의 은행을 이용한다.
   (A) 팔다   (B) 바꾸다
   (C) 빌려주다   (D) 빌리다

5. 굶주린 동물 떼들이 먹이를 찾기 위해 시골지역을 표류했다.
   (A) 유래했다   (B) 연락했다
   (C) 헤맸다   (D) 발견했다

6. 제품의 총 가격은 2,000 미국 달러를 초과하는 것으로 보인다.
   (A) 뛰어넘다 (B) 구성하다
   (C) 삽입하다 (D) 추출하다

Fill in each blank with the correct collocation.
알맞은 연어를 골라 빈칸을 채우시오.

정답 | 1. spread out   2. carried away
     | 3. adapt to   4. a variety of
     | 5. evolved into

해석 |
1. 사막에는 마을이 거의 없으며, 그것들은 흩어져 있다.
2. 작은 음식 조각들이 개미들에 의해 옮겨졌다.
3. 떠돌이 고양이는 새 집에 적응하지 못해서 달아났다.
4. 그 섬에는 다양한 문화들이 나란히 존재한다.
5. 그 작은 가게는 마침내 세계적인 사업으로 진화했다.

STEP 1 pp. 32-33

정답 | 1. (C)   2. (A)

라크로스

야구는 명백히 미국의 국가적인 스포츠라고 여겨지고 있지만, 다른 미국 스포츠가 훨씬 더 오랫동안 존재해왔다. 원래 스틱볼이라고 알려진 그것은 17세기에 북미 원주민들에 의해 최초로 경기를 하게 되었다. 나중에 유럽 정착민에 의해 받아들여졌는데, 그들은 이 스포츠에 '라크로스'라는 프랑스식 명칭을 붙였다.

미국 원주민의 라크로스에서는 수마일 길이의 필드에 수백 명의 선수들이 있었다. 하지만 이것은 시간이 흐르면서 현대의 경기 형태로 바뀌었다. 오늘날, 표준 라크로스 경기장은 길이가 110야드이고 폭은 60야드이다. 각 팀에는 골키퍼를 포함하여 10명의 선수들만 있는데, 선수들은 끝에 느슨한 그물이 달린 기다란 채를 가지고 다닌다. 공은 그물 안에 들어있다가 선수에서 선수로 옮겨진다. 팀은 상대팀의 골에 공을 힘껏 던져서 점수를 올린다. 야구나 농구만큼 인기가 많지는 않지만, 라크로스는 북미에서 가장 빨리 성장하는 스포츠 중 하나이다.

• **Structure Zone**

> 관계대명사가 쉼표 뒤에 쓰이면 선행사나 앞의 전체 문장에 추가적인 정보를 제공하는 계속적 용법으로 쓰인다. 관계대명사는 '접속사+대명사'의 역할을 하는 것이므로 문맥에 맞게 적절한 접속사를 넣어 해석하도록 한다.
> Later, it was adopted by European settlers, **who** gave it the French name "lacrosse."

1. 지문에서 단어 unambiguously와 가장 비슷한 의미는
   (A) 특히   (B) 사실상
   (C) 명백히   (D) 계속하여

   ▶ 접속사 un-은 명사, 형용사, 부사의 앞에 붙어 원래의 의미에 부정의 의미를 부여하는 역할을 한다. 따라서 '모호하게'라는 의미의 ambiguously 앞에 붙어 '모호하지 않게', 즉 '분명히'라는 의미로 바뀌게 되므로 (C)의 obviously와 같은 의미이다.

2. 지문에서 단어 hurling과 의미가 가장 가까운 것은
   (A) 던지다   (B) 차단하다
   (C) 승리하다   (D) 매달다

   ▶ hurl은 무언가를 힘을 실어 힘껏 던지는 행동을 말하므로 '힘껏 내던지다'라는 뜻을 가진 (A)의 pitching과 그 의미가 가장 비슷하다.

• Note-Taking

Lacrosse

In the Past	Today
- known as stickball	- called lacrosse
- field — miles long	- field is 110 yards long & 60 yards wide
- hundreds of players	- 10 players on each team
- played by indigenous tribes in North America	- one of the fastest-growing sports in North America

SUMMARY

Lacrosse has been around much longer than baseball. Native Americans first played it in the 17th century. When Europeans began to play it, they gave it the French name "lacrosse." In the past, the field was miles long, and there were hundreds of players. Today, the field is much smaller, and there are just 10 players on each team. Players carry long sticks and pass a ball as they try to hurl it into the other team's goal. Lacrosse is one of the fastest-growing sports in North America.

라크로스는 야구보다 더 오랫동안 존재해왔다. 미국 원주민들이 17세기에 이 경기를 처음으로 했다. 유럽인들이 이 경기를 하기 시작했을 때, 그들은 이것에 '라크로스'라는 프랑스식 명칭을 붙였다. 과거에는 필드가 수 마일 길이였고 수백 명의 선수들이 있었다. 오늘날, 필드는 훨씬 작아졌고, 각 팀에는 단지 10명의 선수만 있다. 선수들은 기다란 스틱을 가지고 다니며 공을 패스하여 상대팀의 골 안으로 던져 넣는다. 라크로스는 북미에서 가장 빠르게 성장하는 스포츠 중 하나이다.

VOCAB Match each word with the correct definition.
각 단어에 알맞은 뜻을 찾아 연결하시오.

a. tribe – a group of people with a common ancestor, culture, etc. 종족
b. settlers – people who go to live in a new country or region 정착민

c. modern – relating to the present time 현대의
d. loose – not firmly held or fixed in place 느슨한
e. opposing – being in competition with one another 대립하는

STEP 2 pp.34-35
정답 | 1. (B)   2. (D)   3. (C)

압력

스쿠버다이빙은 사람들이 깊은 물속에서 오랫동안 머무를 수 있게 해 준다. 하지만, 사람의 몸은 그렇게 깊은 곳에서는 적응하지 못한다. 염려할 만한 주요 원인은 압력이다. 공기는 1제곱미터의 압력당 대략 14.7파운드 정도가 가해진다. 이것은 압력대기(ATA)라고 불린다. 수심에서, 공기는 1 ATA가 계속 가해진다. 그러나 잠수부는 10미터 하강할 때마다 추가 압력을 경험하는데, 이는 몸 안의 공기를 압축하게 하는 원인이 된다.

잠수부가 상승할 때 공기는 팽창하게 되는데, 이는 잠재적으로 고막과 폐를 터지게 할 수 있다. 이것을 예방하기 위하여, 잠수부는 초과량의 공기가 인체로부터 자연적으로 방출되도록 서서히 표면으로 되돌아와야 한다. 압력의 증가는 인체 조직이 질소 가스를 흡수하는 비율도 증가시킨다. 서서히 상승하는 동안에, 그것은 숨을 내쉼으로써 배출된다. 그러나 만약 잠수부가 너무 빠르게 상승하면, 질소가 배출되기도 전에 팽창하여 조직과 혈액 안에서 작은 기포들을 형성한다. 이것은 보통 잠함병이라고 불리는 고통스런 상태인 감압증을 초래하게 되는데, 뇌졸중과 마비의 원인이 되기도 한다. 하지만 이러한 위험은 잠수부가 하강을 신중히 계획하고 얼마나 깊이 들어갈 것인지와 그곳에서 얼마나 오랫동안 안전하게 머무를 수 있을지를 정확히 계산한다면 피할 수 있다.

• Structure Zone

- 접속사 as는 '~함에 따라'라는 시간의 경과를 나타낼 때 사용할 수 있다.
  As the divers ascend, the air expands, potentially causing their eardrums or lungs to burst.
- 선행사가 전치사의 목적어가 되는 두 문장을 연결할 때 전치사는 관계대명사의 앞에 위치할 수 있다. 이렇게 연결된 문장에서는 관계대명사가 전치사의 목적어가 된다.
  Increased pressure also increases the rate **at which** body tissues absorb nitrogen gas.

1. 지문에서 단어 exerts를 대체하기에 가장 적합한 것은
   (A) 비틀다   (B) (힘을) 가하다
   (C) 주장하다   (D) 길어지다

   ● exert는 '(힘 또는 영향력을) 가하다, 쓰다'라는 의미로, 보기에서 이와 가장 가까운 뜻을 가진 것은 (B) applies이다.

2. 지문에서 단어 discharged와 가장 비슷한 의미는
   (A) 묘사되는   (B) 위치하는
   (C) 쫓기는   (D) 방출되는

   ● discharge는 '내려놓다, 떠나게 하다, 방출하다'라는 뜻을 가지는데, 지문에서는 물 속에서 상승하면서 몸 안의 공기가 배출되는 행위를 의미하고 있으므로 (D)의 released가 가장 가까운 의미이다.

3. 지문에서 단어 it이 가리키는 것은
   (A) 압력   (B) 비율
   (C) 질소   (D) 상승

   ● 바로 앞 문장에서 인체 조직이 질소를 흡수한다는 내용이 있고 해당 문장에서는 이것이 호흡을 통해 배출되고 있다고 말하고 있으므로 배출되는 것은 질소라는 것을 알 수 있다.

• Note-Taking

P1 MI pressure when scuba diving – the primary cause for concern
       SD causes the air inside the body to compress

P2 MI increased pressure in water & its effects
       SD • causes air within the body to compress during ascent
            → eardrums or lungs burst – divers must return gradually
           • increases the rate at which body tissues absorb nitrogen gas
            → can lead to decompression sickness – the bends
           : can be avoided if divers carefully map out their descents

VOCAB Write the correct word for each definition.
각 뜻에 알맞은 단어를 찾아 적으시오.

a. burst 터지다   b. decompression 감압
c. stroke 뇌졸중   d. paralysis 마비
e. calculate 계산하다

• More Info Zone

잠수통에 들어가는 헬륨 가스

질소는 사람의 혈액에 어느 정도 녹아있지만 잠수한 상태에서는 혈액에 녹는 양이 5배가 된다. 이런 상황에서 잠수를 끝내고 물 위로 나올 시 질소는 기포를 형성하게 되는데, 이 기포들이 혈액의 흐름을 방해하고 체내의 통증을 유발한다. 이러한 이유로 잠수부들이 사용하는 산소통에는 질소 대신 헬륨 가스를 넣게 되는데 헬륨은 비활성기체여서 압력에 따른 용해도가 질소보다 낮아 인체에서 불필요한 반응을 하지 않는다고 한다.

STEP 3	pp.36-37
정답	1. (D)　2. (B)　3. (B)　4. (D)

이끼

　지구 진화의 초기단계에는 육지에 생명체가 없었다. 하지만 바다에는 식물과 동물이 풍부했다. 조류는 물 밖에서 살수 있었던 최초의 식물 형태였다. 5억년 훨씬 전에, 이 조류가 이끼로 진화했다.

　초기의 이끼는 육지에서 살 수 있었지만, 여전히 많은 양의 물을 필요로 했다. 게다가 그 당시에 지구에는 흙이 거의 없었다. 그래서 이것은 대개 습한 지역에 있는 바위 위에서 자랐다. 그리고 흙에서 물을 찾기 위한 긴 뿌리 대신, 그것에서는 헛뿌리가 자랐는데 단단한 표면에 달라붙을 수 있는 짧은 뿌리와 같았다. 대부분의 식물과 마찬가지로, 이 이끼는 햇빛을 양분으로 전환하기 위해 광합성을 했다. 그리고 번식을 위하여 작은 씨앗과 비슷하게 생긴 포자를 만들어냈는데, 이것들은 바람에 실려 이동했다.

　1억년 정도 후에, 이러한 이끼의 일부가 보다 발달된 식물로 진화했다. 하지만 단순한 이끼는 여전히 전세계에서 발견된다. 이것은 초기 조상 형태에서 그다지 많이 달라지지 않았다. 이것은 예전과 마찬가지로 바위 위나 나무의 옆 부분과 같은 어둡고 서늘하며 습한 곳에서 자란다. 가뭄이 들면, 이것은 갈색으로 변하여 마치 말라 죽은 것처럼 보인다. 수 주 동안 이런 상태로 있다. 하지만 충분한 양의 비가 다시 내리면, 이끼는 초록으로 변하여 다시 살아난다. 이끼는 나무처럼 키가 크거나 꽃처럼 아름답지는 않지만, 보이는 것보다는 훨씬 회복력이 크다.

• **Structure Zone**

물질명사는 셀 수 없는 명사로 문장 안에서 단수 취급한다. 따라서 동사의 수 일치에 주의해야 한다.

In addition, there **was** little **dirt** on the Earth at that time.

1. 지문의 주제는 무엇인가?
   (A) 육지에 살았던 최초의 동물은 이끼를 먹으면서 생존했다.
   (B) 이끼와 조류는 육지 위와 물 속에서 살 수 있다.
   (C) 이끼가 없었다면, 다른 종류의 식물은 충분한 물을 얻지 못했을 것이다.
   (D) 이끼는 오랫동안 존재해온 단순한 형태의 식물 생명체이다.

   ▶ 지문에서는 이끼가 지구가 진화되기 시작한 초기에 존재한 생물체이며 부분적으로 다른 종으로 발달한 것도 있지만 여전히 지구상에서 발견된다고 말하고 있다. 따라서 지문의 주제로 (D)가 가장 알맞다.

2. 왜 작가는 지문에서 roots를 언급하는가?
   (A) 이끼가 어떻게 물을 얻는지 보여주기 위해서
   (B) 그것들을 헛뿌리와 대조하기 위해서
   (C) 왜 이끼가 진화했는지를 설명하기 위해서
   (D) 광합성을 소개하기 위해서

   ▶ 이끼가 단단한 표면에 달라붙는 것은 헛뿌리가 있기 때문인데 토양에서의 양분 흡수를 위한 식물의 뿌리와는 그 기능이 다른 것이므로 지문에서는 헛뿌리와 뿌리를 서로 대조하여 설명하고 있다. 따라서 (B)가 정답이 된다.

3. 지문에서 단어 cling 을 대체하기에 가장 적합한 것은
   (A) 복사하다　(B) 잡다
   (C) 침식시키다　(D) 닮다

   ▶ cling은 '매달리다, 달라붙다'라는 뜻의 동사로 이와 의미가 가장 비슷한 것은 '잡다'라는 의미를 가진 (B)의 grip이다.

4. 지문에서 단어 resilient 와 의미가 가장 가까운 것은
   (A) 일반적인　(B) 향기로운
   (C) 끊임없는　(D) 끈질긴

   ▶ resilient는 '회복력이 큰'이라는 뜻으로 회복력이 크다는 것은 끈질기게 한 속성을 유지한다는 뜻이 될 수 있다. 따라서 '끈질긴'이라는 의미의 (D) persistent와 그 의미가 가장 유사하다.

VOCAB_ Find the correct word in the passage for each of the given definition.
주어진 뜻에 알맞은 단어를 지문에서 찾으시오.

a. photosynthesis 광합성　b. reproduce 번식하다
c. advanced 진화한　d. ancestor 조상

• **Note-Taking** (Sample Answer)

P1　MI　moss
　　SD　evolved from algae, the first form of plant life out of water

P2　MI　grew mostly on rocks in moist places
　　SD　- had rhizoids to cling to hard surfaces
　　　　- used photosynthesis and reproduced by generating spores

P3　MI　today's moss – not changed much
　　SD　- still grows in dark, cool, & wet places
　　　　- withers during droughts & comes alive in heavy rains: resilient

UNIT TEST	pp.38-39
정답	1. (A)　2. (C)　3. (D)　4. (D)　5. (C) 6. (B)

성간 물질

　우주가 얼마나 광대한지 완전히 이해하기란 불가능하다. 우주의 은하계 수는 1,000억 개가 넘는다고 추정된다. 각각의 은하계 안에는 수천억 개의 행성이 존재한다. 우리의 은하계인 은하수는 2,000억에서 4,000억 정도 되는 행성의 고향이다. 이 행성의 대부분은 태양계의 일부인데, 이는 그것들이 중력에 의해 서로 지탱하고 있는 것을 의미한다. 광대한 공간들이 이 행성계 사이에 존재하지만, 이 공간들이 비어있는 것은 아니다.

　성간 물질은 이러한 행성계 사이의 공간에 존재하는 모든 것에 대한 명칭이다. 성간 물질은 99%의 가스와 1%의 먼지로 이루어져 있다고 추정된다. 성간 물질에서 발견되는 가스는 매우 낮은 밀도를 갖는데, 그래서 가스 분자는 광범위한 범위에 흩어져 있다. 먼

지의 경우, 이것은 다양한 원인 물질에서 오는데 탄소, 얼음, 그리고 다양한 금속 등이 이에 해당된다. 성간 물질의 가스와 마찬가지로 먼지 대부분은 광대하게 흩어져 있다. 백만 입방 미터의 공간마다 겨우 먼지 티끌 하나 정도만 있을 뿐이다.

하지만 성간 물질이 성간 공간에서 아무런 목적 없이 표류하지만은 않는다는 것을 아는 것이 중요하다. 사실 이것은 우주에서 매우 중요한 역할 중 하나를 담당한다. 어떤 곳에서는 성간 물질들이 모이기 시작하여 성간구름이라고 알려진 형태를 만든다. 크기가 가장 크고 밀도가 높은 성운 안에서는 매우 특별한 일이 발생한다. 중력이 물질을 덩어리의 형태로 만드는데, 그 후 이것은 열을 내기 시작한다. 사실 그것은 매우 뜨거워져서 핵 반응이 일어나게 되는데, 그러고 나서 이 덩어리 물질이 밝게 빛을 내기 시작하는 것이다. 성간의 깊은 곳에서는 이렇게 성간 물질이 새 행성의 탄생 원인이 된다.

Glossary vast 광대한

• **Structure Zone**

- 주어가 너무 길 때는 주어 자리에 가주어 it을 주어대신 쓰고, 주어는 뒤로 보낼 수 있다.

  It is impossible to fully comprehend just how immense the universe is.

- something, anything, everything 등의 명사에 형용사가 붙을 경우 앞이 아닌 뒤에서 수식한다.

  Within the largest and densest of these clouds, **something very special** happens.

- 'so + 형용사/부사 + that 구문'은 '너무 ~해서 …하다'라는 원인과 결과를 나타내는 표현이다.

  In fact, it gets **so hot that** nuclear reactions occur, and the ball of matter starts to shine brightly.

1. 지문의 주제는 무엇인가?
   (A) 행성 사이에 존재하는 물질이 새 행성을 탄생시킨다.
   (B) 행성의 수는 성간 물질로 인해 빠르게 감소하고 있다.
   (C) 우리의 은하계는 대부분 가스와 먼지로 구성되는데 이는 성간구름이라고 불린다.
   (D) 우주는 해로운 성간 물질로 인해 매일 밀도가 높아지고 있다.

   ● 주어진 지문은 우주에 존재하는 성간 물질이 무엇인지를 다루고 결론적으로 이 성간 물질이 행성의 탄생에 어떠한 원인이 되고 있는지를 그 과정과 함께 설명하고 있다. 따라서 (A)가 지문의 주제로 가장 알맞다.

2. 지문에서 단어 scattered와 비슷한 의미는
   (A) 사라진   (B) 굵힌
   (C) 흩어진   (D) 계산된

   ● scattered는 '흩뿌려진'이라는 뜻이다. 따라서 이와 가장 비슷한 단어는 '(이리저리) 흩어진'이라는 뜻의 (C) dispersed이다.

3. 지문에서 단어 grain과 의미가 가장 가까운 것은
   (A) 세부사항   (B) 조직
   (C) 전자   (D) 입자

   ● grain은 '알갱이, 티끌'의 의미이다. 따라서 보기 중 이와 비슷한 단어는 '티끌, 입자'라는 뜻의 (D) particle이 된다.

4. 2단락에서 작가의 주요 목적은 무엇인가?
   (A) 성간 물질의 크기를 강조하는 것
   (B) 성간 물질과 은하수를 대조하는 것
   (C) 성간 물질이 어디에서 발견되는지 묘사하는 것
   (D) 성간 물질이 무엇으로 구성되는지 설명하는 것

   ● 주어진 지문의 2단락에서는 성간 물질이 무엇을 의미하며 무엇으로 구성되는지를 설명하고 있다. 따라서 (D)가 답이 된다.

5. 지문에서 단어 it이 가리키는 것은
   (A) 성간 공간   (B) 중력
   (C) 덩어리   (D) 성간 물질

   ● it이 포함된 문장의 바로 앞 문장에는 중력에 의해 생성된 덩어리에 대해 언급하고 있으며, 부연설명이 뒤따라 나오는 형태이다. 따라서 it은 앞 문장의 덩어리를 의미한다.

6. 3단락에 따르면, 성간구름은
   (A) 행성계를 서로 지탱하고 있다.
   (B) 행성이 형성되는 곳이다.
   (C) 성간 물질을 파괴할 수 있다.
   (D) 은하수에는 존재하지 않는다.

   ● 3단락에 따르면 중력에 의해 덩어리로 뭉쳐진 성간 물질이 성간구름이 된 후, 핵 반응을 일으켜 행성으로 탄생된다고 설명하고 있다. 따라서 성간구름은 행성이 형성되는 곳이라고 말할 수 있다.

VOCABULARY TEST   pp. 40-41

Recall the essential words in the unit to reinforce your vocabulary acquisition. Write the meaning of each word in your language.
유닛에서 배운 주요 단어들을 떠올려 각 단어의 뜻을 쓰시오.

dense	조밀한	ascend	오르다
convert	전환하다	calculate	계산하다
stroke	뇌졸중	opposing	대립하는
burst	터지다	reproduce	번식하다
comprehend	이해하다	aimlessly	목적 없이
paralysis	마비	estimate	추정하다
advanced	진화한	abound	풍부하다
disability	장애	exceed	초과하다
moist	습한	decompression	감압
drift	표류하다	loose	느슨한
vast	광대한	settlers	정착민
adopt	쓰다, 채용하다	gesture	몸짓
exhalation	숨을 내쉼	ancestor	조상

indigenous | 토종의
photosynthesis | 광합성
lavish | 풍성한
trace back | 거슬러 올라가다
a variety of | 다양한
combination | 조합
carry away | ~을 가져가다
wither | 시들다
tribe | 종족
modern | 현대의
spread out | 넓게 퍼진
loyalty | 귀족
adapt to | ~에 적응하다
evolve into | ~로 진화하다

Complete each sentence with the correct word or collocation.
문장에 알맞은 단어나 연어를 찾아 쓰시오.

정답 | 1. disabilities 2. drift
3. opposing 4. abounded
5. lavish 6. calculate
7. photosynthesis 8. combination
9. a variety of 10. adopted

해석 |
1. 청각 장애가 있는 사람들은 보통 수화를 통해 의사소통을 한다.
2. 성간 물질은 성간 공간에서 단순히 표류하는 것만은 아니다.
3. 한 팀은 상대팀의 골 안에 공을 던져서 점수를 낸다.
4. 오래 전에, 바다는 육지와 달리 식물과 동물이 풍부했다.
5. 사람들은 바푸 기간에 풍성한 피크닉을 즐긴다.
6. 잠수부들은 얼마나 깊이 들어갈 것인지 정확히 계산해야 한다.
7. 대부분의 식물은 햇빛을 양분으로 전환하기 위해 광합성을 한다.
8. 수화는 손 동작과 몸 동작이 결합된 것이다.
9. 성간 물질의 먼지는 다양한 원인 물질에서 온다.
10. 스틱볼이라고 불리는 스포츠는 후에 유럽 정착민에 의해 받아들여졌다.

UNIT 03
Reference

INTRODUCTION

Reference 문제에서는 주어진 단어가 지칭하는 것이 무엇인지 파악할 수 있어야 한다. 주어지는 단어는 주로 *he*, *she*, *it* 또는 *they*와 같은 대명사이다. 때때로 *which*, *this*, 그리고 *these*와 같은 단어가 쓰일 때도 있다. 수험자는 대명사 앞뒤의 명사들을 주의 깊게 살펴보아야 한다.

TYPICAL QUESTION TYPES

지문에서 단어/어구 _____가 지칭하는 것은
_____ 단락에서 단어/어구 _____가 지칭하는 것은

STRATEGIES

- 지문에서 단어의 역할을 확인하고 그것이 사람을 지칭하는지, 또는 장소나 다른 것을 지칭하는지 결정한다.
- 단어가 있는 문장 또는 앞에 있는 문장에 있는 모든 명사들을 찾아본다.
- 명사가 지칭할 수 있는 범주에 해당하지 않는 단어들을 무시한다.

QUICK CHECKUP p.43
정답 | 1. (B) 2. (B) 3. (D)

Find the word that the highlighted pronoun refers to.
음영 처리된 대명사가 지칭하는 단어를 찾으시오.

1. 웃음은 오직 인간만이 가지고 있는 행동 양식이다. 연구가들은 웃음이 사회적인 유대를 단단히 하는 수단으로 진화했고, 아마도 위험 요소가 사라진 뒤 안도감을 보이는 방법으로 시작했다고 생각한다. 또한 웃음은 사람이 함께 있는 다른 이들에게 편안함을 느낀다는 것을 보여주며 믿음을 나타낸다. 웃음 자체는 의도치 않은 소리와 신체적인 몸짓의 조합이다. 사람들이 웃을 때, 안면 근육이 수축하여 그들이 숨쉬기가 어려워지는데, 이것이 우리에게 친숙한 '하하' 소리를 만들어 낸다.
(A) 몸짓들 (B) 사람들
(C) 안면 근육들 (D) 소리들

➡ 주어진 them은 숨쉬기가 힘들어지는 대상을 지칭하므로, 답은 people이다.

2. 딱정벌레는 대략 400,000 종류가 알려져 있다. 그들의 큰 특징은 한 쌍의 딱딱한 외부 날개이다. 그것들은 나는 데 쓰이는 부드러운 내부 날개를 보호한다. 다른 모든 곤충처럼, 그들은 여섯 개의 다리를 지니고 있고 그들의 몸체는 세 부분으로 나뉘어 있다. 각각의 딱정벌레는 서로 다른 먹이를 먹는다. 어떤 딱정벌레들은 오로지 식물을 먹고 다른 딱정벌레들은 더 작은 곤충을 잡아 먹으며, 또 다른 딱정벌레들은 더 큰 동물들의 배설물을 먹고 산다.
(A) 딱정벌레들 (B) 외부 날개들
(C) 내부 날개들 (D) 곤충들

➡ '그것들'이 부드러운 내부 날개를 보호한다고 하였으므로, 이러한 대상을 앞 문장에서 찾으면 outer wings가 답이 된다.

3. 1980년에, 작가인 Alvin Toffler는 '주도적인 소비자들'의 증가를 예견했는데, 그들은 정기적으로 구입하는 제품들을 발전시키기 위해 적극적으로 회사들과 일을 하는 이들이다. 그들을 지칭하기 위해, 그는 '프로슈머'라는 용어를 만들어냈다. 하지만 시간이 흘러, 그 용어는 변화하는 시장에 맞게 발달했다. 오늘날, 프로슈머는 자신들이 선호하는 상표를 변호하고 그들이 싫어하는 것들을 비판하기 위

해 기술을 이용하는 소비자들을 뜻한다. 어느 정도, 그들은 수동적인 소비자에서 마케팅 과정의 중요한 부분으로 옮겨 갔다.
(A) 프로슈머들 (B) 소비자들
(C) 회사들 (D) 상표들

▶ 주어진 문장에서, 소비자들은 선호하는 상표를 변호하고 싫어하는 '그것들'을 비판하기 위해 기술을 이용한다고 하였다. those는 앞에 나온 brands를 대신 받아 중복을 피하고 있다.

4. 사람들이 회사 창립기념일을 기념하기 위해 왔다.
(A) 모이다 (B) 협상하다
(C) 장식하다 (D) 기념하다

5. 혈구는 결속하여 견고한 덩어리를 형성한다.
(A) 연결하다 (B) 흐르다
(C) 확대하다 (D) 반응하다

6. 그 상관은 그의 사무실로 근로자들을 한 명씩 불렀다.
(A) 호위했다 (B) 칭찬했다
(C) 모았다 (D) 면담했다

VOCABULARY   pp.44-45

Write the number of each word's definition.
각 단어의 뜻을 찾아 번호를 쓰시오.

eccentric / 1 별난
drawback / 5 결점
resultant / 7 그 결과로 생긴
commemorate / 11 기념하다
descend / 8 내려가다
fracture / 6 균열

rural / 9 시골의
bind / 3 결속하다
summon / 10 소환하다
conical / 2 원뿔 모양의
encounter / 12 맞닥뜨리다
soluble / 4 용해성이 있는

Match each collocation with the correct definition.
각 연어에 알맞은 뜻을 찾아 연결하시오.

a. link up – to connect to something else 잇다
b. melt down – to convert a solid to a liquid. usually by heat (열 때문에) 녹다
c. break out – to unexpectedly begin 발발하다
d. a handful of – a small amount of 소수의
e. be attributed to – to be regarded as resulting from a cause ~에 기인하다

Circle the word closest in meaning to each underlined word.
각 밑줄 친 단어의 뜻과 가장 가까운 단어를 찾아 동그라미 하시오.

정답 | 1. (A) 2. (B) 3. (B)
      4. (D) 5. (A) 6. (C)

해석 |
1. 그 계획의 유일한 결점은 높은 비용이다.
(A) 단점 (B) 지지자
(C) 요소 (D) 토대

2. Jane은 항상 그의 남동생이 어떤 면에서 별나다고 생각했다.
(A) 매력적인 (B) 이상한
(C) 추가의 (D) 오르는

3. 폭풍이 친 후에, 모든 이는 뒤따른 피해에 충격을 받았다.
(A) 물질적인 (B) ~의 결과로 일어난
(C) 예상된 (D) 극심한

Fill in each blank with the correct collocation.
알맞은 연어를 골라 빈칸을 채우시오.

정답 | 1. broke out   2. a handful of
      3. link up   4. be attributed to
      5. melted down

해석 |
1. 두 남자 간의 싸움이 관중으로 가득 찬 경기장에서 일어났다.
2. 수백 명의 사람들이 그 행사에 초대되었지만, 소수만이 왔다.
3. 당신은 어떤 길을 택해도 되는데, 몇 킬로미터 후 이어지기 때문이다.
4. 그 여배우의 큰 인기는 그녀의 긍정적인 태도에 기인한다.
5. 장신구를 만들기 위해 그 오래된 금화들은 녹여졌다.

STEP 1   pp.46-47

정답 | 1. (A) 2. (B)

Emily Dickinson (에밀리 디킨슨)

Emily Dickinson은 1830년 매사추세츠에서 태어났다. 그녀의 부유한 가족은 지역 사회에서 활동적이었지만, 그녀는 수줍음을 타는 은둔적인 아이였다. 정규 교육을 받은 후, 그녀는 고향으로 돌아갔는데, 그 곳에서 지역의 괴짜로 알려지게 되었다. 그녀는 거의 흰 옷만 입으며, 집을 떠난 적이 드물었다. 그녀는 열정적으로 편지를 쓰며 몇몇의 가까운 친구들과의 우정을 유지하는 데 시간을 보내기도 했지만, 그것의 대부분을 시를 쓰며 보냈다.

그녀는 일생 동안 거의 2,000편의 시를 썼는데, 그녀가 1886년에 세상을 떠나기 전까지 소수만이 출판되었다. 그녀가 죽은 후, 그녀가 쓴 수백 편의 시를 여동생이 발견하였다. 그녀는 가족끼리 아는 친구였던 Mabel Loomis Todd에게 그 중 일부를 주었고, 그녀가 1890년에 시들을 출판했다. 하지만, 1955년이 되어서야 비로소 Dickinson의 완전한 시 모음집이 출간되었다. 오늘날, 그녀는 동시대에서 가장 훌륭한 시인 중 한 명으로 여겨진다.

Glossary pen (글 등을) 쓰다

• **Structure Zone**

'after + 주어 + 동사'의 형태에서, 주어가 생략되고 동사는 분사형태로 쓰일 수 있다.

After she got an education, she returned to her hometown.
→ **After getting** an education, she returned to her hometown.

1. 지문에서 단어 it 이 가리키는 것은
   (A) 시간   (B) 시
   (C) 우정   (D) 편지 쓰기

   ▶ 그녀는 시간을 편지를 쓰는 데 보내기도 했지만, 대부분의 '그것'은 시를 쓰며 보냈다고 했다. 따라서 주어진 it은 time을 가리킨다.

2. 지문에서 단어 She 가 가리키는 것은
   (A) Emily Dickinson   (B) Dickinson의 여동생
   (C) 가족끼리 아는 친구   (D) 가장 훌륭한 시인 중 한 명

   ▶ 주어진 문장과 바로 앞 문장을 보면, She는 시인의 시를 발견해서 가족이 아는 친구인 Mable Loomis Todd에게 준 사람이다. 따라서 답은 Dickinson의 여동생이다.

• **Note-Taking**

Emily Dickinson

Dickinson's Youth
— shy & reclusive
— known as a local eccentric
— letter writing & writing poetry

Dickinson's Works
— wrote 2,000 poems, but few were published
— published after her death
— a complete collection of her works published in 1955

SUMMARY

Born in 1830, Emily Dickinson was a shy and reclusive child. In her hometown, she spent most of her time exchanging letters with friends and writing poetry. She wrote nearly 2,000 poems, but few were published. After she passed away in 1886, her younger sister found hundreds of her poems. Some were published in 1890, but the complete collection was not available until 1955. She is now thought to be one of the greatest poets of her time.

1830년에 태어난 Emily Dickinson은 수줍음을 타는 은둔적인 아이였다. 고향에서, 그녀는 친구들과 편지를 주고 받으면서 시를 쓰면서 대부분의 시간을 보냈다. 그녀는 거의 2,000편의 시를 썼지만, 소수만이 출판되었다. 그녀가 1886년에 세상을 떠난 후, 그녀의 여동생이 수백 편의 시를 발견했다. 몇몇은 1890년에 출판되었지만, 완전한 모음집은 1955년에야 출간되었다. 그녀는 오늘날 동시대의 가장 훌륭한 시인들 중 한 명으로 간주된다.

VOCAB_ Match each word with the correct definition.
각 단어에 알맞은 뜻을 찾아 연결하시오.

a. reclusive – shut off or apart from the world 은둔한
b. exclusively – of involving only a specific thing 오로지
c. enthusiastic – showing great excitement or interest 열정적인
d. devote to – to give an amount of time to something ~에 바치다
e. collection – the gathered works of a single writer, painter, etc. (시·노래 등의) 모음집

• **More Info Zone**

Emily Dickinson의 시

Emily Dickinson은 약 2,000편의 시를 쓰면서, 어느 시에도 제목을 달지 않았다. 후대의 사람들은 그녀가 보여지기 위한 시를 쓴 것이 아니라, 자신의 심리를 반영하기 위해 시를 썼기 때문에 따로 제목을 달지 않았을 것이라고 추측한다. 현재 그 시들의 제목은 각 시의 첫 구절을 따서 붙인 것이다. Emily Dickinson은 제목 대신 작품마다 번호를 달았다.

STEP 2   pp. 48-49

정답 | 1. (B)   2. (A)   3. (C)

펙틴

교외 지역에서, 사람들은 사과, 오렌지, 그리고 복숭아와 같은 남는 제철 과일을 수확해 잼으로 만든다. 잼을 만드는 첫 번째 과정은 과일과 설탕의 혼합물을 젤 성분의 걸쭉한 농도가 될 때까지 끓이는 것이다. 시간이 오래 소요되는 이 과정은 많은 결점이 있다. 그것은 현저히 많은 과즙이 끓어 없어지게 하고, 잼의 맛에 좋지 않은 영향을 줄 수 있으며, 과일의 자연적 비타민 함량을 상당히 없앨 수 있다. 때문에 대부분의 사람들은 잼을 만들 때 펙틴을 사용한다.

펙틴은 과일에서 찾아볼 수 있는 천연 섬유질이다. 펙틴이 가장 높게 밀집된 과일은 사과와 딸기류이다. 화학적으로, 그것은 각각의 과일 세포를 모이게 만드는 탄수화물의 한 종류이다. 펙틴이 산성이 있는 환경에서 설탕과 함께 열에 가해지면, 펙틴의 큰 분자가 함께 모여 그들의 그물과 같은 구조에 액체를 끌어 모은다. 그 결과, 펙틴은 천연 농후제의 역할을 하고 잼을 만드는 데 걸리는 시간을 크게 단축시키며 과일 고유의 맛을 유지해 준다. 또한 펙틴은 과일의 선명한 색을 지키는 장점이 있어, 눈으로도 잼이 더 맛있게 보이게 한다.

• **Structure Zone**

to부정사는 문장에서 주격보어로 쓰일 수 있는데, 이는 동명사형으로 대체될 수 있다.

The first step to making jam is **to cook** a mixture of fruit and sugar...
→ The first step to making jam is **cooking** a mixture of fruit and sugar...

1. 지문의 주제는 무엇인가?
   (A) 펙틴은 과일에서 발견되는 천연 섬유질이다.
   (B) 펙틴의 특성들은 잼을 만드는 데 유용하다.
   (C) 펙틴은 과일의 비타민과 맛을 지키는 데 도움을 준다.
   (D) 과일에 있는 펙틴은 요리할 때 다양하게 사용된다.

   ◉ 주어진 지문은 펙틴이 어떤 성질을 지니고 있는지와 그것이 잼을 만드는 데에 어떻게 도움을 주는지 설명하고 있다. 따라서 지문의 주제로 알맞은 것은 (B)이다.

2. 지문에서 단어 It이 가리키는 것은
   (A) 과일과 설탕의 혼합물을 조리하는 것
   (B) 잼을 만들 때 펙틴을 사용하는 것
   (C) 걸쭉한 농도를 얻는 것
   (D) 제철 과일을 수확하는 것

   ◉ 주어진 It은 앞 문장에 나온 this time-consuming process, 시간이 오래 소요되는 과정을 뜻하고 그것은 결국 과일과 설탕의 혼합물을 조리하는 것을 가리킨다. 따라서 답은 (A)이다.

3. 지문에서 단어 their가 가리키는 것은
   (A) 세포들   (B) 환경들
   (C) 분자들   (D) 구조들

   ◉ 주어진 their은 그물 같은 구조를 가진 대상으로, 펙틴을 모아 액체가 빠져나가지 않게 하는 복수형의 주체이다. 따라서 답은 (C)가 된다.

• **Note-Taking**

P1 MI the drawbacks to cooking a mixture of jam
    SD - boils away a portion of the fruit's juice
        - can adversely affect the jam's flavor
        - removes the fruit's natural vitamin content

P2 MI pectin — acts as a natural thickening agent
    SD - reduces the required cooking time
        - maintains the distinctive flavor of the fruit
        - preserves the vivid color of the fruit

VOCAB Write the correct word for each definition.
각 뜻에 알맞은 단어를 찾아 적으시오.

a. consistency 농도, 밀도   b. adversely 부정적으로
c. trap 빠져나가지 못하게 하다   d. distinctive 독특한, 고유의
e. preserve 지키다

STEP 3   pp.50-51

정답 | 1. (A)   2. (B)   3. (D)   4. (B)

자유의 종

펜실베이니아 주에 위치한 필라델피아 시에는 자유의 종으로 알려진 금속으로 된 거대한 종이 있다. 자유의 종은 미국의 상징으로 여겨지지만, 사실 그 나라보다 더 오래되었다.

1751년, 펜실베이니아는 대영제국의 식민지였다. 그것의 헌법 50주년을 기념하기 위해 식민지 정부는 구리와 주석으로 된 2,000파운드에 달하는 거대한 종의 건설을 명했다. 독립기념관 첨탑의 서까래에 달려 있는 자유의 종은 특별한 일을 발표하거나 중요한 행사에 사람들을 모으기 위해 울렸다. 대영제국과 미국 식민지 사이에 전쟁이 발발했을 때, 자유의 종은 중요한 전투들의 결과를 알리기 위해 사용되었다. 1776년, 자유의 종은 미국 독립 선언을 최초로 낭독하기 위해 시민들을 모으는 데 울린 것으로 유명하다. 1777년에 영국군이 도시로 진격하면서 자유의 종은 내려져서 근처의 마을에 숨겨졌는데, 녹여져서 무기를 만드는 데 쓰일 수도 있다는 우려 때문이었다. 영국이 패배한 후, 종은 종탑으로 다시 돌아갔다.

자유의 종의 가장 유명한 특징은 그것의 측면에 있는 거대한 균열이다. 그 균열이 처음 생긴 것이 언제인지 아무도 확실히 알지는 못하지만, 1846년에 George Washington의 생일을 기념하기 위해 울렸을 때 그것이 현저히 커졌다. 그 후로, 종은 울리지 않는다. 오늘날, 자유의 종은 필라델피아의 자유의 종 센터에서 국가의 인기 있는 상징으로 남아있다.

Glossary belfry 종탑

• **Structure Zone**

• 주어를 수식하는 구절을 삽입할 때는, 삽입구 앞뒤로 쉼표를 쓴다. 이때 두 쉼표 안에 있는 구절이 생략되더라도 문장이 성립되어야 한다는 것에 유의한다.

The city of Philadelphia, **located in the state of Pennsylvania**, is home to a large metal bell known as the Liberty Bell.

• oneself는 명사의 바로 뒤에 쓰여 명사를 강조하는 역할을 한다.

... it is actually older than **the country itself**.

1. 지문에서 단어 its가 가리키는 것은
   (A) 펜실베이니아   (B) 식민지 정부
   (C) 50주년   (D) 자유의 종

   ◉ 주어진 its는 단수로, '그것의' 헌법 제정이 50주년을 맞이했다는 문맥에 따르면 답은 펜실베이니아이다.

2. 지문에서 단어 it이 가리키는 것은
   (A) 자유의 종   (B) 균열
   (C) 영국군   (D) George Washington의 생일

   ◉ 앞에서 1846에 자유의 종이 울리면서 현저히 커졌다고 하였으므로, 이러한 내용에 알맞은 대상을 찾아보면 (B)가 답이 된다.

3. 다음 중 자유의 종에 대한 내용으로 사실이 아닌 것은 무엇인가?
   (A) 구리와 주석으로 만들어졌다.
   (B) 250년 이상 되었다.
   (C) 1846년부터 울리지 않았다.
   (D) 영국에 의해 도난된 후 숨겨졌다.

   ▶ 자유의 종은 녹여져서 무기를 만드는 데 쓰일 수도 있다는 우려 때문에 숨겨졌다고 했다. 따라서 (D)는 사실이 아니다.

4. 자유의 종에 있는 균열에 대해 언급된 것은 무엇인가?
   (A) 몇 번에 걸쳐 수리되었다.
   (B) 더 이상 종을 울리지 않는 원인이다.
   (C) 종을 만들 때 쓰인 금속들 때문에 생겼다.
   (D) 종을 만든 예술가의 원래 디자인 일부이다.

   ▶ 자유의 종에 있는 균열 때문에 1846년 이후에 종을 울리지 않는다고 했으므로 답은 (B)이다. 나머지는 지문에서 언급되지 않았다.

VOCAB Find the correct word in the passage for each of the given definition.
주어진 뜻에 알맞은 단어를 지문에서 찾으시오.

a. colony 식민지
b. constitution 헌법
c. rafter 서까래
d. ammunition 무기

• **Note-Taking** (Sample Answer)

P1 MI the Liberty Bell – located in Philadelphia
    SD a symbol of the USA which is older than the country

P2 MI the history of the Liberty Bell
    SD - built in 1751 to celebrate the 50th anniversary of Pennsylvania's constitution
        - hung in the steeple of Philadelphia's Independence Hall
        - used to announce the first reading of the Declaration of Independence
        - was taken down & hidden from the British army in 1777

P3 MI rung for the last time in 1846
    SD - a large crack in the Liberty Bell's side, which expanded
        - moved to the Liberty Bell Center

UNIT TEST pp. 52-53

정답 | 1. (C) 2. (C) 3. (B) 4. (D) 5. (D)
     6. (C), (B), (F)

석회동굴

다양한 종류의 동굴들이 있지만, 석회동굴은 세계에서 가장 깊고 길다. 석회동굴에는 인상적인 종유석과 석순이 있는데, 겨울의 고드름처럼 천장으로부터 내려오고 바닥으로부터 올라오는 원뿔모양의 암석 형성대이다. 석회동굴의 평균적 크기와 특징은 그 동굴이 어떻게 생겨났는지에 기인한다.

석회동굴의 형성은 약산성수로부터 시작된다. 이 물은 두 가지 요소 중 한 가지에서 산성을 얻는데, 탄산을 생성하는 공기 중의 이산화탄소나, 황산을 생성하는 것으로 땅 깊은 곳에서 올라오는 황화수소로부터 이다. 이 물이 지면을 따라 움직이면서, 종종 석회암과 만난다. 대부분의 석회암은 오래 전에 고대 대양의 해저에서 형성되었다. 이 때문에, 그것의 주요 성분 중 하나는 조개껍데기에서 발견되고 산성수에 잘 용해되는 무기질인 탄산칼슘이다. 그러므로, 산성수가 석회암에서 발견되는 작은 균열들을 지날 때, 그 물은 작은 구멍을 남기며 암석을 부수고 그것을 옮긴다.

시간이 지나면서, 흐르는 물은 계속해서 구멍을 더 크게 만들어 동굴로 만든다. 동굴이 커지면서, 암석에 있는 다른 틈들과 연결되어 결국 상호 연결된 동굴들과 굴들로 된 지하망을 생성한다. 석회암이 녹은 물에는 용해 가능한 형태의 탄산칼슘이 생긴다. 물이 동굴을 따라 흐를 때, 물은 탄산칼슘을 남기고 그것은 다시 고체 상태가 된다. 천천히 쌓이면서, 그것은 석회동굴 특유의 초자연적인 친숙한 형태를 생성한다. 세계에서 가장 거대한 석회동굴은 베트남에 있으며, 그것은 길이가 9킬로미터, 가로가 200미터, 그리고 세로는 150미터이다.

Glossary icicle 고드름   dissolve 녹다

• **Structure Zone**

> • '전치사 + 관계대명사' 형태인 in which를 써서 앞에 나온 명사를 수식할 수 있고, 이때 in which 뒤에는 '주어 + 동사 (+ 목적어)'의 완전한 문장이 와야 한다.
> The usual sizes and features of limestone caves can be attributed to the manner **in which** the caves themselves are created.
>
> • 동시에 일어나는 일을 쓸 때는 'and + 절' 형태 대신 쉼표와 현재분사를 써서 중복되는 주어를 생략하여 문장을 매끄럽게 쓸 수 있다.
> ... it begins to break the rock down and carry it away **and it leaves** behind a small cavity.
> → ... it begins to break the rock down and carry it away, **leaving** behind a small cavity.

1. 지문에서 단어 which 가 가리키는 것은
   (A) 이산화탄소   (B) 탄산
   (C) 황화수소   (D) 땅

   ▶ 음영 처리된 which는 관계대명사로, 땅 깊은 곳에서 올라와 황산을 생성한다고 하였다. 설명에 맞는 것을 주어진 문장에서 찾으면 (C)가 된다.

2. 지문에서 단어 its 가 가리키는 것은
   (A) 대양   (B) 해저
   (C) 석회암   (D) 탄산칼슘

주어진 its가 가리키는 것은 오래 전 해저에서 형성되었다고 하였으므로 답은 (C) 석회암이다.

3. 2단락에 따르면, 탄산칼슘은
   (A) 물을 산성으로 만든다.
   (B) 석회암에서 발견된다.
   (C) 종유석을 침식시킨다.
   (D) 물을 함유하고 있다.

   ▶ 2단락의 지문을 보면 석회암의 주요 성분이 탄산칼슘이라는 것을 알 수 있다. 따라서 (B)가 답이 된다.

4. 지문에서 단어 it이 가리키는 것은
   (A) 산성수   (B) 동굴
   (C) 석회암   (D) 탄산칼슘

   ▶ it이 가리키는 것은 천천히 쌓여서 석회동굴 특유의 초자연적인 친숙한 형태를 생성하는 요소이다. 이에 맞는 대상을 찾으면 답은 (D)이다.

5. 지문에서 서술되지 않은 것은
   (A) 대부분의 석회암은 오래 전에 해저에서 형성되었다.
   (B) 이산화탄소는 물을 산성으로 만들 수 있다.
   (C) 종유석과 석순은 석회동굴에서 발견된다.
   (D) 황산과 탄산은 근원이 같다.

   ▶ 지문에 따르면, 석회암은 탄산은 공기 중의 이산화탄소로부터 생기고, 황산은 황화수소로부터 생성되므로 (D)가 답이다. 나머지 보기들은 지문에서 모두 서술되었다.

6. 지문의 간단한 요약을 위해 도입 문장이 아래에 주어진다. 지문에서 가장 중요한 내용을 표현하는 세 개의 보기를 선택하여 요약을 완성하라.

   석회동굴은 깊고 길며, 독특한 형태를 지니고 있다.

   보기
   (A) 이산화탄소는 공기 중에 찾아볼 수 있다.
   (B) 산성수는 석회암을 녹이고 구멍을 남긴다.
   (C) 석회암은 높은 수준의 탄산칼슘을 함유하고 있다.
   (D) 석회암은 표면에 많은 균열이 있다.
   (E) 종유석과 얼음은 거의 같은 방법으로 형성된다.
   (F) 탄산칼슘은 흐르는 물에 의해 남겨져 원뿔 형태의 구조를 생성한다.

   ▶ 요약문에는 포괄적이면서도 핵심적인 내용이 포함되어야 한다. (A), (D), (E) 모두 핵심 문장이 되기에는 세부적인 사항이다.

VOCABULARY TEST   pp. 54-55

Recall the essential words in the unit to reinforce your vocabulary acquisition. Write the meaning of each word in your language.
유닛에서 배운 주요 단어들을 떠올려 각 단어의 뜻을 쓰시오.

reclusive	은둔한
rafter	서까래
resultant	그 결과로 생긴
exclusively	오로지
soluble	용해성이 있는
constitution	헌법
coin	(어구 등을) 만들다
abhor	혐오하다
summon	소환하다
dissolve	녹다
eccentric	별난
conical	원뿔 형태의
trap	빠져나가지 못하게 하다
encounter	맞닥뜨리다
involuntary	의도치 않은
distinctive	독특한, 고유의
devote to	~에 바치다
a handful of	소수의
fracture	균열
be attributed to	~에 기인하다
break out	발발하다
bind	결속하다
enthusiastic	열정적인
rural	교외의
preserve	지키다
adversely	부정적으로
descend	내려가다
bond	유대감
consistency	농도
advocate	지지하다
colony	식민지
collection	(시·노래 등의) 모음집
commemorate	기념하다
icicle	고드름
subsist	살아가다
drawback	결점
ammunition	무기
melt down	(열 때문에) 녹다
pen	(글 등을) 쓰다
link up	잇다

Complete each sentence with the correct word or collocation.
문장에 알맞은 단어나 연어를 찾아 쓰시오.

정답 | 1. reclusive   2. subsist
     3. colony   4. icicles
     5. adversely   6. advocate
     7. dissolves   8. melted down
     9. enthusiastic 10. preserving

해석

1. Emily Dickinson의 가족은 지역 사회에서 활발했지만, 그녀는 <u>은둔적인</u> 아이였다.
2. 어떤 딱정벌레들은 오로지 식물을 <u>먹이로 삼고</u>, 다른 딱정벌레들은 더 작은 곤충을 잡아 먹는다.
3. 1751년, 펜실베이니아는 대영제국의 <u>식민지</u>였다.
4. 종유석은 겨울의 <u>고드름</u>처럼 형성된다.
5. 시간이 오래 소요되는 이 과정은 잼의 맛에 좋지 않은 영향을 줄 수 있다.
6. 프로슈머는 선호하는 상표를 <u>변호하기</u> 위해 기술을 이용한다.
7. 석회암이 <u>녹은</u> 물에는 탄산칼슘이 생긴다.
8. 사람들은 그 종이 녹여져서 무기를 만드는 데 쓰일까 봐 두려워했다.
9. Emily Dickinson은 <u>열정적인</u> 편지 쓰기를 통해 가까운 친구들과의 우정을 유지했다.
10. 펙틴은 과일의 선명한 색을 <u>지키는</u> 장점도 있다.

UNIT 04
Fact and Negative Fact

INTRODUCTION
지문에 포함된 사실과 관련된 두 가지 형태의 질문이 있다. 첫 번째 형태에서는 수험자들에게 지문 안에 포함된 정보를 알고 있는지를 묻고, 두 번째 형태에서는 지문 안에 포함되지 않은 정보가 무엇인지를 묻는다.

TYPICAL QUESTION TYPES
_____ 단락에 따르면,
_____ 단락에서 언급된 것은
~는 사실이 아니다.
~는 언급되지 않았다.
다음 중 사실이 아닌 것은

STRATEGIES
- 지문 안에 포함되거나 포함되지 않은 정보를 찾고 있는지의 여부를 잘 이해했는지 확실히 하기 위해 질문을 신중히 읽어라.
- 중요 단어나 어구에 대한 보기를 훑어보아라.
- '부정적인 사실'은 틀린 정보이거나 또는 단순히 지문에서 언급하지 않은 정보일 수 있다는 것을 명심하라.

QUICK CHECKUP   p.57
정답 | 1. (B)   2. (A)   3. (B)

Find the answer that is true according to the passage.
지문에 따라 맞는 답을 고르시오.

1. '소울푸드'라는 말은 남부 미국에서 발달된 아프리카 식의 미국 요리를 나타낸다. 소울푸드의 주재료에는 돼지고기, 콩, 잎 채소, 그리고 옥수수가루가 있다. 소울푸드의 독특한 특징은 필요성에 의해 발전했다. 과거에, 노예들은 그들이 취할 수 있는 음식이면 어떤 것이라도 모두 이용해야 했다. 후에, 이러한 요리법들은 미국 원주민의 요리법뿐만 아니라, 가난한 시골 남부인들의 음식 문화와 합쳐졌다.
   (A) 소울푸드는 미국의 원주민들에 의해 최초로 만들어졌다.
   (B) 원래의 소울푸드 요리법은 가능한 어떤 음식이든지 사용했다.

   ▶ 소울푸드의 기원을 설명하면서 과거에 노예들이 얻을 수 있는 모든 음식을 사용했다는 내용이 지문에 나오므로 (B)가 맞는 내용이다.

2. 동물의 윤리적 대우를 위한 사람들은 약어로 PETA라고 알려져 있는데, 이는 동물의 권리를 보호하는 데 초점을 둔 미국의 비영리단체로 1980년에 설립되었다. 세계에서 가장 큰 동물 권리 단체 중 하나이지만, PETA는 단체의 크기보다는 그 전략으로 더 잘 알려져 있다. 모피와 동물 실험에 반대하는 대립적 캠페인은 사람들을 충격에 빠뜨리고 단체의 명분에 관심을 끌도록 고안된 논란이 많은 광고를 특징으로 한다.
   (A) PETA는 주의를 끌기 위해 극단적인 광고를 사용한다.
   (B) PETA는 작지만 효과적인 캠페인 전략을 갖고 있다.

   ▶ PETA는 동물 실험이나 모피와 같은 주제에 관해 사람들의 주의를 끌기 위해 충격적인 내용을 광고로 사용한다는 내용이 지문에 나온다. 따라서 (A)가 지문의 내용과 일치한다.

3. 2000년 1월 1일, 세계기상학회(WMO)는 북서 태평양과 남부 중국해에서 발생하는 태풍 지역에 새로운 작명 체계를 시행했다. 이는 그 지역의 각기 다른 나라들로부터 모아진 140개의 이름 목록을 사용한다. 과거에 그랬던 것처럼 오로지 여자의 이름에 의존하기보다 그 목록은 남자들의 이름, 식물, 동물, 장소, 신화적 인물, 그리고 그 지역에서 중요시하는 것들의 다른 단어들도 포함한다. 이러한 이름들과 함께, 태풍을 식별하기 위해 숫자를 붙이는 전통적인 방법도 계속해서 사용된다.
   (A) WMO는 태풍에 이름 붙이는 방법을 숫자를 붙이는 방법으로 대체했다.
   (B) 2000년 이래로 140개의 이름 목록이 태풍을 식별하기 위해 사용되었다.

   ▶ WMO에서는 태풍에 이름을 붙이기 위하여 근처의 해당국들로부터 이름을 모아 140개의 이름 목록을 만들어 사용한다는 내용이 지문에 있으므로 (B)가 정답이 된다.

VOCABULARY   pp.58-59

Write the number of each word's definition.
각 단어의 뜻을 찾아 번호를 쓰시오.

depict / 11 묘사하다   grasp / 2 움켜쥐다
harness / 1 (동력원으로) 이용하다   respiratory / 8 호흡기의
acute / 6 극심한   contagious / 3 전염성의
abate / 9 약화시키다   refrain / 12 삼가다
controversial / 4 논란이 많은   excavation / 7 발굴
futility / 5 무익, 헛수고   skeptical / 10 회의적인

Match each collocation with the correct definition.
각 연어에 알맞은 뜻을 찾아 연결하시오.

a. be derived from – to have come from something else
   ~로부터 유래되다
b. in leaps and bounds – increasing or progressing very quickly 급속히
c. be credited with – to be considered responsible for (a task, achievement, etc.) ~로 인정받다
d. participate in – to take part in (an event, activity, etc.) 참여하다
e. be evicted from – to be legally forced to leave a place
   ~로부터 쫓겨나다

Circle the word closest in meaning to each underlined word.
각 밑줄 친 단어의 뜻과 가장 가까운 단어를 찾아 동그라미 하시오.

정답 | 1. (B)   2. (A)   3. (D)
     4. (C)   5. (A)   6. (B)

해석 |
1. 어떤 영장류들은 나뭇가지를 움켜쥐고 나무에서 나무로 매달려 다닌다.
   (A) 이해하다   (B) 움켜잡다
   (C) 발견하다   (D) 낮추다

2. 이 벽화들은 고대 도시를 파괴했던 사건들을 묘사한다.
   (A) 설명하다   (B) 과장하다
   (C) 창조하다   (D) 위장하다

3. 태양판들은 태양 에너지를 이용하기 위해 고안되었다.
   (A) 높이다   (B) 보호하다
   (C) 분석하다   (D) 활용하다

4. 대통령은 연설하기 전에 박수가 잦아들기를 기다렸다.
   (A) 시작하다   (B) 계속하다
   (C) 진정되다   (D) 확대하다

5. 근육통을 앓고 있는 운동선수들은 운동하는 것을 삼가라는 충고를 받았다.
   (A) 자제하다   (B) 쉬다
   (C) 약을 투여하다 (D) 상담하다

6. 그 과학자는 자신이 치유법을 찾았다고 주장하지만, 그녀의 동료들은 회의적이다.
   (A) 유연한   (B) 의심하는
   (C) 폭력적인   (D) 낙관적인

Fill in each blank with the correct collocation.
알맞은 연어를 골라 빈칸을 채우시오.

정답 | 1. is derived from   2. is credited with
     3. participated in   4. in leaps and bounds
     5. be evicted from

해석 |
1. 그 약은 희귀한 열대나무의 열매에서 추출되었다.
2. 그 현지인은 고대 밀림 마을을 발견했다고 인정받는다.
3. 그 뛰어난 운동선수는 몇몇 올림픽 행사에 참여했다.
4. 더딘 시작 후, 그녀의 사업은 급속히 팽창하기 시작했다.
5. 가난한 가족들은 임대료를 내지 못해 그들의 집에서 쫓겨날 수 있다.

STEP 1   pp. 60-61

정답 | 1. (B)   2. (D)

카잔루크의 트라키아인 무덤

중부 불가리아 지역에 위치한 카잔루크의 트라키아인 무덤은 유네스코 세계문화유산이다. 이 무덤은 복도와 둥근 묘실로 구성되는데, 죽은 사람을 매장하기 위해 사용된 거대한 집합체인 공동묘지의 일부이다.

무덤은 인상 깊게 잘 보존된 기원전 4세기경의 벽화로 장식되어 있는데, 그 무렵은 헬레니즘 시대로 고대 그리스 제국의 문화적 영향이 유럽과 인접 지역의 예술품에서 발견되는 시기이다. 카잔루크의 트라키아인 무덤 벽화는 장례식을 묘사하고 있다. 벽화에서 족장과 그의 아내는 나란히 앉아있는데, 서로의 손목을 꼭 잡고 감동적인 이별을 보여주는 듯하다. 그들 앞에는 하녀들과 하인들, 그리고 말들의 의식 행렬이 정중히 다가오고 있다.

매우 잘 보존된 상태와 더불어, 그 벽화의 뛰어난 구성과 자연적인 세부묘사는 무덤을 역사적 중요성을 가진 예술공간으로 만든다.

Glossary chamber 방, 실

• **Structure Zone**

> 5형식 동사로 쓰이는 make는 'make + 목적어 + 목적보어'의 형태로 나타내며, 이때 목적보어 자리에 명사가 오면 '~을 …로 만들다'라는 뜻이다.
> Naturalistic details **make** the tomb **an artistic site** of historical importance.

1. 다음 중 사실이 아닌 것은
   (A) 무덤은 상당히 크다.
   (B) 무덤은 일부분은 심하게 훼손되었다.
   (C) 묘실은 둥글다.
   (D) 무덤은 문화적으로 중요하다고 여겨진다.

   ➡ 카잔루크의 트라키아인 무덤 보존 상태에 대해서는 벽화가 매우 잘 보존되었다는 것 외에 무덤의 훼손 정도에 대해서는 언급되지 않았다. 따라서 (B)는 지문의 내용과 일치하지 않는다.

2. 벽화에 대해 언급된 것은
   (A) 그리스 문화에 크게 영향을 주었다.
   (B) 묘실에 있다.
   (C) 축제에서의 남자와 여자를 보여준다.
   (D) 훌륭히 구성되었다고 여겨진다.

   ➡ 벽화는 그 구성과 자연적인 세부묘사로 인해 역사적 중요성과 더불어 예술성까지 인정받고 있다는 내용이 지문에 나오므로, (D)가 정답이 된다.

• **Note-Taking**

The Thracian Tomb of Kazanlak

Where It Is	— central Bulgaria
What It Consists of	— a corridor & a round burial chamber; part of a necropolis
Its Murals	— are impressively well-preserved
	— were painted in the 4th century B.C. – Hellenistic period
	— depict a Thracian chieftain & his wife at a funeral feast
	— have the remarkable composition & naturalistic details

SUMMARY

The Thracian Tomb of Kazanlak is part of a necropolis in central Bulgaria. It consists of a corridor and a round burial chamber. The tomb contains murals from the 4th century B.C. The murals depict a Thracian chieftain and his wife with maids, servants and horses at a funeral feast. The murals are well-preserved and are notable for their remarkable composition and naturalistic details.

카잔루크의 트라키아인 무덤은 중부 불가리아에 있는 공동묘지의 일부이다. 이것은 복도와 둥근 묘실로 구성되었다. 무덤은 기원전 4세기의 벽화들을 포함한다. 벽화는 장례식에서 하녀들, 하인들, 그리고 말들과 함께 있는 트라키아 족장과 그의 아내를 묘사하고 있다. 벽화는 잘 보존되었으며 뛰어난 구성과 자연적인 세부묘사로 유명하다.

VOCAB_ Match each word with the correct definition.
각 단어에 알맞은 뜻을 찾아 연결하시오.

a. adjacent – lying near or close 근접한
b. chieftain – the chief of a clan 족장
c. procession – the act of moving along in order 행렬
d. state – the condition that a person or a thing is in 상태
e. composition – manner of being composed and placed 구성

• **More Info Zone**

유적지와 도굴

세계에서 가장 오래된 건축물 8위로 알려진 카잔루크 트라키아인 무덤은 1944년 4월 방공호를 파던 병사들이 우연히 발견하여 세상에 알려졌다. 카잔루크의 고분은 다른 많은 고분들과 마찬가지로 발견되기 오래 전에 도굴되었는데, 금은 장식품과 호화로운 보석 등은 대부분 사라진 상태였다. 하지만 목관에 매장된 두 남녀의 유골, 단도, 작은 금장식품, 그리스식 항아리 조각들이 남아서 트라키아 시대의 생활상을 조금이나마 엿볼 수 있다.

STEP 2 pp. 62-63

정답 | 1. (A) 2. (C) 3. (D)

전기

전기는 인류에 의해 동력원으로 이용되고 있는 자연 발생 현상으로, 현대 문명에 박차를 가하고 있는 과학기술을 매우 빠른 속도로 발달할 수 있게 해 준다.

전기는 양전하를 전달하는 양성자와 음전하를 전달하는 전자로 알려진 원자구성입자 안의 전하로 시작된다. 전하가 한 물체에서 다른 물체로 이동할 때, 이것을 전류라고 부른다. 전류의 흐름을 조절하기 위하여 전기회로가 만들어질 수 있는데, 이는 세 가지 요소로 구성된다. 구리선과 같은 도체, 전지와 같은 전기원, 전구와 같은 전기를 필요로 하는 장치가 그것이다.

전선 안의 구리는 전류를 '전도'하는데 이는 전기가 전지에서 전구로 흐르도록 해 준다. 전류가 얼마나 강하게 흐르게 되는지는 두 가지 요인에 의해 달라진다. 전하를 이동하게 하는 전류의 전압과 흐름을 밀어내는 도체의 저항이 그것이다. 금속은 가장 흔하게 사용되는 도체인데, 이는 금속이 낮은 저항을 가지는 경향이 있기 때문이다. 그들의 양성자는 움직이지 않는데, 이는 회로를 통해 전하를 전달하는 것이 그들의 전자라는 것을 의미한다.

• **Structure Zone**

• to부정사의 부사적 용법 중에서 '~하기 위하여'라는 의미의 표현은 'in order to + 동사원형'을 이용하여서도 나타낼 수 있다.

In order to control the movement of a current, an electric circuit can be constructed.

• 의문사를 포함하는 문장이 명사절의 형태가 되어 주어로 쓰이는 경우에는 '의문사 + 주어 + 동사'의 어순을 가진다.

How powerfully **an electric current flows** depends on two factors.

1. 지문에서 단어 their 가 가리키는 것은
   (A) 금속   (B) 도체
   (C) 양성자   (D) 전자

   ▶ their가 쓰인 해당 문장은 도체로 쓰이는 금속의 특징에 대해 설명하고 있으므로 their는 metals를 의미한다.

2. 3단락에서 언급된 것은
   (A) 강한 전류를 위해서 도체의 전압은 낮아야 한다.
   (B) 높은 전압은 높은 금속 저항을 일으킨다.
   (C) 전자는 금속 도체를 통해 쉽게 이동하는 경향이 있다.
   (D) 회로는 전자와 양성자 둘 다 포함할 수 없다.

   ▶ 3단락에서는 도체를 통해 어떻게 전류가 흐르게 되는지, 그리고 도체로 흔히 쓰이는 금속은 어떤 성질을 가지는지에 대해 설명하고 있다. 따라서 금속 도체의 특징을 말하고 있는 (C)가 답이 된다.

3. 다음 중 사실이 아닌 것은
   (A) 양성자는 원자구성입자이다.
   (B) 전류는 전하의 이동이다.
   (C) 구리 선은 도체의 역할을 할 수 있다.
   (D) 전하는 회로를 필요로 한다.

   ➲ 전류의 이동을 전류라고 하며, 이 전류의 흐름을 조정하기 위해 전기회로가 필요하다고 했으므로, 전하 자체가 전기회로가 필요한 것은 아니다. 따라서 (D)는 본문의 내용과 일치하지 않는다.

• Note-Taking

P1 MI electricity
    SD a naturally occurring phenomenon

P2 MI requires three elements to begin:
    SD • electric charge – protons & electrons
        • electric current – the transfer of a charge
        • electric circuit – consists of a conductor, a source & a device

P3 MI two factors that influence the power of electric current
    SD • the voltage of the current: the force that moves the charge
        • the resistance of the conductor: pushes against the flow

VOCAB_ Write the correct word for each definition.
각 뜻에 알맞은 단어를 찾아 적으시오.

a. civilization 문명
b. particle 입자
c. circuit 회로
d. resistance 저항
e. immobile 움직이지 않는

STEP 3   pp. 64-65

정답 | 1. (C)   2. (A)   3. (D)   4. (B)

노로 바이러스

노로 바이러스는 RNA 바이러스의 일종으로, 수많은 변종을 가진 하나의 종으로 구성된다. 이것의 이름은 미국 도시인 Norwalk에서 기인한 것인데, 이곳은 1968년 최초의 바이러스 발생 지역으로 알려진 곳이다. 이것은 흔히 '위장 독감'이라는 말로 알려져 있지만, 이것은 호흡기 질환인 독감 바이러스와는 관련이 없다. 반면에 노로 바이러스는 위장과 장의 염증인 급성 위장염의 원인이 된다.

노로 바이러스는 전염성이 매우 강한데, 사람에게 전염되는 경로가 여러 가지이다. 이것은 오염된 음식을 통해, 또는 오염된 표면을 만짐으로써 사람과 사람간에 전염된다. 일부의 가장 심각한 노로 바이러스는 사람들이 쉽게 오고 가지 못하는 고립된 집단에서 발생한다. 병원, 교도소, 학교 기숙사, 그리고 아마도 가장 악명 높게는 유람선 등이 여기에 속한다. 노로 바이러스의 가장 흔한 증상은 메스꺼움, 구토, 설사, 그리고 위장 통증이다. 이러한 증상들은 종종 위험한 탈수증으로 이어지기도 한다.

노로 바이러스에 대한 백신이나 효과적인 치료가 없다는 사실에도 불구하고, 취할 수 있는 예방 단계는 많다. 적절한 위생을 실천하는 것이 이에 포함되는데, 손을 자주 씻는 것, 음식을 내기 전에 충분히 씻고 익히는 것이 해당된다. 이 질병 자체는 주로 하루에서 삼일 정도 지속될 뿐이지만, 노로 바이러스를 앓고 있는 사람들은 증상이 약해진 이후에도 며칠 동안 전염성이 계속된다. 따라서 이들은 이 기간 동안에 음식을 요리하거나 만지고 내는 것을 삼가해야 한다.

Glossary RNA 리보 핵산

• Structure Zone

> 등위 접속사는 문법적으로 동일한 구조를 대등하게 연결하는 것이다. 따라서 등위접속사로 연결되는 것들은 동일한 품사, 문법적으로 동일한 형태의 어구, 문장과 문장이 되는 것에 유의한다.
>
> These include practicing proper hygiene, such as frequently **washing one's hands, and cooking and washing food** thoroughly before serving it.

1. 지문에서 단어 colloquially와 의미가 가장 가까운 것은
   (A) 일시적으로   (B) 상당히
   (C) 구어(口語)로   (D) 옮기 쉽게

   ➲ colloquially는 '구어체로'라는 뜻인데 이는 '형식을 따지지 않는 구어(口語)'라는 뜻으로도 사용된다. 따라서 (C)가 답이 된다.

2. 1단락에서 언급한 것은
   (A) 위장염은 노로 바이러스 때문에 생긴다.
   (B) RNA 바이러스는 호흡기 질환으로 이어질 수 있다.
   (C) 노로 바이러스는 위장 독감과는 관련이 없다.
   (D) 독감 바이러스는 위장염의 한 형태이다.

   ➲ 1단락의 후반부에 노로 바이러스가 위와 장의 염증 원인이 된다는 내용이 있으므로 (A)가 정답이다.

3. 3단락에서 작가의 주요 의도는
   (A) 노로 바이러스가 전염성이 강하다는 것을 보여주는 것
   (B) 노로 바이러스 백신이 왜 없는지 설명하는 것
   (C) 노로 바이러스와 다른 질병을 비교하는 것
   (D) 노로 바이러스를 피하는 방법에 대해 조언하는 것

   ➲ 3단락에서는 손을 자주 씻거나 음식을 깨끗이 씻고 충분히 익히는 등의 노로 바이러스 예방법에 대해 기술하고 있다. 따라서 (D)를 작가의 의도라고 볼 수 있다.

4. 사실이 아닌 것은
   (A) 노로 바이러스의 심각한 발생은 유람선에서 일어날 수 있다.
   (B) 노로 바이러스의 치료에는 손을 씻는 것이 포함된다.
   (C) 노로 바이러스는 한 사람에서 다른 사람으로 옮겨질 수 있다.
   (D) 노로 바이러스의 증상은 탈수증의 원인이 된다.

   ➲ 3단락에서 노로 바이러스에 대한 백신이나 효과적인 치료법은 없다고 하였으며, 손을 씻는 것은 치료법이 아닌 예방법으로 소개되고 있다. 따라서 (B)가 사실이 아니다.

VOCAB Find the correct word in the passage for each of the given definition.
주어진 뜻에 알맞은 단어를 지문에서 찾으시오.

a. inflammation 염증
b. transmit 전하다
c. dehydration 탈수
d. hygiene 위생

• **Note-Taking** (Sample Answer)

P1 MI norovirus – a type of RNA virus
    SD causes an inflammation of the stomach & intestines

P2 MI the infection process & symptoms of norovirus
    SD transmitted from person to person via contaminated food or surfaces
        → causes nausea, vomiting, diarrhea, stomach pain, & dehydration

P3 MI preventative steps for norovirus
    SD practice proper hygiene & refrain from cooking, handling, or serving food

• **More Info Zone**

생명력이 강한 노로 바이러스

노로 바이러스는 다른 바이러스들과는 달리 온도가 낮을수록 활발해진다. 영하 20도에서도 생존이 가능하며 심지어 냉장, 냉동온도에서 수년간 감염력이 유지되기도 한다. 따라서 날씨가 쌀쌀해지는 가을부터 기승을 부리기 시작하여 겨울철 식중독의 3분의 1은 이 노로 바이러스가 원인이 된다. 노로 바이러스는 다른 바이러스들과 달리 소량의 바이러스 입자(18~20 molecules)만으로도 감염이 되며, 수많은 변종이 있기 때문에 한번 감염되었다 하더라도 이후에 또 다른 종류의 노로 바이러스에 감염될 수 있다. 이 때문에 백신 개발이 힘든 것이므로 무엇보다 개인 위생과 같은 예방법이 매우 중요하다.

UNIT TEST	pp.66-67
정답	1. (B) 2. (A) 3. (B) 4. (C) 5. (D) 6. Hissarlik (C), (G) Troy (A), (E), (F)

Heinrich Schliemann (하인리히 슐리만)

19세기 독일 고고학자인 Heinrich Schliemann은, 일부에게는 그 분야의 위대한 개척자로 여겨지기도 하는 논란이 많은 인물이다. 그는 고대 트로이의 위치를 발견해낸 인물로 가장 유명한데, 많은 이들이 단지 신화에 불과하다고 믿었던 도시의 존재를 입증했다.

Schliemann은 젊은 시절에 모험으로 가득한 삶을 살았다. 그는 전세계를 여행했는데, 조난사고에서도 살아남았으며 캘리포니아의 골드러시에도 참여했다. 46세의 지긋한 나이가 되어서야 그는 고고학자가 되기로 결심했다. 유년시절부터 그리스 신화에 관심이 많았던 그는 Homer(호머)의 서사시인 일리아드와 오디세이

에서 묘사된 트로이 도시를 찾는 데 주력했다. 그 당시에는 역사가들 사이에서 이 시들이 역사적인 기술인지 아니면 허구 작품인지에 관해 격렬한 논쟁이 있었다. 그것들이 전자라고 믿었으므로, Schliemann은 트로이가 한 때 세워져 있던 장소로 그를 인도하는 데 Homer의 작품들을 사용했다.

그는 결국 트로이의 잔재들이 로마 정착지의 유적 아래, 서부 터키에 있는 언덕인 히살리크에서 발견될 수 있을 것이라고 결론 지었다. 1871년에, 그는 그 장소에서 주요 발굴을 시작했다. 2년 이상의 헛수고 후에, Schliemann은 은과 금 공예품 은닉처를 발견했다. 그는 이것들을 'Priam(프리아모스)의 보물'이라고 불렀는데, 그것들이 한때 트로이의 왕인 Priam에게 속해있었다고 믿었기 때문이다. 그의 동료들은 회의적이었으며, Schliemann은 곧 터키 정부와 충돌했다. 나중에는 돌아오는 것이 허용되기는 했지만, 그는 그 장소에서 쫓겨나게 되었다. Schliemann은 1890년 그가 죽을 때까지도 그의 작업을 계속했다.

오늘날, Schliemann이 주장했던 많은 것들이 부정확하다고 여겨지고 있으며, 다이너마이트의 이용을 포함한 그의 일부 발굴 기술들은 신랄히 비판 받아왔다. 그러나 그는 수세기에 걸친 미스터리를 풀고, 그의 동료 고고학자들을 사라진 도시가 있던 자리로 안내한 대단한 업적을 이룬 것으로서는 인정받고 있다.

Glossary cache 은닉처

• **Structure Zone**

> • 분사구문은 부사절에서 '접속사 + 주어'는 생략하고 현재분사나 과거분사를 이용하여 표현을 단순화시킨 것을 말한다. 시간, 이유, 양보, 조건, 부대상황 등을 나타내는 접속사가 생략되었으므로 문맥을 통해 그 의미를 이해해야 한다. 분사구문에서 being과 having been은 생략되는 경우가 많다.
>
> **Because he had been interested** in Greek mythology since childhood, he focused on finding the city of Troy.
> → **Interested** in Greek mythology since childhood, he focused on finding the city of Troy.
>
> **Because Schliemann believed** they were the former, Schliemann used Homer's works to guide him to the place where Troy once stood.
> → **Believing** they were the former, Schliemann used Homer's works to guide him to the place where Troy once stood.
>
> • be considered는 '~로 여겨지다'라는 뜻으로 뒤에 to부정사가 뒤따른다.
>
> Heinrich Schliemann, a 19th-century German archaeologist, **was** a controversial figure **considered** by some **to be** a great pioneer in his field.
>
> Many of Schliemann's claims **are considered to be** inaccurate.

1. 지문의 주제는 무엇인가?
    (A) Heinrich Schliemann은 트로이가 신화라는 것을 입증했다.
    (B) Heinrich Schliemann은 트로이의 위치를 밝혀냈다.
    (C) Heinrich Schliemann은 가장 중요한 고고학적 유물을 발견했다.
    (D) Homer의 가장 위대한 서사시들은 Heinrich Schliemann에 의해 발견되었다.

    ◉ Heinrich Schliemann에 대한 지문의 내용 중 보다 강조되는 주제는 그가 신화로만 알려졌던 트로이의 실제 위치를 발견했다는 것이므로 (B)가 답이 된다.

2. 왜 작가는 지문에서 the California Gold Rush를 언급하는가?
    (A) Schliemann의 모험이 가득한 삶의 예로 들기 위해서
    (B) Schliemann이 가보았던 최초의 역사적 장소들을 알려주기 위해서
    (C) Schliemann이 어떻게 트로이에 관한 세계를 찾았는지 보여주기 위해서
    (D) Schliemann이 어떻게 신화에 관심을 가지게 되었는지 설명하기 위해서

    ◉ 골드러시를 언급한 앞 문장을 보면 Schliemann이 모험으로 가득한 삶을 살았다는 이야기가 나온다. 조난사고나 골드러시에 대한 내용은 모험으로 가득한 삶을 부가설명하기 위한 것이라 해석할 수 있으므로 (A)가 정답이다.

3. 지문에서 어구 ran afoul of와 가장 비슷한 의미는
    (A) ~로 달아나다   (B) ~와 갈등을 겪다
    (C) ~로부터 탈출하다   (D) ~와 동맹하다

    ◉ run afoul of는 '~와 대립하다, 충돌하다'라는 의미이므로 '~와 충돌하다'라는 뜻의 (B) conflicted with가 가장 알맞다.

4. 3단락에서 언급한 것은
    (A) 히살리크는 로마시의 서부에 위치한 언덕이다.
    (B) 터키 정부는 Schliemann이 그의 작업을 끝내는 것을 도왔다.
    (C) Schliemann이 히살리크 아래에서 보물을 찾는 데 2년 정도가 걸렸다.
    (D) Schliemann은 Priam 왕의 보물을 찾다가 죽었다.

    ◉ 3단락은 Schliemann이 트로이의 위치를 히살리크라고 보고 유적지를 발굴해내는 과정을 그리고 있다. 발굴을 시작하고 2년 동안 헛수고를 했다는 내용으로 미루어 Priam 왕의 보물이라 믿었던 것을 찾는 데 2년이 걸렸음을 알 수 있다.

5. 다음 중 사실이 아닌 것은
    (A) Schliemann은 트로이가 로마 유적 아래에 있다고 생각했다.
    (B) Schliemann이 Priam 왕의 보물을 찾았다고 모든 사람들이 믿은 것은 아니었다.
    (C) Schliemann은 40대가 되어서야 고고학자가 되었다.
    (D) 역사학자들은 Homer의 서사시가 허구 작품이라는 것에 동의했다.

    ◉ Homer의 서사시에 대해서는 역사적 기술이라는 의견과 허구 작품이라는 의견이 팽팽 대립하고 있었다는 내용이 지문에 나오므로, (D)는 사실이 아니다.

6. 보기에서 적당한 구를 찾아서 그것들과 관련된 카테고리에 넣어라. 보기 중에서 두 개는 사용되지 않을 것이다.

    히살리크   /   트로이

    보기
    (A) Homer의 서사시에서 묘사됨
    (B) 치명적인 조난사고 장소
    (C) 서부 터키에 있는 언덕
    (D) 골드러시로 유명함
    (E) 존재했는지에 대한 논란이 있던 도시
    (F) 한때 Priam이라는 이름의 왕에 의해 통치를 받음
    (G) 로마 유적의 장소

    ◉ 히살리크는 서부 터키의 언덕이며 로마 유적지이고 Homer의 서사시에서 묘사된 트로이는 역사학자들 사이에서 존재 여부에 대한 논쟁이 있었던 곳으로 한때 Priam 왕의 통치 아래 있었던 곳이다.

VOCABULARY TEST   pp. 68-69

Recall the essential words in the unit to reinforce your vocabulary acquisition. Write the meaning of each word in your language.
유닛에서 배운 주요 단어들을 떠올려 각 단어의 뜻을 쓰시오.

particle ǀ 입자	adjacent ǀ 근접한
contagious ǀ 전염성의	inflammation ǀ 염증
circuit ǀ 회로	skeptical ǀ 회의적인
state ǀ 상태	respiratory ǀ 호흡기의
refrain ǀ 삼가다	depict ǀ 묘사하다
resistance ǀ 저항	chieftain ǀ 족장
transmit ǀ 전하다	pioneer ǀ 선구자
acute ǀ 극심한	tactic ǀ 전략
civilization ǀ 문명	abate ǀ 약화시키다
hygiene ǀ 위생	futility ǀ 무익, 헛수고
cache ǀ 은닉처	harness ǀ (동력원으로) 이용하다
procession ǀ 행렬	immobile ǀ 움직이지 않는
composition ǀ 구성	confrontational ǀ 대립을 일삼는
controversial ǀ 논란이 많은	fierce ǀ 격렬한
dehydration ǀ 탈수	staple ǀ 주요한
contribute ǀ 기여하다	excavation ǀ 발굴
merge with ǀ 병합하다	be evicted from ǀ ~로부터 쫓겨나다
participate in ǀ 참여하다	grasp ǀ 움켜쥐다
culinary ǀ 요리의	in leaps and bounds ǀ 급속히
be derived from ǀ ~로부터 유래되다	
be credited with ǀ ~로 인정받다	

Complete each sentence with the correct word or collocation.
문장에 알맞은 단어나 연어를 찾아 쓰시오.

정답 ǀ 1. tactics   2. fierce
        3. procession   4. cache

5. dehydration 6. resistance
7. particles 8. staple
9. chieftain 10. merged with

해석

1. PETA는 규모보다는 전략으로 더 잘 알려져 있다.
2. 역사학자들 사이에서 격렬한 논쟁이 있었다.
3. 하녀들, 하인들, 그리고 말들의 의식 행렬이 다가온다.
4. Schliemann은 은과 금 공예품의 은닉처를 발견했다.
5. 노로 바이러스의 증상은 종종 위험한 탈수로 이어진다.
6. 금속은 흔히 도체로 이용되는데, 그것들이 낮은 저항을 갖기 때문이다.
7. 전기는 원자구성입자에서 발견되는 전하로 시작된다.
8. 소울푸드의 주요 재료에는 돼지고기, 콩, 그리고 잎 채소가 있다.
9. 벽화에서 트라키아 족장과 그의 아내는 나란히 앉아있다.
10. 노예들의 요리법은 가난한 시골 남부인들의 요리 문화와 통합되었다.

UNIT 05
Sentence Simplification

INTRODUCTION

문장 단순화 문제에서는 빠지는 내용 없이, 주어진 문장 안의 내용 순서를 바꾸거나 더 단순한 동의어로 바꾼 문장을 찾는다. 문장의 중요한 내용이 빠지거나 다른 내용이 담긴 보기들은 오답이 된다.

TYPICAL QUESTION TYPE

아래 문장 중 지문에서 음영 처리된 문장의 핵심 정보를 가장 잘 나타낸 것은 어느 것인가? *잘못된* 보기들은 중요한 의미를 바꾸거나 핵심 정보를 생략한다.

STRATEGIES

- 음영 처리된 문장들은 주로 한 개 이상의 절로 구성되어 있다. 주어진 문장의 주어들, 동사들, 그리고 목적어들을 집중해서 찾아야 한다.
- 등위접속사와 종속접속사를 찾고, 절 간의 관계(첨가, 대조, 선택, 조건, 순서)를 파악한다.
- 주어진 보기들을 확인하라. 중요하다고 인지한 정보를 포함하고 있지 않은 구절과 동사의 능동태, 수동태나 시제의 변화를 찾아라. 또한 중요한 정보를 빠뜨려 문장의 의미가 바뀐 부분을 찾아라.

QUICK CHECKUP p.71

정답 | 1. (C) 2. (B)

Find the answer that best expresses the essential information in the highlighted sentence.
음영 처리된 문장의 주요 정보를 가장 잘 나타낸 답을 찾으시오.

1. 눈을 즐겁게 해 주는 글쓰기 예술인 캘리그라피는 독특하고 오래 사용되어온 시각적 예술이다. 영어 단어인 '캘리그라피'는 '미'를 뜻하는 그리스어인 *kallos*와 '글쓰기'를 뜻하는 *graphy*에서 기원했다. 캘리그라피는 적어도 기원전 2세기부터 중요한 예술이었다. 캘리그라퍼들은 끝이 아주 정교한 붓, 펜, 그리고 조각용 연장을 사용해서 어떤 면에서 보면 아름답고 조화롭지만, 항상 읽기 쉽지만은 않은 글씨들을 쓴다.
   (A) 캘리그라피로 쓰인 글자들과 단어들은 캘리그라퍼들이 아주 좋은 붓과 연장을 사용할 때 더 읽기 쉽다.
   (B) 캘리그라퍼들은 글자들과 단어들을 예술적이고 흥미로운 방식으로 표현하는데, 모든 이가 항상 그것들을 읽을 수 있는 것은 아니다.
   (C) 캘리그라피에는 글자들과 단어들을 보기 좋게 만들어내기 위해 연장들이 사용되는데, 항상 읽기 쉬운 것은 아니다.
   (D) 캘리그라퍼들은 글자들이 아름답고 읽기 쉽게 하기 위해 몇몇 특별한 글쓰기 도구들을 사용한다.

   ▶ 음영 처리된 문장을 살펴보면, 캘리그라퍼들은 연장을 써서 아름다운 글씨를 만들어 내지만, 그것들이 항상 읽기 쉬운 것은 아니라고 하였다. 이러한 내용을 모두 담은 문장을 찾으면 (C)가 답이 된다.

2. Nelson Mandela는 남아프리카에서 처음으로 온전히 민주적인 방법으로 대통령에 뽑힌 이이며, 그 국가의 첫 번째 흑인 대통령이다. Mandela의 대통령 임기는 남아프리카의 아파르트헤이트(예전 남아프리카공화국의 인종 차별 정책)에 종지부를 찍었다. 혁명 운동으로 27년 이상을 감옥에서 보내야 했지만, Mandela는 감옥에 있는 동안 조직적인 남아프리카 흑인의 시민권 박탈에 대항하였다. 감옥에서 풀려난 후, 그는 1994년에 대통령으로 선출되었고 인종적 화해의 시작을 총괄했다.
   (A) Nelson Mandela는 남아프리카 흑인의 권리를 박탈한 정부를 향해 27년 동안 시위했다.
   (B) 정부에 대항한 이유로 감옥에서 27년을 보내면서, Nelson Mandela는 남아프리카 흑인의 권리를 위해 시위했다.
   (C) Nelson Mandela는 남아프리카 흑인의 권리가 박탈당하는 방식에 시위한 이유로 27년 동안 감옥살이를 했다.
   (D) Nelson Mandela는 평화적으로 정부에 대항했던 많은 흑인들을 감옥에 가둔 체제에 시위하면서 27년을 보냈다.

   ▶ 지문에 따르면, Nelson Mandela는 27년 수감된 동안 남아프리카 흑인의 시민권을 위해 투쟁했다고 하였으며, 그것이 수감된 이유는 아니었다. 주어진 문장을 가장 잘 나타낸 보기를 찾으면 (B)이다.

VOCABULARY   pp. 72-73

Write the number of each word's definition.
각 단어의 뜻을 찾아 번호를 쓰시오.

herbivorous / 5 초식의   predator / 10 포식동물
flourish / 6 번창하다
gritty / 11 불쾌한 현실을 그대로 보여주는
luminary / 1 전문가   privileged / 2 특권을 가진
compress / 4 압축하다   fascinate / 9 매료하다
speculate / 3 추측하다   determine / 8 결정하다
constrain / 12 강요하다   devastating / 7 엄청난 손상을 가하는

Match each collocation with the correct definition.
각 연어에 알맞은 뜻을 찾아 연결하시오.

a. in captivity – being held in or kept in a cage
   갇혀진 상태의
b. prey upon – to hunt another animal for food
   ~을 먹이로 삼다
c. in favor of – arguing for, supporting, or choosing
   ~을 지지하여
d. be torn apart – to break into many small pieces
   부서지다
e. stand out – to be prominent or easy to notice 두드러지다

Circle the word closest in meaning to each underlined word.
각 밑줄 친 단어의 뜻과 가장 가까운 단어를 찾아 동그라미 하시오.

정답 | 1. (C)   2. (A)   3. (B)
     4. (B)   5. (D)   6. (C)

해석 |
1. 그 고객은 신용 카드 요금의 청구지가 어디인지 추측했다.
   (A) 낙서했다   (B) 묘사했다
   (C) 추정했다   (D) 애원했다

2. 그 왕국은 천연자원 덕분에 기원전 12세기에 번성했다.
   (A) 번창했다   (B) 상기됐다
   (C) 녹았다   (D) 영양분을 공급했다

3. 그 회의는 나노테크놀로지 분야의 몇몇 전문가들의 강의를 포함했다.
   (A) 악기들   (B) 전문가들
   (C) 장애인들   (D) 포유류들

4. 그 여자는 가족이 부유했기 때문에 아주 특권적인 어린 시절을 보냈다.
   (A) 드러난   (B) 혜택 받은
   (C) 값비싼   (D) 빈곤한

5. 지난 주말에 남아메리카에 엄청난 지진이 있었다.
   (A) 간섭하는   (B) 과장하는
   (C) 번영한   (D) 처참한

6. 많은 사람들은 밤하늘에 나타나는 별들에 매혹된다.
   (A) 흩뿌려졌다   (B) 방치됐다
   (C) 매료됐다   (D) 어지럽혀졌다

Fill in each blank with the correct collocation.
알맞은 연어를 골라 빈칸을 채우시오.

정답 | 1. in captivity   2. was torn apart
     3. prey upon   4. stood out
     5. in favor of

해석 |
1. 어떤 야생동물은 동물원에 가둬져서 길러지고 있다.
2. 그 시계탑은 내전 중에 부서졌다.
3. 많은 연구들에 따르면 황소개구리는 더 작은 개구리들도 먹는다.
4. 그 교수의 지성은 그의 동료들 사이에서 두드러진다.
5. 배심원은 그 화재 사건에서 피해자를 지지하는 판결을 내렸다.

STEP 1   pp. 74-75

정답 | 1. (D)   2. (C)

갈라파고스땅거북

　갈라파고스땅거북은 세계에서 가장 큰 거북이고 지구상에서 가장 오래 사는 동물 중 하나이다. 갈라파고스땅거북들은 무게가 400킬로그램에 달하고, 사육되면 170년 동안 산다고 알려져 있다.
　갈라파고스땅거북은 철저히 초식성이다. 그들은 선인장, 풀, 산딸기류를 먹고 하루에 8~9시간을 먹이를 찾아 다닌다. 다른 거북들처럼 갈라파고스땅거북은 아주 느리게 움직이고 보호를 위해 두꺼운 등껍질에 의존한다. 다 자란 갈라파고스땅거북은 자연적 포식자가 없지만, 어린 거북은 갈라파고스매의 먹이가 되고, 거북의 알은 쥐와 멧돼지의 일상적인 먹이가 된다. 갈라파고스땅거북이 현재 멸종 위기에 처한 것은 아니지만, 한때 그들의 아종들이 살고 있던 갈라파고스 제도의 열 개 섬 중 다섯 곳에서만 생존하는 거북들의 수가 여전히 분포하고 있다.

Glossary cactus 선인장
Galapagos Archipelago 갈라파고스 제도

• **Structure Zone**

현재분사를 써서 동시 동작을 나타낸다. 이때 분사형은 'as + 주어 + 동사'로 풀어 쓸 수 있다.

Galapagos tortoises... can spend 8 or 9 hours per day **searching** for food.
→ Galapagos tortoises... can spend 8 or 9 hours per day **as it searches** for food.

1. 아래 문장 중 지문에서 첫 번째 음영 처리된 문장의 핵심 정보를 가장 잘 나타낸 것은 어느 것인가?
   (A) 갈라파고스땅거북은 천적이 없지만, 어린 거북은 때때로 쥐와 멧돼지의 먹이가 되는 매의 알을 빈번히 먹는다.
   (B) 새들은 갈라파고스땅거북을 먹이로 삼는데, 그들의 껍질은 그 거북을 다른 동물들로부터 안전하게 해 준다.
   (C) 갈라파고스땅거북은 천적이 없지만, 매, 돼지, 그리고 쥐와 같이 원래부터 섬에 있었던 것이 아닌 몇몇 동물들은 거북을 먹는다.
   (D) 새들은 빈번히 어린 갈라파고스땅거북을 먹고, 다른 동물들은 보통 갈라파고스땅거북의 알을 먹지만, 다 자란 거북은 다른 동물로부터 안전하다.

   ◉ 음영 처리된 문장을 살펴보면 다 자란 갈라파고스땅거북을 먹는 동물은 없지만, 어린 거북과 거북의 알은 다른 동물들의 먹이가 된다고 하였다. (D)를 제외한 다른 보기들의 내용은 지문의 문장과 조금씩 다르다.

2. 아래 문장 중 지문에서 두 번째 음영 처리된 문장의 핵심 정보를 가장 잘 나타낸 것은 어느 것인가?
   (A) 갈라파고스땅거북은 갈라파고스 제도의 열 개 섬 중 다섯 곳에서 멸종 위기에 처해있다.
   (B) 몇몇 아종은 갈라파고스 제도의 몇 군데 섬에서 죽을 위기에 처해있다.
   (C) 갈라파고스땅거북의 아종이 살고 있는 열 개의 섬 중 다섯 곳에서만 여전히 몇몇의 거북이 있다.
   (D) 갈라파고스 제도의 모든 섬 중, 열 곳에서만 거북이 생존하고 있다.

   ◉ 음영 처리된 문장의 내용은 갈라파고스 제도의 열 곳의 섬 중 다섯 곳에서만 갈라파고스땅거북의 아종이 살고 있다는 내용이다. 따라서 답은 (C)가 된다.

• Note-Taking

The Galapagos Tortoise

• the largest species of tortoise
• reach weights of 400 kilograms & live for 170 yrs.
• are herbivorous, move slowly, & have a thick shell for protection
• young tortoises & eggs – prey for some animals
• the populations of living tortoises have decreased

SUMMARY
The Galapagos tortoise is the largest tortoise in the world. Its weight is about 400 kilograms, and its lifespan is 170 years. It is herbivorous, moves slowly, and has a thick shell to protect it. Young tortoises and eggs are often eaten by other animals. About half of its subspecies have died out.

갈라파고스땅거북은 세계에서 가장 큰 거북이다. 그것의 무게는 약 400킬로그램이고, 수명은 170년이다. 그것은 초식성이고, 느리게 움직이며 자신을 보호하는 두꺼운 껍질을 지니고 있다. 어린 거북과 알은 다른 동물들에게 종종 먹이가 된다. 그것의 아종 중 반 정도가 없어졌다.

VOCAB Match each word with the correct definition.
각 단어에 알맞은 뜻을 찾아 연결하시오.

a. creature – a living thing that is not a plant 생물
b. strictly – of one particular type 철저히
c. rely on – to need or depend on something ~에 의지하다
d. protection – a prevention from harmful elements 보호
e. population – the number of a group of specific animals (동물 등의) 개체 수

• More Info Zone

갈라파고스 제도

갈라파고스 제도는 남아메리카 동태평양에 있는 제도로서, 아메리카 대륙으로부터 1,000킬로미터 떨어져 있다. 1535년 에스파냐의 T. 데 베를랑가가 발견하였는데, 그 당시 무인도로서 많은 거북들이 살고 있었다. 바다거북을 에스파냐어로 galápago라고 하는데, 섬 이름은 이 단어에서 따온 것이다. 갈라파고스땅거북 이외에도 바다도마뱀, 갈라파고스펭귄, 코바네우, 각종 파충류 등 많은 독특한 생물들이 살고 있다.

STEP 2
pp. 76-77

정답 | 1. (C)   2. (B)

미국 사실주의

　미국 사실주의는 미술, 음악, 그리고 문학에서 나타난 운동으로, 20세기 초반에 미국에서 번성하였다. 이전 세기의 고결한 이상과 반대로, 이 운동은 미국 삶의 불쾌한 현실을 그대로 보여주었다. George Bellows, John French Sloan, 그리고 Edward Hopper와 같은 화가들은 권투 시합, 혼잡한 술집, 그리고 늦은 밤의 비어있는 식당과 같이 노동자 계층의 도시 생활 장면들을 담아냈다. W.C. Handy와 Scott Joplin 같은 음악가들은 1910년대의 정신 없는 도시의 삶만큼이나 블루스와 재즈와 같은 흑인 음악 형식에 의해서도 많은 영향을 받은, 빠르고 혼란스러운 작품들을 썼다.

　하지만 미국 사실주의는 흔히 Mark Twain, Henry James, F. Scott Fitzgerald, 그리고 Ernest Hemingway와 같은 전문가들을 아우르는 문학계의 운동으로 기억되고 있다. 미국 내전 후, 작가들은 현실적인 인물들과 어려운 도덕적 선택을 묘사하는 단순한 언어를 지지하며, 꾸밈이 심한 19세기 소설의 산문체와 복잡한 줄거리를 버리기 시작했다. 이들 이야기의 주제는 부유하고 특혜받은 엘리트의 삶을 극적으로 표현하는 것에서, 보통 사람들의 극히 현실적인 분투로 옮겨갔다.

• **Structure Zone**

'as much A as B'는 'B만큼 A에 의해서도 많이'라는 의미이며 A와 B의 품사는 동일해야 한다.

Musicians including W.C. Handy and Scott Joplin wrote... pieces influenced **as much** by African-American musical forms such as the blues and jazz
　　　　　　　　　　　　　A
as by the frantic pace of city life in the 1910s.
　　　　　　　　　　　B

1. 아래 문장 중 지문에서 첫 번째 음영 처리된 문장의 핵심 정보를 가장 잘 나타낸 것은 어느 것인가?
   (A) 재즈와 블루스 음악가들은 도시의 일상적인 삶과 함께 W.C. Handy와 Scott Joplin 같은 20세기 초반의 작곡가들을 고무했다.
   (B) 블루스와 재즈는 1910년대의 W.C. Handy와 Scott Joplin 같은 음악가들이 쓴 음악에 영향을 준 주요 요소 두 가지였다.
   (C) W.C. Handy, Scott Joplin과 다른 작곡가들은 블루스, 재즈, 그리고 대도시의 빠른 삶 등의 세 가지에 영감을 받았다.
   (D) 20세기에, Scott Joplin과 W.C. Handy 같은 작곡가들은 블루스와 재즈 음악을 쓰기 위해 도시 삶의 빠른 속도에 영감을 받았다.

   ▶ 음영 처리된 문장은 W.C. Handy와 Scott Joplin 같은 음악가들이 블루스, 재즈, 그리고 도시 삶에 영향을 받아 빠른 속도의 곡들을 만들었다고 하였다. 이와 같은 내용이 담긴 문장을 보기에서 찾으면 (C)이다.

2. 아래 문장 중 지문에서 두 번째 음영 처리된 문장의 핵심 정보를 가장 잘 나타낸 것은 어느 것인가?
   (A) 미국 사실주의 소설들은 단순한 언어와 현실적인 인물들을 담았던 내전 전의 소설들과 대조하여 복잡한 내용을 담고 있다.
   (B) 미국 내전 이전, 책들은 복잡한 줄거리와 장식적인 단어들로 적혀 있었는데, 내전 후에는 덜 복잡해지고 더 현실적이 되었다.
   (C) 19세기에, 소설들은 짧은 문장들과 평범한 단어들로 쓰였지만 미국 내전 후에 작가들의 단어 선택은 좀 더 시적이고 비현실적이 되었다.
   (D) 미국 내전 전과 끝난 이후에 이르는 시간 동안, 미국 소설의 언어는 좀 더 복잡해지고 인물들과 도덕관념은 덜 복잡해졌다.

   ▶ 음영 처리된 문장의 내용을 정리해 보면, 미국 내전 이전의 글들은 복잡하고 꾸밈이 심했고, 그 이후의 글들은 현실적인 인물들과 어려운 도덕적 선택을 간단한 언어로 나타냈다. 따라서 답은 (B)가 된다.

• **Note-Taking**

P1　MI　American Realism – a movement that flourished in the 20th century
　　SD　portrayed the gritty reality of American life
　　　　• painters – showed scenes of working class city life
　　　　• musicians – wrote fast-paced & chaotic pieces

P2　MI　American Realism – remembered as a movement in literature
　　SD　• writers – used simple language w/ realistic characters & difficult moral choices
　　　　– wrote about real struggles of regular ppl.

VOCAB _ Write the correct word for each definition.
각 뜻에 알맞은 단어를 찾아 적으시오.

a. preceding 앞선　　b. chaotic 혼란스러운
c. complicated 복잡한　　d. moral 도덕의
e. struggle 분투

STEP 3	pp. 78-79
정답	1. (D)　　2. (A)

토성

　태양계의 모든 행성들이 천문학자들에게는 각기 흥미롭지만, 토성만큼 독특한 행성도 드물다. 근처에 있는 목성처럼, 토성은 소위 가스체 거대 행성이다. 대부분의 덩어리는 가스로 된 수소와 헬륨으로 되어 있다. 이 가스들은 액체 형태의 금속성 수소 층을 감싼다. 이 층에 있는 수소는 토성의 핵이 중력적인 압력을 받아 액체의 금속으로 압축된 것이다.

　하지만 토성은 그것을 둘러싼 아름다운 얼음 고리로 가장 잘 알려져 있다. 다른 행성들도 고리 체계가 있지만, 토성의 고리만큼 거대한 것은 없다. 이 고리들은 토성의 표면 위 7,000킬로미터의 높이에서 우주를 향해 73,000킬로미터나 뻗어 있다. 이 고리들이 어떻게 형성되었는지 천문학자들이 확실히 알지는 못하지만, 몇 가지 가설이 존재한다. 이 고리들은 토성의 중력에 의해 떨어진 달이 남아 있는 것일 수도 있고, 토성이 본래 형성되었던 구름의 잔여물일 수도 있으며, 토성의 달 중 하나인 얼음 성분으로 된 외층일 수도 있다.

　토성의 고리들은 17세기부터 천문학자들을 매료시켜왔지만, 토성은 1940년대에 다른 이유로 유명해지기 시작했다. 바로 그것의 달인 타이탄의 독특함 때문이었다. 토성의 51개 달 중, 타이탄은 두 가지 이유로 천문학자들에게 두드러진다. 그것은 태양계에서 대기를 지닌 유일한 달이고, 지구를 제외하면 표면에 안정된 상태의 액체를 지닌 유일한 물체이다. 이 두 가지 사실은 천문학자들로 하여금 타이탄의 얼음 성분의 표면 아래 깊은 곳에 생명체가 살 수도 있다고 추측하게 해왔다.

• **Structure Zone**

> • '대부분의'이라는 뜻으로 쓰이는 most는 단수로 취급한다.
> **Most** of its mass **comes** from gaseous hydrogen and helium.
>
> • 앞에 나온 명사를 다시 쓸 때는 관계대명사 that을 써서 중복을 피할 수 있다.
> Though other planets have ring systems, none is as extensive as **that(=the ring system)** of Saturn.

1. 아래 문장 중 지문에서 첫 번째 음영 처리된 문장의 핵심 정보를 가장 잘 나타낸 것은 어느 것인가?
   (A) 토성 고리들은 아마도 중력 때문에 달이 부서져 구름이 되어, 그것이 달의 표면으로부터 떨어져 나온 얼음과 결합하여 형성되었을 것이다.
   (B) 얼음과 다른 물질들은 중력에 의해 압축된 구름을 토성을 만들었고, 그 행성을 둘러싼 고리들을 만들었다.
   (C) 토성의 고리들은 그 행성의 중력과 본래 토성이 형성된 물질의 구름, 그리고 얼음 층이 달을 부수었을 때 만들어졌다.
   (D) 토성의 고리들은 달을 부순 중력, 토성의 형성이 남긴 잔여물, 또는 달의 얼음 층에 의해 만들어졌을 수 있다

   ◉ 지문에서 첫 번째 음영 처리된 문장에 따르면, 토성의 고리가 어떻게 형성되었는지에 대해 몇 가지 가설이 존재한다고 하였다. 그것은 토성의 중력으로 인해 생긴 달의 잔여물일 수도 있고, 구름 층의 잔여물일 수도 있으며 토성의 달 중 하나의 얼음 형태의 외층일 수도 있다. 이 같은 내용을 찾으면 (D)가 답이 된다.

2. 아래 문장 중 지문에서 두 번째 음영 처리된 문장의 핵심 정보를 가장 잘 나타낸 것은 어느 것인가?
   (A) 토성의 고리들은 오래 전부터 과학자들에게 흥미로웠지만, 토성의 달인 타이탄도 아주 흥미롭다.
   (B) 천문학자들은 1600년대부터 토성의 고리에 매료되었지만, 1940년대에 천문학자들은 타이탄의 고리들에 더 큰 관심을 쏟기 시작했다.
   (C) 1940년대, 천문학자들은 토성의 고리 중 하나인 디이탄에 흥미를 갖기 시작했는데, 그것이 고리들 중 가장 독특하기 때문이다.
   (D) 천문학자들이 1600년대부터 연구해오긴 했지만, 타이탄의 독특한 성질은 그들이 토성의 고리들에 더 관심을 갖게 만들었다.

   ◉ 두 번째 음영 처리된 문장의 내용은, 천문학자들이 오래 전부터 토성의 고리에 관심을 가졌지만, 1940년대에 타이탄으로 인해 토성이 유명해지기 시작했다는 것이다. 이를 가장 잘 나타낸 문장은 (A)이다.

VOCAB_ Find the correct word in the passage for each of the given definition.
주어진 뜻에 알맞은 단어를 지문에서 찾으시오.

a. extensive 아주 넓은   b. hypothesis 가설
c. remnant 남은 부분   d. stable 안정된

• **Note-Taking** (Sample Answer)

P1 MI Saturn – so-called "gas giant"
    SD hydrogen & helium surround metallic hydrogen compressed into a liquid metal

P2 MI Saturn's extensive rings of ice
    SD could be the remains of a moon torn apart by Saturn's gravity, remnants of the cloud, or the icy outer layer of one of Saturn's moons

P3 MI one of Saturn's 51 moons, Titan
    SD has an atmosphere & stable bodies of liquid on its surface

• **More Info Zone**

타이탄

토성의 가장 큰 위성인 타이탄은 질량이 크고 표면온도가 낮기 때문에 태양계 행성의 위성 54개 중 유일하게 대기를 갖고 있어 지구와 가장 흡사한 위성으로 알려져 있다. 목성의 위성인 가니메데에 이어 태양계에서 두 번째로 큰 위성이며, 1655년에 네덜란드 천문학자인 Christiaan Huygens에 의해 발견되었다. 그는 이 위성을 '토성의 위성'이라 불렀으며, 후에 영국인 천문학자인 William Herschel이 그리스 신화의 티탄족에서 이름을 따서 '타이탄'이라는 이름을 붙였다.

UNIT TEST pp.80-81

정답 | 1. (B) 2. (A) 3. (D) 4. (C)
5. Classical Economics (A), (C), (F)
Keynes' Theory (E), (G)

유효수요와 유효공급

고전 경제학에서, 상품의 가격은 상품에 대한 공급과 수요에 의해 결정된다. 많은 사람들이 어떤 것을 구매하기를 원하지만 소수의 사람만이 그것을 팔고자 하거나 팔 수 있으면, 상품의 가격은 상승할 것이다. 반면에, 소수의 사람들이 어떤 것을 사고 싶어하지만 많은 사람들이 그것을 팔고 싶어하거나 팔아야 하면, 상품의 가격은 하락할 것이다. 구매자와 판매자가 가격의 합의점에 이르렀을 때, 그 제품에 대한 시장은 평형에 도달했다고 한다. 고전 경제학자들은 평형이 시장의 자연적인 상태이며 시장에서 한 상품에 대한 수요가 지나치게 많으면, 다른 시장에서는 지나치게 많은 공급이 이루어진다고 믿었다.

하지만, 1930년대의 대공황은 세계 많은 경제의 기반을 흔들었고, 고전 경제학 이론들이 비난 받았다. 이 위기에 대한 정부의 반응은 Keynes의 경제 이론과 그것의 중심 사상 중 하나인 유효수요와 관념적 수요에 대한 흥미를 다시 불러일으켰다.

Keynes는 한 시장의 수요가 다른 시장의 수요 부족으로 생기는 것이 가능하다고 주장했다. 예를 들어, 만약 교사에 대한 수요가 낮다면, 교사에 대한 보수도 낮을 것이다. 이것은 교사의 급료가 하락하는 원인이 된다. 교사의 급료가 하락하면, 그들의 자유 재량

물건들에 대한 수요도 하락한다. 한 교사가 새 텔레비전(관념적 수요)에 많은 돈을 쓰고 싶어하지만, 그녀는 하락한 급료 때문에 걱정스러워서 사실상 아주 적은 돈을 쓰게 된다(유효수요). 이것은 경제에 아주 좋지 않은 결과를 줄 수 있는데, 노동에 대한 수요가 감소하면, 노동자가 물건을 사려는 수요도 감소하기 때문이다. 물건 수요 감소는 공급자들이 물건을 더 적게 생산하게 하고, 그것은 노동자에 대한 수요를 낮춰 악순환이 반복된다. Keynes의 이론은 고전 경제학을 반박하며 현대 사회에서 나타나는 새로운 경제의 전형적인 예를 보여준다.

Glossary　equilibrium 평형 상태　notional 관념적인
　　　　　　 discretionary 자유재량에 의한

• **Structure Zone**

> • 관계대명사 which는 앞에 나온 명사 뿐 아니라, 구를 대신해서 쓰일 수 있다.
> The dropping demand for goods causes <u>suppliers to produce less</u>, **which** further reduces the demand for labor and the cycle repeats.
>
> • 동시에 일어나는 일을 쓸 때는 'and + 절' 형태 대신 쉼표와 현재분사를 써서 나타낼 수 있다.
> The Keynes' theory shows new economic paradigms in modern society, **refuting** the classical economics.

1. 아래 문장 중 지문에서 음영 처리된 문장의 핵심 정보를 가장 잘 나타낸 것은 어느 것인가?
   (A) 구매자들은 판매자로부터 물건을 사는 것을 거부하여 시장의 평형을 이룰 수 있다.
   (B) 구매자들과 판매자들이 물건의 가격에 동의했을 때 시장의 평형이 이루어진다.
   (C) 판매자들이 물건을 팔기를 원할 때, 그들이 가격에 동의할 때까지 구매자들과 협상해야 한다.
   (D) 구매자들과 판매자들은 그들이 물건을 사거나 팔고 싶어할 때 시장 평형을 이룰 수 있다.

   ◉ 음영 처리된 문장의 내용은 시장의 평형에 대해 설명하고 있다. 구매자와 판매자가 가격에 대해 합의했을 때 시장의 평형이 이루어진다고 하였으므로, 이를 가장 잘 나타낸 문장은 (B)이다.

2. 작가는 the Great Depression 에 대해 무엇을 나타내는가?
   (A) Keynes의 경제 이론은 그 위기에 대한 원인과 결과를 설명할 수 있다.
   (B) 그 위기는 평형에 이르지 못한 시장들 때문에 생겼다.
   (C) 높은 유효수요는 대부분의 사람들이 감당하기에 너무 높은 가격으로 이어진다.
   (D) 그 위기는 주로 선진 경제국의 낮은 관념적 수요 때문에 생겼다.

   ◉ 지문에 따르면, 1930년에 일어난 경제 대공황은 고전 경제학 탓으로 여겨졌고, 정부들은 Keynes의 경제 이론에 관심을 다시 가지게 되는 계기가 되었다고 하였다. 따라서 답은 (A)이다.

3. 지문에서 단어 This 가 가리키는 것은
   (A) 하락하는 급료에 대한 교사의 걱정
   (B) 새 텔레비전과 같은 자유재량 물건에 대한 교사의 수요
   (C) 한 개인이 감당할 수 있는 것보다 더 많은 돈을 상품에 쓰는 것
   (D) 한 개인이 쓰고 싶은 것보다 더 적은 돈을 상품에 쓰는 것

   ◉ 대명사 This가 가리키는 것은 바로 앞 문장에서 찾는 것이 좋다. 문맥을 살펴보면 주어진 This가 결과적으로 노동자의 수요를 감소시키고, 노동자의 물건에 대한 수요도 감소시키는 것을 알 수 있다. 이러한 문맥에 맞는 내용을 찾으면 (D)가 답이 된다.

4. 3단락의 주제는 무엇인가?
   (A) 노동력에 대한 수요는 자유재량 물건에 대한 수요와 공급에 영향을 미친다.
   (B) Keynes의 경제 이론은 정부들이 경제 위기에 대응하는 데 도움을 준다.
   (C) 유효수요는 한 시장의 수요 부족이 다른 시장의 수요를 어떻게 하락시킬 수 있는지 설명해 준다.
   (D) 유효공급과 유효수요는 물건에 대한 시장의 가격이 어떻게 평형에 이르는지 설명해 준다.

   ◉ 3단락에서 한 시장의 수요 부족이 다른 시장에 어떠한 영향을 미치는지 교사의 수요와 급료, 그리고 자유재량 물건을 예를 들어 설명한다. 교사의 수요 부족은 결국 교사의 급료의 하락으로 이어지고 이는 결국 경제에 좋지 않은 영향을 준다고 하였다. 따라서 이를 가장 잘 나타낸 문장은 (C)가 된다.

5. 보기에서 적당한 구를 찾아서 그것들과 관련된 카테고리에 넣어라. 보기 중에서 두 개는 사용되지 않을 것이다.

   고전 경제학　/　Keynes 이론

   보기
   (A) 공급과 수요가 가격을 결정한다고 주장한다.
   (B) 평형이 공급을 결정한다고 추정한다.
   (C) 평형은 시장의 자연적인 상태라고 여긴다.
   (D) 유효수요가 관념적 수요보다 더 중요하다고 주장한다.
   (E) 유효수요에 중점을 둔다.
   (F) 경제 대공황의 원인으로 여겨진다.
   (G) 한 시장의 수요 부족이 다른 시장의 수요를 만든다고 주장한다.

   ◉ 고전 경제학에서는 공급과 수요가 가격을 결정하고, 판매자와 구매자가 가격에 동의해서 만들어진 평형이 시장의 자연적인 상태라고 여겨진다. 또한 고전 경제학은 경제 대공황의 원인으로 여겨졌다. 한편 Keynes의 경제 이론의 주요 사상은 유효수요로, 그는 한 시장의 수요 부족이 다른 시장의 수요에 영향을 미친다고 주장하였다. (B)와 (D)는 지문에서 언급되지 않은 사실이다.

VOCABULARY TEST　　　　pp.82-83

Recall the essential words in the unit to reinforce your vocabulary acquisition. Write the meaning of each word in your language.
유닛에서 배운 주요 단어들을 떠올려 각 단어의 뜻을 쓰시오.

predator | 포식동물
compress | 압축하다
speculate | 추측하다
fascinate | 매료하다
protection | 보호
remnant | 잔여물
protest | 대항하다
elect | 선출하다
moral | 도덕의
constrain | 강요하다
struggle | 분투
extensive | 거대한
hypothesis | 가설
notional | 관념적인
complicated | 복잡한
strictly | 철저히
rely on | ~에 의존하다
be torn apart | 부서지다
stable | 안정적인
in captivity | 가둬진 상태의

population | 개체 수
gritty | 불쾌한 현실을 그대로 보여주는
herbivorous | 초식성의
devastating | 엄청난 손실을 가하는
preceding | 앞선
chaotic | 혼란스러운
privileged | 특권적인
flourish | 번성하다
racial | 인종적인
luminary | 전문가
determine | 결정하다
reconciliation | 화해
discretionary | 자유재량에 의한
legible | 읽을 수 있는
creature | 생물
imprisoned | 수감된
in favor of | ~을 지지하여
equilibrium | 평형 상태
prey upon | ~을 먹이로 삼다
stand out | 두드러지다

Complete each sentence with the correct word or collocation.
문장에 알맞은 단어나 연어를 찾아 쓰시오.

정답 | 1. hypotheses   2. determined
3. struggles   4. reconciliation
5. chaotic   6. preyed upon
7. discretionary   8. imprisoned
9. preceding   10. constrained

해석 |
1. 토성의 고리들이 어떻게 형성되었는지에 대해 몇 가지 가설들이 있다.
2. 물건의 가격은 그것에 대한 공급과 수요에 의해 결정된다.
3. 그 소설은 보통 사람들의 아주 현실적인 분투를 보여주었다.
4. Nelson Mandela는 인종적 화해의 시작을 총괄했다.
5. 그 음악가들은 빠르고 혼란스러운 작품들을 썼다.
6. 어린 갈라파고스땅거북은 갈라파고스매의 먹이가 된다.
7. 교사들의 급료가 하락하면, 그들의 자유재량 물건들에 대한 수요도 하락할 것이다.
8. 그 정치인은 27년 이상 수감되었다.
9. 이전 세기와 반대로, 미국 사실주의는 불쾌한 현실을 그대로 보여주었다.
10. 한 시장의 수요는 다른 시장의 수요의 부족에 의해 강요될 수 있다.

PROGRESS TEST ❶

pp.86-93

정답 | 1. (D)   2. (A)   3. C   4. (B)   5. (C)
6. (A)   7. (C)   8. (A)   9. (D)   10. (B)
11. (D), (C), (E)

바이칼 호수

흔히 '러시아의 갈라파고스'라고 일컬어지는 바이칼 호수는 세계에서 가장 독특한 지리적 형태를 지닌 곳 중 하나이다. 그것의 크기, 연대, 그리고 지리학적 고립 때문에 독특한 식물군과 동물군을 아주 다양하게 지니고 있어서 의미 있는 과학적 호기심을 이끌어내는 곳이다. 불행히도, 그곳은 인간 활동에 의해 끊임없이 훼손될 위협에 처해있다.

A 그 호수는 모스크바 동쪽으로 4,350킬로미터 떨어져 있는 시베리아 남동쪽에 위치하고, 모든 면이 산으로 둘러싸여져 있다. B 길이는 640킬로미터, 깊이는 거의 1,700미터로, 세계에서 가장 깊은 호수이다. C 또한 2천만년에서 2천5백만년 전에 형성된 것으로 보이는 지구에서 가장 오래된 민물 호수일 것이다. D

호수 안과 주변에는 1,340의 동물 종(種)이 사는데, 그 중 745종은 그 지역의 토종이다. 이 동물들 중에는 민물 환경에서만 발견되는 유일한 표범 종류인 바이칼 물범이 있다. 호수는 또한 그 지역의 아주 별미인 흰 물고기종인 오믈의 서식지이기도 하다. 어부들이 오믈을 많이 찾으면서 수산업계는 이 호수에서 왕성히 활동했다. 이것이 오믈 수의 위험한 하락을 초래했지만, 엄격한 쿼터제(할당)가 부과되면서 그 수가 다시 늘어났다.

그 호수는 또한 다른 심각한 환경적 위협에서도 벗어나고 있다. 그것의 물에 직접적으로 폐기물을 배출했던 제지공장은 2013년에 파산했고, 호숫가를 따라 파이프라인을 세우려고 계획했던 정유회사는 다른 경로를 이용하라는 정부의 압력을 받았다. 바이칼 호수에 지장을 주는 또 다른 인간 활동에는, 지속적인 지역관광사업의 발달 및 그 지역에 방사성 폐기물을 저장하게 될까봐 많은 사람들이 두려워하는 우라늄 발전소를 지으려는 계획 등이 있다.

바이칼 호수를 안전하고 순수하게 지키려는 노력은 계속되고 있다. 호수의 아름다움과 생물학적인 다양성은 러시아와 외국의 많은 이들로 하여금 그것의 보존에 앞장서게 하고 있다.

Glossary endemic 고유의, 풍토적인   quota 한도(량)

• **Structure Zone**

• 관계대명사 which는 앞에 나온 사물뿐만 아니라, 절 전체를 받아 부연 설명하는 데 쓰일 수 있다.
  ... it is home to a vast array of unique flora and fauna, which makes it a site of significant scientific interest.

• 'to + 현재완료' 시제는 주절보다 앞선 과거를 나타낼 때 쓰인다.
  ... it is believed to have formed between 20 and 25 million years ago.

1. 지문의 주제는 무엇인가?
   (A) 바이칼 호수에는 수많은 종류의 동물들이 있다.
   (B) 바이칼 호수에는 많은 수의 식물이 있다.
   (C) 다양한 인간 활동이 바이칼 호수를 오염시켜왔다.
   (D) 바이칼 호수는 독특하지만 위협받고 있는 생태계이다.

   ● 주어진 지문은 바이칼 호수에 살고 있는 생물들과 이를 위협하고 있는 인간 활동들을 설명하고 있다. 따라서 지문의 주제로 알맞은 것은 (D)이다.

2. 지문에서 단어 despoiled를 대체하기에 가장 적합한 것은
   (A) 파괴된   (B) 발달한
   (C) 중단된   (D) 개조된

   ● despoiled는 '훼손된'이라는 의미이다. 따라서 이를 대체하기에 적절한 것은 '파괴된'이라는 의미를 지닌 (A) ravaged이다.

3. 주어진 문장이 2단락에 들어갈 수 있는 곳을 가리키는 네 개의 네모 [■]를 보시오.
   사실, 바이칼 호수는 지구의 얼지 않은 민물 중 20%를 포함하고 있다고 추정된다.
   이 문장이 어디에 가장 적절한가?

   ● 주어진 문장은 바이칼 호수가 지구의 민물 중 많은 부분을 차지하고 있다는 것을 서술하고 있으므로, 바이칼 호수의 규모를 중점으로 다루고 있는 문장 바로 뒤인 C 에 위치하는 것이 알맞다.

4. 다음 중 바이칼 호수에 대해 사실이 아닌 것은 무엇인가?
   (A) 그 주위 모두 산으로 둘러싸여 있다.
   (B) 모스크바로부터 640km 떨어져 있다.
   (C) 다른 어떤 호수보다도 더 깊다.
   (D) 적어도 2천만년 이상 되었다.

   ● 지문에 따르면, 바이칼 호수는 모스크바로부터 동쪽으로 4,350킬로미터 떨어져 있고, 그것의 길이가 640킬로미터이다. 따라서 답은 (B)이다.

5. 2단락에서 작가의 주요 목적은
   (A) 시베리아 남동쪽에 있는 민물 호수를 소개하는 것이다.
   (B) 바이칼 호수의 먼 위치를 강조하는 것이다.
   (C) 바이칼 호수의 물리적 특징을 묘사하는 것이다.
   (D) 바이칼 호수가 어떻게 변화해왔는지 보여주는 것이다.

   ● 작가는 2단락에서 바이칼 호수의 위치와 규모, 깊이 등의 특징을 설명하고 있다.

6. 오믈의 어업에 대해 무엇을 추론할 수 있는가?
   (A) 과거보다 더 작은 규모로 일어난다.
   (B) 정부의 도움으로 크게 성장했다.
   (C) 특별히 디자인된 낚시 그물을 쓴다.
   (D) 호수의 물개 수 하락을 이끌었다.

   ● 지문에 따르면, 오믈 어업이 바이칼 호수에서 왕성하였지만 엄격한 쿼터제가 부과되었다고 하였다. 이러한 내용을 바탕으로, 과거보다 그 규모가 작아졌다는 것을 알 수 있다.

7. 지문에서 단어 discharging과 의미가 가장 가까운 것은
   (A) 반복하다   (B) 묵살하다
   (C) 분출하다   (D) 여과하다

   ● discharge는 '방출하다'라는 뜻을 가지고 있다. 보기 중 이와 가장 가까운 뜻을 가진 단어는 (C)이다.

8. 지문에서 단어 its와 의미가 가장 가까운 것은
   (A) 호수   (B) 제지공장
   (C) 폐기물   (D) 정유회사

   ● 지문에서, 제지공장이 폐기물을 '그것의' 하수로 방출했다고 하였다. 따라서 답은 (바이칼) 호수임을 알 수 있다.

9. 아래 문장 중 지문에서 음영 처리된 문장의 핵심 정보를 가장 잘 나타낸 것은 어느 것인가? 잘못된 보기들은 중요한 의미를 바꾸거나 핵심 정보를 생략한다.
   (A) 그 호수의 관광사업은 우라늄 발전소를 지으려는 계획에 의해 지장 받았다.
   (B) 사람들은 관광업에서 나오는 돈이 방사능 저장지역을 대체하는 데 도움을 줄 거라고 기대한다.
   (C) 그 호수 근처에 저장된 방사능 물질은 우라늄 발전소에 의해 처리될 것이다.
   (D) 발달하는 관광사업과 우라늄 발전소 계획은 그 호수를 위협하고 있다.

   ● 음영 처리된 문장의 내용은 호수를 위협하는 인간 활동 중 관광사업 발달과 우라늄 발전소 건설 계획이 있다고 하였으므로, 이를 가장 잘 나타낸 문장은 (D)이다.

10. 사실이 아닌 것은
    (A) 바이칼 호수에는 민물 물개들이 있다.
    (B) 바이칼 호수는 세계에서 가장 큰 호수이다.
    (C) 오믈은 바이칼 호수에 사는 종 중 하나이다.
    (D) 산업시설이 바이칼 호수 주변 지역에 지어질 수도 있다.

    ● 지문에 따르면, 바이칼 호수는 세계에서 가장 깊은 호수이며, 가장 큰 호수라는 것은 언급되지 않았다.

11. 지문의 간단한 요약을 위해 도입 문장이 아래에 주어진다. 지문에서 가장 중요한 내용을 표현하는 세 개의 보기를 선택하여 요약문을 완성하라.

> 다양한 독특한 생물들이 사는 바이칼 호수는 인간 개발에 따른 위험에 직면해 있다.

보기
(A) 그 호수에는 745 종의 토종 동물들이 산다.
(B) 그 호수는 시베리아 남쪽의 산악 지역에 위치해 있다.
(C) 그 호수에는 몇몇의 토종 생물들이 있고, 엄격한 쿼터제가 부과되었다.
(D) 그 호수는 세계에서 가장 깊고 오래된 민물 호수이다.
(E) 몇몇 인간 활동들이 호수를 위험에 빠트렸지만, 그 지역을 보존하려는 계획들이 있다.
(F) 그 지역의 여행산업은 우라늄 발전소를 지어 호수를 보호하려고 하고 있다.

◉ 지문은 바이칼 호수의 지리적, 지형적 특징, 그리고 그 지역 고유의 생물들을 소개하면서, 인간 활동으로 위험에 처해있지만 오늘날 그 지역과 고유 생물들을 보호하려는 노력들이 계획되고 있다고 설명하고 있다. 따라서 (D), (C), (E)를 차례로 선택하면 된다.

정답 | 12. (B) 13. (A) 14. (A) 15. (C) 16. B
17. (C) 18. (D) 19. (B) 20. (B) 21. (C)
22. Parenchyma Cells (A), (E), (H)
　　Collenchyma Cells (B), (I)
　　Sclerenchyma Cells (D), (F)

식물 세포

많은 부분에서 동물의 세포와 비슷하기는 하지만, 식물 세포는 다른 진핵 세포와 구별되는 여러 가지 특징을 가지고 있다. 어느 식물 세포에나 있는 가장 현저한 특징은 그것의 세포벽이다. A 세포벽의 강도가 종종 과대평가되기는 하지만, 이 강한 조직은 팽압을 통해 식물 세포가 그들의 특징인 사각형 모양이나 정육면체 모양을 지니도록 도와준다. B 세포를 위한 저장 공간격인 세포의 거대한 중심 액포와, 세포 안쪽을 채우는 액인 세포의 세포질 사이의 물의 흐름은, 세포막이 세포벽에 닿아 더 확장될 수 없을 때까지 팽창하게 한다. C 그 액포 자체는 동물 세포에 있는 액포보다 훨씬 더 크고, 다 자란 식물 세포 안에는 단 하나의 액포만이 있다. D 이 한 개의 세포기관은 식물 세포 내부 공간의 30%에서 80%까지 차지한다. 액포의 크기는 식물 세포에서 가장 잘 알려진 부분들이 자신의 역할을 하게 돕는다. 그것의 크기 때문에, 액포는 엽록체를 세포벽 쪽으로 미는데, 거기서 엽록체는 세포와 기관을 위한 에너지를 생성하는 데 쓰이는 태양빛에 노출된다.

식물의 생물학적 요구 대부분은 유세포에 의해 통제된다. 이 세포들은 광합성을 통해 에너지를 생성하고 분열을 계속해서 식물의 생 전반 동안 자란다. 두 번째 식물 세포 종류는 후각 세포로, 가소성을 지닌 강하고 두꺼운 세포벽을 가지고 있다. 그들은 넓게 퍼져서 자라고 있는 식물 부분을 지탱해준다. 이와 대조적으로, 기본 조직 세포들은 단단하고 강하다. 이 세포들은 나무에 힘을 주는 탄소 분자인 리그닌으로 가득 찬 방수 세포벽을 가지고 있다. 물이 이 세포들 안에 침투하지 못하므로, 그들은 빨리 사라진다. 하지만 식물에 있어 그들의 가치는 그들이 죽고 난 후에도 오랫동안 계속된다. 기본조직 세포는 목질 식물의 구조에 많은 부분을 기여한다. 이 세 가지 종류의 세포들은 식물의 대부분에서 발견되고, 식물의 조직은 함께 제 역할을 하는 이 세포들 중 하나 또는 하나 이상으로 구성된다.

Glossary turgor pressure 팽압   vacuole (세포질 속의) 액포

- **Structure Zone**

> • before, after, although, though 등의 접속사가 쓰인 문장에서, 앞의 절과 뒤의 절에 나오는 주어가 같을 경우 선행절에서 주어와 be 동사를 생략하고 형용사를 바로 쓸 수 있다.
>
> Though (they are) similar to animal cells in many ways, plant cells share a number of features that distinguish them from other eukaryotic cells.

12. 지문에서 단어 salient와 가장 비슷한 의미는
(A) 견고한　　(B) 현저한
(C) 간섭하는　(D) 복잡한

◉ 음영 처리된 단어 salient는 '핵심적인, 현저한'이라는 의미이다. 이와 가장 비슷한 단어를 보기에서 찾으면 (B) prominent가 된다.

13. 지문에서 동물 세포에 대해 추론할 수 있는 것은?
(A) 그들은 진핵 생물이다.
(B) 그들은 보통 한 개의 액포를 가지고 있다.
(C) 그들에게는 세포질이 없다.
(D) 그들 안에 있는 액포는 세포 밖으로 세포 기관을 민다.

◉ 지문에서, '식물 세포는 동물 세포와 비슷하지만, 다른 진핵 세포와 다른 특성을 가지고 있다'고 하였다. 이를 바탕으로, 동물 세포와 식물 세포 모두 진핵 세포라는 것을 알 수 있다. 따라서 답은 (A)이다.

14. 지문에서 어구 this tough structure가 가리키는 것은
(A) 세포벽　　(B) 동물 세포
(C) 진핵 세포　(D) 특성적 모양

◉ 음영 처리된 '이 강한 조직'의 앞선 문장에서, 식물 세포의 세포벽이 언급되었다. 어구가 포함된 문장의 문맥을 살펴 보면, 이 세포벽에 대한 설명이라는 것을 알 수 있다.

15. 왜 작가는 지문에서 turgor pressure를 언급하는가?
(A) 세포 안 액포의 중요성을 주장하기 위해서
(B) 사각형 모양을 지닌 식물 세포의 예를 들기 위해서
(C) 식물 세포가 어떻게 그들의 모양과 힘을 얻는지 설명하기 위해서
(D) 물리적인 힘이 어떻게 식물 세포와 상호작용하는지 묘사하기 위해서

◉ 지문에 따르면, 팽압은 액포와 세포질 사이의 물의 흐름으로, 식물 세포는 팽압을 통해 사각형이나 정육면체의 모양을 하게 되고, 또한 팽압은 세포막을 팽창하게 한다고 하였다 따라서 답은 (C)이다.

16. 주어진 문장이 1단락에 들어갈 수 있는 곳을 가리키는 네 개의 네모 [■]를 보시오.

    팽창을 유지함으로써, 식물 세포는 많은 동물 세포 안에 존재하는 간단한 펌프 없이 내부 압력을 조절할 수 있다.

    이 문장이 어디에 가장 적절한가?

    ● 주어진 문장은, 식물 세포가 지닌 팽압의 원리에 대해 간단히 설명하고 있다. 따라서 팽압이 언급된 바로 뒤인 B에 위치하게 하여, 그 후에 나오는 문장에서 본격적으로 팽압이 하는 일이 자세히 나오게 하는 것이 자연스럽다.

17. 지문에 따르면, 다음 중 엽록체에 대해 사실인 것은 무엇인가?
    (A) 모든 식물 세포에서 발견된다.
    (B) 생존하기 위해 액포의 물을 필요로 한다.
    (C) 에너지를 생산하기 위해 태양빛을 필요로 한다.
    (D) 식물 세포에서 가장 흔한 부분이다.

    ● 지문에 따르면, 액포가 엽록체를 세포벽으로 밀어 태양빛에 노출되게 함으로서 에너지가 생성된다고 하였다. 따라서 사실인 것은 (C)이다.

18. 지문에서 광합성에 대해 암시하는 것은 무엇인가?
    (A) 한 가지의 식물 세포 종류에서만 이뤄진다.
    (B) 엽록소와 액포에서 모두 일어난다.
    (C) 더 작은 세포들은 그것을 통해 더 많은 에너지를 생산한다.
    (D) 식물 세포에 더 작은 액포가 있었다면, 그것을 해내지 못했을 것이다.

    ● 2단락의 후반부에 따르면, 액포의 크기 덕분에 엽록소를 세포벽으로 밀어 광합성을 일으킬 수 있다고 하였다. 따라서 크기가 더 작았다면, 광합성을 할 수 없었을 것이라고 추측할 수 있다.

19. 지문에서 단어 plasticity 를 대체하기에 가장 적합한 것은
    (A) 두께   (B) 유연성
    (C) 탄소   (D) 점착성

    ● plasticity는 가소성, 즉 탄성을 뜻한다. 따라서 이를 대체하기에 가장 알맞은 것은 유연성을 뜻하는 flexibility이다.

20. 2단락에 따르면, 다음 중 식물 세포의 역할이 아닌 것은 무엇인가?
    (A) 에너지를 생성하기
    (B) 질병에 대항하기
    (C) 식물에 모양을 잡아 주기
    (D) 식물 조직을 만들기

    ● 2단락에서 언급된 식물 세포의 역할로는 에너지 생성하기, 식물 성장 부분 지탱하기, 식물 조직 제공하기 등이 있다. 언급되지 않은 것은 (B)이다.

21. 아래 문장 중 지문에서 음영 처리된 문장의 핵심 정보를 가장 잘 나타낸 것은 어느 것인가? 잘못된 보기들은 중요한 의미를 바꾸거나 핵심 정보를 생략한다.
    (A) 기본조직 세포는 탄소 분자로 되어 있는 리그닌이라는 물질 덕분에 방수가 된다.
    (B) 모든 식물 세포들이 단단하지만, 기본조직 세포는 그들을 방수해 주는 탄소 리그닌이라는 물질을 통해 더 강한 힘을 얻는다.
    (C) 리그닌이라고 불리는 특정한 탄소 물질이 기본조직 세포의 방수 세포벽을 채워 그것이 강해지고 목질이 되게 만든다.
    (D) 후각 세포와 기본조직 세포는 리그닌이라는 강한 탄소 물질로 세포 안을 채우는 방수 세포벽을 지니고 있다.

    ● 음영 처리된 문장의 내용은 기본조직 세포들의 세포벽에 대해 설명하고 있다. 탄소 분자인 리그닌으로 차 있는 방수 세포벽을 가지고 있다고 하였으므로, 이를 가장 잘 나타낸 문장은 (C)이다.

22. 보기에서 적당한 구를 찾아서 그것들과 관련된 카테고리에 넣어라. 보기 중에서 두 개는 사용되지 않을 것이다.

    유세포 / 후각 세포 / 기본조직 세포

    보기
    (A) 분열을 멈추지 않는다.
    (B) 식물이 성장하는 부분에서 발견된다.
    (C) 단 하나의 액포를 지니고 있다.
    (D) 다 성장한 식물에서는 죽어 있다.
    (E) 식물의 에너지를 생산한다.
    (F) 식물의 뼈와 같다.
    (G) 식물 조직의 대부분을 구성한다.
    (H) 식물의 생물적인 욕구를 조절한다.
    (I) 강하고 단단한 세포벽을 가지고 있다.

    ● 지문에 따르면, 유세포는 에너지를 생성하고 분열을 계속하며 생물학적 요구를 조절한다. 그리고 후각 세포는 식물의 자라는 부분을 지탱해 주며 강하고 두꺼운 세포벽이 있다. 반면, 기본조직 세포는 다 자란 식물에서는 죽어 있지만 목질 식물 구조에 기여한다. 이 같은 사실에 따라 보기를 선택한다.

PART 2
TOEFL iBT® Reading Skills 02

Understanding Sentence Structure

문장들은 여러 가지 문법적 부분으로 나뉠 수 있다. 각 부분은 의사를 분명하게 소통하는 데 있어 개별의 역할을 한다. 대부분의 문장은 주어, 동사, 목적어, 또는 보어로 구성되어 있다.

Type 1: S + V

The boy runs (quickly).
　주어　 동사
소년은 (빨리) 달린다.

Type 2: S + V + C

Some of my friends are Hispanics.
　　　주어　　　　　동사　　보어
내 친구 중 몇몇은 히스패닉계이다.

Type 3: S + V + O

The shell on the back protects the turtle.
　　　주어　　　　　동사　　　목적어
등에 있는 껍질은 거북을 보호한다.

Type 4: S + V + I.O. + D.O.

The novel gave the author a great fortune.
　주어　　동사　간접목적어　　직접목적어
그 소설은 소설가에게 엄청난 부를 주었다.

Type 5: S + V + O + O.C.

The detective persuaded the man to reveal the secret.
　　주어　　　　동사　　　목적어　　　　목적격보어
그 탐정은 그 남자가 비밀을 털어놓도록 설득했다.

Find the subject (S), verb (V), complement (C), direct object (D.O.), indirect object (I.O.) or objective complement (O.C.) in each sentence and write which sentence type it is.
각 문장에서 주어, 동사, 보어, 직접목적어, 간접목적어, 또는 목적격보어를 찾고, 그 문장이 몇 형식인지 적으시오.

1. Mystras was a fortified city built in 1249 by a prince
　　S　　V　　　C
   of Achaea.　Type 2

2. Keynes' theory shows us new economic paradigms
　　　S　　　　V　I.O.　　　D.O.
   in modern society.　Type 4

3. Major depressive disorder causes people
　　　　　S　　　　　V　　O
   to experience feelings of sadness.　Type 5
   　　　　　　O.C.

4. Claude Monet spent much of his time in painting in
　　　　S　　　V　　　　O
   the garden.　Type 3

5. Peter Durand made a process using tin cans that he
　　　S　　　V　　　O
   patented in 1810.　Type 3

6. Mystras became a cultural center known for its
　　S　　V　　　　C
   scholars.　Type 2

7. The gases surround a layer of liquid metallic
　　　S　　V　　　　O
   hydrogen.　Type 3

8. Motion capture technology allows animated
　　　　　　S　　　　　　V　　O
   characters to move like actual actors.　Type 5
   　　　　　O.C.

해석

1. 미스트라스는 1249년 아카이아의 왕자에 의해 건설된 요새도시이다.
2. Keynes의 이론은 현대 사회에서 나타나는 새로운 경제의 전형적인 예를 보여준다.
3. 주요우울장애는 사람들로 하여금 깊은 슬픔과 절망을 느끼게 한다.
4. Claude Monet는 많은 시간을 정원에서 그림을 그리며 보냈다.
5. Peter Durand는 1810년에 특허 받은 통조림을 이용하는 과정을 만들었다.
6. 미스트라스는 그곳의 학자들로 알려진 문화적 중심이 되었다.
7. 그 가스들은 액체 형태의 금속성 수소 층을 감싼다.
8. 모션 캡처 기술은 애니메이션화 된 등장인물들이 실제 배우처럼 움직이게 한다.

Understanding Transition Words

연결 단어와 어구는 문장 간이나 문단 간의 관계를 나타낸다. 그것들은 논리적인 구성을 제공하여 문장들과 문단들이 서로 자연스럽게 흐르게 해 준다.

연결어와 구

첨가(부연)	in addition, moreover, furthermore, as well as, on top of that
비교	similarly, as ~ as, likewise, by comparison, compared to
대조	on the other hand, on the contrary, in contrast, whereas
증명	evidently, obviously, that is
요약	in brief, briefly, overall, in short, to sum up, to summarize
결론	therefore, consequently, thus, in conclusion, as a result
원인과 결과	because (of), since, due to, owing to, hence, for the reason that
예시	for example, for instance, such as, namely, to illustrate
순서	first, next, afterward, subsequently, consequently, later
강조	in fact, indeed, definitely, without doubt, certainly, absolutely
시간(때)	at that time, during, for, in, until

Fill in each blank with the appropriate transition word or phrase.
알맞은 연결 어구를 골라 빈칸에 적으시오.

1. for example
2. Afterward
3. compared to
4. Because of
5. as well as
6. during

해석

1. 리트머스는 다양하게 사용된다. 예를 들면, 식물학자들은 토양의 산성도를 확인하기 위해 그것을 쓴다.
2. Claude Monet는 교외에 농가를 빌렸다. 그 후에, 그는 그 정원에서 많은 그림을 그렸다.
3. 겨울 계절풍에 비교했을 때, 여름 계절풍은 더 강력하다.
4. 모션 캡처 기술 때문에, 현대 영화는 혁명적인 발전을 이뤘다.
5. 천문학자들은 메이저뿐 아니라 퀘이사도 발견했다.
6. 낭만주의는 19세기 동안 예술 분야를 지배했다.

UNIT 06
Inference

INTRODUCTION

추론적 질문은 지문에서 직접적으로 언급하지 않은 정보와 관련이 있다. 수험자는 드러난 사실들을 분석하고, 그 사실들을 논리적 결론을 도출해내는 데 이용해야 한다. 수험자는 지문에 나타난 단서와 함께, 함축된 내용을 찾아내기 위하여 상식과 논리를 이용해야 한다. 따라서 수험자는 구체적인 세부사항이나 전체 지문에 기반하여 추론하여야 한다.

TYPICAL QUESTION TYPES

~에 대해 추론할 수 있는 것은?
_____ 단락에서 추론할 수 있는 것은
~ 이후에 어떤 일이 일어났을 것 같은가?

STRATEGIES

- 질문에서 중심 단어들을 찾고 해당 단어의 위치를 파악하기 위해 지문을 훑어 보아라. 이것은 중요한 정보가 있는 곳을 결정하는 데에 도움이 될 것이다.
- 중요 정보를 찾은 후에는, 확실히 긍정적이거나 부정적인 단어들을 찾아라. 이것으로 분위기와 어울리지 않는 보기를 제거할 수 있다.
- 추론된 정보는 직접적으로 언급되지 않는다는 점을 기억하라. 암시하고 있는 것이 무엇인지를 알아내기 위해 논리를 이용해야 한다.

QUICK CHECKUP p. 99

정답 | 1. (A)　　2. (A)　　3. (B)

Choose the sentence that makes the correct inference.
올바른 추론을 한 문장을 고르시오.

1. 미스트라스는 1249년 아카이아의 왕자에 의해 건설된 요새도시이다. 이것은 곧 비잔틴 제국에 의해 정복당했으며, 이 새로운 비잔틴 지방의 수도는 미스트라스 봉건왕국으로 만들어졌다. 이때는 미스트라스의 영광에 있어 최고의 정점이었는데, 아름다운 교회와 커다란 도서관, 그리고 위대한 학자들로 알려진 문화 중심지가 되었다. 이후에 그 도시는 터키인들, 그 다음에는 베네치아인들의 수중에 들어갔다. 1832년에 그 도시는 버려지게 되어 오늘날에는 유적으로만 남아있다.
 (A) 여러 문화가 미스트라스 시를 수세기 동안 지배했다.
 (B) 미스트라스 시는 터키와의 전투에서 파괴되었다.

 ▶ 미스트라스는 비잔틴에 의해 정복된 후에도 터키와 베네치아의 수중에 들어갔다는 내용이 나오므로, 여러 문화가 도시에 유입되었다는 사실을 알 수 있다. 따라서 (A)가 정답이 된다.

2. 주요우울장애는 사람들로 하여금 깊은 슬픔과 절망을 끊임없이 느끼게 하는 심각한 질병이다. 환자들은 수면과 식이 문제도 겪는 경향이 있는데, 이는 그들의 육체적 건강에 있어 심각한 결과를 초래할 수 있다. 정상적인 우울 감정과는 달리 주요우울장애는 정확한 원인에서 초래되는 것이 아니며, 빨리 사라지지도 않는다. 일반적으로, 완전히 회복되려면 자격을 갖춘 의료종사자에 의한 치료가 필요하다.
 (A) 주요우울장애는 긴 시간 동안 지속될 수 있다.
 (B) 주요우울장애는 육체적 질병 때문에 생길 수 있다.

 ▶ 주요우울장애는 정확한 원인도 없고 빨리 사라지지도 않는다는 내용을 통해 해당증상이 긴 기간 동안 계속됨을 알 수 있다. 따라서 (A)의 내용을 추론할 수 있다.

3. 카구는 뉴칼레도니아 섬에서만 발견되는 날지 못하는 새이다. 숲 바닥에 살면서 포식자로부터 위장하기 위해 짙은 색에 의존하는 다른 새들과는 달리, 카구는 밝은 오렌지색 부리와 다리가 있고 연회색이다. 카구의 커다랗고 완전히 형성된 날개들은 날지 못하는 새들에게 있어서는 또 다른 특이한 모습이다. 불행히도, 인간에 의해 뉴칼레도니아로 도입된 외래종 동물들은 카구를 먹이로 삼았으며, 카구를 멸종위기에 처한 동물로 만들었다.
 (A) 카구는 자신을 방어하기 위해 커다란 날개를 사용한다.
 (B) 뉴칼레도니아의 카구 수는 줄고 있다.

 ▶ 카구가 외래종의 먹이가 되어 멸종위기 동물이 되었다는 사실로 미루어 보아, 그 수가 계속 감소하고 있음을 추론할 수 있다. 따라서 (B)가 답이 된다.

VOCABULARY   pp. 100-101

Write the number of each word's definition.
각 단어의 뜻을 찾아 번호를 쓰시오.

reverse / 1 반대
forgo / 5 포기하다
abstract / 10 추상적인
cosmetic / 4 미용의
polish / 2 광내다
interact / 12 교류하다
ferment / 8 발효되다
orient / 9 맞추다
decay / 3 부패, 부식
scrape / 6 긁다
ingest / 7 삼키다, 먹다
prevalent 11 / 만연한

Match each collocation with the correct definition.
각 연어에 알맞은 뜻을 찾아 연결하시오.

a. be applied to – to be spread on a surface ~에 발라지다
b. be made up of – to consist of ~로 구성되다
c. be placed in – to be put into something ~에 자리잡다
d. in conjunction with – working together with ~와 함께
e. be treated with – to be put with a substance for a specific purpose ~로 처리되다

Circle the word closest in meaning to each underlined word.
각 밑줄 친 단어의 뜻과 가장 가까운 단어를 찾아 동그라미 하시오.

정답 | 1. (D)   2. (A)   3. (C)
       4. (B)   5. (B)   6. (C)

해석 |
1. 그 남자는 항상 교류의 중요성을 강조했다.
   (A) 단언   (B) 창안
   (C) 주입   (D) 소통

2. 공부 모임을 포기하기로 선택한 사람들은 시험을 잘 보지 못할 것이다.
   (A) 그만두다   (B) 결합하다
   (C) 선택하다   (D) 강화하다

3. 어떤 이들은 영화에서 폭력이 만연해졌다고 한다.
   (A) 동등한   (B) 신선한
   (C) 널리 퍼진   (D) 정확한

4. 의사는 아이에게 음식을 삼키기 전에 잘 씹으라고 말했다.
   (A) 끝나다   (B) 삼키다
   (C) 새로 꾸미다   (D) 살균하다

5. 집 벽의 부식이 시작되면, 그것들을 대체해야 한다.
   (A) 확장   (B) 악화
   (C) 강화   (D) 건설

6. 자동차의 아랫면이 노면을 따라 긁혀서 불꽃이 튀었다.
   (A) 정의하다   (B) 갈망하다
   (C) 끌다   (D) 손질하다

Fill in each blank with the correct collocation.
알맞은 연어를 골라 빈칸을 채우시오.

정답 | 1. be applied to   2. is made up of
       3. be treated with   4. in conjunction with
       5. be placed in

해석 |
1. 두꺼운 자외선 차단제가 피부에 발라져야 한다.
2. 학교 위원회는 학생들, 부모들, 그리고 교사들로 구성된다.
3. 나무는 방수되기 위해 화학 물질로 처리되어야 한다.
4. 회사는 정부와 함께 그 서비스를 만들어냈다.
5. 불법 이민자들은 경찰이 도착할 때까지 유치장에 있게 될 것이다.

STEP 1   pp. 102-103

정답 | 1. (A)   2. (D)

리트머스

　유기원료로 만들어진 염료인 리트머스는 용액이 산성인지 염기성인지를 알아보기 위해 화학자들에 의해 가장 많이 사용된다. 산성 용액에 노출되면, 파란 리트머스는 붉게 변한다. 붉은 리트머스가 염기성 용액에 놓여지면 반대의 현상이 발생한다.

　화학자들은 일반적으로 리트머스 처리된 종이를 사용한다. 리트머스 자체는 바위나 나무에서 자라는 식물과 비슷한 유기체인 지의류로 만들어진다. 지의류는 분해된 후, 암모니아와 탄산칼륨과 혼합되어 발효된다. 마지막으로 백악질이 가미되는데, 혼합물은 건조되어 가루로 만들어진다. 리트머스는 14세기 초기에 최초로 사용되었다고 믿어진다. 오늘날, 리트머스는 다양하게 사용된다. 예를 들어, 식물학자는 토양의 산성을 검사하는 데 이것을 사용하여 식물에 적합한지를 확인하고, 의사들은 임신한 여성의 건강을 확인하는 데 사용한다.

Glossary potash 탄산칼륨

• **Structure Zone**

재귀대명사는 주어가 어떠한 행위를 했다는 것을 강조할 때 쓰이며, 생략하여도 문장은 성립한다.

The litmus **itself** is made from lichens, small plantlike organisms that grow on rocks and trees.

1. 리트머스가 가루로 만들어진 후에 어떤 일이 일어나겠는가?
   (A) 화학적 사용을 위해 종이에 발라진다.
   (B) 발효되어 식물을 다루는 데 사용된다.
   (C) 용액에서 용해되어 파랗거나 붉게 변한다.
   (D) 다른 가루들로 되어 있는 백악질에 첨가된다.

   ▶ 리트머스의 제조 과정으로 분해, 혼합, 발효, 건조 과정을 거쳐 가루가 되는 것까지 기술하고 있고, 리트머스 처리된 종이를 화학자들이 사용한다는 언급이 있으므로, 가루가 된 리트머스는 종이 위에 덧붙여진다는 것을 알 수 있다. 따라서 (A)가 정답이다.

2. 지문에서 추론할 수 있는 것은?
   (A) 리트머스 종이는 몇몇 화학자들에 의해 발명되었다.
   (B) 용액이 중성이면, 리트머스는 투명해진다.
   (C) 리트머스를 만들기 위해 푸른색과 붉은색의 지의류가 사용된다.
   (D) 토양은 각기 다른 산성 수준을 지닐 수 있다.

   ▶ 식물학자들이 리트머스를 사용하는 방법 중, 토양이 식물에 적합한지를 알아보기 위해 산성 여부를 확인한다는 내용이 있으므로, (D)의 사실을 추론할 수 있다.

• Note-Taking

Litmus

What It Is	— a dye made from organic sources
What It Does	— determine whether a solution is an acid or base
	— an acid makes blue litmus red / a base makes red litmus blue
How It Is Made	— lichens — crushed, mixed, fermented, dried → becomes a powder
How It Is Used	— to test soil or to check the health of pregnant women

SUMMARY
Litmus is used to tell if a solution is an acid or a base. It changes color from blue to red and vice versa. Paper that has been treated with litmus is usually used. Litmus is made from lichens. They are crushed and mixed with ammonia and potash. After they are fermented, chalk is added, and the entire mixture is turned into a powder. Litmus is used to test soil and to check the health of pregnant women.

리트머스는 용액이 산성인지 염기성인지를 알아보기 위해 사용된다. 이것은 파란색에서 붉은색으로, 또는 그 반대로 색이 변한다. 주로 리트머스 처리가 된 종이가 사용된다. 리트머스는 지의류로 만들어진다. 그것들은 분해되어 암모니아와 탄산칼륨과 혼합된다. 그것이 발효된 후, 백악질이 첨가되며 완전한 혼합체는 가루가 된다. 리트머스는 토양을 검사하고 임신한 여성의 건강을 확인하는 데 사용된다.

VOCAB Match each word with the correct definition.
각 단어에 알맞은 뜻을 찾아 연결하시오.

a. dye – a substance that is used to change something's color 염료
b. organic – pertaining to only to natural elements 유기체의
c. solution – a liquid in which a solid substance has been dissolved 용액
d. exposed – left or being without cover or protection 노출된
e. lichen – a group of tiny plants that look like moss 지의류

STEP 2   pp. 104-105

정답 | 1. (D)   2. (B)   3. (B)

지베르니에서의 Monet(모네)

Claude Monet는 인상주의의 창시자로 가장 잘 알려진 유명한 프랑스 화가이다. 1883년, 도시를 벗어나기를 바랐던 그는 지베르니라는 작은 마을에 재정착했는데, 그곳에서 그와 그의 가족은 농가와 주변 땅 2에이커를 빌렸다. 그들은 함께, 화가에게 영감과 일부 위대한 작품에 대한 주제를 제공했던 정성들인 정원을 만들었다.

Monet는 대부분의 시간을 정원에서 그림을 그리며 보냈으며, 야외에서의 작업을 위해 전통적인 화가의 작업실은 포기했다. 그의 초기 인상주의 그림들이 그러하듯, 그는 (그림) 소재들 전반의 색채와 빛의 움직임에 초점을 맞췄는데, 그 소재들에는 아이리스, 달리아, 그리고 수양버들이 포함되었다.

1893년에 Monet는 아름다운 수련이 있는 연못을 가진 일본식 수생 식물정원을 포함하기 위해 그의 정원을 확장했다. 그 꽃들을 그린 그의 작품들은 그 당시 가장 위대한 작품들 중 일부라고 여겨지고 있다. 관람자를 (그림에) 맞추는 지평선이 없는 그 그림들은 연못 표면의 하늘과 구름의 반영을 배경으로, 수련의 거친 묘사를 창조해냈다. 이러한 작품들의 추상적 본질은 현대 미술의 영향에 기인하지만, 일부는 Monet의 악화된 시력도 한 역할을 했다고 믿는다.

• Structure Zone

> • '주격관계대명사 + be 동사'는 문장에서 생략될 수 있는데, 이때 남은 현재분사나 과거분사는 앞의 단어를 수식하는 형용사적 역할을 한다.
> Claude Monet was a famous French painter (who is) best **known** as the founder of the Impressionist Movement.
>
> • 관계부사는 문장 안에서 '접속사 + 부사'의 역할을 하며 '전치사 + 관계대명사'로 바꿀 수 있다. 관계부사의 선행사는 시간, 장소, 이유, 방법이며 각 의미에 따라 when, where, why, how의 관계부사를 사용한다.
> He relocated to the small village of Giverny, **where**(=in which) he and his family rented a farmhouse and two acres of surrounding land.

1. 지베르니에 대해 추론할 수 있는 것은 무엇인가?
   (A) Monet의 고향이며 프랑스의 교외에 있었다.
   (B) Monet는 파리와 매우 가까워서 이 지역을 좋아했다.
   (C) 지베르니의 많은 주민들은 일본식 정원을 가지고 있었다.
   (D) 이곳은 시골에 있으며 아름다운 자연 풍경을 가지고 있었다.

   ▶ Monet가 도시로부터 탈출을 꿈꾸며 재정착한 곳이므로 지베르니는 시골임을 알 수 있으며, 외부에서 그림 그리며 영감을 얻었다는 내용에서 자연 풍경이 아름다웠다는 것을 추론할 수 있다.

2. 지문에서 단어 elaborate와 의미가 가장 가까운 것은
   (A) 조건이 맞는   (B) 경이로운
   (C) 활발한   (D) 큰 충격을 받은

   ● elaborate는 공들여 만들어 매우 뛰어나다는 의미가 있는 단어이므로 보기 중에서는 (B)와 의미가 가장 가깝다.

3. Monet의 수련 그림에 대해 추론할 수 있는 것은 무엇인가?
   (A) 그것들은 여전히 지베르니 마을에서 전시되고 있다.
   (B) 그것들은 다른 그림들보다 다소 흐릿하다.
   (C) 그것들은 어두운 색감을 다양하게 나타낸다.
   (D) 그것들은 화가의 작업실에서 완성되었다.

   ● Monet의 수련 그림은 연못 위에 비친 하늘과 구름의 반영을 배경으로 하여 거칠게 묘사되었다고 하였고, Monet의 악화된 시력이 그림에 영향을 미쳤을 수도 있다고 하였으므로, 그림이 사실적이라기보다는 흐릿하다는 사실을 알 수 있다.

• Note-Taking

P1 MI Claude Monet – relocated to Giverny in 1883
    SD created a garden which offered the inspiration & subjects

P2 MI painted in the garden
    SD focused on colors & the movement of light across his subjects

P3 MI his masterpieces
    SD paintings of flowers – created rough representations of the water lilies, the reflections of the sky & clouds on the surface of the pond

VOCAB_ Write the correct word for each definition.
각 뜻에 알맞은 단어를 찾아 적으시오.

a. inspiration 영감   b. weeping 축 늘어진
c. contain 포함하다   d. representation 묘사
e. reflection 반영

STEP 3			pp. 106-107
정답	1. (A)	2. (B)	3. (C)	4. (D)

치약

전통적으로, 치약은 일반적인 구강 위생법의 기초 역할을 한다. 칫솔에 묻혀 치아에 바르면, 이것은 플라그와 음식찌꺼기를 제거하고 구취를 감소시키며 충치와 잇몸질환을 예방한다. 또한 이것은 얼룩을 제거하고 치아를 하얗게 하는 미용효과도 있다.

치약은 주로 수산화알루미늄과 탄산칼슘과 같은 연마제로 구성된다. 화학적 단계에서 반응하기보다, 이 입자들은 칫솔의 기계적 움직임과 결합되어 작용한다. 본질적으로, 그들(입자들)은 치아로부터 원치 않는 물질을 긁어내고 저단계의 광택도 제공하는데, 이는 치아를 더 밝게 만들 수 있다.

대부분의 상업적 치약의 유효성분은 불소이다. 이것은 뼈와 치아 외부 표면인 법랑질을 튼튼히 한다고 알려진 자연적으로 발생하는 물질이다. 불소는 충치와, 잇몸의 염증을 일으키는 구강질환인 치은염의 예방에 도움이 되도록 치약에 첨가된다. 적은 양을 삼켰을 때는 해가 되지 않지만, 많은 양의 불소를 삼키게 되면 심각한 건강상의 위험이 될 수 있다. 상업적 치약의 다른 성분들은 치약이 거품을 내어 입안에 골고루 퍼지게 하는 계면활성제와 구취를 감소시키기 위해 주로 첨가되는 항균제이다. 또한 대부분의 치약은 천연 또는 인공 향료 중 하나를 함유한다. 오늘날에는 비록 실용적인 목적이 되지는 않더라도, 다양한 좋은 맛의 치약들이 많이 있다.

• Structure Zone

> • 전치사의 목적어로는 명사나 명사구, 명사절이 오므로 전치사 뒤에 오는 동사는 동명사의 형태를 취해야 한다.
>
> It can also have the cosmetic effect **of removing** stains and **whitening** teeth.
>
> • 명사 앞에 수식하는 말로 부사와 형용사가 나올 때는 부사가 형용사 앞에 위치한다. 이는 형용사는 명사를 수식하는 역할, 부사는 형용사, 동사, 다른 부사 등을 수식하는 역할을 하기 때문이다.
>
> This is a **naturally occurring** material known to strengthen bones and enamel, which is the outer covering of teeth.

1. 왜 작가는 mechanical motions에 대해 언급하는가?
   (A) 연마제가 어떻게 작용하는지 보여주기 위해서
   (B) 연마제가 어떻게 만들어지는지 설명하기 위해서
   (C) 광택효과를 피하는 것에 대해 조언하기 위해서
   (D) 치아를 닦는 몇 가지 해로운 방법에 대해 경고하기 위해서

   ● 연마제는 반복적으로 칫솔질을 통해 치아의 음식찌꺼기나 플라그 등을 제거하는 것이므로, mechanical motions는 연마제가 어떤 움직임을 통해 치아에 작용하는지를 설명하기 위한 장치라 할 수 있다.

2. 불소에 대해 사실이 아닌 것은 무엇인가?
   (A) 그것은 인공 물질이 아니다.
   (B) 그것에는 미백 효과가 있다.
   (C) 그것은 뼈와 법랑질을 튼튼하게 한다.
   (D) 그것을 너무 많이 삼키는 것은 건강을 해칠 수 있다.

   ● 치약을 사용하는 것에 약간의 미백 효과는 있으나 이것이 불소로부터 기인한다는 말은 없다. 불소의 효과로는 충치와 치은염 예방만이 언급되었으므로 (B)는 답이 아니다.

3. 향료에 대해 추론할 수 있는 것은 무엇인가?
   (A) 그것들은 대부분의 상업적 치약에 포함되지 않는다.
   (B) 그것들은 어린 아이들이나 노인들에게는 건강상의 위험이 된다.
   (C) 그것들은 양치질이 더 기분 좋은 경험이 되도록 첨가된다.
   (D) 그것들은 치약에서 발견되는 인공 화학 물질에 의해 활성화된다.

   ● 향료에는 실용적인 목적이 없다고 했으므로 의학적 효과는 없으며, 좋은 맛의 치약들이 다양하게 존재한다는 것으로 보아, (C)의 사실을 추론할 수 있다.

4. 지문에서 추론할 수 있는 것은 무엇인가?
   (A) 천연 치약은 인공 치약보다 더 좋다.
   (B) 연마제는 치약의 효과를 감소시킨다.
   (C) 치약 거품은 치아의 법랑질에 해가 된다.
   (D) 부주의하게 불소를 섭취하는 것은 몸을 해롭게 할 수 있다.

   ▶ 불소를 적게 섭취하는 것은 괜찮으나, 많이 섭취하면 몸에 해롭다고 했으므로, (D)를 추론할 수 있다.

VOCAB Find the correct word in the passage for each of the given definition.
주어진 뜻에 알맞은 단어를 지문에서 찾으시오.

a. regimen 요법   b. halitosis 구취
c. abrasive 연마제   d. artificial 인공의

• **Note-Taking** (Sample Answer)

P1 MI toothpaste – used for standard oral hygiene
    SD removes plaque, reduces halitosis & tooth decay & whitens teeth
P2 MI how toothpaste is applied while brushing one's teeth
    SD scrapes material & polishes to make teeth brighter
P3 MI ingredients of commercial toothpastes
    SD • fluoride – aids in the prevention of cavities & gingivitis
        • surfactants – help toothpaste to foam & spread
        • antibacterial agents – reduce bad breath

• **More Info Zone**

┌─ 치약에 관한 사실 ─────────────────────────┐
│ 치약은 기원전 5000년 이집트에서 처음 사용되었다. 초기 치약은 계란과 굴의 껍질, 화산재의 부석 등을 혼합한 가루였는데, 이집트인들은 이를 손에 묻혀 치아에 묻은 찌꺼기를 닦아냈다. 현대의 치약에는 거품을 내기 위해 계면활성제가 포함되는데, 구취의 원인이 되기도 한다. 이는 계면활성제를 과다 복용할 시 위염의 원인이 되어 구취를 초래하기 때문이다. 따라서 양치할 때는 잘 헹구어내는 것이 무엇보다 중요하다. │
└───────────────────────────────────┘

UNIT TEST				pp. 108-109
정답	1. (B) 2. (C) 3. (D) 4. (C) 5. (C)				
	6. Mutualism (A) Commensalism (F), (G)				
	Parasitism (B), (D)				

식물과 동물의 공생

공생은 두 개의 서로 다른 종이 양쪽에 영향을 미치면서 규칙적으로 상호작용할 때 발생한다고 알려져 있다. 이것은 일반적으로 두 동물 종 사이에서 일어나지만, 공생관계는 식물과 동물 종 사이에서도 일어난다.

공생의 가장 일반적인 형태 중 하나는 두 종이 상호작용을 통해 서로 유익한 효과를 얻는 관계인 상리공생이다. 상리공생의 전형적인 예는 꽃과 꿀벌에서 볼 수 있다. 꿀벌은 꽃에서 꽃가루와 꿀을 모아 그것들을 그들의 유충을 위한 먹이로 사용한다. 그렇게 함으로써 그들은 꽃에서 꽃으로 꽃가루를 무심히 퍼뜨리게 되는데, 이는 꽃을 번식하게 한다. 이런 방법으로 각 종은 생존을 위해 서로 의존한다.

편리공생은 공생의 다른 유형이다. 편리공생에서는 한 종이 상호작용을 통해 이익을 얻는 반면, 두 번째 종은 어떤 중요 방식으로든 도움을 얻지 못하거나 해를 입지도 않는다. 예를 들어, 어떤 나무들은 자랄 때 나무의 몸통에 커다란 구멍이 생긴다. 이 구멍들은 많은 종류의 새들에 의해 둥지를 짓는 장소로 사용된다. 그렇게, 나무들은 새들의 존재에 의해 크게 영향 받지 않으면서, 새들에게 포식자로부터의 은신처와 안전을 제공한다.

마지막으로, 한 종은 도움을 받고 다른 종은 해를 입거나 심지어 죽게 되는 식물과 동물간의 공생이 있다. 기생으로 알려진 이것은 작은 곤충으로 식물에 붙어 살면서 수액을 빨아먹는 진딧물의 행태에서 발견된다. 하지만 식물도 기생할 수 있다. 균류 기생은 많은 종류의 포유류, 곤충, 그리고 물고기의 내부 또는 표면에서 서식하는 것으로 발견된다. 이것들 중 가장 극단적인 것은 오피오코디셉스 곰팡이인데, 곤충에 영향을 미쳐서 결국 그들의 뇌를 조절하게 하는 균류이다. 균류는 이 운 나쁜 곤충을 죽이기 전에 균류가 자라기 적합한 장소로 개미를 걸어가게 한다.

Glossary pollen 꽃가루   sap 수액

• **Structure Zone**

> • neither A nor B는 상관접속사이며 접속사가 문장에서 동일한 형태를 대등하게 연결하듯이, A와 B의 자리에도 대등한 문법 형태가 와야 한다.
> In commensalism, one species benefits from the interaction while the second is **neither helped nor harmed** in any significant way.
>
> • force는 사역동사의 한 형태로 5형식 문장에 사용하며 목적보어의 자리에는 to부정사가 온다.
> The fungus **forces** ants **to walk** to suitable places for the fungus to grow before killing the unfortunate insects.

1. 지문의 주제는 무엇인가?
   (A) 공생은 같은 종의 두 개체 사이에서 일어난다.
   (B) 식물과 동물의 관계는 몇몇 다른 형태를 취한다.
   (C) 동물들은 대부분의 상호 종 관계에서 식물보다 더 이익을 얻는다.
   (D) 상호공생은 가장 흔한 식물과 동물간의 공생 유형이다.

   ▶ 지문은 식물과 동물의 관계를 상리공생, 편리공생, 기생 등 여러 형태로 보여주고 있으므로 (B)가 지문의 주제로 가장 알맞다.

2. 지문에서 단어 them이 가리키는 것은
   (A) 꽃들
   (B) 꿀벌들
   (C) 꽃가루와 꿀
   (D) 꿀벌들과 그들의 유충들

   ▶ 대명사는 바로 앞서서 나오는 문장이나 표현에 나오는 명사를 받는다. 해당 문장에서는 벌들이 꽃가루와 꿀을 모은다는 말이 나오므로 유충의 먹이로 사용하는 '그것들'은 꽃가루와 꿀이 된다.

3. 2단락에서 추론할 수 있는 것은 무엇인가?
   (A) 꿀은 꿀벌이 꽃을 해치는 것을 막는다.
   (B) 꿀벌은 그들의 유충에 먹이를 공급하기 위해 협력한다.
   (C) 몇몇 꽃 종은 꿀벌과 같은 곤충들에 해를 입힌다.
   (D) 꽃들은 번식을 위하여 꽃가루를 나눠야 한다.

   ▶ 벌들은 유충을 위해 꿀을 필요로 하고 이 때 꽃가루가 이동하며 꽃이 번식되는 것이라고 했으므로, 꽃의 번식을 위해서는 꽃가루가 나눠져야 한다는 것을 알 수 있다.

4. 진딧물에 대해 추론할 수 있는 것은 무엇인가?
   (A) 그들은 몇몇 식물의 먹이가 된다.
   (B) 그들은 식물을 기생물로부터 보호하도록 돕는다.
   (C) 그들은 식물을 이용함으로써 그것들에 해를 미친다.
   (D) 그들은 어떤 식물에 살면서 이익을 주고받는다.

   ▶ 한 종이 이익을 얻으면서 다른 종에는 해를 끼치는 기생관계로 진딧물의 예를 든 것이므로, 진딧물은 식물을 이용하지만 동시에 해도 끼친다는 사실을 추론할 수 있다.

5. 다음 중 사실이 아닌 것은
   (A) 공생은 두 동물 종 사이에서 일어나는 것이 가능하다.
   (B) 벌과 꽃은 그들의 공생관계에서 이익을 얻는다.
   (C) 구멍에 새 둥지가 있는 나무들은 다른 포식자로부터 보호받는다.
   (D) 오피오코디셉스 곰팡이는 개미를 먹이로 하는 기생물이다.

   ▶ 나무의 몸통에 있는 구멍에 새 둥지가 있게 되면 포식자로부터 새가 보호받는다는 내용이 있으므로, 나무가 보호받는다는 내용의 (C)는 사실이 아니다.

6. 보기에서 적당한 구를 찾아서 그것들과 관련된 카테고리에 넣어라 보기 중에서 한 개는 사용되지 않을 것이다.

   상리공생 / 편리공생 / 기생

   보기
   (A) 꿀벌과 꽃의 관계와 관련 있다.
   (B) 한 종에는 도움이 되나 다른 종을 해칠 수 있다.
   (C) 진딧물이 동물의 뇌를 흡입했을 때 발생한다.
   (D) 일부 식물과 진딧물 사이에서 발생할 수 있다.
   (E) 다른 종이 죽을 때 한 종은 해를 입는 결과가 될 수 있다.
   (F) 한 종은 영향을 미치지 않게 할 수 있다.
   (G) 새가 나무 구멍에 둥지를 지을 때 발생한다.

   ▶ 상리공생은 두 서로 이익을 주고 받는 것이므로 (A)가 이에 해당한다. 편리공생은 한 종만 이익을 받고 다른 종은 별 영향을 받지 않는 것이므로 (F)와 (G)가 해당된다. 기생은 한 종이 이익을 보는 반면 다른 종에게는 심한 피해를 입히므로 (B)와 (D)가 해당된다.

• **More Info Zone**

상리공생과 편리공생의 다양한 형태

상리공생
- 진딧물과 개미: 진딧물은 개미에게 단맛의 액체를 제공하고 개미는 진딧물을 무당벌레와 같은 천적으로 보호해준다.
- 유카나방과 유카식물: 나방은 유카식물의 씨 꼬투리에 알을 낳으면서 수분을 지켜주고 나방의 유충은 부화되어 씨의 일부를 먹는다.
- 개미와 아카시아나무: 개미는 아카시아나무의 큰 가시에 구멍을 뚫어 서식지를 만들고 잎을 먹으며 아카시아나무에 뿌리 내리려는 다른 식물의 싹을 제거한다.

편리공생
- 어치와 개미: 일부 어치는 개미를 자기 몸에 기어오르게 하여 몸에 붙은 기생 생물을 없앤다.
- 해삼과 숨이고기: 숨이고기는 위험에 닥쳤을 때 해삼 속으로 숨었다가 나온다.
- 빨판상어: 빨판상어는 상어, 고래, 바다거북 등의 다른 동물에 붙어 이동한다.

VOCABULARY TEST pp.110-111

Recall the essential words in the unit to reinforce your vocabulary acquisition. Write the meaning of each word in your language.
유닛에서 배운 주요 단어들을 떠올려 각 단어의 뜻을 쓰시오.

exposed	노출된	dye	염료
cosmetic	미용의	interact	상호작용하다
sap	수액	ingest	삼키다
halitosis	구취	contain	포함하다
abandon	버리다	dissipate	소멸되다
artificial	인공의	regimen	요법
polish	광내다	organic	유기체의
solution	용액	ferment	발효되다
inspiration	영감	reverse	반대
suck	빨다	orient	맞추다
pollen	꽃가루	decay	부패, 부식
fortified	요새화 된	lichen	지의류
representation	묘사	prevalent	만연한
scholar	학자	camouflage	위장하다
conquer	정복하다	weeping	축 늘어진
forgo	포기하다	scrape	긁다
abrasive	연마제	in conjunction with	~와 함께
be applied to	~에 발라지다	abstract	추상적인
reflection	반영	be placed in	~에 자리잡다
be made up of	~로 구성되다		
be treated with	~로 처리되다		

Complete each sentence with the correct word or collocation.
문장에 알맞은 단어나 연어를 찾아 쓰시오.

정답 | 1. exposed 2. made up of
3. scholars 4. prevalent
5. pollen 6. contain
7. inspiration 8. conquered
9. lichens 10. dissipate

해석 |
1. 산성 용액에 노출되면, 파란 리트머스는 붉게 변한다.
2. 치약은 수산화알루미늄 같은 연마제들로 주로 구성된다.
3. 미스트라스는 위대한 학자들로 알려진 문화 중심지가 되었다.
4. 공생의 가장 만연한 형태 중 하나는 상리공생이다.
5. 꿀벌들은 꽃으로부터 꽃가루와 꿀을 모은다.
6. 대부분의 치약은 천연 또는 인공 향료 중 하나를 함유한다.
7. Monet는 그에게 영감을 주었던 아름다운 정원을 만들었다.
8. 미스트라스는 곧 비잔틴에 의해 정복당했다.
9. 리트머스는 바위 위에서 자라는 작은 식물과 비슷한 유기체인 지의류로 만들어진다.
10. 주요우울장애는 정확한 원인에서 초래되는 것이 아니며 빨리 사라지지도 않는다.

UNIT 07
Rhetorical Purpose

INTRODUCTION
수사학적 목적 문제는 작가가 지문에 어떤 특정한 내용을 담았는지 그 의도나 목적을 묻는다. 또한 한 단락 전체가 의도하는 바가 무엇인지 묻는 문제가 나오기도 한다.

TYPICAL QUESTION TYPES
_____ 단락에서 작가의 주요 목적은
왜 작가는 _____ 단락에서 _____을 언급하는가?
작가는 무엇을 나타내기 위해 지문에서 _____을 언급하는가

STRATEGIES
- 문제를 자세히 읽고, 한 단락 전체의 목적을 묻고 있는지, 또는 특정한 부분이 의도하는 바를 묻는 것인지 파악한다.

- 특정한 부분을 묻는 문제에서는 그 세부 정보가 쓰인 목적을 잘 살펴 보라. 그 목적은 두 가지 내용을 비교하기 위한 것이거나, 예를 제시하기 위한 것이거나, 의견을 강조하기 위한 것일 수도 있고, 또는 어떤 정보의 사실 여부를 알려주기 위한 것일 수도 있다.
- 한 단락 전체의 목적을 묻는 문제에서는, 도입 부분과 마무리 문장을 집중해서 본다. 그 부분들에 충분한 단서가 없다면, 단락 중간 부분을 살펴서 중심 어휘들을 찾아 본다.

QUICK CHECKUP p. 113
정답 | 1. (B) 2. (A) 3. (A)

Choose the reason why the author mentioned the highlighted sentence.
작가가 음영 처리된 문장을 언급한 의도로 알맞은 것을 찾으시오.

1. 유대교에서, 바 미츠바는 한 소년이 어른으로 이행하는 의식이다. 바 미츠바는 소년들이 13살이 될 때 거행된다. 이 나이는 그들이 자신의 행동에 책임을 지게 되는 때로 여겨진다. 그 의식은 소년이 기도를 주도하는 것과, 율법의 구절을 낭독하거나 율법에 대해 연설을 하는 것을 익히는 몇 개월의 준비 과정을 거친다. 의식 후에는 보통 음식과 음료를 곁들인 호화로운 파티가 열린다.
(A) 바 미츠바의 중요성을 강조하기 위해서
(B) 바 미츠바가 열리는 시점에 대한 이유를 들기 위해서

▶ 주어진 문장은 '바 미츠바가 13살이 될 때 거행된다'를 부연 설명하며, 왜 그때 열리는지 알려주고 있다.

2. 밴드왜건 효과는 조사를 하지 않거나 증권 중개인의 상담을 받지 않고 주식을 구매하는 투자자들의 행동을 설명하기 위해 쓰이는 용어이다. 대신, 그들은 간단히 다른 많은 이들이 이미 구매한 주식에 투자한다. 이것이 이성적이지 못한 행동으로 보일 수도 있지만, 시장의 집합적 지식을 활용하는 전략적인 방법이 될 수 있다. 하지만, 이러한 행동은 투자자들의 이성적인 선택을 막는 경향이 있어서 좋지 않은 투자의 결과를 낳을 수 있다.
(A) 밴드왜건 효과의 긍정적인 면을 보여주기 위해서
(B) 밴드왜건 효과의 주된 원인을 묘사하기 위해서

▶ a strategic way of utilizing the collective knowledge of the market이라는 표현을 통해, 음영 처리된 문장이 밴드왜건 효과의 이점을 알려준다는 것을 알 수 있다.

3. 19세기 동안, 낭만주의는 유럽 예술계를 지배했다. 특히 낭만주의 음악은 독일에서 번영하였는데, Beethoven, Mendelssohn, 그리고 Wagner와 같은 작곡가들은 서양 고전 음악 역사에서 가장 훌륭한 작품들 중 몇몇을 썼다. 이러한 작곡가들은 소나타와 심포니 같은 전통적인 구성을 사용하면서도, 풍성한 화성과 새로운 종류의 선율도 썼다. 궁극적으로, 그들의 목표는 관객으로부터 감정적인 반응을 이끌어낼 만큼 강한 느낌을 표출하는 것이었다.
(A) 낭만주의 음악의 특성을 설명하기 위해서
(B) 낭만주의 음악과 다른 음악스타일을 비교하기 위해서

▶ 주어진 문장은 낭만주의 음악가들이 사용한 구성과 화성, 선율에 대해서 설명하고 있다. 따라서 답은 (A)이다.

VOCABULARY
pp. 114-115

Write the number of each word's definition.
각 단어의 뜻을 찾아 번호를 쓰시오.

imperative / 1 긴요한 것
contaminate / 2 오염시키다
substitute / 4 대체물
insulation / 3 절연
emit / 11 (빛·소리 등을) 내다
thermal / 7 열을 내는
deduce / 10 추론하다
replicate / 12 모사하다
elasticity / 8 탄성
regulate / 6 조절하다
celestial / 9 천체의
proponent / 5 지지자

Match each collocation with the correct definition.
각 연어에 알맞은 뜻을 찾아 연결하시오.

a. flake off – to fall off a surface in flat pieces 떨어져 나오다
b. in terms of – as related to a specific subject ~에 관하여
c. embark on – to begin something long and difficult ~에 착수하다
d. the majority of – the greater number or part of 대부분의
e. be concerned with – to address as a topic ~에 관계가 있다

Circle the word closest in meaning to each underlined word.
각 밑줄 친 단어의 뜻과 가장 가까운 단어를 찾아 동그라미 하시오.

정답 | 1. (D) 2. (D) 3. (A)
4. (A) 5. (B) 6. (C)

해석 |
1. 그 형사는 범죄자의 신원에 대해 추측할 수 있었다.
   (A) 발표하다   (B) 철회하다
   (C) 손상시키다 (D) 추측하다

2. 그 예술가는 박물관에서 본 그림을 모사하려고 했다.
   (A) 구매하다   (B) 저작권을 얻다
   (C) 분석하다   (D) 복제하다

3. 그 공장의 배출물들이 강을 오염시키고 있다.
   (A) 오염시키다 (B) 굳히다
   (C) 넘쳐나게 하다 (D) 잠입하다

4. 그 기계는 배터리가 얼마 없을 때 삐 하는 소리를 낸다.
   (A) 발하다   (B) 기록하다
   (C) 이용하다 (D) 설치하다

5. 그 요리법에 따르면, 요거트는 우유의 대용품이 될 수 있다.
   (A) 자막   (B) 대체(물)
   (C) 제거   (D) 도움

6. 몸 안의 혈액 순환을 조절하는 것이 심장의 역할이다.
   (A) 응고하다   (B) 복잡하게 하다
   (C) 조정하다   (D) 종합하다

Fill in each blank with the correct collocation.
알맞은 연어를 골라 빈칸을 채우시오.

정답 | 1. In terms of   2. the majority of
3. flake off   4. are concerned with
5. embarks on

해석 |
1. 급여에 관해서는, 이것이 추구하기에 가장 좋은 직업 중 하나이다.
2. 그 투표 결과는 대부분의 유권자들이 대통령을 지지한다는 것을 보여주었다.
3. 페인트가 이 오래된 집에서 떨어져 나가기 시작한다.
4. 그 조사 항목들은 종교에 관한 사고방식에 관계 있다.
5. 여정에 착수하기 전에, 몇몇 준비 과정이 있어야 한다.

STEP 1
pp. 116-117

정답 | 1. (B)   2. (D)

통조림 식품

　역사를 통틀어, 추후 사용을 위해 음식을 보존하는 효과적인 방법을 찾는 일은 생존에 있어서 긴요하게 여겨졌다. 어떤 문화에서는 염장에 의존했고, 다른 곳에서는 다양한 절임 방법이 활용되었다. 하지만, 18세기 후반이 되어서야 밀폐된 용기에 음식을 저장하는 개념이 생겨났다.

　1810년에, Peter Durand라는 영국인이 통조림을 이용하는 과정을 특허 받았다. 3년 뒤, 긴 항해 여정에 나서는 선원들을 위한 통조림에 담긴 음식들을 대량 생산하기 위해, 최초의 통조림 공장이 건설되었다. 오늘날처럼, 통조림은 음식으로 채워져 밀봉된 후 가열되었다. 흥미롭게도, 통조림 음식이 상하지 않고 오래가는 이유는 이 시기에 완전히 파악되지 않았다. 50년 뒤에야 과학자인 Louis Pasteur가 열이 음식을 상하게 하는 박테리아를 없애고, 밀폐 통조림이 추후 음식을 오염시키는 박테리아를 막는다는 것을 추론했다.

Glossary　practice 행하다

• **Structure Zone**

prevent A from B를 써서 'B로부터 A를 막다'라는 표현을 할 수 있다. 이때 B 자리에는 명사 또는 동명사형이 와야 한다.

...the airtight cans **prevent** <u>further bacteria</u> from
                                      A
<u>contaminating the food</u>.
         B

1. 왜 작가는 지문에서 염장 과 절임 을 언급하는가?
   (A) 통조림 작업 때문에 일어나는 문제점들을 묘사하기 위해서
   (B) 초기 (음식) 보존 방법들의 예를 들기 위해서
   (C) 두 가지 종류의 통조림 방법을 대조하기 위해서
   (D) 잘 보존되지 못한 음식이 상하는 이유를 설명하기 위해서

   ➲ 지문의 첫 부분에서 작가는 역사적으로 추후에 먹기 위해 음식을 보존하는 것이 중요했다고 밝히며, 이를 뒷받침하기 위해 염장과 절임 이라는 방법을 예로 들고 있다.

2. 작가는 무엇을 나타내기 위해 지문에서 선원들 을 언급하는가
   (A) 통조림 음식은 세계로 수출되었다.
   (B) 통조림 공장 노동자들이 부족했다.
   (C) 어떤 사람들은 통조림에 보존된 음식을 신뢰하지 않았다.
   (D) 통조림 음식은 장기간 여행에 도움이 되었다.

   ➲ 음영 처리된 sailors가 속한 문장을 살펴 보면, 장기 항해에 나서는 그들을 위해 통조림 음식을 대량 생산하는 공장이 지어졌다고 하였다. 이를 통해 통조림 음식이 그들에게 도움이 되었음을 알 수 있으므로, 답은 (D)이다.

• **Note-Taking**

The Timeline of Canned Food

Before 18th	— relied on <u>salting</u> & <u>pickling</u> to <u>preserve</u> food for later use
In 1810	— used <u>tin cans</u> — <u>patented</u> by Peter Durand
In 1813	— <u>established</u> the first <u>canning factory</u>
50 Years Later	— found out <u>heat</u> killed the <u>bacteria</u> & the <u>airtight cans</u> prevented further <u>bacteria</u>

SUMMARY

In the past, food was <u>preserved</u> through <u>salting or pickling</u>. Then, people realized that food could be stored in <u>airtight containers</u>. In <u>1810</u>, a process using <u>tin cans</u> was <u>patented</u>. A <u>canning factory</u> was <u>established</u> three years later. It mass-produced <u>canned</u> goods that could be eaten by <u>sailors</u> on ships. About <u>fifty years</u> later, Louis Pasteur figured out that <u>heat</u> killed the <u>bacteria</u> that cause food go bad and that <u>the airtight cans</u> protected the food from other <u>bacteria</u>.

과거에, 음식은 염장이나 절임을 통해 보존되었다. 그 후, 사람들은 음식이 밀폐 용기에 저장될 수 있다는 것을 깨달았다. 1810년에, 통조림을 사용하는 과정이 특허 받았다. 3년 뒤에 통조림 공장이 건설되었다. 그 공장은 배의 선원들이 먹을 수 있도록 통조림 음식들을 대량 생산했다. 약 50년 뒤에, Louise Pasteur가 열이 음식을 상하게 하는 박테리아를 없애고 밀폐 통조림이 다른 박테리아로부터 음식을 지킨다는 것을 알아냈다.

VOCAB Match each word with the correct definition.
각 단어에 알맞은 뜻을 찾아 연결하시오.

a. conceive – to form a notion or idea 생각을 품다
b. patent – to make or sell a new product 특허를 받다
c. edible – fit to be eaten as food 먹을 수 있는
d. seal – to cover something to prevent from other materials 밀봉하다
e. spoil – to go bad 상하다

STEP 2 pp.118-119

| 정답 | 1. (C) | 2. (D) | 3. (B) |

모션 캡처

모션 캡처 기술은 시각 영상 기록 체계의 한 종류이다. 그것의 기본적인 기능은 사람이나 물체의 정확한 움직임을 기록하는 것이다. 그것은 또한 사람의 미묘한 얼굴 표정을 포착하는 데도 쓰인다. 이러한 움직임과 표현들은 컴퓨터의 3D 가상 모델에 적용되어 아주 정확하게 모사된다.

모션 캡처 기술로 기록되는 대상은 먼저 무수히 많은 작은 표시물로 뒤덮이게 된다. 그 대상이 인간일 경우, 모든 신체의 주요 관절 부분 가까이에 표시물이 장착된 특수 모션 캡처 보디수트를 입게 된다. 얼굴 표정을 포착하기 위해, 300개에 달하는 작은 표시물들이 사람 얼굴의 피부에 직접적으로 얹혀진다.

모션 캡처 기술이 스포츠, 게임, 군사와 의학 부분에서 응용되기는 하지만, 영화 산업에서 가장 많이 쓰인다. 특수 효과에 있어서, 그것은 보통 전통적인 컴퓨터 애니메이션의 대체물로 쓰인다. 그것의 주된 이점은 과거에는 이루지 못했던 차원의 현실감을 만화로 된 등장인물들에게 제공하여 실제 연기자들처럼 움직이고 감정을 표현하게 한다는 것이다. 이러한 점 때문에, 많은 이들은 모션 캡처 기술을 현대 영화계에 혁명적인 발전으로 여긴다.

• **Structure Zone**

'with + 명사'는 부사형과 동일하게 쓰일 수 있다.
These movements and expressions can then be...
replicated **with** great **accuracy**.
→ These movements and expressions can then be...
  replicated **accurately**.

1. 지문에서 단어 subtle 을 대체하기에 가장 적합한 것은
   (A) 선명한   (B) 초기의
   (C) 섬세한   (D) 눈에 잘 띄는

▶ 음영 처리된 단어 subtle은 '미묘한, 감지하기 힘든'이라는 뜻을 지니고 있다. 보기 중 이것과 가장 비슷한 뜻을 지닌 단어는 delicate 이다.

2. 2단락에서 작가의 주요 목적은
   (A) 컴퓨터 애니메이션의 다양한 형태들을 대조하는 것이다.
   (B) 모션 캡처 기술의 높은 비용을 보여주는 것이다.
   (C) 모션 캡처 기술의 장점을 묘사하는 것이다.
   (D) 모션 캡처 과정이 어떻게 준비되는지 설명하는 것이다.

   ▶ 2단락에서는 모션 캡처 기술을 사용할 때 무수히 많은 작은 표시물들이 쓰이며, 특히 인간의 경우 표시물들로 뒤덮인 보디수트를 입거나 얼굴에 300개에 달하는 표시물들이 쓰인다고 설명하였다. 따라서 2단락에서 작가가 의도하는 바는 모션 캡처가 준비되는 과정을 알려주는 것이다.

3. 왜 작가는 지문에서 actual actors를 언급하는가?
   (A) 기술적인 어려움에 대한 해결 방안을 제시하기 위해서
   (B) 모션 캡처 등장인물들이 얼마나 사실적으로 보이는지 강조하기 위해서
   (C) 누가 모션 캡처 기술로부터 이득을 받는지 보여주기 위해서
   (D) 전통적인 컴퓨터 애니메이션의 기원들을 설명하기 위해서

   ▶ 작가가 actual actors를 언급한 이유는 모션 캡처 기술로 탄생한 등장인물들은 실제 배우들처럼 움직이고, 감정 표현을 할 수 있을 만큼 사실적이라는 것을 밝히기 위해서이다.

• **Note-Taking**

P1　MI　motion capture technology – a type of visual recording sys.
　　 SD　records the exact movements of a prsn. or object

P2　MI　what is needed for motion capture technology
　　 SD　human – a bodysuit w/ built-in markers

P3　MI　motion capture technology in the film industry
　　 SD　special effects – a substitute for TD computer animation

VOCAB_ Write the correct word for each definition.
각 뜻에 알맞은 단어를 찾아 적으시오.

a. accuracy 정확함　　b. application 응용
c. primary 주된　　　 d. unachievable 이룰 수 없는
e. revolutionary 혁명적인

STEP 3　　　　　　　　　　　　　　pp. 120-121
정답 | 1. (B)　 2. (D)　 3. (D)　 4. (B)

인간의 피부

피부는 인간의 신체에서 가장 거대한 기관으로, 대략 2제곱미터의 크기에 무게는 3.6킬로그램에 달한다. 세 층으로 되어 있으며, 신체의 외층으로써 많은 유용한 역할들을 한다.

방수가 되는 외층인 표피는 신체를 박테리아 감염으로부터 지켜준다. 대부분의 다른 인체 조직과는 달리, 표피에는 혈관이 없고 공기 중의 산소로부터 많은 영양을 공급받는다. 각질로 불리는 표피 세포의 대부분은 표피의 중간에 형성되어 점차적으로 표면으로 움직인다. 그곳에서, 그것들은 없어지고 결국에는 떨어져 나가면서 신체를 보호하는 최전선이 된다. 진피는 그 다음 층으로, 표피의 바로 아래에 위치해 있다. 결합조직으로 이루어져 있으며, 피부에 힘과 탄성을 준다. 모낭과 모공 또한 진피에 있고, 수많은 혈관과 접촉 감각과 외부 온도를 감지하는 능력을 주는 신경 종말도 마찬가지이다. 피부의 가장 깊은 층은 하피, 다른 용어로는 피하 조직이다. 물리적인 접촉의 충격으로부터 몸을 막아주고 필수적인 절연 역할을 하는 지방으로 주로 이루어져 있으며, 피부를 신체의 뼈와 근육에 고정시킨다. 이 층에 있는 지방은 음식 공급이 부족할 때 신체의 연료로도 쓰인다.

종합적으로, 세 층으로 된 피부는 우리를 외부 위협으로부터 지켜주고, 신체 온도를 조정하며, 접촉 감각으로 하여금 외부 세상에 연결할 수 있게 하고, 필수적인 절연 역할을 한다.

Glossary　follicle 모낭

1. 각질에 대해 추론할 수 있는 것은?
   (A) 평균 세포들보다 더 크다.
   (B) 계속해서 교체되어야 한다.
   (C) 대부분의 인체 기관에서 발견된다.
   (D) 내부의 박테리아로부터 신체를 지킨다.

   ▶ 지문에 따르면, 각질은 표피 중간에서 형성되어 점차적으로 표면으로 움직이다가 결국 떨어져 나간다고 하였다. 이러한 내용을 바탕으로, 원래의 각질이 떨어져 나가면 다시 중간에서 형성된 표피가 표면으로 올라오는 것을 추측할 수 있다.

2. 왜 작가는 지문에서 our sense of touch를 언급하는가?
   (A) 피부에 혈관이 없는 이유를 설명하기 위해서
   (B) 모낭과 모공을 비교하기 위해서
   (C) 진피가 어디에 위치하는지 보여주기 위해서
   (D) 진피의 역할 중 하나를 제시하기 위해서

   ▶ 작가는 진피에 있는 신경 종말을 설명하면서, 접촉 감각을 지니게 해 주고 외부 온도를 느끼게 해 준다고 하였다. 따라서 답은 (D)이다.

3. 왜 작가는 지문에서 fuel을 언급하는가?
   (A) 지방의 원인 중 하나를 제시하기 위해서
   (B) 지방이 피부에 어떻게 해를 가하는지 보여주기 위해서
   (C) 지방이 어떻게 피부에 쌓이는지 묘사하기 위해서
   (D) 지방의 또 다른 역할을 소개하기 위해서

   ▶ 작가는 지방의 여러 가지 유익한 역할을 소개하며, 음식 섭취량이 부족할 때 인체의 연료 역할을 하기도 한다고 덧붙였다.

4. 다음 중 인간 피부의 층들에 대해 사실이 아닌 것은 무엇인가?
   (A) 가장 깊은 층은 대부분 지방으로 이루어져 있다.
   (B) 피부의 중간 부분에는 혈관이 없다.
   (C) 하피는 진피의 밑에 위치한다.
   (D) 표피는 외부 위협으로부터 우리를 지켜준다.

◉ 혈관이 없는 것은 가장 바깥에 있는 층인 표피이다. 중간 층인 진피에는 수많은 혈관과 신경 종말이 있다고 하였다.

VOCAB Find the correct word in the passage for each of the given definition.
주어진 뜻에 알맞은 단어를 지문에서 찾으시오.

a. infection 감염   b. nourishment 영양분
c. anchor 고정시키다   d. external 외부의

• **Note-Taking** (Sample Answer)

P1 MI human skin
    SD made up of three layers & serves valuable functions

P2 MI the three layers of human skin
    SD • epidermis – the waterproof outer layer
          - protects us from bacteria, nourishes from oxygen, has keratinocytes
        • dermis – located beneath the epidermis
          - gives the skin its strength & elasticity, has hair follicles & sweat glands
        • hypodermis – the skin's deepest layer
          - made up of fat – cushions the body, provides vital insulation, anchors the skin & can be used as fuel by the body

P3 MI the roles of the skin with three layers
    SD protects us, regulates body temperature, helps the sense of touch & acts as a vital insulation

---

UNIT TEST   pp. 122-123
정답   1. (C)   2. (B)   3. (D)   4. (C)   5. (A)
       6. (D), (A), (E)

전파 천문학

행성과 별들의 과학적인 연구인 천문학의 하위 분야로서, 전파 천문학은 전파 망원경을 써서 우주에 있는 물체들을 연구하는 것과 관련이 있다. 이들은 우리 행성 너머에서 발산되는 전파를 감지하고 기록하기 위해 쓰인다. 가장 거대한 전파 망원경은 푸에르토 리코의 아레시보 관측소에 있으며, 지름이 300미터가 넘는다.

전파 천문학은 1930년대에 Karl Jansky라는 미국인 물리학자가 우리 은하계 일부에서 전파가 전송되는 것을 관측하면서 시작되었다. 그 이후로, 전파 천문학자들은 우주가 전파로 가득 차 있으며, 어떤 전파들은 우주 깊은 곳에서 나온다는 것을 깨닫게 되었다. 그들은 또한 퀘이사, 펄서, 그리고 메이저와 같이 완전히 새로운 천체를 상당수 발견했다.

천문학자들이 쓰는 전파 망원경은 전파 근원지의 방향을 가리킬 수 있는 기본적으로 거대한 접시 모양의 안테나이다. 그것들은 흔히 천체를 살피고, 과학자들이 전파 신호의 근원지를 끝내 찾게 해 주는 자료를 찾는 데 쓰인다. 태양은 우리 은하계에서 가장 활발한 전파 발산지 중 한 곳이지만, 수십억 광년이 떨어진 곳에 위치한 더 강력한 다른 근원지들도 있다. 전파 천문학의 탁월한 점은 과학자들로 하여금 이렇게 알려지지 않은 천체들을 실제로 보지는 않아도 '관측할' 수 있게 한다는 것이다.

전파 천문학의 가장 중요한 과학적 업적 중 하나는 '우주 마이크로파 배경'을 감지했다는 것이었다. 1964년에 발견된 이 열복사는 우주가 창조되었을 때 남겨져 있던 것으로 여겨지며, 빅뱅이론의 지지자들에게 유용한 증거를 제공한다. 그리고 당연히 전파 망원경이 언젠가 지능을 가진 근원으로부터 신호를 감지하여, 인간만이 우주에 있는 것이 아니라는 것을 증명할 것이라는 기대도 있다.

Glossary cosmic 우주의

• **Structure Zone**

부사 far는 '멀리'라는 뜻 이외에, 비교급 등을 꾸며주며 '훨씬 더'라는 강조의 의미로 쓰이기도 한다.

... there are other **far** more powerful sources located billions of light years away.

1. 지문의 주제는 무엇인가?
   (A) 전파 천문학은 일반적으로 제대로 이해받지 못하는 과학 분야이다.
   (B) 전파 천문학은 천체를 파악하는 데 중요하다.
   (C) 전파 천문학은 과학에 중요한 기여를 해왔다.
   (D) 전파 천문학의 궁극적인 목표는 새로운 행성들을 찾는 것이다.

   ◉ 작가는 과학자들이 전파 천문학을 통해 새로운 천체를 발견해왔고, 그것이 빅뱅이론의 중요한 근거를 발견하였으며, 외계 생명체를 감지하게 될 수도 있다고 하였다. 이러한 내용을 모두 포함하고 있는 (C)가 답이다.

2. 퀘이사, 펄서, 그리고 메이저에 대해 추론할 수 있는 것은?
   (A) 그것들은 우주 사이를 움직인다.
   (B) 그것들은 전파를 발산한다.
   (C) 그것들은 아주 거대하다.
   (D) 그것들은 빅뱅을 일으켰다.

   ◉ 지문에 따르면, 전파 천문학자들은 전파 천문학을 사용하여 우주 깊은 곳에서 오는 전파를 감지하였고, 이러한 방식을 통해 퀘이사, 펄서, 그리고 메이저 등을 발견하였다. 이를 통해, 지시문에 언급된 천체들이 전파를 발산한다는 것을 알 수 있다.

3. 2단락에서 작가의 주요 목적은
   (A) 전파의 일반적인 근원지를 묘사하는 것이다.
   (B) 전파 천문학과 천문학을 비교하는 것이다.
   (C) 전파 망원경이 어떻게 작동하는지 설명하는 것이다.
   (D) 전파 천문학의 간단한 역사를 제시하는 것이다.

   ◉ 2단락에서는 전파 천문학이 언제, 누구에 의해 어떻게 시작되었고, 어떠한 천체들이 발견되었는지 간단히 설명하고 있다. 따라서 답은 (D)이다.

4. 지문에서 단어 they가 가리키는 것은
   (A) 천체들   (B) 천문학자들
   (C) 전파 망원경들   (D) 전파 근원지들

   ● 음영 처리된 they는 천체를 살피고, 과학자들로 하여금 새로운 전파 근원지를 발견하게 해 주는 주체이다. 따라서 답은 앞 문장에서 나온 전파 망원경이다.

5. 왜 작가는 지문에서 an intelligent source를 언급하는가?
   (A) 전파 천문학이 언젠가 외계 생명체를 감지할 수도 있다는 점을 제시하기 위해서
   (B) 전파 천문학 기술의 복잡함을 강조하기 위해서
   (C) 전파 천문학이 높이 평가되지 못하는 이유를 보여주기 위해서
   (D) 빅뱅이론의 창시자를 칭찬하기 위해서

   ● 작가는 언젠가 전파 천문학을 통해 지능을 가진 진원을 감지하여 인간들이 지구에 있는 유일한 존재가 아닌 것으로 밝혀질 것이라는 기대가 있다고 하였다. 그러므로 답은 (A)이다.

6. 지문의 간단한 요약을 위해 도입 문장이 아래에 주어진다. 지문에서 가장 중요한 내용을 표현하는 세 개의 보기를 선택하여 요약문을 완성하라.

   전파 천문학은 전파를 발산하는 우주의 물체를 연구하는 것이다.

   보기
   (A) 전파 망원경을 사용하여 전파를 감지하고 먼 물체들을 연구하게 해 준다.
   (B) Karl Jansky는 미국인 물리학자였다.
   (C) 천문학의 하위 분야로 여겨진다.
   (D) 많은 중요한 발견들이 전파 천문학을 통해 이루어졌다.
   (E) 중요한 증거들을 제공하며 빅뱅이론을 뒷받침하고, 외계 생명체에 대한 기대를 높인다.
   (F) 세계에서 가장 큰 전파 망원경은 푸에르토리코에 있다.

   ● 요약문에는 포괄적이면서도 핵심적인 내용이 포함되어야 한다. (B), (C), (F) 모두 핵심 문장이 되기에는 세부적인 사항이다.

- **More Info Zone**

  빅뱅이론

  우주가 태초의 대폭발로 시작되었다는 이론이다. 빅뱅이론에 따르면, 처음에 우주는 상상할 수 없을 만큼 작고 뜨거웠다. 그러나 밀도가 너무나 높았던 우주는 폭발하였고 그 후 계속 팽창해 나가고 있다. 이 팽창 과정에서 우주의 일부가 뭉쳐 별들이 생성되었다. 빅뱅이론의 지지자들은, 온도와 밀도가 높았던 초기 우주가 급격히 팽창하면서 점차 식기 시작하였고, 이 과정에서 수소, 헬륨 같은 가벼운 원소가 만들어져 지금까지 우주의 대부분을 차지하게 되었다고 주장한다. 현재까지 빅뱅이론은 우주의 생성을 설명할 수 있는 가장 적합한 모형으로 알려져 있다.

VOCABULARY TEST pp. 124-125

Recall the essential words in the unit to reinforce your vocabulary acquisition. Write the meaning of each word in your language.
유닛에서 배운 주요 단어들을 떠올려 각 단어의 뜻을 쓰시오.

edible | 먹을 수 있는
substitute | 대체물
nourishment | 영양분
cosmic | 우주의
spoil | 상하다
emit | (빛·소리 등을) 내다
deduce | 추론하다
accuracy | 정확함
elasticity | 탄성
proponent | 지지자
primary | 주된
strategic | 전략적인
revolutionary | 혁명석인
follicle | 모낭
unachievable | 이룰 수 없는
conceive | 생각을 품다
thermal | 열을 내는
be concerned with | ~에 관계가 있다
dominate | 지배하다
flake off | 떨어져 나오다
embark on | ~에 착수하다

infection | 감염
celestial | 천체의
external | 외부의
patent | 특허를 받다
contaminate | 오염시키다
regulate | 조정하다
brilliance | 탁월
imperative | 긴요한 것
anchor | 고정시키다
animated | 만화로 된, 생기 있는
transition | 이행
seal | 밀봉하다
elicit | 끌어내다
application | 응용
irrational | 비이성적인
replicate | 모사하다
in terms of | ~에 관하여
insulation | 절연
the majority of | 대부분의

Complete each sentence with the correct word or collocation.
문장에 알맞은 단어나 연어를 찾아 쓰시오.

정답 | 1. elasticity   2. embarking on
      3. dominated   4. emitted
      5. applications   6. transition
      7. elicit   8. strategic
      9. imperative   10. unachievable

해석 |
1. 결합조직으로 이루어진 진피는 피부에 탄성을 준다.
2. 통조림 음식은 긴 항해 여정에 나서는 선원들을 위해 이용되었다.
3. 낭만주의는 유럽 예술계를 지배했다.
4. 전파 망원경은 우리 행성 너머에서 발산되는 전파를 감지한다.
5. 모션 캡처 기술은 스포츠, 군사와 의학 부분에서도 응용된다.
6. 유대교에서, 바 미츠바는 한 소년이 어른으로 이행하는 의식이다.
7. 그 작곡가들의 목표는 관객으로부터 감정적인 반응을 이끌어내는 것이었다.
8. 그것은 시장의 집합적 지식을 활용하는 전략적인 방법이 될 수 있다.
9. 음식을 보존하는 효과적인 방법을 찾는 일은 긴요한 것으로 여겨졌다.

10. 그것은 과거에는 이루지 못했던 차원의 현실감을 만화로 된 등장인물에게 제공한다.

UNIT 08
Insertion

INTRODUCTION
문장 삽입 문제는 주어진 문장을 지문 중 가장 알맞은 부분에 넣는 유형이다. 가장 정확한 위치를 찾기 위해서는 지문의 흐름이 문맥적으로 타당한지 살펴보고 문법적으로도 올바른지 파악할 수 있어야 한다.

TYPICAL QUESTION TYPE
주어진 문장이 지문에 들어갈 수 있는 곳을 가리키는 네 개의 네모 [■]를 보라.

더욱이, 그들은 조국에서 땅을 사는 것조차도 금지되었다.

이 문장이 어디에 가장 적절한가?

STRATEGIES
- 주어진 문장과 접속사와 접속 어구에 맞는 위치를 살펴 보고 어울리는 곳을 찾는다. 이것들은 문장이 어디에 속하는지 단서를 준다.
- 주어진 문장 안이나 단락 안의 보기 위치들에서 대명사가 있는지 파악한다. 그러고 나서, 대명사가 가리키는 명사를 찾는다.
- 주어진 문장을 각 보기 위치에 넣어 주의 깊게 읽어 보며, 글의 흐름이 매끄러운지 살펴 본다. 지문 안의 연결된 두 문장이 분리될 수 없는 경우라면, 그 보기 위치는 배제한다.

QUICK CHECKUP   p. 127

정답 | 1. C   2. D   3. A

Check the square where the given sentence fits.
주어진 문장이 들어갈 곳으로 알맞은 네모를 고르시오.

1. 예술에 있어서 표절의 정의는 더욱 모호하다.

   다른 이의 창의적인 생산물을 가져다 자신의 것으로 내세우는 것은 표절이라고 알려져 있다. A 표절은 많은 전문 분야에 광범위하게 퍼져 있는데, 특히 저널리즘과 예술계에서 심하다. B 기자들은 그들이 사용하는 주제에 대한 집필물을 사전에 참고해야 하지만, 이러한 출처를 정확히 밝히지 않는 것은 비윤리적이라고 여겨진다. C **예술에 있어서 표절의 정의는 더욱 모호하다.** 예술가들은 정기적으로 서로의 작품을 차용하는데, 이러한 과정에서 영감과 저작권의 침해가 모호해진다. D

   ▶ 주어진 문장은 예술계에서의 표절을 설명하고 있으며, more ambiguous라는 표현을 통해 앞에 나온 내용과 비교되는 문장인 것을 알 수 있다. 따라서 이 문장이 들어갈 위치는 C 이다.

2. 이 인구 이동은 토양의 염분이 높아져 농작물 재배가 급격히 감소한 것이 원인이 되었다고 알려져 있다.

   수메르는 메소포타미아 지역의 초기 문명 중 하나로, 현재 쿠웨이트와 이라크 남부의 위치에 자리잡고 있었다. A 고대 그리스처럼, 수메르는 원래 수많은 도시국가로 이루어져 있었다. B 기원전 2900년에 왕조시대가 시작되었는데, 강력한 왕조들이 연속해서 그 지역을 통합하고 있었다. C 하지만 사람들이 북쪽으로 옮겨가면서, 수메르는 대략 800년 후에 몰락에 빠졌다. D **이 인구 이동은 토양의 염분이 높아져 농작물 재배가 급격히 감소한 것이 원인이 되었다고 알려져 있다.**

   ▶ this population shift라는 표현을 통해, 앞선 문장에 인구 이동의 내용이 있다는 것을 추측할 수 있다. 따라서 주어진 문장은 마지막 문장 뒤에 위치해야 한다.

3. 그것은 전통적으로 그들이 이 힘과 조화로운지 확실히 하기 위해 건물들의 방향을 지정하는 데 사용되었다.

   문자 그대로라면 '바람과 물'을 뜻하는 풍수는 보이지 않는 힘이 우주를 다 함께 지탱하고 있다는 중국의 사상이다. A **그것은 전통적으로 그들이 이 힘과 조화로운지 확실히 하기 위해 건물들의 방향을 지정하는 데 사용되었다.** 이것은 별들, 지리적 특성, 또는 나침반 방향과 관련이 있다. B 풍수는 3,000년 이상 되었지만, 오늘날에도 활용된다. C 몇몇 현대 가정과 사무실은 이 원칙을 바탕으로 배열된다. D

   ▶ 문장의 내용과 this energy라는 표현으로 미루어 보아, 주어진 문장은 풍수지리에 대한 문장의 부연설명이라는 것을 알 수 있다. 따라서 답은 A 이다.

VOCABULARY   pp. 128-129

Write the number of each word's definition.
각 단어의 뜻을 찾아 번호를 쓰시오.

aquatic / 7 수생의
emigrate / 11 이주하다
tariff / 12 관세
proclamation / 4 선언
neutralize / 8 중화시키다
induce / 6 유발하다

famine / 3 기근
severity / 10 혹독함
harbor / 5 (생각을) 품다
immune / 9 면역성이 있는
detect / 1 감지하다
irrigate / 2 관개하다

Match each collocation with the correct definition.
각 연어에 알맞은 뜻을 찾아 연결하시오.

a. be ruled by – to be under the control of 지배 당하다

b. take control – to have the power to dominate
지배권을 잡다
c. take steps – to figure out a measure or solution
조치를 취하다
d. vary in – to have a wide range of ~이 여러 가지다
e. associated with – linked or related to ~와 관련된

Circle the word closest in meaning to each underlined word.
각 밑줄 친 단어의 뜻과 가장 가까운 단어를 찾아 동그라미 하시오.

정답 | 1. (B) 2. (A) 3. (D)
     4. (B) 5. (A) 6. (D)

해석 |
1. 그 수학자는 방정식에서 오류를 감지할 수 있었다.
   (A) 분석하다   (B) 확인하다
   (C) 정정하다   (D) 설명하다

2. 그 여자는 그녀 인생의 혹독함이 끝나기를 바랐다.
   (A) 가혹함   (B) 다양함
   (C) 받아들임   (D) 뜻밖의 기쁨

3. 이 서류는 새로운 현 정부의 선언서이다.
   (A) 장애물   (B) 형성
   (C) 집행   (D) 법령

4. 전쟁 후, 수천 명의 사람들이 그 나라로부터 인접 나라들로 이주했다.
   (A) 접했다   (B) 이동했다
   (C) 대조했다   (D) 축적했다

5. 그 소년은 음악가가 되려는 꿈을 품곤 했다.
   (A) 품다   (B) 버리다
   (C) 빈정대다   (D) 약을 투여하다

6. 이 약은 독성의 효과를 중화시킬 것이다.
   (A) 분류하다   (B) 발표하다
   (C) 수분하다   (D) 무효화하다

Fill in each blank with the correct collocation.
알맞은 연어를 골라 빈칸을 채우시오.

정답 | 1. took control   2. vary in
     3. associated with   4. take steps
     5. was ruled by

해석 |
1. 그 당은 총선에서 크게 승리하여 지배권을 잡았다.
2. 그 새의 깃털은 짙은 파란색으로부터 선명한 빨간색까지 색이 다양하다.
3. 비만은 보통 건강에 해로운 식단과 관련이 있다.
4. 경영진은 그 회사의 위기를 극복하기 위해 조치를 취하기 시작했다.
5. 그 식민지는 수년 동안 먼 왕국에 의해 지배 당했다.

STEP 1 pp. 130-131

정답 | 1. 1C   2. 2B

아홀로틀

아홀로틀은 멕시코 중부의 두 호수에 사는 도롱뇽의 일종이다. 1A 그것은 약 30센티미터의 길이까지 자란다. 1B 변태라는 과정을 통해 수중 유충에서 육지 생물로 변화하는 다른 대부분의 양서류와는 달리, 아홀로틀은 수중에서 일생을 보낸다. 1C 아마도 아홀로틀의 가장 특이한 성질은 사지 부분 전체를 다시 자라나게 할 수 있는 재생 능력일 것이다. 1D

2A 불행하게도, 아홀로틀은 자연 서식지인 두 개의 호수를 잃었다. 2B 야생에서 약 1,000마리만이 존재한다고 추정된다. 2C 그럼에도 불구하고, 현재 아홀로틀은 이 특이한 생물을 애완용으로 기르는 사람들에 의해 흔히 사육된다. 2D 아홀로틀은 또한 실험실에서 그것의 치유 능력의 비밀을 알게 되기를 바라는 과학자들에 의해 연구된다.

1. 주어진 문장이 1단락에 들어갈 수 있는 곳을 가리키는 네 개의 네모 [■]를 보시오.

이것 때문에, 그것은 깃털과 닮은 외부 아가미를 지니고 있다.

이 문장이 어디에 가장 적절한가?

▶ 주어진 문장은 아홀로틀이 외부 아가미를 기르는 이유가 되는 내용 뒤에 들어가야 한다. 지문에서 그 근거가 되는 문장을 찾아보면 '아홀로틀은 수중에서 평생을 보낸다'이다. 따라서 답은 1C 이다.

2. 주어진 문장이 2단락에 들어갈 수 있는 곳을 가리키는 네 개의 네모 [■]를 보시오.

그 토종 호수 중 하나는 완전히 말랐고, 다른 하나는 굉장히 오염되었다.

이 문장이 어디에 가장 적절한가?

▶ 'one of ~, and the other'이라는 표현이 쓰이려면 앞의 내용에서 두 가지 대상이 나와야 한다. 문맥상, 두 가지 호수를 소개한 다음 주어진 문장이 들어가는 것이 가장 적절하므로 답은 2B 가 된다.

• Note-Taking

Axolotls

What They Are	— a type of salamander w/ a length of about 30 centimeters
Where They Live	— spend their whole lives in the water
What They Have	— regenerative powers — capable of growing back limbs
Today	— only about 1,000 exist in the wild
	— kept in captivity by ppl. as pets
	— found in laboratories where scientists learn about its healing abilities

SUMMARY

The axolotl is a salamander found in central Mexico. It grows to a length of 30 centimeters. Most amphibians change from aquatic larvae into land-dwelling adults. But the axolotl spends its entire life in the water. It can also grow back lost limbs. Sadly, it has lost its habitats, and there are a few left in the wild. However, the axolotl is often kept as a pet. It is also studied by scientists interested in its healing abilities.

아홀로틀은 멕시코 중부에서 발견되는 도롱뇽이다. 그것은 30센티미터의 길이까지 자란다. 대부분의 양서류는 수중 유충에서 육지 생물로 변화한다. 하지만 아홀로틀은 수중에서 일생을 보낸다. 또한 그것은 잃은 사지를 다시 기를 수 있다. 슬프게도, 그것은 서식지들을 잃었고 야생에는 소수만이 남아있다. 하지만, 아홀로틀은 흔히 애완 동물로 길러진다. 그것은 치유 능력에 관심 있는 과학자들에 의해서도 연구된다.

VOCAB_ Match each word with the correct definition.
각 단어에 알맞은 뜻을 찾아 연결하시오.

a. amphibian – an animal that can live both on land and in water 양서류
b. metamorphosis – an animal's change between life stages 변태
c. trait – a particular characteristic or quality 특성
d. regenerative – growing again after being lost, damaged, etc. 재생시키는
e. limb – an arm or a leg 사지

STEP 2			pp. 132-133
정답	1. 1B	2. (C)	3. 3C

아일랜드 감자 기근

1845년을 시작으로, 아일랜드는 100만명의 사람들이 죽고 100만명이 넘는 사람들이 다른 나라로 이주하게 한 심각한 기근에 시달렸다. 기근의 직접적인 원인은 감자의 병충해였지만, 그 재앙의 시련에 원인이 된 사회적, 정치적인 요소들이 많이 있었다.

1A 19세기 중반에 아일랜드는 신교였던 대영제국에 의해 지배 당했고, 아일랜드의 구교도들은 제도적인 차별에 맞닥뜨렸다. 1B 소규모의 농장만을 임대할 수 있게 되면서 그들은 주로 감자를 재배했는데, 그것이 곡물보다 더 적은 공간을 차지했기 때문이다. 1C 병충해가 닥쳤을 때, 인구의 반은 감자에 의지해서 살아 남았다. 1D

기근이 시작된 후, 영국 정부는 수입 곡물에 높은 관세를 내리는 곡물 조령을 폐지하였으나, 효과가 거의 없었다. 이후, 새로운 정당이 권력을 장악했고 위기를 끝내는 데 성의 없는 시도만을 했다. 구호 활동의 수장은 '신은 아일랜드인들에게 교훈을 주기 위해 이런 재앙을 보냈다'라는 도를 넘은 발언까지 했다.

3A 기근은 몇 년 후에 끝났다. 3B 하지만 아일랜드인들은 영국에 대한 쓰라림과 불신의 감정을 계속해서 품었다. 3C 결국, 그들의 노력은 1949년에 아일랜드 공화국 선언으로 이어졌다. 3D

• **Structure Zone**

'leave + 목적어 + 형용사[현재분사]'는 '…을 ~하게 하다'라는 의미로 쓰인다.

…a devastating famine that **left a million people dead** and caused a million more to emigrate…

1. 주어진 문장이 2단락에 들어갈 수 있는 곳을 가리키는 네 개의 네모 [■]를 보시오.

더욱이, 그들은 조국에서 땅을 사는 것조차도 금지되었다.

이 문장이 어디에 가장 적절한가?

➊ 주어진 문장은 아일랜드인들이 영국으로부터 당했던 시련을 보여주고 있다. Moreover라는 접속사를 통해, 앞선 문장도 이러한 맥락의 내용을 담고 있을 것이라는 것을 알 수 있다. 따라서 영국의 박해 내용이 나온 뒤이며, 아일랜드인들의 농작에서의 어려움을 나타낸 문장 앞인 1B 가 가장 적절하다.

2. 3단락에서 작가의 주요 목적은
(A) 기근이 영국 정치 체제에 미친 영향을 묘사하는 것이다.
(B) 곡물에 부과된 관세와 감자에 부과된 관세를 비교하는 것이다.
(C) 영국 정부가 기근을 막기 위하여 얼마나 적은 노력을 했는지 보여주는 것이다.
(D) 아일랜드인들의 수준 낮은 농장 기술의 예를 드는 것이다.

➊ 작가는 3단락에서 영국이 기근 해결을 위해 내놓은 여러 가지 대안들을 설명하면서, 효과가 미미한 것들이었다는 것을 보여주고 있다. 따라서 답은 (C)이다.

3. 주어진 문장이 4단락에 들어갈 수 있는 곳을 가리키는 네 개의 네모 [■]를 보시오.

아일랜드인들은 대영제국으로부터 독립을 얻기 위해 분투를 시작했다.

이 문장이 어디에 가장 적절한가?

➊ 주어진 문장 뒤에는 아일랜드인들 분투의 결과가 나오는 것이 문맥에 알맞다. 내용상 가장 잘 어울리는 자리는 3C 이다.

• **Note-Taking**

P1 MI the outbreak of Irish famine in 1845
 SD caused due to a potato blight w/ social & political factors

P2 MI discrimination against Irish Catholics by Great Britain
 SD allowed only small farm plots → mostly grew potatoes

P3 MI British government's actions
 SD abolished the Corn Law & made halfhearted attempts to end the crisis

P4 MI the proclamation of the Republic of Ireland
 SD the Irish: harbored feelings of bitterness & distrust toward the British

VOCAB_ Write the correct word for each definition.
각 뜻에 알맞은 단어를 찾아 적으시오.

a. blight 병충해
b. discrimination 차별
c. halfhearted 열성이 없는
d. calamity 재앙
e. distrust 불신

STEP 3			pp. 134-135
정답	1. (D) 2. 2D	3. 3A	4. (C)

알레르기

알레르기는 알레르기 유발 항원으로 알려진, 다른 점에서 보면 무해한 물질에 대한 면역 체계의 부적절한 반응으로 일어나는 흔한 장애이다. 세계의 30%에 달하는 인구가 몇몇 종류의 알레르기를 겪고 있으며, 그 수가 늘어나는 것으로 추정된다.

2A 인체 면역 체계의 주된 역할은 위험한 외부 물질을 파악하여 그것들을 중화시키려고 조치를 취하는 것이다. 2B 그것은 물질을 추적하여 신체에 해를 가하기 전에 파괴하는 항체들을 생산함으로써 이를 실행한다. 2C 이 항체들은 히스타민이라는 화학 물질을 신체에 방출한다. 2D

3A 하지만, 한번 그러고 나면 항원이 감지될 때마다 이러한 반응을 계속 일으킬 것이다. 3B 알레르기 반응은 가벼운 것에서 목숨을 위협하는 것까지 심각성이 다양하다. 3C 자연적으로 공기로 운반되는 항원은 가벼운 증상들을 일으키지만, 음식 알레르기와 곤충에게 쏘인 것은 발진, 목 부음, 그리고 혈압 강하를 유발하는 과민증을 일으킬 수 있다. 3D

무조건 피하는 것이 알레르기에 대처하는 가장 효과적인 방법이지만, 다양한 알레르기용 약도 있다. 하지만, 이러한 제품들은 알레르기 증상을 처치할 뿐, 치료하는 것이 아니라는 점을 알아두는 것이 중요하다. 어떤 알레르기의 경우, 의사들은 항원 면역 요법을 권할 수도 있는데, 이것은 인체가 소량의 항원에 노출될 수 있도록 연속적으로 주사를 맞고, 결국에는 그에 따르는 반응을 최소화하는 것이다.

• Structure Zone

- 부사 so를 써서 이미 언급된 것을 다시 가리키는 '그렇게'라는 의미로 쓸 수 있다.

  ... it will continue to do **so** every time the allergen is detected.

- while은 상반된 두 내용을 대조하는 문장에서 쓰일 수 있다.

  Natural airborne allergens normally cause mild symptoms **while** food allergies and insect stings can cause anaphylaxis,...

- 주어가 너무 길 때, 'it is + 형용사 + to부정사'의 형태를 쓸 수 있다. 이때 it은 가주어이고 to 이하가 진주어이다.

  However, **it is important to note** that these products merely treat the symptoms of allergies and are not cures.

---

1. 다음 중 항원에 대해 사실인 것은 무엇인가?
   (A) 항체를 처리하기 위해 신체가 생산한다.
   (B) 신체가 과민증을 일으킬 때 배출된다.
   (C) 대부분의 흔한 알레르기보다 더 심각하다.
   (D) 항원 면역 요법으로 약물치료를 받을 수 있다.

   ▶ 지문에 따르면, 항원은 면역 체계의 반응을 일으키는 물질이다. 이에 대처하기 위해 항원 면역 요법의 도움을 받을 수 있다고 하였다. 따라서 답은 (D)이고, 나머지 보기들은 사실과 다르다.

2. 주어진 문장이 2단락에 들어갈 수 있는 곳을 가리키는 네 개의 네모 [■]를 보시오.

   그것은 콧물, 따가운 눈, 그리고 피부의 간지러움 등 많은 흔한 알레르기 증상들을 일으킨다.

   이 문장이 어디에 가장 적절한가?

   ▶ 주어진 문장의 주어인 It은 여러 가지 알레르기 증상을 일으키는 주체이고, 문맥상 히스타민임을 알 수 있다. 따라서 답은 2D이다.

3. 주어진 문장이 3단락에 들어갈 수 있는 곳을 가리키는 네 개의 네모 [■]를 보시오.

   왜 면역 체계가 무해한 항원을 심각한 위협으로 오인하는지 아무도 확실히 알지 못한다.

   이 문장이 어디에 가장 적절한가?

   ▶ 3단락에서는 항원이 감지된 후 나타나는 알레르기 반응들에 대해 설명하고 있다. 문맥상, 주어진 문장을 단락의 제일 앞에 삽입하는 것이 적절하다. 따라서 답은 3A이다.

4. 지문에서 단어 minimize와 의미가 가장 가까운 것은
   (A) 근절하다   (B) 안정시키다
   (C) 줄이다   (D) 격려하다

   ▶ 단어 minimize는 '최소화하다, 축소하다'라는 뜻을 지니고 있다. 따라서 가장 비슷한 의미의 단어를 찾으면 diminish가 된다.

VOCAB Find the correct word in the passage for each of the given definition.
주어진 뜻에 알맞은 단어를 지문에서 찾으시오.

a. disorder 장애
b. airborne 공기로 운반되는
c. swelling 부어 오른 곳
d. dose (약의) 투여량

• Note-Taking (Sample Answer)

P1   MI   allergies
      SD   caused by an improper reaction of the immune system

P2   MI   the primary function of the immune system
      SD   producing antibodies → causes many common allergy symptoms

P3   MI   allergic reactions
      SD   mild symptoms to serious reactions of anaphylaxis

P4 MI effective methods of dealing w/ allergies
    SD avoidance, a variety of allergy medications & allergen immunotherapy

UNIT TEST   pp. 136-137

정답 | 1. (B) 2. (D) 3. 3D 4. 4B 5. (C)
     6. Summer Monsoons (B), (E), (G)
        Winter Monsoons (A), (C)

계절풍

전통적으로 인도양 지역과 관계된 '계절풍'이라는 용어는 오늘날 매년 건조기가 지속되게 하거나 폭우 기간이 길어지게 하는, 바람 방향의 변화에 일반적으로 적용된다. 그 용어 자체는 '계절'을 뜻하는 아랍 단어인 *mausem*에서 파생되었다.

이 현상에는 일반적으로 두 가지 종류가 있는데, 여름 계절풍과 겨울 계절풍이다. 이 두 가지 사이의 차이를 이해하려면, 기억해야 할 두 가지 중요한 핵심이 있다. 첫 번째는 계절풍의 바람은 항상 추운 지역에서 따뜻한 지역으로 분다는 것이고, 두 번째는 육지가 해상보다 더 빨리 열이 오르고 식는다는 것이다.

3A 그러므로, 햇빛이 강한 여름 동안에는 육지 위에 있는 공기가 해안 위에 있는 공기보다 더 따뜻하다. 3B 이것은 육지 위에 저기압 지역을, 그리고 해상 위에 고기압 지역을 형성한다. 3C 습한 해안 공기는 고기압 지역에서 저기압 지역으로 옮겨간다. 3D

겨울 동안, 반대의 현상이 일어난다. 4A 강한 햇빛이 없을 때, 육지는 해안보다 더 빠르게 열을 잃는다. 4B 그곳에서, 공기가 상승해서 많은 양의 강수가 일어난다. 4C 그 결과, 육지 지역은 건기를 겪고 때때로 가뭄을 경험한다. 4D

일반적으로, 여름 계절풍은 겨울 계절풍보다 더 강력하다. 열대 지역의 많은 이들은 곡물에 물을 대고, 수력발전소를 가동하기 위해 여름 계절풍의 호우에 의존한다. 하지만, 아주 심한 계절풍에 동반되는 강풍과 폭우는 홍수와 심각한 재산 피해를 초래할 수 있다.

Glossary dry spell 건기   undergo 겪다   drought 가뭄

• Structure Zone

비교급 more는 형용사뿐만 아니라 부사에도 쓰일 수 있다.
...land both heats up and colds down **more quickly** than water.
...the land loses its warmth **more rapidly** than the ocean does.

1. 지문의 주제는 무엇인가?
   (A) 지구온난화가 계절풍 형성에 미치는 영향
   (B) 계절풍을 일으키는 기후적 조건들
   (C) 다양한 계절풍으로 일어나는 피해와 이점
   (D) 여름 계절풍이 겨울 계절풍보다 더 강력한 이유

▶ 습도와 기압 등을 들어 여름 계절풍과 겨울 계절풍이 각각 어떻게 일어나는지 설명하고 있다. 이에 가장 적합한 답은 (B)이다.

2. 지문에서 단어 shift와 의미가 가장 가까운 것은
   (A) 증가   (B) 기온 상승
   (C) 감소   (D) 편차

▶ 음영 처리된 단어 shift는 '변화'라는 뜻을 가지고 있다. 이에 가장 비슷한 단어는 (D) deviation이다.

3. 주어진 문장이 3단락에 들어갈 수 있는 곳을 가리키는 네 개의 네모 [■]를 보시오.

그것이 육지에 도달하면, 더 따뜻한 기온이 공기를 가열하고 상승하게 만들어, 습기가 비의 형태로 지상에 떨어진다.

이 문장이 어디에 가장 적절한가?

▶ 먼저 주어진 문장을 살펴 보면, '그것'이 육지에 도달하여 결과적으로 비가 내리게 된다고 하였다. 지문에서 해안 공기가 저기압 지역, 즉 육지로 움직인다고 하였으므로, 문맥상 이러한 내용 뒤에 문장이 위치하는 것이 적합하다. 따라서 답은 3D이다.

4. 주어진 문장이 4단락에 들어갈 수 있는 곳을 가리키는 네 개의 네모 [■]를 보시오.

그에 상응하는 변화들이 압력에서 일어나 육지 위의 공기가 더 따뜻한 해안지역으로 옮겨가게 한다.

이 문장이 어디에 가장 적절한가?

▶ 4단락의 전체적인 내용은 겨울 계절풍에 관한 것으로, 육지가 해안보다 기온 변화가 더 크다고 하였으므로, 육지 부분이 고기압이 된다는 것을 알 수 있다. 이러한 내용이 주어진 문장에 담겨 있고, 문맥상 어울리는 자리를 찾으면 답은 4B이다.

5. 왜 작가는 지문에서 hydroelectric power plants를 언급하는가?
   (A) 계절풍 때문에 생기는 문제에 대한 대안을 제시하기 위해서
   (B) 계절풍들이 어떻게 연구되는지 설명하기 위해서
   (C) 계절풍의 장점을 강조하기 위해서
   (D) 기온 변화의 현상을 보여주기 위해서

▶ 작가는 5단락에서 계절풍의 장점들과 단점들을 서술하고 있다. 장점 중 하나로 언급된 것이 수력발전소로, 그것을 가동하는 데 여름 계절풍이 쓰인다고 하였다. 따라서 답은 (C)이다.

6. 보기에서 적당한 구를 찾아서 그것들과 관련된 카테고리에 넣어라. 보기 중에서 두 개는 사용되지 않을 것이다.

여름 계절풍   /   겨울 계절풍

보기
(A) 덜 강력한 종류이다.
(B) 곡물에 물을 대는 데 사용된다.
(C) 종종 가뭄을 초래할 수 있다.
(D) 따뜻한 지역에서 차가운 지역으로 옮겨가는 바람이 여기에 속한다.
(E) 해안 위에 고기압 지역이 있다.

(F) 일년에 여러 번 일어난다.
(G) 습기가 있는 공기가 육지로 움직인다.

▶ 지문에 따르면, 여름 계절풍은 겨울 계절풍보다 더 강력하고 관개와 수력발전소 가동을 위해 쓰이며, 해상 위에 고기압을 내륙 지역에는 저기압을 형성하여 습한 해안 공기가 내륙으로 옮겨가면서 생긴다. 반면에, 겨울 계절풍은 여름 계절풍과 반대의 경우에 일어나며 건기와 가뭄을 초래할 수 있다고 하였다. 이 같은 사실에 따라 보기를 선택한다.

4. 알레르기는 면역 체계의 부적절한 반응으로 일어난다.
5. 19세기 중반에 아일랜드는 대영제국에 의해 지배 당했다.
6. 아흘로톤은 사지 부분 전체를 다시 자라나게 할 수 있다.
7. 수메르는 대략 800년 후에 몰락에 빠졌다.
8. 표절은 오늘날 예술계와 저널리즘에 광범위하게 퍼져 있다.
9. 양서류는 수중 유충에서 육지 생물로 변화한다.
10. 신체의 체계는 위험한 외부 물질을 중화시키려고 조치를 취한다.

VOCABULARY TEST   pp. 138-139

Recall the essential words in the unit to reinforce your vocabulary acquisition. Write the meaning of each word in your language.
유닛에서 배운 주요 단어들을 떠올려 각 단어의 뜻을 쓰시오.

irrigate	관개하다
proclamation	선언
harbor	(생각을) 품다
detect	감지하다
dynasty	왕조
decline	하락
dry spell	건기
unethical	비윤리적인
calamity	재앙
consult	참고하다
severity	혹독함
distrust	불신
emigrate	이주하다
undergo	겪다
blight	병충해
plagiarism	표절
drought	가뭄
take steps	조치를 취하다
blur	흐릿해지다
be ruled by	지배 당하다
dose	(약의) 투여량
amphibian	양서류
swelling	부어 오른 곳
immune	면역성이 있는
limb	사지
trait	특성
halfhearted	열성이 없는
tariff	관세
famine	기근
aquatic	수생의
airborne	공기로 운반되는
metamorphosis	변태
neutralize	중화시키다
disorder	장애
regenerative	재생시키는
induce	유발하다
associated with	~와 관련된
discrimination	차별
vary in	~이 여러 가지로
take control	지배권을 잡다

Complete each sentence with the correct word or collocation.
문장에 알맞은 단어나 연어를 찾아 쓰시오.

정답 | 1. famine   2. unethical
       3. undergo   4. immune
       5. was ruled by 6. limbs
       7. decline   8. Plagiarism
       9. aquatic   10. takes steps

해석 |
1. 1845년을 시작으로, 아일랜드는 심각한 기근에 시달렸다.
2. 출처를 정확히 밝히지 않는 것은 비윤리적이라고 여겨진다.
3. 그 결과, 육지 지역은 건기를 겪는다.

PART 3
TOEFL iBT® Reading Skills 03

Summarizing

요약은 지문을 주제와 가장 중요한 세부사항들로 줄이는 것이다. 그렇게 하기 위해서, 수험자는 주어진 내용을 의미 변함 없이 자신만의 표현으로 바꿔 써야 한다. 보통 지문의 서두 부분에 위치하고 있는 주제문을 찾는 것부터 (요약을) 시작할 수 있다. 수험자는 작가가 주제 문장을 뒷받침하기 위해 사용한 주요 핵심 내용들을 찾아보아야 한다. 마지막으로 주제 문장과 세부사항들을 다른 말로 바꾸어 짧은 문단으로 배열해야 한다.

Find the topic sentence and major points of the passage. Then complete the summary.
지문의 주제 문장과 주요 핵심 내용들을 찾은 후, 요약문을 완성하시오.

고고학자들은 멕시코의 비밀스러운 도시인 테오티우아칸이 어떻게 지어졌는지 정확히 알지 못한다. 첫째로, 기원전 100년까지 거슬러 올라간다고 여겨지는 테오티우칸을 누가 지었는지 아무도 알지 못한다. 비록 그것의 이름이 아즈텍 언어에서 온 '신들이 태어난 장소'이지만, 그 도시는 아즈텍 왕국보다 훨씬 더 오래되었다. 더욱이, 테오티우칸 사람들은 8세기경에 흔적도 없이 사라졌다. 왜 그들이 도시를 버렸는지, 그들이 어디로 갔는지는 불분명하다.

- **Main Idea**   The city of Teotihuacan remains mysterious to archaeologists.
- **Supporting Details**
  - Nobody knows who built the city.
  - It has an Aztec name but far precedes the Aztec Empire.
  - It is uncertain why the people of Teotihuacan disappeared.

- Summary The city of Teotihuacan in ancient Mexico remains mysterious to archaeologists. First, nobody knows who built the city. Even though it has an Aztec name, it far precedes the Aztec Empire. Additionally, it is uncertain why the people of Teotihuacan disappeared or where they went.
- 주제 테오티우칸 도시는 고고학자들에게 비밀스럽게 남아있다.
- 세부사항 - 그 도시를 누가 지었는지 아무도 모른다.
  - 아즈텍식 이름이 있지만 아즈텍 왕국보다 훨씬 오래되었다.
  - 테오티우칸 사람들이 왜 사라졌는지 불분명하다.
- 요약문 고대 멕시코 도시인 테오티우칸은 고고학자들에게 비밀스럽게 남아있다. 첫째로, 누가 그 도시를 지었는지 아무도 모른다. 아즈텍식 이름이 있지만, 아즈텍 왕국보다 훨씬 오래되었다. 더욱이, 테오티우칸 사람들이 왜 사라졌는지, 어디로 갔는지 불분명하다.

➤ 주어진 지문의 주제는 테오티우칸 도시가 사람들에게 비밀스럽게 남겨져 있다는 것으로, 이에 대한 세 가지 세부사항들이 제시되어 주제를 뒷받침한다. 지문에 알맞은 내용들을 찾아 요약문을 완성할 수 있다.

Categorizing

범주 나누기는 중요한 구성적 기술인데, 더 분명한 이해를 위해 지문에 나타난 정보를 취해서 두 개 이상의 범주로 나누는 것이다. 지문이 두 가지 소재에 대한 것이라는 것을 수험자가 인지하면, 그들은 서로 비교되고 있는 것들이나 대조되는 것들에 주목해야 한다.

Write the correct information for each category.
각 범주에 알맞은 정보를 골라 적으시오.

쌍봉낙타는 두 개의 혹으로 쉽게 구분될 수 있다. 그것의 더 흔한 사촌격인 단봉낙타는 오로지 한 개의 혹을 가지고 있다. 중앙아시아 지역 토종인 쌍봉낙타는 그 개체수가 200만으로 줄었는데, 그들 중 대부분은 사육된다. 단봉낙타 또한 대체적으로 사육된다. 개체수가 1,500만에 달하는 그것들은 주로 북아프리카와 남서아시아 부분에 퍼져 있다.

- Bactrian Camel: two large humps, native to the Central Asia region, population of about 2 million
- Dromedary Camel: a single hump, population of about 15 million, scattered across North Africa and parts of Southwest Asia

➤ 쌍봉낙타는 두 개의 혹을 지니고 있고, 중앙아시아 지역 토종이며 200만 마리 정도가 남아 있다. 한 개의 혹을 가지고 있는 단봉낙타는 1,500만 마리가 살고 있고, 북아프리카와 남서아시아 지역에 퍼져 있다. 이와 같은 내용을 찾아 쓴다.

Select the appropriate phrases from the answer choices.
보기에서 적당한 구를 찾아 적으시오.

Short Programs (A), (C), (D)
Free Skating (B), (E)

여자 피겨 스케이팅 경기들은 쇼트 프로그램과 프리 스케이팅의 두 가지 부문으로 나뉘어진다. 쇼트 프로그램은 2분 50초 안에 완성되어야 하고, 8가지의 의무적인 (동작) 요소를 포함해야 한다. 프리 스케이팅은 4분에 달하며, 스케이트 선수들은 가능한 한 많은 어려운 동작들을 포함해야 한다. 쇼트 프로그램에 쓰이는 음악은 특정 리듬에 따라야 하지만, 프리 스케이팅의 음악은 그러한 제한들이 없다.

쇼트 프로그램 / 프리 스케이팅

(A) 특정한 음악적 제한들이 있다.
(B) 가능한 한 많은 복잡한 동작들을 포함한다.
(C) 3분 미만의 시간 제한이 있다.
(D) 8가지의 필수적인 (동작) 요소를 포함한다.
(E) 길이가 4분이 될 수 있다.

➤ 쇼트 프로그램은 2분 50초 안에 완성되어야 하고 8가지의 동작이 포함되어야 하며, 특정 리듬에 따라야 한다. 반면 프리 스케이팅은 4분의 길이에, 가능한 한 많은 동작이 포함되어야 하고 음악적인 제한이 없다. 이를 바탕으로 쇼트 프로그램과 프리 스케이팅의 세부사항을 분류한다.

UNIT 09
Prose Summary

INTRODUCTION
요약 문제의 목적은 수험자로 하여금 지문의 가장 중요한 핵심 내용들을 파악하게 하는 것이다. 제시된 여러 가지의 사실들과 주장들 중, 주제를 뒷받침하는 세 가지 핵심 내용을 찾을 수 있어야 한다.

TYPICAL QUESTION TYPE
지문의 간단한 요약을 위해 도입 문장이 아래에 주어진다. 지문에서 가장 중요한 내용을 표현하는 세 개의 보기를 선택하여 요약문을 완성하라. 어떤 문장들은 지문에 제시되지 않거나 중요하지 않은 내용을 표현하므로 요약문에 포함되지 않는다.

STRATEGIES

- 주어진 도입 문장은 지문의 주제나 주장을 나타내고 있으므로 주의 깊게 읽는다. 그 문장을 완전히 이해하면 뒷받침 내용들을 파악하는 데 도움이 된다.
- 사실과 다른 문장들만을 골라내는 것이 아니라, 중요하지 않은 세부 사항이나 지문에 포함되지 않은 정보를 골라내서 제거할 수 있어야 한다.
- 지문에 있는 주요 뒷받침 내용들은 보기에서 다른 말로 바꾸어 표현된다. 그러므로, 핵심 단어들의 유의어를 찾아야 한다.

QUICK CHECKUP p.145

정답 | 1. (A), (E), (C)   2. (B), (D), (C)   3. (C), (A), (E)

Read each passage and choose the three major ideas in order to complete the summary.
지문을 읽고 요약을 완성하는 세 개의 주요 문장을 순서대로 고르시오.

1. 스미싱은 개인을 속여 개인 정보를 노출하게 하는 범죄 행동이다. 스미싱은 휴대폰의 문자를 사용하는데, 이 문자들은 마치 합법 금융기관에서 보내진 것처럼 보이게 되어 있다. 하지만, 그것들은 발신자 번호로 뜨는 특정한 번호들로 인해 식별될 수 있다.

   스미싱은 위법 행위의 한 종류이다.

   보기
   (A) 스미싱은 개인 정보를 훔치기 위해 사용된다.
   (B) 스미싱에는 특별한 휴대폰이 필요하다.
   (C) 스미싱 문자는 종종 특정한 번호를 포함한다.
   (D) 은행은 종종 문제를 해결하기 위해 스미싱을 사용한다.
   (E) 스미싱은 문자를 사용한다.

   ● 지문은 스미싱이 문자를 이용해 개인 정보를 유출시키는 불법 행위이며, 특정한 번호들로 확인될 수 있다고 하였다.

2. 출판인인 Joseph Pulitzer의 유언장 조항에 의해 1917년에 설립된 퓰리처 상은 작가들, 기자들, 그리고 작곡가들을 기리는 상이다. 그것은 21개 부문들에 매년 수여되고 현금 10,000달러가 함께 주어진다. 각각 5명이나 7명의 구성원들로 된 102명의 심사위원단이 수상자들을 선정한다.

   퓰리처 상은 매년 수여되는 상이다.

   보기
   (A) 퓰리처 상은 기자에 의해 시작되었다.
   (B) 퓰리처 상은 작가들, 기자들, 그리고 작곡가들에게 수여된다.
   (C) 일정한 금액의 상금이 퓰리처 상과 함께 주어진다.
   (D) 21개의 퓰리처 상 부문들이 있다.
   (E) 어떤 퓰리처 상의 심사위원단은 오직 5명의 구성원들로 되어있다.

   ● 지문은 퓰리처 상에 대해 설명하고 퓰리처 상은 작가들, 기자들, 작곡가들에게 주어지며 21개 부문으로 되어 있다고 하였다. 그리고 현금 10,000달러가 함께 수여된다.

3. 세계에서 가장 거대한 천문대는 하와이 섬의 휴화산인 마우나케아에 위치해있다. 이 위치는 그것의 어두운 하늘, 깨끗한 공기, 낮은 습도, 그리고 높은 고도 때문에 선정되었는데, 이 모든 것이 우주를 대단히 깨끗하게 볼 수 있게 기여한다. 천문대에는 세계에서 가장 거대한 적외선 망원경들을 포함해 제 기능을 하는 13개의 망원경들이 있다.

   세계에서 가장 거대한 천문대는 하와이에 있다.

   보기
   (A) 천문대의 위치는 훌륭한 조망을 제공한다.
   (B) 화산의 이름은 마우나케아이다.
   (C) 그 천문대는 휴화산에 있다.
   (D) 하와이에는 많은 천문대들이 있다.
   (E) 그 천문대에는 13개의 망원경들이 있다.

   ● 하와이의 마우나케아에 있는 천문대에 대한 지문이다. 휴화산에 위치해 있고, 여러 가지 요인으로 인해 조망이 좋으며, 13개의 망원경이 있다는 내용의 보기들을 고른다.

VOCABULARY pp.146-147

Write the number of each word's definition.
각 단어의 뜻을 찾아 번호를 쓰시오.

differentiate / 3 구별하다
incorporate / 2 포함하다
acclaim / 8 칭송
erect / 6 세우다
mimic / 12 모방하다
assess / 1 평가하다

accentuate / 7 강조하다
apprentice / 10 견습생
conservation / 5 보존
consequence / 11 결과
pose / 9 제기하다
absorb / 4 흡수하다

Match each collocation with the correct definition.
각 연어에 알맞은 뜻을 찾아 연결하시오.

a. be renowned as – to be famous and respected as something ~로 명성이 높다
b. coincide with – to occur at the same time as ~와 동시에 일어나다
c. be engraved with – to be carved with (words or symbols) ~가 새겨지다
d. be designated as – to be given an official title ~로 지정되다
e. be advised to – to be recommended to take a certain action ~하도록 충고를 받다

Circle the word closest in meaning to each underlined word.
각 밑줄 친 단어의 뜻과 가장 가까운 단어를 찾아 동그라미 하시오.

정답 | 1. (D)   2. (A)   3. (C)
       4. (B)   5. (A)   6. (C)

해석 |

1. 여성들은 그들의 자연적 특징을 강조하기 위해 화장품을 바른다.
   (A) 근절하다   (B) 복제하다
   (C) 포기하다   (D) (좋은 점을) 높이다

2. 흉내지빠귀는 다른 새들의 노랫소리를 흉내 낼 수 있다.
   (A) 모방하다   (B) 인지하다
   (C) 악화되다   (D) 분석하다

3. 어린 아이들은 그들 행동의 결과들을 예측할 수 없다.
   (A) 모습들   (B) 정도
   (C) 결과들   (D) 전략들

4. 과학자들은 그들의 도약에 대해 국제적인 칭송을 받았다.
   (A) 탁월함   (B) 칭찬
   (C) 자금   (D) 협력

5. 그의 생각들은 결국 제작 과정에 포함되었다.
   (A) 통합되었다   (B) 구식이 되었다
   (C) 특허를 받았다   (D) 분리되었다

6. 그 여자의 업무는 그 골동품들이 보존될 가치가 있는지 평가하는 것이다.
   (A) 버리다   (B) 완화하다
   (C) 추정하다   (D) 접근하다

Fill in each blank with the correct collocation.
알맞은 연어를 골라 빈칸을 채우시오.

정답 | 1. is renowned as   2. is designated as
      3. coincided with   4. is advised to
      5. is engraved with

해석 |

1. 그 정치인은 탁월한 토론자로 명성이 높다.
2. 그 캠퍼스 전체가 금연구역으로 지정되었다.
3. 불행히도, 악천후가 그 학생의 방학 시기와 겹쳤다.
4. 모든 외국인 방문자는 대사관에 등록할 것을 충고 받는다.
5. 그 반지의 안쪽에는 세공인의 머리글자들이 새겨져 있다.

STEP 1　　　　　　　　　　　　　　　　pp. 148-149

정답 | 1. (D)　　2. (F), (D), (C)

뮤지컬과 오페라

뮤지컬과 오페라를 구별하는 선은 특히 근대극에서 때때로 모호할 수 있지만, 두 장르 사이에는 몇몇의 분명한 차이점들이 있다.

그 중 하나는 보통 뮤지컬의 줄거리가 동작과 대사를 통해 발전해 나가고, 노래는 극에서 성립된 분위기와 감정을 강조하는 부수적인 요소라는 점이다. 반면, 오페라에서는 대부분 노래 자체가 줄거리를 말한다. 즉, 줄거리의 원문은 음악에 직접적으로 포함된다.

뮤지컬의 또 다른 특징들은 쉽게 다른 언어로 번역되고, 표현 방식으로 노래와 연기 외에 춤이 사용되는 일이 많다는 것이다. 하지만 오페라에서 노래는 명백히 중심이 되고, 전통적으로 그것이 쓰인 언어로 공연된다.

• **Structure Zone**

> 'with + 명사 + 현재분사' 형태는 앞에 나온 내용만으로는 전달하고자 하는 취지를 충분히 전달하지 못할 때 보충설명어를 추가함으로써 부대상황을 표현하는 구조이다.
>
> One of these is that the storyline of a musical generally progresses through action and dialogue, **with songs serving** as accessories that accentuate the established mood and emotions of the play.

1. 지문에서 단어 **blurred**와 의미가 가장 가까운 것은
   (A) 꺼리는   (B) 전례 없는
   (C) 다용도의   (D) 모호한

   ➡ 음영 처리된 단어 blurred는 '애매한, 모호한'이라는 뜻을 지니고 있다. 따라서 이에 가장 가까운 뜻을 지닌 것은 (D) ambiguous 이다.

2. 지문의 간단한 요약을 위해 도입 문장이 아래에 주어진다. 지문에서 가장 중요한 내용을 표현하는 세 개의 보기를 선택하여 요약문을 완성하라.

   유사점에도 불구하고, 뮤지컬과 오페라는 두 개의 구분되는 장르이다.

   보기
   (A) 오페라는 뮤지컬보다 더 긴 역사를 가지고 있다.
   (B) 오페라가 많은 줄거리를 지니고 있는 것에 반해 뮤지컬에는 하나의 줄거리만이 있다.
   (C) 오페라는 보통 다른 언어로 번역되지 않는다.
   (D) 뮤지컬은 노래와 연기와 함께 춤이 가미된다.
   (E) 오페라와 뮤지컬 모두 강당에서 대부분 상연된다.
   (F) 오페라와 달리, 뮤지컬은 줄거리 흐름을 위해 대사와 동작에 의존한다.

   ➡ 지문에 따르면, 뮤지컬은 여러 언어로 번역되어 노래, 연기, 춤이 모두 가미된다. 반면에 오페라는 원래 그것이 쓰인 언어로 공연되는 것이 일반적이고, 노래 자체가 줄거리를 이끌어간다. (E)는 지문에 언급되지 않았으므로 답에 해당되지 않는다.

• **Note-Taking**

	Musicals	Operas
Storyline	• progress through <u>action</u> & <u>dialogue</u> • songs – serve as <u>accessories</u>	• use songs to <u>tell</u> the story • the <u>text</u> of the plot – <u>incorporated</u> directly

Performance	• use dancing as a form of expression	• use singing as the centerpiece
Language	• are easily translated into other languages	• are performed in the language in which they were written

SUMMARY

There are some distinctions between musicals and operas. For example, musicals use music to accentuate the established mood and emotions while operas use music to tell the story. In addition, musicals can be performed in many languages, but operas are only performed in their original language. Finally, dancing, singing, and acting are all featured in musicals, but it is music that is clearly the centerpiece of operas.

뮤지컬과 오페라에는 몇 가지 차이점들이 있다. 예를 들면, 뮤지컬은 성립된 분위기와 감정을 강조하는 데 음악을 사용하지만, 오페라는 줄거리를 말하기 위해 쓴다. 더욱이, 뮤지컬은 많은 언어들로 공연되지만, 오페라는 원래의 언어로만 공연된다. 마지막으로, 춤, 노래, 그리고 연기는 모두 뮤지컬에 가미되지만, 오페라에서는 명백히 노래가 중심이 된다.

VOCAB_ Match each word with the correct definition.
각 단어에 알맞은 뜻을 찾아 연결하시오.

a. distinction – a clear difference between two things
  차이점
b. accessory – something added to improve something else 부대용품
c. translate – to change one language into another
  번역하다
d. undeniably – in an unquestionable or obvious manner
  명백히
e. centerpiece – the main feature of something 중심

STEP 2			pp. 150-151
정답	1. (C)	2. (B)	3. (A), (D), (C)

Michelangelo (미켈란젤로)

간단히 Michelangelo로 가장 잘 알려진 Michelangelo di Lodovico Buonarroti Simoni(미켈란젤로 디 로도비코 부오나로티 시모니)는 16세기 이탈리아의 르네상스 예술가이다. 주로 조각가였던 그는 그림, 건축, 시 등 여러 가지 분야에서 뛰어났고, 많은 이들에게 지금껏 가장 훌륭하고 영향력 있는 예술가 중 한 명으로 여겨진다.

1475년에 이탈리아 도시인 카프레제에서 태어난 Michelangelo는 12살에 플로렌스 근처의 존경 받는 화가인 Domenico Ghirlandajo(도미니코 기를란다이오)의 견습생이 되었다. Ghirlandajo는 이내 어린 견습생의 싹트는 재능에 질투를 느껴, 대신 조각가와 함께 일하도록 보내버린 것으로 알려져 있다. Michelangelo의 조각 재능은 곧 그에게 명성을 가져다 주었다.

사후에 명성을 얻은 많은 예술가들과는 달리, Michelangelo는 그의 생애에 예술 천재로 명성이 높았다. 동료들에게 Il Divino (신성한 존재)라고 불리었던 그는, 살아 있는 동안 그에 대한 두 권의 전기가 출판될 정도로 유명했다. 그는 30살이 되기 전에 피에타와 다비드 상을 조각했고, 시스티나 예배당의 천장에 있는 걸작을 그렸다. 많은 다른 예술가들은 Michelangelo의 스타일이 보여주는 열정과 조화를 되살리기 위해 노력했고, 그들의 노력은 결국 새로운 거대한 예술운동인 매너리즘을 이끌었다.

1. 지문에서 단어 budding을 대체하기에 가장 적합한 것은
  (A) 유혹적인   (B) 쇠약하게 하는
  (C) 떠오르는   (D) 짜증스러운

  ▶ budding은 '싹트기 시작하는'이라는 뜻을 지니고 있다. 보기 중 유의어를 찾으면 '떠오르는'이라는 의미를 가진 (C) emerging이 답이 된다.

2. Michelangelo에 대해 사실이 아닌 것은
  (A) Domenico Ghirlandajo라는 유명한 화가를 위해 일했다.
  (B) 천재라고 여겨졌지만 동료들에 의해 미움 받았다.
  (C) 그의 생애에 그에 대한 두 권의 책이 쓰여졌다.
  (D) 30살이 되기 전에 두 개의 유명한 조각상을 만들었다.

  ▶ 지문에 따르면, Michelangelo는 동료들에 의해 Il Divino, 즉 신성한 존재라고 불릴 만큼 그들에게 존경 받았다.

3. 지문의 간단한 요약을 위해 도입 문장이 아래에 주어진다. 지문에서 가장 중요한 내용을 표현하는 세 개의 보기를 선택하여 요약문을 완성하라.

  Michelangelo는 역사상 가장 훌륭하고 영향력 있는 예술가 중 한 명이다.

  보기
  (A) 그는 젊은 시절 조각가와 화가와 함께 일했다.
  (B) 그는 1475년 플로렌스 근처의 도시에서 태어났다.
  (C) 그의 스타일은 새로운 거대 예술운동의 영감이 되었다.
  (D) 그는 그의 생애에 명성과 칭송을 누렸다.
  (E) 그는 종종 그 자신을 Il Divino라고 칭했다.
  (F) 그가 견습생으로 일했던 화가는 그의 재능을 질투했다.

  ▶ 주어진 문장은 지문의 주제를 담고 있다. 이를 뒷받침하는 중심 내용을 고르면 (A), (D), (C)가 된다. (B)와 (E)는 지문의 내용과 다르고, (F)는 세부적인 사항이다.

• Note-Taking

P1 MI Michelangelo – Italian Renaissance artist
   SD one of the greatest and most influential artists of all time

P2 MI became an apprentice to Domenico Ghirlandajo

	SD	developed <u>sculpting abilities</u> which earned him acclaim
P3	MI	<u>renowned</u> as an artistic <u>genius</u> during his lifetime
	SD	• <u>sculpted</u> the *Pieta* and *David* before he was 30 • <u>painted</u> the <u>ceiling</u> of the Sistine Chapel • inspired many other artists and led to the art movement <u>Mannerism</u>

VOCAB_ Write the correct word for each definition.
각 뜻에 알맞은 단어를 찾아 적으시오.

a. excel 뛰어나다
b. posthumously 사후에
c. peer 동료
d. biography 전기
e. recreate 되살리다

STEP 3 pp. 152-153

정답 | 1. (D) 2. (A) 3. (D), (E), (C)

퀴리과의 고고유적공원

현재 과테말라의 남동쪽에 위치한 퀴리과는 거의 2,000년 전에 건설된 고대 마야 도시이다. 오늘날, 그 유적지는 퀴리과 고고유적 공원으로 알려진 34헥타르의 보호구역 안에서 보존되고 있다.

그 도시는 8세기 초에 가장 강력한 힘에 도달했는데, 이때 마야 왕국의 귀족상, 그리고 행정상의 중심이 되었지만 분명치 않은 이유들로 인하여 이내 급격한 쇠락 시기에 빠졌다. 하지만 이 쇠락은 마야 문명 전체의 불가사의한 몰락과 시기가 같다고 여겨진다. 퀴리과 유적지는 오늘날 마야에 대한 정보를 얻을 수 있는 중요한 자원으로 여겨진다.

건축적으로, 퀴리과는 대광장이라고 불리는 거대한 공공 지역을 중심으로 하고 있었다. 이 지역은 계단, 피라미드, 그리고 테라스 등의 복잡한 구조로 둘러싸여 있었다. 퀴리과 유적지에는 사암으로 된 17개의 비석들이 있는데, 그것들의 대부분은 8세기에 만들어졌고 상형문자가 새겨져 있다. 이 비석들 중 하나는 간단히 석주 E라고 불리며, 마야가 세운 단독 비석 중 가장 거대하다고 알려져 있다. 비석들에 새겨진 것들 중 어떤 것들은 중요한 날짜를 표시하고 식(蝕) 등의 자연적 현상을 기록하는 달력으로 쓰인다. 다른 것들은 그 당시의 중요한 정치적, 그리고 사회적 행사뿐 아니라 고대 마야의 신화를 묘사한다.

퀴리과가 유네스코 세계 문화유산 보호지역으로 지정된 것은 부분적으로 이 비석들이 제공하는 가치 있는 통찰력이 마야 문명의 분명한 이해를 도운 덕분이다.

• **Structure Zone**

• 명사를 꾸며주는 현재분사의 형태는 두 개 이상일 경우 서로 동급이어야 한다.

Some of the engravings on these monuments act as **calendars marking** important dates and **recording** natural events such as eclipses.

• '주격대명사 which + 절' 형태는 앞서 등장한 사물을 부연 설명할 때 쓰이는데, 이때 'which + 절' 부분이 없어도 전체 문장은 완전해야 한다.

It is partly because of the valuable insights provided by these monuments, **(which have helped shape our understanding of Mayan civilization,)** that Quirigua has been designated as a UNESCO World Heritage Site.

1. 왜 작가는 지문에서 the Great Plaza 를 언급하는가?
   (A) 마야 문명의 몰락을 강조하기 위해서
   (B) 사암 비석의 예를 들기 위해서
   (C) 서로 다른 두 가지의 건축 스타일을 비교하기 위해서
   (D) 도시가 어떻게 배열되었는지 설명하기 위해서

   ▶ 대광장은 계단, 피라미드, 테라스로 구성된 복잡한 체계로 둘러싸여 있다. 작가는 대광장을 통해 도시가 건축학적으로 어떻게 되어있는지 설명하고 있다.

2. 마야의 상형문자에 대해 추론할 수 있는 것은 무엇인가?
   (A) 현대 고고학자들에 의해 이해될 수 있다.
   (B) 퀴리과의 유적지에서만 발견된다.
   (C) 다른 문명들이 쓴 상형문자와 비슷하다.
   (D) 8세기 전반에 걸쳐서만 사용되었다.

   ▶ 지문에 따르면, 비석에 새겨진 상형문자들은 날짜를 표시하고, 자연적 현상을 기록하고 있으며 그 당시의 중요한 행사들과 고대 마야의 신화를 묘사하고 있다고 하였다. 이를 바탕으로, 현대 고고학자들이 상형문자를 해석할 수 있다는 것을 추론할 수 있다.

3. 지문의 간단한 요약을 위해 도입 문장이 아래에 주어진다. 지문에서 가장 중요한 내용을 표현하는 세 개의 보기를 선택하여 요약문을 완성하라.

   고대 마야 도시인 퀴리과의 유적지는 오늘날 중요한 고고학적 지역이다.

   보기
   (A) 그 유적지는 과테말라의 남동쪽에 위치하고 있다.
   (B) 그 도시는 자연재해로 인해 파괴된 것으로 보인다.
   (C) 그 유적지는 오늘날 유네스코 세계 문화유산 보호지역이다.
   (D) 그 유적지는 대부분 8세기에 만들어진 많은 비석들을 포함하고 있다.
   (E) 비석들에는 신화, 중요한 날짜, 그리고 주요 행사들이 새겨져 있다.
   (F) 그 도시에는 피라미드, 테라스, 그리고 계단으로 둘러싸인 거대한 왕실 소유의 땅이 있었다.

▶ 작가는 고대 마야 도시인 퀴리과의 유적지를 소개하며, 그곳에 있는 17개의 비석들을 중점으로 도시를 설명하고 있다. 그리고 퀴리과가 유네스코 세계 문화유산 보호지역이 된 데는 그 비석들의 비중이 컸다고 밝히고 있다. 따라서 답은 (D), (E), (C)가 된다.

VOCAB_ Find the correct word in the passage for each of the given definition.
주어진 뜻에 알맞은 단어를 지문에서 찾으시오.

a. administrative 행정상의   b. sharp 급격한
c. monument 기념비   d. hieroglyphic 상형문자

• **Note-Taking** (Sample Answer)

P1 MI Quirigua's ruins
    SD preserved in the Archaeological Park & Ruins of Quirigua

P2 MI the city's decline
    SD believed to have coincided w/ the mysterious collapse of the entire Mayan civilization

P3 MI Quirigua's ruins & their features
    SD • the Great Plaza – surrounded by a complex system of staircases, pyramids, & terraces
        • 17 sandstone monuments – engraved w/ hieroglyphics

P4 MI Quirigua as a UNESCO World Heritage Site
    SD helped shape our understanding of Mayan civilization

• **More Info Zone**

퀴리과 고고공원의 비석들

퀴리과 고고유적공원의 비석들 중에는 771년에 세운 비석인 석주 E가 있다. 이 비석의 높이는 10.6미터, 너비는 1.5미터, 그리고 두께는 1.2미터이며, 이 석주의 무게는 59,000킬로그램에 달한다. 비석 전체에는 왕의 초상과 전설적인 인물상, 특이한 무늬들과 상형문자가 새겨져 있다. 이 비석 옆에는 고전기 마야 문명 시대를 대표하는 정교한 석각 12개가 함께 있다.

UNIT TEST   pp.154-155

정답 | 1. (B)   2. (D)   3. (A)   4. D   5. (A)
     6. (F), (E), (A)

환경호르몬

현대 사회에서 가장 심각한 건강상의 위험이 될 가능성이 있는 것 중 하나는 환경호르몬이라고 알려진 화학 종류로부터 나온다. 이 화학물질 중 몇몇은 인공적이고 다른 것들은 자연적으로 발생한다. 그것들의 공통분모는 그것들 모두 호르몬의 생성과 분포를 담당하는 신체의 내분비계에 해로운 영향을 미친다는 것이다.

내분비계는 주로 신체 전반에 위치하고 있는 선(腺)들로 되어 있으며, 뇌하수체, 갑상선, 그리고 생식샘을 가지고 있다. 무엇보다도, 그것은 성장과 성적 발달을 맡고 있다. 환경호르몬은 이 체계에 다양한 영향을 미치는데, 모두 부정적인 결과를 낳는다. 어떤 환경호르몬은 호르몬으로 둔갑하여 내분비계를 속이는가 하면, 호르몬이 원래 기능을 수행하지 못하게 막는다. 또한 어떤 호르몬을 감소시키거나 생성을 촉진하는 환경호르몬도 있다.

A 내분비계의 성질 때문에, 환경호르몬은 어린이, 태아, 그리고 임산부에게 가장 심각한 위험을 제기한다. B 과학자들은 여전히 이 화학물질들이 인간에게 얼마나 많은 영향을 주는지 가늠하고 있지만, 그것들이 야생, 특히 어류와 양서류에 해로운 영향을 미친다는 증거가 늘어나고 있다. C 환경호르몬은 농약, 플라스틱, 그리고 세제에서 가장 많이 발견된다. D

(환경호르몬에 대한) 노출의 위험을 줄이기 위해, 사람들은 유기농 과일과 채소를 구입하고 가정용 농약의 사용을 제한할 것을 충고 받는다. 또한 그들은 치즈와 육류 같은 고지방 식품을 피해야 하는데, 그것들이 이 화학물질들을 더 많이 흡수하기 때문이다. 이러한 이유로, 고지방 음식은 플라스틱(비닐)으로 싸서는 안 된다. 사실, 섭취를 위한 어떤 것도 플라스틱 용기 안에 담아 열을 가하면 안 되며, 유리나 도자기 용기로 대체되어야 한다. 더욱이, 씹을 수 있는 부드러운 플라스틱 장난감들은 어린이들에게 주어져서는 안 된다.

Glossary common denominator 공통분모   pesticide 농약
             receptacle 그릇, 용기

1. 지문에서 단어 **they** 가 가리키는 것은
   (A) 건강상 위험들   (B) 환경호르몬들
   (C) 해로운 영향들   (D) 호르몬들

   ▶ 음영 처리된 they의 바로 전 문장을 보면, 이 화학물질 중 어떤 것은 인공적이고 다른 것들은 자연적으로 발생하는 것이라고 하였다. 이 화학물질들은 환경호르몬들이므로, 답은 (B)이다.

2. 왜 작가는 **the pituitary gland**를 언급하는가?
   (A) 환경호르몬의 부정적인 결과를 보여주기 위해서
   (B) 환경호르몬이 어떻게 분포되는지 보여주기 위해서
   (C) 신체가 어떻게 성장을 조절하는지 설명하기 위해서
   (D) 내분비계 구성의 예를 들기 위해서

   ▶ 작가는 내분비계를 설명하며 뇌하수체, 갑상선, 그리고 생식샘으로 구성되어 있다고 하였다. 따라서 답은 (D)이다.

3. 지문에서 단어 **detrimental**과 가장 비슷한 의미는
   (A) 해로운   (B) 감소하는
   (C) 비정상적인   (D) 부인할 수 없는

   ▶ detrimental은 '해로운'이라는 의미를 가지고 있다. 따라서 보기 중 이를 대신할 수 있는 단어는 (A) damaging이 된다.

4. 주어진 문장이 3단락에 들어갈 수 있는 곳을 가리키는 네 개의 네모 [■]를 보시오.

   그것들 모두는 상수도로 유입되어 인간이 오염된 음식을 먹거나 오염된 물을 마시게 할 수 있다.

   이 문장이 어디에 가장 적절한가?

   ▶ 주어진 문장을 살펴 보면, '그것들'이 상수도로 유입되어 인간이 오염된 것을 섭취하게 한다고 하였다. 문맥상 '그것들'이 가리키는 것은 농약, 플라스틱, 세제이다. 따라서 답으로는 D 가 가장 적합하다.

5. 4단락에 따르면, 사실인 것은
   (A) 환경호르몬은 고지방 식품에서 발견될 가능성이 더 높다.
   (B) 환경호르몬은 유리와 도자기 용기에서도 발견된다.
   (C) 농약은 플라스틱에 싸여진 음식에 영향을 미치지 않는다.
   (D) 부드러운 플라스틱은 단단한 플라스틱보다 건강상의 위험이 더 적다.

   ▶ 작가는 4단락에서 고지방 식품이 화학물질을 더 많이 흡수하기 때문에 피해야 한다고 하였다. 따라서 답은 (A)이다.

6. 지문의 간단한 요약을 위해 도입 문장이 아래에 주어진다. 지문에서 가장 중요한 내용을 표현하는 세 개의 보기를 선택하여 요약문을 완성하라.

   환경호르몬은 신체에 해로운 영향을 미칠 수 있는 화학물질이다.

   보기
   (A) 농약과 고지방 음식을 피하는 것은 환경호르몬 노출의 위험을 줄일 수 있다.
   (B) 과학자들은 환경호르몬이 인간에게만 영향을 미치고 어류나 양서류에는 영향을 미치지 않는 이유를 알지 못한다.
   (C) 환경호르몬은 때때로 인공적이지만 자연적으로 생기는 화학물질도 있다.
   (D) 내분비계는 신체 전반에 위치하고 있는 선들의 망이다.
   (E) 환경호르몬은 오염된 물질의 소모를 통해 신체에 유입될 수 있다.
   (F) 환경호르몬은 호르몬을 생성하고 조절하는 체계에 부정적인 영향을 미친다.

   ▶ 지문은 환경호르몬이 어떻게 신체에 해로운 영향을 미치는지, 야생에서는 어떻게 작용하는지, 그리고 어떻게 피할 수 있는지를 설명하고 있고, 주어진 문장은 환경호르몬을 정의하고 있으므로 2, 3, 4단락 각각의 요지인 (F), (E), (A)를 차례로 선택하면 된다.

VOCABULARY TEST
pp.156-157

Recall the essential words in the unit to reinforce your vocabulary acquisition. Write the meaning of each word in your language.
유닛에서 배운 주요 단어들을 떠올려 각 단어의 뜻을 쓰시오.

accentuate | 강조하다
peer | 동료
accessory | 부대용품
dormant | 휴면기의
erect | 세우다
sharp | 급격한
posthumously | 사후에
centerpiece | 중심
pose | 제기하다
differentiate | 구별하다
receptacle | 그릇
reveal | 드러내다
monument | 기념비
distinction | 차이점
excel | 뛰어나다
consequence | 결과
undeniably | 명백히
pesticide | 농약
jury | 심사위원단
be jealous of | ~을 질투하다
be engraved with | ~가 새겨지다
be designated as | ~로 지정되다
acclaim | 칭송
be renowned as | ~로 명성이 높다
coincide with | ~와 동시에 일어나다
be advised to | ~하도록 충고를 받다
trick | 속이다
conservation | 보존
recreate | 되살리다
absorb | 흡수하다
translate | 번역하다
incorporate | 포함하다
biography | 전기
provision | 제공
assess | 평가하다
administrative | 행정상의
mimic | 모방하다
apprentice | 견습생
legitimate | 합법적인
hieroglyphic | 상형문자

Complete each sentence with the correct word or collocation.
문장에 알맞은 단어나 연어를 찾아 쓰시오.

정답 |
1. apprentice
2. conservation
3. centerpiece
4. monuments
5. trick
6. translated
7. pesticides
8. excelled
9. mimicking
10. designated as

해석 |
1. Michelangelo는 존경 받는 화가의 <u>견습생</u>이 되었다.
2. 그 유적지는 <u>보존</u> 지역에서 잘 보호되어 있다.
3. 노래는 명백히 오페라의 <u>중심</u>이다.
4. 퀴리과의 유적지에는 17개의 사암 <u>비석</u>들이 있다.
5. 스미싱은 개인을 <u>속이려</u> 하는 범죄 행동이다.
6. 뮤지컬은 쉽게 다른 언어로 <u>번역될</u> 수 있다.
7. 환경호르몬은 가정용 <u>농약</u>과 플라스틱에서 가장 많이 발견된다.
8. 주로 조각가였지만, Michelangelo는 여러 가지 분야에서 <u>뛰어났다</u>.
9. 어떤 환경호르몬은 호르몬으로 <u>둔갑하여</u> 내분비계를 속인다.
10. 퀴리과는 유네스코 세계 문화유산 보호지역으로 <u>지정되었</u>다.

UNIT 10
Category Chart

INTRODUCTION
차트 문제에서는 두 개 또는 세 개의 일반적인 카테고리와 지문에서의 몇 가지 중요한 세부사항이 제시된다. 수험자는 각 세부사항이 어떤 카테고리에 속하는지 알아냄으로써 지문 이해력을 입증해야 한다.

TYPICAL QUESTION TYPE
보기에서 적당한 구를 찾아서 그것들과 관련된 카테고리에 넣어라. 보기 중에서 두 개는 사용되지 않을 것이다.

STRATEGIES
- 두 카테고리를 읽는 것으로 시작하여 지문과 연관시키면서 그것들을 이해하는지 확인하라.
- 각 카테고리와 관련된 주요 단어를 생각하라. 그리고 이 단어들이나 그들의 동의어를 찾아 보기들을 훑어보라.
- 두 개의 보기들은 사용되지 않는다는 것을 기억하라. 이것들을 골라내는 것으로 다른 세부사항에 맞는 정확한 카테고리를 쉽게 선택할 수 있을 것이다.

QUICK CHECKUP   p. 159
정답 | 1. Violin (B), (F) Viola (C), (E)
     2. Deciduous Trees (C), (F)
        Coniferous Trees (A), (D)

Select the appropriate phrases from the answer choices and match them to the category to which they relate.
보기에서 적당한 어구를 골라 그와 관련된 카테고리와 연결하시오.

1. 바이올린은 같은 계열의 크기가 약간 더 큰 비올라와 흔히 혼동된다. 둘 다 네 개의 현을 가지고 있지만 바이올린에는 A, D, G, 그리고 C현이 있다. 비올라에는 C현이 E현으로 대체된다. 또한, 바이올린 활의 손잡이가 직각의 모서리인 반면, 비올라 활의 손잡이에는 곡선의 모서리가 있다. 마지막으로, 고음을 내는 바이올린이 일반적으로 멜로디를 위해 사용되는 반면, 비올라는 깊고 그윽한 소리를 내어 전통적으로 하모니를 위해 사용된다.

보기
(A) 활 없이 연주된다.
(B) C현이 있다.
(C) 다른 것보다 조금 더 크다.
(D) 다섯 번째 현이 있다.
(E) 곡선 모서리의 활을 가진다.
(F) 멜로디를 연주하기 위해 사용된다.

▶ 바이올린에는 A, D, G, C현이 있으며 고음을 내어 멜로디 연주에 사용되고, 비올라에는 C현 대신 E현이 있으며 활의 모서리가 곡선이다. 따라서 바이올린에 알맞은 내용은 (B)와 (F)이고, 비올라에는 (C)와 (E)가 해당된다. 활 없이 연주된다거나 다섯 번째 현이 있다는 내용은 지문에 나와있지 않으므로 (A)와 (D)는 제외한다.

2. 참나무와 단풍나무 같은 활엽수는 넓은 잎을 지니고 있는데, 가을이면 떨어져서 이듬해 봄에 다시 돋는다. 그것들은 침엽수와 비교되는데, 침엽수는 일년 내내 자라는 가는 침 잎을 지니고 있다. 침엽수에는 원뿔 모양 열매도 나는데, 이것을 씨 대신 번식의 수단으로 사용한다. 활엽수 잎의 넓은 표면은 고효율적으로 광합성하게 한다. 하지만 침 잎들은 곤충과 폭풍우에 더 저항력이 있는 장점이 있다.

보기
(A) 곤충에 덜 취약하다.
(B) 생존을 위해 햇빛을 필요로 하지 않는다.
(C) 참나무와 단풍나무가 포함된다.
(D) 원뿔 모양 열매를 통해 번식한다.
(E) 더 가는 나뭇가지를 가지고 있다.
(F) 보다 효과적으로 광합성을 한다.

▶ 활엽수는 그 종류로 참나무와 단풍나무를 언급했으며, 넓은 잎으로 고효율적으로 광합성을 한다고 했으므로 (C)와 (F)가 답이 된다. (A)의 vulnerable은 '취약한' 이라는 의미의 형용사로 곤충에 덜 취약한 것은 침엽수에 해당하며, 침엽수는 원뿔 모양 열매를 통해 번식하므로 (D)도 답이 된다.

VOCABULARY   pp. 160-161

Write the number of each word's definition.
각 단어의 뜻을 찾아 번호를 쓰시오.

retain / 4 유지하다
predate / 9 ~보다 앞서다
circumvent / 10 피하다
monarchy / 2 군주제
endeavor / 11 시도
mutual / 3 상호간의

infest / 5 들끓다
surrender / 12 항복
dismiss / 6 해산시키다
inflict / 1 ~을 가하다
discipline / 7 학문 분야
interior / 8 내정

Match each collocation with the correct definition.
각 연어에 알맞은 뜻을 찾아 연결하시오.

a. in earnest – with increased effort in a serious way
   본격적으로
b. be mistaken for – to be misunderstood as ~로 오인되는
c. be divided into – to be broken up into (smaller groups)
   ~로 나뉘어지다
d. rallying point – a symbol that makes scattered groups gather together 결집시키는 계기
e. replace ~ with – to remove one thing and to put another in its place ~을 …로 대체하다

Circle the word closest in meaning to each underlined word.
각 밑줄 친 단어의 뜻과 가장 가까운 단어를 찾아 동그라미 하시오.

정답 | 1. (A)   2. (C)   3. (B)
　　　4. (A)   5. (D)   6. (A)

해석 |
1. 그 정치인의 인기가 권력에 오른 시점보다 앞섰다.
   (A) 선행했다   (B) 착수하게 했다
   (C) 재촉했다   (D) 당혹하게 했다

2. 그 관리인은 무능을 이유로 몇 사람을 해고했다.
   (A) 규제를 풀었다   (B) 분석했다
   (C) 끝냈다   (D) 촉진했다

3. 다중의 학문 분야들은 교수의 연구에 의해 영향을 받을 것이다.
   (A) 처벌들   (B) 분야들
   (C) 추종자들   (D) 졸업생들

4. 참담한 패배는 군대의 최종 항복으로 이어졌다.
   (A) 항복   (B) 승리
   (C) 결정   (D) 통일

5. 조직의 최근 시도는 국제적으로 확장하는 것을 포함한다.
   (A) 경영진   (B) 전환
   (C) 의욕   (D) 시도

6. 회사들은 규제를 피하는 방법들을 찾고 있다.
   (A) 피하다   (B) 강화하다
   (C) 협상하다   (D) 부수다

Fill in each blank with the correct collocation.
알맞은 연어를 골라 빈칸을 채우시오.

정답 | 1. rallying point   2. are mistaken for
　　　3. are divided into   4. replace ~ with
　　　5. in earnest

해석 |
1. 해고는 노동자들을 파업을 위해 결집시키는 계기가 되었다.
2. 치타는 종종 재규어나 표범으로 오인된다.
3. 고용인들은 여섯 개의 분리된 팀으로 나뉘어진다.
4. 반역 지도자는 협박을 협상으로 대체하기로 결심했다.
5. 몇 주의 준비 후, 그 프로젝트는 마침내 본격적으로 시작되었다.

STEP 1   pp.162-163

정답 | 1. (C)   2. National League (A), (B), (D)
　　　American League (C), (G)

MLB

전세계 최고의 야구 리그인 메이저리그 야구(MLB)는 1876년에 창설되었으며, 현재는 서른 개의 팀이 있다. 이 팀들은 내셔널 리그와 아메리칸 리그, 두 개의 리그로 더 나누어진다.

원래 MLB는 내셔널 리그만 포함하고 있었는데, 1901년 아메리칸 리그가 독립 조직으로 구성되었다. 두 개의 리그는 2년 후에 경쟁하기 시작해서 1921년에는 공식적으로 합병되었다. 하지만 그들에게는 몇몇 차이점이 있는데 그 중 가장 중요한 것은 아메리칸 리그의 지명타자 제도로, 투수 대신에 한 명의 선수가 타격에 나서는 것이다.

시즌의 마지막에, 각 리그는 1위 팀을 월드시리즈에서 경기하도록 보낸다. 2013년을 기준으로, 내셔널 리그의 46회 우승에 비해 아메리칸 리그는 63회의 승리를 차지했다. 또한 두 리그의 최고 선수들은 시즌 중반에 올스타전에서 만나게 된다. 내셔널 리그는 이 경기에서 43대 39로 우세하다.

1. 지문에서 단어 merged 를 대체하기에 가장 적합한 것은
   (A) 용해했다   (B) 협상했다
   (C) 통합했다   (D) 구별했다

   ● merge는 '합병하다, 통합하다'의 뜻이므로 (C)의 consolidated 와 대체하여 쓸 수 있다.

2. 보기에서 적당한 구를 찾아서 그것들과 관련된 카테고리에 넣어라. 보기 중에서 두 개는 사용되지 않을 것이다.

   내셔널 리그   /   아메리칸 리그

   보기
   (A) MLB의 유일한 리그로 시작되었다.
   (B) 2013년까지 월드시리즈에서 더 적게 승리했다.
   (C) 1901년에 만들어졌다.
   (D) 투수 자신이 직접 타격을 하도록 한다.
   (E) 1921년에 규칙을 바꾸었다.
   (F) 각 팀에 선수를 더 적게 두도록 한다.
   (G) 2013년까지 39번의 올스타전에서 승리했다.

   ● 내셔널 리그는 MLB 유일 리그로 시작되었으며, 2013년까지 46회 월드시리즈에서 우승하여 63회 우승한 아메리칸 리그보다 승리 횟수가 적다. 또한 지명타자 제도가 없으므로 (A), (B), (D)가 내셔널 리그에 해당한다. 아메리칸 리그는 1901년에 만들어졌고 내셔널 리그의 43회 올스타전 승리에 비교하여 39회의 승리 기록이 있으므로, (C)와 (G)가 아메리칸 리그에 해당된다.

• **Note-Taking**

	National League	American League
Differences	• started as the only league in MLB • formally merged with the American League in 1921	• formed as an independent organization in 1901 • has the designated hitter rule

Common Grounds	• sends its top team to play in the World Series • sends the best players to the All-star Game midseason

SUMMARY

MLB began in 1876 and has 30 teams divided into two leagues. It started with only the National League. The American League formed in 1901, and the two leagues formally merged in 1921. They have some differences. Only the American League allows a player to bat in place of the pitcher. The two leagues' best teams play in the World Series at the season's conclusion. Their best players also meet in the All-Star Game midseason.

MLB는 1876년에 시작되었으며 두 개의 리그로 나뉜 서른 개의 팀이 있다. 이것은 내셔널 리그로만 시작되었다. 아메리칸 리그는 1901년에 구성되었고, 이 두 리그는 1921년에 공식적으로 합병되었다. 그들에는 몇몇의 차이점들이 있다. 단지 아메리칸 리그에서만 한 선수가 투수 대신 타격에 나서도록 한다. 시즌 마지막에, 두 리그의 최고 팀은 월드시리즈에서 경기한다. 또한 그들의 최고 선수들은 시즌 중반 올스타전에서 만난다.

VOCAB_ Match each word with the correct definition.
각 단어에 알맞은 뜻을 찾아 연결하시오.

a. league – a group of teams that play a sport against one another (스포츠 경기의) 리그
b. premier – the most important or admired 최고의
c. notable – worthy of noticing 유명한
d. claim – to gain or win something 차지하다
e. advantage – a superior position 우세

• **More Info Zone**

┌─ 메이저리그 올스타전 ─┐

메이저리그의 올스타전은 1933년 시카고 트리뷴지의 스포츠 담당 기자의 제안에 의해 처음 시작되었다. 처음에는 국제 박람회 행사 중 하나인 일회성 행사였지만 대단한 성공을 거두어 매년 정례화되어 열리고 있다. 올스타전에 나갈 선발 야수들은 인터넷 투표와 서른 개 메이저리그 구장에서 실시되는 현장 투표로 결정되는데, 투표권은 미국에만 국한되지 않고 멕시코, 캐나다, 푸에르토리코, 일본 등의 나라에도 주어진다. 올스타전의 감독은 전년도 월드시리즈 진출 팀의 감독들이 각각 맡게 되며, 각 감독은 투표로 뽑힌 야수들을 제외하고 투수와 교체 야수는 직접 지명할 수 있다. 올스타전에서 승리한 리그는 월드시리즈의 첫 두 경기와 필요할 경우 마지막 두 경기를 홈 구장에서 치를 수 있는 혜택을 얻는다.

STEP 2 pp. 164-165

정답 | 1. (A) 2. (B) 3. Lice (D), (F) Mites (A), (C), (G)

이와 진드기

사람들을 괴롭히는 경향으로 인해 혐오감을 불러일으키는 작은 생명체인 이와 진드기는 흔히 서로 오인되기도 한다. 하지만, 그들은 차이점이 공통점보다 훨씬 더 많다.

이는 사실상 거의 모든 종의 포유류와 조류에서 발견되는 기생 곤충이다. 청소곤충인 그것들은 숙주를 먹이 공급원으로 의존하는데, 피부와 피, 그리고 신체 분비물을 먹고 산다. 그들은 일반적으로 회색이며 약 3밀리미터의 크기에 수명은 대략 30일 정도이다. 반면, 진드기는 곤충이 아니라 실제로는 절지동물이다. 그것들은 동물뿐 아니라 식물에서 흔히 활물기생균으로 사는 매우 작은 무척추동물이다. 하지만, 거의 50,000여 종으로 알려진 진드기 중 많은 수가 물이나 육지에서 자유롭게 서식한다.

이는 서캐라고 알려진 알을 분비물을 이용해 털 가닥에 붙이면서 숙주의 몸에 직접 낳는다. 이는 가려움과 불편함을 주기는 하지만, 사람들에게 어떤 심각한 건강상의 위험을 가하지는 않는다. 하지만, 진드기는 천식과 습진을 포함한 많은 알레르기 질병의 원인이 된다. 또한 사람의 피부를 파고들어가 알을 낳아서 옴이라고 알려진 질환을 일으키는 진드기 종도 있다.

• **Structure Zone**

• 'A뿐만 아니라 B도'라는 뜻의 not only A but also B는 상관접속사로, 접속사는 문법적으로 대등한 두 표현을 연결하므로 A와 B는 문법적으로 서로 동일한 표현이어야 한다.

They are microscopic invertebrates that sometimes live as parasites, **not only** on animals **but also** on plants.

• 삽입구는 수식하고자 하는 것에 추가적인 정보를 주기 위해 끼워 넣는 것으로, 명사 뒤에 삽입되어 앞의 명사를 보충 설명하는 경우가 많다. 삽입구의 앞 뒤로는 콤마가 쓰이므로 쉽게 구분할 수 있다.

Lice lay their eggs, **known as nits**, directly on their host by using saliva to attach them to hair shafts.

1. 지문에서 단어 revulsion 을 대체하기에 가장 적합한 것은
   (A) 혐오   (B) 호기심
   (C) 혼란   (D) 의견차이

   ▶ revulsion은 '혐오감, 역겨움'이라는 뜻의 단어로 '혐오감'을 나타내는 (A) disgust와 의미가 가장 가깝다.

2. 이의 분비물에 대해 추론할 수 있는 것은?
   (A) 냄새가 없다.
   (B) 끈적거린다.
   (C) 진드기도 가지고 있다.
   (D) 질병의 원인이 된다.

➡ 지문에서 이가 분비물을 이용해 알을 털 가닥에 붙인다고 했으므로 분비물은 끈적이는 성질이라는 것을 추론할 수 있다.

3. 보기에서 적당한 구를 찾아서 그것들과 관련된 카테고리에 넣어라. 보기 중에서 두 개는 사용되지 않을 것이다.

이   /   진드기

보기
(A) 무척추동물이다.
(B) 곤충을 먹이로 삼는다.
(C) 식물에서 살 수도 있다.
(D) 알을 털에 붙인다.
(E) 멸종 위기에 처한 종이다.
(F) 한 달 가량 산다.
(G) 옴의 원인이 될 수 있다.

➡ 이는 털에 알을 낳고 한 달 가량의 수명을 가진다고 했으므로, (D)와 (F)가 이에 해당한다. 진드기는 곤충이 아닌 무척추동물이며 동식물 모두에 서식하고 옴의 원인이 된다고 했으므로, (A), (C), (G)가 정답이다. 곤충을 먹이로 한다거나 멸종 위기에 처했다는 것은 지문에서 언급되지 않은 내용이다.

• Note-Taking

P1 MI lice & mites
    SD have more differences than similarities

P2 MI the features of lice & mites
    SD • lice: parasitical insects — depend on their hosts as sources of food
        • mites: arthropods which mostly live freely in water or on land

P3 MI their harmful effects on humans
    SD • lice: cause itching & discomfort ← lay their eggs on their hosts
        • mites: cause allergic diseases – include asthma, eczema, & scabies

VOCAB_ Write the correct word for each definition.
각 뜻에 알맞은 단어를 찾아 적으시오.

a. propensity 경향   b. outnumber 수적으로 우세하다
c. parasitical 기생(충)의   d. secretion 분비물
e. burrow 파고들다

• More Info Zone
살인진드기라 불리는 작은소참진드기

집의 침구류 등에서 발견되는 진드기가 대개 알레르기 질환의 원인이 되는 것과 달리, 수풀 등에서 주로 발견되는 작은소참진드기는 바이러스의 매개체가 되기도 한다. 특히 이 진드기에 의해 중증 열성 혈소판 감소 증후군 바이러스에 감염되었을 때는 사망까지도 이를 수 있으므로 주의가 필요하다. 작은소참진드기는 한국뿐 아니라 일본, 중국, 호주 등지에서도 서식한다. 보통 3밀리미터 정도의 크기지만, 사람의 몸에 달라붙어 흡혈하기 시작하면 약 10밀리미터까지도 커진다. 살인진드기는 피부에 달라붙으면 피부를 뚫고 피부 아래까지 들어가 흡혈하는 경우도 있으므로 야외 활동시에는 풀숲에 피부가 노출되는 것을 최대한 막아야 한다.

STEP 3   pp. 166-167

정답 | 1. (D)   2. (B)
     3. German Militarism (A), (C), (E)
        Japanese Militarism (F), (G)

독일 군국주의

두 세계대전 배후의 다양한 이유를 고찰해 볼 때, 강하고 공격적인 군대를 유지하려는 독일의 뿌리깊은 태도에 예외 없이 상당한 초점이 맞추어진다는 사실에 주목해야 한다.

독일 군국주의의 기원은 국가 자체보다도 더 앞서는데, 1806년 나폴레옹이 프러시아를 무찌른 것에 뿌리를 내리고 있기 때문이다. 항복 조건으로 프러시아는 42,000명 이하의 군사들만 유지하도록 요구되었다. 이러한 조항을 피해가기 위해, 프러시아의 왕은 매년 42,000명의 군사들을 훈련시키고 즉시 그들을 내보낸 다음, 새로운 그룹으로 그들의 자리를 대체하였다. 1871년 독일이 통일될 때까지, 남성 인구의 상당부분이 군사 훈련을 받았다. 일본의 군국주의는 사람들을 결집하게 하는 계기로서 국가 황제에 의지했는데, 프러시아의 장군을 1885년부터 1888년까지 군사자문으로 복무하도록 하면서 프러시아의 군국주의를 본보기로 이용했다. 독일 군국주의는 1918년 군주제의 몰락에서 살아남아 나치의 통치 아래에서 사실상 힘을 얻게 되었다. 나치는 전능한 황제를 두기보다, 제1차 세계대전에서의 패배와 그 결과에 따른 패배에 가해진 엄벌에 초점을 맞추면서, 국가의 상처 입은 자존심을 군국주의를 강화하는 계기로 이용했다. 독일 군국주의와 일본 군국주의의 공통점은 두 나라가 군사적 공격성의 배후 원동력으로 민족주의를 이용했다는 것이다.

오늘날, 독일은 여전히 대규모의 군사를 가지고 있고, 세계에서 가장 큰 방위 예산 중의 하나이다. 하지만 현대 여론은 군국주의에 대해 강하게 반전으로 돌아섰으며, 독일이 국제적인 군사적 노력에 어떤 형태로든 개입하는 것은 신중히 행해지고 있다.

• **Structure Zone**

> • 과거의 습관적 동작은 조동사 would로 표현할 수 있다.
> The King of Prussia **would** train 42,000 soldiers for a year and then immediately dismiss them.
>
> • 과거의 어떤 시점보다 더 이전의 일을 표현할 때는 대과거라 하여 'had + p.p.'의 과거완료를 사용한다. 대과거를 사용할 때는 문장 안에 기준시점이 되는 과거에 대한 언급이 있다.
> By the time Germany unified in 1871, a significant portion of the male population **had received** military training.

• **Note-Taking** (Sample Answer)

P1 MI German militarism
   SD one of the reasons behind the two world wars
P2 MI German militarism vs. Japanese militarism
   SD • German: received military training (male) by 1871, acted under Nazi rule
       • Japanese: relied on the nation's emperor, used Prussian militarism as a model
       — both used racism as a driving force
P3 MI modern public opinion
   SD firmly against it

1. 지문에서 단어 subsequent 와 의미가 가장 가까운 것은
   (A) 불공평한   (B) 증가하는
   (C) 열등한   (D) 다음의

   ● subsequent는 '(어떤 일의) 차후의, 다음의'라는 뜻으로 '다음의'라는 의미 ensuing과 의미가 가장 비슷하다.

2. 언급되지 않은 것은
   (A) 프러시아는 군사의 크기에 제한이 있었다.
   (B) 독일은 프러시아 군대를 패배시켰다.
   (C) 오늘날 독일은 여전히 대규모의 군사를 가지고 있다.
   (D) 프러시아 장군은 일본에 조언해 주었다.

   ● 프러시아를 패배시킨 것은 독일이 아닌 Napoleon이므로 (B)는 본문의 내용과 다르다.

3. 보기에서 적당한 구를 찾아서 그것들과 관련된 카테고리에 넣어라. 보기 중에서 두 개는 사용되지 않을 것이다.

   독일 군국주의   /   일본 군국주의

   보기
   (A) Napoleon이 프러시아를 패배시켰을 때 시작되었다.
   (B) 제1차 세계대전 직후에 끝났다.
   (C) 이전의 패배와 처벌로 인해 힘을 얻었다.
   (D) 남자와 여자 모두 훈련시켰다.
   (E) 군주제가 끝난 이후에 계속되었다.
   (F) 황제를 상징으로 이용했다.
   (G) 프러시아 군국주의를 모방했다.

   ● 독일 군국주의는 프러시아가 Napoleon에 패했을 때 시작되었으며, 군주제의 몰락 후에도 살아남아 제1차 세계대전에서 패배한 후에 더욱 강화되었다. 따라서 (A), (C), (E)가 답이 된다. 일본 군국주의에서 황제는 국민들을 결집시키는 하나의 상징이었고, 프러시아의 군국주의를 모델로 하였다고 했으므로 (F)와 (G)가 답이다.

VOCAB Find the correct word in the passage for each of the given definition.
주어진 뜻에 알맞은 단어를 지문에서 찾으시오.

a. stipulation 조항   b. unify 통일하다
c. wounded 상처 입은   d. impetus 계기, 자극(제)

UNIT TEST   pp. 168-169

정답 | 1. (D) 2. (A) 3. (C) 4. (A) 5. (C)
     6. *Exposition du Systéme du Monde* (A), (D), (F), (H)
        Théorie Analytique des Probabilités (B), (E), (I)

Pierre-Simon Laplace (피에르시몽 라플라스)

프랑스 수학자이자 천문학자인 Pierre-Simon Laplace의 업적은 다중 학문 분야에 중대한 영향을 미쳤으며, 많은 이들로 하여금 그를 시대의 가장 위대한 과학자 중 하나라고 여기게 한다.

Laplace는 1749년에 농부의 아들로 태어났으며, 부유한 이웃들의 재정적 도움으로 교육을 받았다. 1771년에 그는 통계학과, 특히 태양계의 안정성에 초점을 맞춘 천문학에 대해 본격적으로 연구를 시작했다. Isaac Newton의 연구를 기반으로 하여, 그는 어떤 두 개의 행성과 태양은 반드시 상호 평형 상태에서 존재한다는 수학적인 결론을 이끌어냈다.

그는 후에 그 스스로 말한 '태양계에 의한 최대 기계적 결함의 완전한 해결방법'을 추구하고자 천체역학으로 옮겨갔다. 1796년에 그의 (연구) 결과들은 *우주의 체계*에 실렸으며, 이는 현재 과학 학술 문학의 걸작품 중 하나라고 여겨지고 있다. 그의 이전 출판물 중 하나인 *천체역학*을 기초로 하였으며, 그의 잘 알려진 성운설을 소개한 것이 바로 이 책인데, 성운설은 거대한 성간 가스 구름이 응축했을 때 태양계가 생성되었다는 이론을 제시한 것이었다.

다음으로 통계학과 확률학으로 옮겨가서, Laplace는 1812년에 *확률해석론*을 출판했다. 이는 통계학적으로, 모든 가능한 결과는 동일 발생 가능성을 가진다고 언급한 것으로 가장 잘 알려져 있을 것이다. 그것은 또한 모함수도 소개했는데, 모함수는 확률 방정식에서 긴 합의 계산을 돕기 위해 사용될 수 있다. Laplace는 결론에서 '이 에세이를 보는 사람들은 기본적으로 가능성 이론이란 축소된 미적분학이라는 당연한 상식을 발견할 것이다'라고 썼다.

말년에 Laplace는 정치에 관여하여 1799년에 Napoleon의 내무부 장관으로 잠시 봉직했으며, 1817년 부르봉 왕정복고시기에는 후작의 직위를 받았다.

Glossary nebular 성운의   equation 방정식

• **Structure Zone**

> • 접속사 that은 절을 이끌어서 앞에 나오는 명사를 설명하기도 하는데, 이때 that절 이하는 앞의 명사와 동격의 관계가 된다. 동격의 that은 접속사일 뿐, that 절 안에서 어떠한 문장 성분도 되지 않는다.
>
> Building on the work of Isaac Newton, he came to the mathematical conclusion **that any two planets and the sun must exist in a state of mutual equilibrium.**
>
> • 'it is ~ that'은 강조구문으로 it is와 that 사이에 문장에서 강조하고자 하는 표현을 넣어 그 의미를 더욱 강하게 나타낼 수 있다.
>
> ... **it is** this book **that** introduced his well-known nebular hypothesis.

1. 아래 문장 중 지문에서 음영 처리된 문장의 핵심 정보를 가장 잘 나타낸 것은 어느 것인가?
   (A) 1771년을 시작으로, 그는 태양계의 안정성에 초점을 맞추기 위해 통계학과 천문학을 포기했다.
   (B) 1771년은 그가 태양계의 안정성에 관한 기록을 출간하고 통계학과 천문학에 초점을 맞춘 해이다.
   (C) 1771년에 그는 통계학에서 천문학, 특히 태양계의 안정성으로 초점을 바꾸었다.
   (D) 1771년에, 그는 천문학과 통계학의 다른 요소뿐만 아니라, 태양계의 안정성에도 집중하기 시작했다.

   ● 음영 처리된 문장에서 Laplace는 통계학과 천문학, 특히 태양계의 안정성에 대한 연구를 본격적으로 시작했다고 했으므로, 그는 두 학문을 모두 연구하면서 태양계의 안정성을 더욱 탐구했다는 사실을 알 수 있다. 따라서 문장의 의미와 가장 비슷한 것은 (D)이다.

2. 지문에서 단어 contracted와 뜻이 가장 가까운 것은
   (A) 압축했다   (B) 흩어졌다
   (C) 진동했다   (D) 폭발했다

   ● contract는 '응축하다, 수축하다'라는 뜻의 동사로 '압축하다'라는 뜻의 (A) compressed와 의미가 가장 가깝다.

3. 3단락에서 언급된 것은
   (A) 다른 과학자들은 Laplace의 연구 결과에 동의하지 않았다.
   (B) 천체역학은 성운설에 반대했다.
   (C) 우주의 체계는 천체역학을 기초로 쓰여졌다.
   (D) Laplace는 결국 천체역학에 대한 흥미를 잃었다.

   ● Laplace는 그가 연구한 것의 결론을 우주의 체계에 썼는데, 이는 천체역학을 기초로 한 것이라는 내용이 있으므로 (C)가 정답이다.

4. 지문에서 It이 가리키는 것은
   (A) 이론   (B) 결과
   (C) 동일한 가능성 (D) 계산

   ● 해당 문장에서 It은 '통계학적으로 말해 모든 가능한 결과는 동일한 발생 가능성을 가진다'라는 언급을 포함한 확률해석론이라는 그의 확률 이론을 말하는 것으로, 그 이론에서 모함수도 소개했다는 내용을 덧붙여 설명하고 있다.

5. 5단락에서 작가의 주요 목적은
   (A) Laplace와 Napoleon을 비교하는 것이다.
   (B) Laplace가 직면했던 문제들을 설명하는 것이다.
   (C) Laplace 삶의 세부적인 내용을 첨가하여 제공하는 것이다.
   (D) Laplace 성공의 원인을 설명하는 것이다.

   ● 5단락에서는 수학자이자 과학자로서의 Laplace의 삶 외에 관직에 올랐던 다른 모습도 보여주고 있다. 따라서 작가는 Laplace의 학문적 업적 외에 다른 삶의 모습을 덧붙여서 보여주고자 했음을 알 수 있다.

6. 보기에서 적당한 구를 찾아서 그것들과 관련된 카테고리에 넣어라. 보기 중에서 두 개는 사용되지 않을 것이다.

   우주의 체계 / *확률해석론*

   보기
   (A) 성운설을 포함했다.
   (B) 긴 합의 계산 방법을 소개했다.
   (C) 정치인들에 반대했다.
   (D) 과학적 학술 문학의 걸작품이라고 여겨진다.
   (E) 1812년에 출판되었다.
   (F) Laplace의 초기 작업에 기초한다.
   (G) 태양의 평형을 논의했다.
   (H) 1796년에 출판되었다.
   (I) 결과와 발생 가능성 사이의 연관성을 나타냈다.

   ● Laplace가 1796년에 낸 *우주의 체계*는 그의 초기 작업을 기반으로 쓰여진 것으로, 그가 주장한 성운설을 포함하며 과학 학술 문학의 걸작품 중 하나로 여겨지고 있으므로, 이에 해당하는 (A), (D), (F), (H)가 답이다. 그 이후 1812년에 발간된 *확률해석론*은 결과와 발생 가능성 간의 연관성에 관한 이론과, 긴 계산시에 도움이 되는 모함수라는 개념을 소개한 것이므로 (B), (E), (I)가 답이 된다.

• **More Info Zone**

Napoleon과 Laplace

Laplace는 젊었을 때 파리 군관학교에서 학생들을 가르쳤는데, 그의 제자 중에는 Laplace가 직접 졸업논문을 심사했던 Napoleon이 있었다. Napoleon은 과학에 대해서 지대한 관심을 가진 통치자 중 하나였는데 독일 침략시 천재 수학자 Gauss의 마을만은 파괴하지 않도록 명령했을 정도로 과학자들을 존경하는 마음이 매우 강했다. Laplace는 이런 Napoleon을 찾아가 그의 저서인 *천체물리학*을 선물하게 되고, 저명한 수학자와의 만남을 대단히 기뻐했던 Napoleon은 그를 내무부 장관으로 발탁한다. 하지만 Laplace가 오랫동안 공직에 있던 것은 아니다. 자신의 학문에 대한 대단한 자부심과 고집이 있던 Laplace는 공직을 수행함에 있어 객관적이지 못하고 사소한 것에도 트집을 잡는 경향이 있었는데, 결국 행정가로서의 능력을 입증받지 못하고 6주 만에 물러나고 말았다.

VOCABULARY TEST   pp. 170-171

Recall the essential words in the unit to reinforce your vocabulary acquisition. Write the meaning of each word in your language.
유닛에서 배운 주요 단어들을 떠올려 각 단어의 뜻을 쓰시오.

propensity | 경향
secretion | 분비물
racism | 민족 우월 의식
outnumber | 수적으로 우세하다
surrender | 항복
equation | 방정식
retain | 유지하다
infest | 들끓다
parasitical | 기생(충)의
dismiss | 해산시키다
burrow | 파고들다
interior | 내정
nebular | 성운의
curved | 굽은
mutual | 상호간의
coniferous | 침엽수의
in lieu of | ~ 대신에
replace ~ with | ~을 …로 대체하다
circumvent | 피하다
be contrasted with | ~와 비교하여
be mistaken for | ~로 오인되다
rallying point | 결집시키는 계기
be divided into | ~로 나누어지다

notable | 주목할 만한
predate | ~보다 앞서다
impetus | 원동력, 자극
league | (스포츠) 리그
inflict | ~을 가하다
stipulation | 조항
monarchy | 군주제
mellow | 그윽한
premier | 최고의
endeavor | 노력
claim | 차지하다
discipline | 학문 분야
wounded | 상처 입은
unify | 통일하다
bow | 활
advantage | 우세
in earnest | 본격적으로

Complete each sentence with the correct word or collocation.
문장에 알맞은 단어나 연어를 찾아 쓰시오.

정답 | 1. curved   2. outnumber
      3. coniferous 4. endeavor
      5. mellow   6. burrows
      7. are divided into 8. monarchy
      9. in lieu of 10. interior

해석 |
1. 비올라 활의 손잡이에는 곡선의 모서리가 있다.
2. 두 생명체는 차이점이 공통점보다 훨씬 더 많다.
3. 활엽수는 침엽수와 비교될 수 있다.
4. 독일이 국제적인 군사적 노력에 어떤 형태로든 개입하는 것은 신중히 행해지고 있다.
5. 비올라는 깊고 그윽한 소리를 내며 전통적으로 하모니를 위해 사용된다.
6. 사람의 피부를 파고 들어가는 진드기 종이 있다.
7. 미국의 서른 개 야구팀은 두 개의 리그로 나뉘어진다.
8. 독일 군국주의는 1918년 군주제의 몰락에서 살아남았다.
9. 어떤 나무들은 원뿔 모양 열매를 지니고 있는데, 씨 대신 사용한다.
10. Laplace는 1799년에 Napoleon의 내무부 장관으로 봉직했다.

PROGRESS TEST ❷   pp. 174-181

정답 | 1. (B)   2. B   3. (C)   4. (B)   5. (D)
       6. (D)   7. (A)   8. (C)   9. (B)   10. (C)
       11. (A), (F), (B)

쿠르드족

대략 아라비아 반도 북쪽의 거대한 산악 지역에 거주하는 쿠르드족은 국적 없는 민족으로 구성되어 있다. A '쿠르디스탄'으로 흔히 불리는 쿠르드족의 고향은 동쪽의 이란부터 이라크와 시리아를 거쳐 서쪽의 터키까지 네 국가를 걸쳐 뻗어 있다. B 쿠르드족의 기원에 대해서는 논란의 여지가 있다. 하지만, 일반적으로 쿠르드족이 2,000년 이상 전에 이란으로부터 쿠르디스탄 지역으로 이주했다고 여겨진다. C 언어학적, 유전적, 그리고 인류학적 근거들은 쿠르드족이 아프가니스탄의 파슈툰족과 아제르바이잔인들 같은 다른 이란 민족들과 친밀한 관계임을 나타낸다. D 쿠르드족의 문화는 그것의 주변에 있는 아랍, 터키, 그리고 페르시아 문화와 여러 방면으로 눈에 띄게 다르다. 예를 들면, 쿠르드족은 *Hilperké*라는 노래와 춤을 춘다. 수세기의 역사가 이 노래들과 연관된 가사와 동작을 통해 전해지고, 춤은 보존적인 역할을 한다.

쿠르드인들을 함께 묶는 언어학적, 그리고 문화적 공통점에도 불구하고, 그들은 국가가 없는 국민들로 남아 있다. 역사적으로 소수의 쿠르드족은 쿠르디스탄을 포함하고 둘러싼 국가들의 다수 인종에 의해 박해당해왔다. 20세기에, 쿠르드족은 이라크에서의 대학살, 터키에서의 문화적 진압과 학살, 그리고 이란과 시리아에서의 차별을 견뎌야 했다. 터키에서만 오스만 왕국이 끝난 후 100,000명이 넘는 쿠르드족이 죽임을 당한 것으로 보인다.

이와 대조적으로, 21세기에는 독립된 쿠르드 국가로 발전할 전망이 보인다. 미국과 연합군에 의한 2003년 침입에 따른 이라크 정부의 몰락은 이라크 북부가 이라크 쿠르디스탄으로 불리는 자율 정치체가 되는 것을 이끌었다. 이라크로부터 완전히 분리된 나라는 아니지만, 이라크의 쿠르드족은 바그다드의 간섭 없이 이 지역에서 자치할 수 있게 되었다. 2012년에, 시리아 내전이 일어났다. 그 일로 서쪽 쿠르디스탄에 있는 쿠르드족은 비슷한 기회를 얻었는데, 쿠르드 민병대가 2012년에 시리아의 북동쪽을 장악한 것이었다. 이러한 움직임들이 독립된 국가 건설로 이어질지는 지켜보아야 한다.

Glossary massacre 대학살   coalition 연합

1. 다음 중 쿠르드족과 다른 민족들의 차이점으로 언급된 것은 무엇인가?
   (A) 그들의 언어
   (B) 그들의 문화
   (C) 그들의 유전학
   (D) 그들의 인류학적 특징

   ➲ 지문에 따르면, 쿠르드족은 다른 이란계 민족들과 언어학적, 유전적, 인류학적 근거를 공유하고 있지만, 그들의 문화는 다른 이웃 민족들과 다르다고 하였으므로 답은 (B)이다.

2. 주어진 문장이 1단락에 들어갈 수 있는 곳을 가리키는 네 개의 네모 [■]를 보시오.

   그것의 국경은 명확하지 않지만, 쿠르디스탄은 일반적으로 서쪽의 타우루스 산맥으로부터 동쪽의 자그로스 산맥까지 뻗어 있다고 여겨진다.

   이 문장이 어디에 가장 적절한가?

   ➲ 주어진 문장은 쿠르디스탄이 어느 지역에 걸쳐있는지 밝히고 있으므로, 지리적 위치를 밝히고 있는 문장 바로 뒤인 B 에 있는 것이 알맞다.

3. 지문에서 단어 its 가 가리키는 것은
   (A) 아프가니스탄
   (B) 아제르바이잔
   (C) 쿠르드 문화
   (D) 페르시아 문화

   ➲ 지문에서, '그것의' 이웃인 아랍, 터키, 페르시아의 문화와 다른 면들이 있다고 하였으므로, its가 가리키는 것은 (C)이다.

4. 지문에 따르면, 다음 중 Hilperké에 대해 사실인 것은?
   (A) 쿠르드족, 파슈툰족, 그리고 아제르바이잔인들에 의해 행해진다.
   (B) 예술임과 동시에 쿠르드 역사를 기억하는 한 방법이다.
   (C) 쿠르드인들에 의해 2,000년 동안 행해져 왔다.
   (D) 아랍, 터키, 그리고 페르시아 정부에 의해 금지되었다.

   ➲ 지문에 따르면, Hilperké의 노래에 수세기의 역사가 담겨 있고 춤은 보존의 역할을 한다고 하였으므로 답은 (B)이다.

5. 지문에서 단어 persecuted 와 의미가 가장 가까운 것은
   (A) 공격했다
   (B) 기소했다
   (C) 계속시켰다
   (D) 희생시켰다

   ➲ persecute는 '박해하다'라는 뜻을 가지고 있다. 보기 중 이와 가장 가까운 뜻을 가진 단어는 (D)이다.

6. 2단락에서 쿠르드인들에 대한 탄압에 대해 추론되는 것은 무엇인가?
   (A) 쿠르드족은 시리아와 이란의 다수인종에게 살해당했다.
   (B) 쿠르드족을 향한 폭력은 20세기가 끝날 무렵 멈춰졌다.
   (C) 몇몇의 쿠르드족은 독립된 쿠르디스탄을 원치 않는다.
   (D) 쿠르드인에 대한 차별은 쿠르디스탄이 위치한 나라들에서 일반적이다.

   ➲ 지문에 따르면, 쿠르디스탄이 위치한 이라크, 터키, 이란, 그리고 시리아에서는 다양한 형태로 쿠르드인들이 차별 받고 박해 받았다. 따라서 답은 (D)이다.

7. 지문에서 단어 autonomous 를 대체하기에 가장 적합한 것은
   (A) 독립된
   (B) 익명의
   (C) 인기 없는
   (D) 존경 받는

   ➲ autonomous는 '자주적인, 자치의'라는 뜻을 가지고 있다. 따라서 이를 대체하기에 적절한 것은 (A) independent이다.

8. 왜 작가는 지문에서 the Syrian Civil War 를 언급하는가?
   (A) 쿠르드족이 차별 받았던 한 방법을 묘사하기 위해서
   (B) 쿠르디스탄이 위치한 네 나라에서 쿠르드족이 위협받는 존재라는 것을 주장하기 위해서
   (C) 쿠르드 국가 건설로 이어질 수도 있는 일의 예를 들기 위해서
   (D) 시리아에 있는 쿠르드족이 독립된 조국을 원하는 이유를 설명하기 위해서

   ➲ 2003년 이라크 정부의 몰락에 따라, 시리아 내전으로 인해 쿠르드 민병대가 시리아 북동쪽을 장악했다고 하였다. 이러한 움직임이 쿠르드의 독립 국가 건설로 이어질지는 지켜보아야 한다고 하였으므로, 답은 (C)이다.

9. 아래 문장 중 지문에서 음영 처리된 문장의 핵심 정보를 가장 잘 나타낸 것은 어느 것인가? *잘못된* 보기들은 중요한 의미를 바꾸거나 핵심 정보를 생략한다.
   (A) 2013년부터 이라크 쿠르드족의 도움을 받은 쿠르드 혁명군은 시리아 북동쪽을 장악하기 위해 시리아 정부와 싸웠다.
   (B) 2013년부터, 쿠르드 군인들은 시리아의 쿠르디스탄 지역을 장악했고, 이라크 쿠르디스탄 지역의 이라크 쿠르드족이 한 것처럼 자치를 시작했다.
   (C) 비록 시리아 군대와 힘겹게 싸워야만 했지만, 시리아 쿠르드족은 2013년에 자치할 기회를 얻었다.
   (D) 2013년부터, 서쪽 쿠르디스탄 지역에 있는 쿠르드족은 시리아 정부와 시리아 북동쪽의 지배권을 놓고 싸워왔다.

   ➲ 음영 처리된 문장의 내용은 쿠르드 민병대가 2013년에 시리아 북동쪽을 장악했다고 하였다. 이를 가장 잘 나타낸 문장은 (B)이다.

10. 지문에 따르면, 다음 중 쿠르디스탄에 대해 사실인 것은?
    (A) 혈전으로 인해 나뉘어졌다.
    (B) 많은 비(非) 쿠르인들의 조국이다.
    (C) 그것을 둘러싼 나라들에 의해 고통 받았다.
    (D) 오스만 왕국 시기 동안 단일국가였다.

    ➲ 지문에 따르면, 네 나라에 걸쳐 있는 쿠르디스탄은 여러 나라에 의해 대학살, 차별, 문화적 진압을 당했다. 따라서 답은 (C)이다.

11. 지문의 간단한 요약을 위해 도입 문장이 아래에 주어진다. 지문에서 가장 중요한 내용을 표현하는 세 개의 보기를 선택하여 요약문을 완성하라.

    쿠르드족은 쿠르드의 조국을 지배하는 네 나라에 분포되어 있는 소수 민족이다.

    보기
    (A) 쿠르드족에게는 그들만의 고유 문화가 있다.
    (B) 쿠르드족은 자주적이고 독립된 조국을 건립하려는 움직임을 시작했다.

(C) *Hilperke*는 쿠르드 춤과 노래의 형태이다.
(D) 100,000명이 넘는 쿠르드족이 터키에서 죽임을 당했다.
(E) 미군과 연합군이 북부 이라크가 독립하는 것을 도왔다.
(F) 오랜 기간 동안, 쿠르드족은 그들이 사는 나라에서 폭력과 차별에 직면했다.

➲ 지문은 쿠르드족이 사는 곳과 문화 등을 설명하고, 그들이 분포된 나라에서 박해 당했으며 여러 가지 사건을 통해 자치 국가를 설립하려는 전망이 보인다고 하였다. 따라서 (A), (F), (B)를 차례로 선택하면 된다.

정답	12. (A) 13. (B) 14. (D) 15. (B) 16. (D)
	17. (D) 18. B 19. (D) 20. (C) 21. (A)
	22. Sami Shamanism (A), (D), (E)
	Hmong Shamanism (B), (F), (H), (I)

샤머니즘

'샤머니즘'이라는 용어는 샤먼(주술사)이라고 불리는 개인들이 정신적인 영역과 소통하거나 상호작용하기 위해 가수(假睡) 상태로 들어가는, 다양한 문화권에 걸쳐 발견되는 관습을 뜻한다. 그 용어 자체는 최초로 터키와 몽골 고대 지역에서 특히 쓰였지만, 이후에 더 일반적으로 사용되어왔다.

그 의도와 모습이 아주 다양하기는 하지만, 주술 양식들에는 공통적인 요소들이 있다. 샤먼의 가장 중요한 역할은 산 자와 죽은 자의 세계 사이를 연결하는 다리가 되는 것이다. 일반적으로, 이것은 나쁜 것들로부터 지역사회를 지키거나 여러 가지 요인들로 고통 받는 개인들을 치유하기 위해 수행된다. 이 초자연적인 연결을 위해서 샤먼은 변조된 의식 상태로 들어가야 하는데, 환각제를 먹는 것에서부터 간단히 구호를 외치는 것까지 다양한 방법으로 행해진다.

A 사미족으로 알려진 북유럽의 민족은 18세기 초까지 샤머니즘을 행했다. B 그들은 그들을 신, 영혼, 그들 조상의 유령들과 교섭하는 곳인 최면 상태로 두기 위해 드럼과 플루트를 이용해 의식을 거행했다. C 그들의 노력을 통해 부족의 안녕이 보장되었다. 또한 사미족은 동물의 영혼, 특히 곰의 그것들을 숭상했다. D

사미족의 샤머니즘이 기독교로 교체된 지 오래되었지만, 중국 민족인 몽족은 오늘날에도 샤머니즘을 계속해서 행하고 있다. 그들은 특별한 신이 개인을 선별해 샤먼으로 삼는다고 믿는다. 트립닙이라고 알려진 이 샤먼들은 병을 치료하기 위해 금·은 종이를 태우고, 동물을 의식의 제물로 삼는 등 특별 의식을 진행한다. 이 샤먼들은 남자와 여자 모두 될 수 있고 지역사회에서 매우 존경 받는 경향이 있다.

몇몇 사람들은 샤머니즘을 과거에 원시적인 종교 관습으로 치부할 수도 있지만, 오늘날 현대 문화에서도 많은 이들은 치유, 편안, 그리고 죽은 자와 소통 방법으로 그것에 의지한다.

Glossary trance 가수(假睡) 상태 affliction 고통, 고통의 요인
intoxicant 취하게 하는 것

12. 지문의 주제는 무엇인가?
(A) 많은 문화에서 발견되는 샤머니즘은 우리의 세계를 영계로 연결하는 관습이다.
(B) 샤머니즘은 터키에서 시작하였지만, 샤먼이라는 사람들에 의해 세계로 퍼졌다.
(C) 종교로 불리긴 하지만, 샤머니즘은 사실 사회적인 현상이다.
(D) 과거에는 넓게 퍼져 있는 문화들을 연결하는 것이 샤먼의 일이었다.

➲ 지문은 샤머니즘의 정의와 함께 어떻게 행해지는지에 대해 설명하고 있다. 따라서 답은 (A)가 된다.

13. 지문에서 단어 realm을 대체하기에 가장 적합한 것은
(A) 방법   (B) 구역
(C) 유령   (D) 짜증

➲ realm은 '영역'이라는 뜻을 가지고 있다. 따라서 이를 대체하기에 가장 알맞은 것은 (B) territory이다.

14. 2단락에서 언급된 것은
(A) 샤먼들은 지역사회에서 규칙을 만든다.
(B) 샤머니즘은 몇몇의 바람직하지 않은 효과를 낳는다.
(C) 각기 다른 문화들의 샤먼들은 종종 교류한다.
(D) 세계 각지의 샤머니즘은 어떤 특징들을 공유한다.

➲ 작가는 2단락에서 샤먼의 역할과 샤머니즘이 행해지는 방법 등을 설명하고 있고, 이 단락의 주제 문장은 단락의 초반부에 명시되어 있다. 따라서 답은 (D)이다.

15. 아래 문장 중 지문에서 음영 처리된 문장의 핵심 정보를 가장 잘 나타낸 것은 어느 것인가? 잘못된 보기들은 중요한 의미를 바꾸거나 핵심 정보를 생략한다.
(A) 샤먼의 의식과 그들이 일반적으로 행동하는 방식 사이에는 직접적인 연결고리가 있다.
(B) 샤먼들은 다른 세계와 소통하기 위해 그들의 의식 상태를 바꾸는 여러 가지 방법을 쓴다.
(C) 다른 세계와 소통하고 난 후, 샤먼은 구호를 외치고 특수 약을 먹어 현실을 바꾼다.
(D) 구호를 외치는 것과 한각제를 마시는 것은 샤먼이 다른 사람들의 의식과 연결하고 세상을 인지하는 방식을 바꾸게 한다.

➲ 음영 처리된 문장의 내용은 샤먼이 환각제와 구호 등을 이용해서 다른 의식 상태가 되어 다른 세계를 접한다고 하였다. 이를 가장 잘 나타낸 문장은 (B)이다.

16. 지문에서 단어 venerated와 가장 비슷한 의미는
(A) 피했다   (B) 유예했다
(C) 포기했다   (D) 숭배했다

➲ 음영 처리된 단어 venerate는 '숭상하다'라는 뜻을 지니고 있다. 이와 가장 비슷한 단어는 '숭배하다'라는 뜻의 (D) worshiped이다.

17. 지문에서 단어 those가 가리키는 것은
(A) 신들   (B) 노력들
(C) 사미족   (D) 영혼들

● 음영 처리된 'they'의 선행절에서, 동물의 영혼들을 숭상한다고 하였다. 주어진 those는 '영혼들'을 대신하여 쓰였음을 알 수 있다.

18. 주어진 문장이 3단락에 들어갈 수 있는 곳을 가리키는 네 개의 네모 [■]를 보시오.

노에디라고 알려진 그들의 샤먼들은 저승 세계를 연결하는 중재인의 역할을 한다.

이 문장이 어디에 가장 적절한가?

● 주어진 문장은 사미족의 샤먼인 노에디에 관한 설명이며, 문장의 도입 부분에 있는 Their은 사미족을 지칭한다. 따라서 노에디의 역할이 소개되는 부분 바로 전인 B 에 위치하게 하는 것이 자연스럽다.

19. 티브 닙에 대해 추론할 수 있는 것은 무엇인가?
(A) 그들은 혼인이 금지되어 있다.
(B) 그들의 역할은 계속해서 바뀐다.
(C) 그들은 더 이상 몽 문화의 한 부분이 아니다.
(D) 그들은 탐나는 지위를 가지고 있다.

● 티브 닙이 몽족 사회에서 매우 존경 받는다는 사실을 통해, (D)의 내용을 추론할 수 있다.

20. 작가는 무엇을 나타내기 위해 지문에서 a primitive religious practice 를 언급하는가
(A) 샤머니즘은 일반적으로 장점보다 단점이 많았다.
(B) 다른 종교들이 샤머니즘을 대신했다.
(C) 어떤 사람들은 샤머니즘에 대해 좋지 않은 의견을 가지고 있다.
(D) 샤머니즘은 시간이 흐르면서 많이 바뀌었다.

● 작가는 마지막 단락에서 어떤 이들이 샤머니즘을 과거의 원시적인 종교 관습으로 무시하였다고 하였다. 이를 통해, 그들이 샤머니즘에 대해 좋지 않은 의견을 가지고 있음을 알 수 있다.

21. 지문에서 단어 it 이 가리키는 것은
(A) 샤머니즘   (B) 과거
(C) 현대 문화   (D) 치유

● 많은 이들이 치유하고, 편안함을 찾으며, 죽은 자와 소통하는 방법으로 '그것'에 의지한다는 것을 보아, it은 (A) shamanism을 가리킨다.

22. 보기에서 적당한 구를 찾아서 그것들과 관련된 카테고리에 넣어라.
보기 중에서 두 개는 사용되지 않을 것이다.

사미족 샤머니즘   /   몽족 샤머니즘

보기
(A) 최면 상태를 만들기 위해 악기들이 사용되었다.
(B) 양성(兩性) 모두 샤먼이 될 수 있었다.
(C) 샤먼들 사이에 경쟁이 있었다.
(D) 북유럽에서 샤머니즘을 행했다.
(E) 그들은 동물의 영혼을 숭배했다.
(F) 그들은 의식 중에 동물을 희생시켰다.
(G) 기독교를 기원으로 한다.
(H) 샤먼들은 티브 닙으로 알려졌다.
(I) 오늘날까지 행해진다.

● 지문에 따르면, 북유럽의 사미족은 드럼과 플루트 등을 통해 최면 상태에 빠졌고, 동물의 영혼을 숭배했다. 반면, 몽족은 남녀 모두 티브 닙이라고 불리는 샤먼이 될 수 있었고, 의식을 위해 동물을 희생시켰으며 오늘날에도 샤머니즘을 행하고 있다. 이 같은 사실에 따라 보기를 선택한다.

ACTUAL TEST
pp.184-195

정답 | 1. (B)   2. (C)   3. (D)   4. (A)   5. (A)
6. D   7. (C)   8. (B)   9. (B)   10. (A)
11. (D)   12. (D), (C), (F)

무술

로마 전쟁의 신 이름인 Mars(마르스)에서 유래된 단어인 'martial'은 '전투 또는 군사와 관련된'이라는 의미이다. 따라서 무술은 문자 그대로 전술 교육이라는 말이 된다. 유럽에서 이 용어는 일찍이 16세기에 펜싱과 같은 운동들을 나타내기 위해 사용되었다. 하지만 오늘날 그것은 일반적으로 실제 전투보다는 신체단련과 영성, 그리고 정신적 수양 면에 더 깊이 자리잡고 있는 태권도와 가라데 같은 동아시아의 싸움 기술을 위해 사용된다.

아시아 무술은 중국의 하 왕조까지 4,000년 이상을 거슬러 올라간다. 고대 중국의 전투 체계는 아마도 불교의 확산과 더불어 고대 인도의 그것들과 최종적으로 융합된 것이라고 믿어지고 있다. 한편, 유럽에서는 고대 그리스의 신체단련과 경쟁에 집중한 것이 종국에는 올림픽 게임이 되어 많은 유럽 무술의 토대가 되었다.

현대의 무술은 무기를 사용하는 수련법과 무기를 사용하지 않는 수련법으로 나뉠 수 있다. 무기를 사용하는 무술에는 유럽의 펜싱과 일본의 검도가 포함되는데, 둘 다 전통적으로 검술을 가르치기 위해 사용되었다. A 무기를 사용하지 않는 무술은 무기를 사용하는 것보다는 훨씬 더 인기가 많은데, 타격에 의존하는 것과 겨루기에 의존하는 것, 두 개 그룹으로 더 분류될 수 있다. B 타격은 주먹이나 편 손, 무릎 또는 발로 강타하는 것을 나타낸다. C 타격을 포함하는 무술은 또한 공격을 막아내는 기술도 가르치는데, 스탠드업 스타일이라고 불리기도 한다. D 이러한 기술들은 힘, 균형, 레버리지(신체 한 부분을 지탱하여 더 큰 힘을 내기), 그리고 서브미션 홀드(상대방에게 고통을 주기 위한 잡기방식)를 이용하는 것에 초점을 맞춘다.

사실상 모든 무술의 궁극적 목적은 수련자가 물리적 공격을 피하고, 공격자를 물리치는 능력을 증진시키는 것이다. 하지만 훈련 과정을 통해 일어나는 정신적이고 영적인, 심지어 철학적이기까지 한 발전이야말로 진정한 주안점임에 틀림없다. 예를 들어, 일본의 무술은 인간의 마음을 정화시키고 신체 내부 기의 적절한 흐름을

만들어내는 데 초점을 맞추고 있으므로, 불교적 영향을 강하게 받는다. 마찬가지로 한국의 무술은 명상의 개념과 내적인 평화 습득에 밀접한 연관이 있다.

무술 산업은 1970년대에 시작되어, 아시아 무술 영화의 성장하는 인기에 힘입어 급속히 팽창했다. 오늘날 무술은 모든 대륙과 모든 연령의 사람들에게 대단한 인기를 끌고 있다.

Glossary culminate ~로 끝나다

• Structure Zone

> • '~하는 것들'이라는 표현으로 those that[which] ~ 구문을 쓸 수 있다. 이때 those는 선행사이며 that[which]는 관계대명사이다. '~하는 사람들'은 those who ~가 된다.
>
> Unarmed martial arts, which are far more popular than their armed counterparts, can be further categorized into two smaller groups: **those that** rely on striking and **those that** emphasize grappling.
>
> • 분사구문에서 현재분사는 능동의 의미를, 과거분사는 수동의 의미를 나타낸다.
>
> **Beginning**(= the martial arts industry began…) in the 1970s, and **spurred**(= the martial arts industry was spurred…) by the growing popularity of Asian martial arts films, the martial arts industry began to expand in leaps and bounds.

1. 지문에서 단어 it 이 가리키는 것은
   (A) 유럽　　　　　(B) 용어
   (C) 세기　　　　　(D) 펜싱

   ● 지문에서 '그것'이 동아시아의 싸움 기술과 관련되어 사용된다고 하였으므로, '그것'은 martial art, 즉 무술이라는 용어를 나타낸다는 것을 알 수 있다.

2. 지문에서 단어 entrenched 를 대체하기에 가장 적합한 것은
   (A) 폐지된　　　　(B) 발굴된
   (C) 뿌리내린　　　(D) 추출된

   ● entrench는 '단단히 자리잡다'라는 의미이다. 따라서 이를 대체하기에 적절한 것은 '뿌리내리다'라는 의미를 지닌 (C) rooted이다.

3. 1단락에서 추론할 수 있는 것은 무엇인가?
   (A) '무술'이라는 용어는 16세기에 가장 많이 사용되었다.
   (B) 무술은 실제 전투에서는 사용되지 않는다.
   (C) 로마 전쟁의 신은 무술을 최초로 연마했다고 알려져 있다.
   (D) '무술'이라는 용어는 시간에 따라 나타내는 바가 바뀌었다.

   ● '무술'이라는 용어는 16세기 유럽에서는 펜싱과 같은 운동을, 현재는 동아시아의 싸움 기술인 태권도와 가라데를 나타내는 데 사용되므로, 시대마다 지칭하는 바가 다르다는 것을 알 수 있다. 따라서 (D)가 답이 된다.

4. 왜 작가는 Buddhism 을 언급하는가?
   (A) 중국과 인도의 무술이 만나게 된 가능한 원인을 제시하기 위해서
   (B) 왜 과거 인도 무술이 영성에 좀 더 초점을 맞췄는지 설명하기 위해서
   (C) 동양의 종교 교육과 서양 무술 훈련을 비교하기 위해서
   (D) 무술의 인기가 천천히 사라지기 시작했다는 것을 나타내기 위해서

   ● 인도의 불교가 널리 퍼졌다는 것은 인도와 고대 중국이 서로 문화적, 종교적으로 영향을 주고 받았다는 것을 의미하므로, 중국과 인도의 무술 또한 이러한 과정을 통해 융합하는 계기가 되었음을 알 수 있다.

5. 2단락에서 언급된 것은
   (A) 무술은 아시아와 유럽에서 독립적으로 발전했다.
   (B) 중국의 영향으로 그리스에서 올림픽이 발전했다.
   (C) 무술은 중국에서 인도를 거쳐 유럽까지 퍼졌다.
   (D) 고대 인도인들은 전투보다는 종교에 보다 더 초점을 두었다.

   ● 작가는 2단락에서 무술이 동양에서는 중국과 인도의 싸움 기술이 혼합하면서 발전했고, 유럽에서는 신체적 경쟁의 일환으로 발전했다고 언급했으므로, 무술은 아시아와 유럽에서 서로 영향을 받지 않고 독립적으로 발전했음을 알 수 있다.

6. 주어진 문장이 3단락에 들어갈 수 있는 곳을 가리키는 네 개의 네모 [■]를 보시오.

   반면에, 겨루기 무술은 지상 전투 스타일이라고 알려져 있다.

   이 문장이 어디에 가장 적절한가?

   ● 3단락에서는 무술을 타격과 겨루기로 나누어 설명하고 있다. 주어진 문장은 겨루기 무술에 대해 언급하고 있으므로, 이 내용은 타격 무술에 대한 설명이 끝나고 바로 연결되는 것이 두 무술을 비교 설명하는 방식으로 볼 때 가장 적합하다. 따라서 타격 무술에 대한 설명 바로 뒤인 D 위치가 답이 된다.

7. 겨루기 무술에 관해 사실이 아닌 것은 무엇인가?
   (A) 상대방을 잡는 것을 포함한다.
   (B) 무기를 사용하지 않는 무술로 분류된다.
   (C) 타격 공격을 방어하는 법에 조점을 맞춘다.
   (D) 힘과 균형의 사용이 요구된다.

   ● 타격 공격을 방어하는 것은 겨루기 무술이 아닌 타격 무술에 해당하는 것이므로 (C)가 정답이다.

8. 지문에서 어구 ward off 와 가장 비슷한 의미는
   (A) 모방하다　　　(B) 피하다
   (C) 무시하다　　　(D) 맡기다

   ● ward off는 '피하다, 막다'라는 의미이므로 '모면하다, 막다'라는 의미의 (B) deflect로 대체할 수 있다.

9. 아래 문장 중 지문에서 음영 처리된 문장의 핵심 정보를 가장 잘 나타낸 것은 어느 것인가? *잘못된* 보기들은 중요한 의미를 바꾸거나 핵심 정보를 생략한다.
   (A) 훈련과 발전에 초점을 맞춤으로서 무술 수련자는 집중력을 증진시킬 수 있다.
   (B) 개인의 정신적 발전이 무술의 실제 목적이라고 말할 수 있다.
   (C) 많은 사람들은 어떤 무술이 영적, 그리고 정신적 발달에 가장 좋은지를 논쟁한다.
   (D) 어떤 종류의 발전이 무술을 배우는 데 가장 적합한지는 아무도 모른다.

   ◉ 지문의 음영 처리된 문장에서는 무술 수련 과정을 통해 정신적, 영적, 철학적으로 발전할 수 있으며, 이러한 발전이야말로 무술의 가장 중요한 핵심이라 했으므로, (B)가 문장의 핵심 정보에 가장 가깝다.

10. 왜 작가는 지문에서 martial arts films를 언급하는가?
    (A) 무술에 대한 관심이 커지고 있는 이유를 제시하기 위해서
    (B) 무술에 대한 보편적인 오해를 나타내기 위해서
    (C) 실제로 무술을 단련하는 사람은 거의 없다는 것을 제시하기 위해서
    (D) 1970년대에 무술이 극적으로 변화한 이유를 설명하기 위해서

    ◉ 무술 영화의 인기와 더불어 사람들의 무술에 대한 관심도 커졌으므로, 이를 나타내기 위해 언급했음을 알 수 있다.

11. 다음 중 사실이 아닌 것은
    (A) 단어 'martial'은 로마 전쟁의 신에서 기인했다.
    (B) 고대 그리스인들은 운동과 신체적 경쟁을 즐겼다.
    (C) 펜싱과 검도는 모두 검술을 가르친다.
    (D) 유럽 무술은 불교의 영향을 받았다.

    ◉ 불교의 영향을 받은 것은 유럽 무술이 아니라, 아시아 무술이므로 (D)가 사실이 아니다.

12. 지문의 간단한 요약을 위해 도입 문장이 아래에 주어진다. 지문에서 가장 중요한 내용을 표현하는 세 개의 보기를 선택하여 요약문을 완성하라.

    무술은 전술을 교육하는 것이다.

    보기
    (A) 최초의 무술은 로마 전쟁의 신에게 바치는 것이었다.
    (B) 무술은 일본의 검도와 유럽의 펜싱을 포함한다.
    (C) 무술은 다양한 범주들로 나뉘어질 수 있다.
    (D) 무술은 고대 중국, 인도, 그리고 그리스에서 발달되었다.
    (E) 1970년대에 무술 영화는 상당한 인기를 끌게 되었다.
    (F) 신체적인 방어와 개인적인 발전이 무술의 주안점이다.

    ◉ 지문은 무술이 전술 교육의 한 형태로 고대 중국과 인도, 그리스에서 발달되었으며, 무기를 사용하는 무술과 무기를 사용하지 않는 무술로 나뉜다고 설명하고 있다. 또한 무술의 궁극적 목적은 자신의 몸을 보호하고 수련 과정에서 정신적으로도 발전할 수 있는 계기가 된다고 하였으므로 (D), (C), (F)를 차례로 선택하면 된다.

정답	13. (B)	14. (A)	15. (D)	16. (C)	17. (B)
	18. (A)	19. C	20. (B)	21. (D)	22. (D)
	23. (C)	22. School of Fontainebleau (C), (E), (F), (H)			
		Barbizon School (A), (G), (I)			

두 예술 학파

북부 중앙 프랑스에는 바르비종이라는 작은 마을이 광활한 퐁텐블로 숲의 가장자리에 자리잡고 있다. 이 지역의 수수한 모습과는 달리, 이곳은 두 개의 중요 예술 운동의 중심 역할을 해오고 있다.

이들 중 첫 번째 것은 퐁텐블로파라고 알려진 것으로 두 시기에 걸쳐 진행되었다. 첫 번째 시기는 1531년에 시작되었는데, 대부분의 관련 화가들은 Rosso Fiorentino(로소 피오렌티노)와 Francesco Primaticcio(프란체스코 프리미티치오)를 포함한 이탈리아인들이었다. 그들은 프랑스 왕인 Francis 1세에게 초청되어 퐁텐블로 숲에 위치한 사냥용 숙소와 관련된 일을 하였다. 왕의 목표는 위대한 화가와 건축가들을 불러모아 그것을 화려한 왕궁으로 개조하는 것이었다.

그 이탈리아인들은 매너리즘 화가들로 Michelangelo의 스타일에 강한 영향을 받았다. 그들의 작품은 치장 벽토를 많이 사용하는 특징이 있었으며, 밝은 색채와 강한 선을 표현한 그들의 그림에는 주로 가늘고 긴 인물이 포함되었다. 1584년부터 1594년까지, 계속되는 종교전쟁으로 인해 작업은 방치되었다. 폭력이 종식되자 새로운 화가 집단이 모여서 개조를 계속했다. 이 제2학파는 주로 프랑스와 플랑드르 화가들이었으며, 제1학파와 스타일은 유사하지만, 그들의 작품은 구성에 있어 더 깊이가 있었으며, 빛과 그림자 사이에 더 강한 대조가 나타났다.

A 그 지역의 두 번째 예술 운동은 수세기 이후에 두각을 나타내어 대략 1830년부터 1870년까지 존재하였다. **B** 후에 바르비종파라는 이름이 붙은 이 운동의 시작은 1824년 파리의 John Constable(존 콘스타블) 그림 전시회에서 찾아볼 수 있다. **C** 역사적으로 중요한 장면들을 그리는 것을 고집했던 전 시대를 따르는 대신, 그들은 자연에 초점을 맞추기 시작하여 야외에서 그림을 그리고자 도시 밖으로 여행했는데, 퐁텐블로 숲이 가장 선호되는 지역이었다. **D**

1848년의 유럽 혁명 기간 동안, Théodore Rousseau(테오도르 루소)와 Jean-François Millet(장프랑수아 밀레)를 포함한 이 많은 젊은 화가들은 모두 파리를 벗어나 바르비종 마을에 모이게 되었다. 그곳에서 그들은 풍경을 그리는 것에 계속해서 초점을 맞추었지만, 많은 작품 속에 주로 농부와 소작농 같은 인물들도 넣기 시작했다. 바르비종파는 Monet(모네)와 Renoir(르느와르)를 포함하여 많은 젊은 화가들에게 영향을 주었으며, 이들은 추후 위대한 예술 운동인 인상주의를 만들어냈다.

오늘날 바르비종과 퐁텐블로는 인기 있는 관광지이다. 마을은 많은 화랑들의 본고장이지만 당대의 예술보다는 그 지역의 유명한 과거를 기념하는 데 초점이 더 맞추어진다.

Glossary stucco 치장 벽토 dub 별명을 붙이다

• **Structure Zone**

> • despite과 instead of는 '~임에도 불구하고'라는 뜻으로 접속사 although와 뜻이 같으나, 둘은 접속사가 아닌 전치사(구)이므로 뒤에 문장이 아닌 명사(구)가 나온다.
> **Despite** this region's unassuming appearance, it has ...
> **Instead of** following the period's rigid insistence on painting scenes of historical importance, they began ...

13. 지문의 주제는 무엇인가?
    (A) 프랑스는 많은 예술 운동의 현장이다.
    (B) 두 개의 예술 운동이 같은 시골 지역에서 일어났다.
    (C) 두 개의 경쟁 예술 학파가 프랑스 마을에서 생겨났다.
    (D) 바르비종은 많은 화가 학교의 본고장이다.

    ◎ 지문에서는 프랑스의 퐁텐블로파와 바르비종파를 언급하면서 두 학파가 같은 지역에서 생겨나게 된 역사적 배경에 대해 설명하고 있으므로, (B)가 정답이 된다.

14. 지문에서 단어 it이 가리키는 것은
    (A) 숙소   (B) 숲
    (C) 왕   (D) 목표

    ◎ 왕은 예술가와 건축가를 모아서 이것을 화려한 왕궁으로 개조하려 했으므로, '그것'은 사냥꾼들의 숙소임을 알 수 있다.

15. 왜 작가는 지문에서 Wars of Religion을 언급하는가?
    (A) 그것이 Francis 1세의 탐욕에 따른 결과라는 것을 제시하기 위해서
    (B) 퐁텐블로에 초청된 것이 왜 대부분 이탈리아 예술인들이었는지 보여주기 위해서
    (C) 그 운동의 예술적 주제에 대한 예를 제시하기 위해서
    (D) 제1학파와 제2학파의 공백을 설명하기 위해서

    ◎ 종교 전쟁을 거치는 동안 제1학파의 작업이 중단되고, 그 후에 제2학파가 나타났으므로, 종교 전쟁은 두 학파의 공백을 설명하기 위한 것임을 알 수 있다.

16. 지문에서 단어 cessation을 대체하기에 가장 적합한 것은
    (A) 연락   (B) 확대
    (C) 중지   (D) 보급

    ◎ cessation은 '중단, 중지'라는 뜻으로 '중지'라는 뜻의 termination으로 대체할 수 있다.

17. 아래 문장 중 지문에서 음영 처리된 문장의 핵심 정보를 가장 잘 나타낸 것은 어느 것인가? *잘못된* 보기들은 중요한 의미를 바꾸거나 핵심 정보를 생략한다.
    (A) 그 학파의 프랑스 화가들은 플랑드르 화가들보다 깊이와 대조에 더 초점을 맞추었다.
    (B) 제2학파의 작품은 제1학파의 것과 닮았지만, 더 깊이 있고 더 대조적이다.
    (C) 프랑스와 플랑드르 예술은 제1학파 화가들의 작품과 더욱 닮았다.
    (D) 제1학파의 화가들은 제2학파의 화가들에게 구성의 깊이를 증진시키기 위해 빛을 사용하도록 가르쳤다.

    ◎ 음영 처리된 문장에서는 제2학파의 작품들이 스타일 면에서는 제1학파의 그림들과 닮았지만, 구성요소가 더욱 깊어지고 빛과 그림자의 대조 또한 더욱 강해졌음을 말하고 있다. 따라서 (B)가 답이 된다.

18. 다음 중 제2퐁텐블로파에 대해 사실이 아닌 것은 무엇인가?
    (A) 이것은 제1학파로부터 수세기 이후에 발생했다.
    (B) 이것은 제1학파와 비슷한 스타일을 가진다.
    (C) 이것은 빛과 어둠의 대조에 보다 더 초점을 맞추었다.
    (D) 이것은 주로 플랑드르와 프랑스 화가들로 구성되었다.

    ◎ 퐁텐블로파는 종교전쟁 이전과 이후 두 시대에 걸쳐 완성된 학파인데 제1학파는 1531에 제2학파는 종교전쟁이 끝난 1594년 이후에 시작되었다. 제1학파로부터 수세기 이후에 발생된 것은 바르비종파이므로 (A)는 사실이 아니다.

19. 주어진 문장이 4단락에 들어갈 수 있는 곳을 가리키는 네 개의 네모 [■]를 보시오.

    > Constable의 시골 주제는 많은 젊은 파리 화가들이 그 당시의 인기 있는 예술기법이었던 형식주의를 버리게 했다.

    이 문장이 어디에 가장 적절한가?

    ◎ 주어진 문장은 파리의 젊은 화가들이 Constable의 영향으로 형식주의를 버리게 된 이유를 제시하는 것이므로, Constable의 그림 전시회에서 바르비종파가 처음 소개되었다는 내용 뒤에 연결되는 것이 가장 자연스럽다.

20. 1848년 유럽 혁명에 대해 무엇을 추론할 수 있는가?
    (A) 프랑스와 이탈리아의 갈등에 의해 초래되었다.
    (B) 화가들이 파리 이외의 다른 곳에서 살기를 원하게 하였다.
    (C) 종교 혁명에 그 기원을 두었다.
    (D) 대개 시골 지역에서 발생했다.

    ◎ 유럽 혁명 기간 동안 많은 젊은 화가들이 파리를 떠나 바르비종 마을에 모여 살면서 시골 풍경을 그렸다고 했으므로, 그 당시에 화가들이 파리 이외의 다른 지역에서도 활동했음을 알 수 있다.

21. 바르비종파에 대해 사실이 아닌 것은 무엇인가?
    (A) 19세기 동안에 존재했다.
    (B) Monet와 Renoir에게 영향을 미쳤다.
    (C) 자연적 주제에 초점을 맞추었다.
    (D) 인상주의에 반대했다.

    ◎ 바르비종파는 후에 Monet와 Renoir를 포함한 많은 젊은 화가들에게 영향을 주었으며, 그들이 인상주의를 만들어 냈으므로 (D)는 사실이 아니다.

22. 지문에서 단어 storied와 의미가 가장 가까운 것은
    (A) 부끄러운   (B) 과장된
    (C) 다층의   (D) 저명한

> storied는 '유명한'이라는 뜻으로 '저명한'이라는 뜻의 illustrious가 가장 비슷하다.

23. 지문에서 언급되지 않은 것은 무엇인가?
    (A) 바르비종과 퐁텐블로 숲은 가까이 있다.
    (B) Michelangelo는 퐁텐블로 제1학파 화가들에게 영향을 주었다.
    (C) John Constable은 바르비종파의 창립 멤버이다.
    (D) 인상주의가 바르비종파 예술 운동을 뒤따랐다.

    > John Constable의 그림들이 바르비종파가 시작하게 된 계기가 된 것은 맞지만, 그가 바르비종파의 창립 멤버라는 언급은 지문에 없으므로 (C)가 답이다.

24. 보기에서 적당한 구를 찾아서 그것들과 관련된 카테고리에 넣어라. 보기 중에서 두 개는 사용되지 않을 것이다.

    퐁텐블로파   /   바르비종파

    보기
    (A) John Constable에 의해 영감을 받았다.
    (B) 주로 귀족들을 그렸다.
    (C) 이탈리아 매너리즘 화가들을 포함했다.
    (D) 형식주의의 발흥으로 이어졌다.
    (E) 가늘고 긴 인체를 표현했다.
    (F) 치장용 벽토를 사용하는 경향이 있었다.
    (G) 야외에서 그림을 그렸다.
    (H) 프랑스 왕을 위해 일했던 화가들을 포함했다.
    (I) 19세기에 나타났다.

    > 지문에 따르면 퐁텐블로파는 프랑스 왕에 의해 초청된 화가들을 주축으로 이탈리아 매너리스트를 포함했는데, 그들은 주로 치장용 벽토를 사용하는 경향이 많았으며, 가늘고 긴 인체를 그림 속에 표현했다. 19세기에 시작된 바르비종파는 John Constable의 풍경 그림에 영감을 받은 것으로, 시골의 자연 같은 야외 풍경을 주로 그렸으며, 인상주의 화가들에게 영향을 주었다. 이를 바탕으로 해당 문구를 답으로 고른다.

정답	25. (A)	26. (B)	27. (C)	28. (B)	29. (D)
	30. C	31. (A)	32. (A)	33. (C)	34. (C)
	35. (A)	36. (D), (F), (A)			

Kepler(케플러)의 법칙

Johannes Kepler(요하네스 케플러)는 16세기 후반부터 17세기 초반까지 태양계의 행성 운동 배후의 역학들을 발견하는 데 집중했던 독일의 수학자이다. 그는 존경 받는 덴마크 천문학자인 Tycho Brahe(티코 브라헤)의 조수로서 그와 긴밀히 작업했는데, 그는 결국 실질적으로 Kepler의 멘토 역할을 했었다.

1601년 Brahe가 사망하고 나서 Kepler는 그의 후임으로 신성 로마 제국의 왕실 수학자가 되었다. 그는 천문학자(Tycho Brahe)가 공들여 모아놓은 정보와 세부적인 관측 자료들을 이용하여, 행성 운동에 관한 세 개의 법칙을 발전시켰다. 대부분의 과학적 지식에 있어 Kepler가 위대한 공헌을 했다고 여겨지는 이 법칙들은, 후에 Isaac Newton으로 하여금 그의 유명한 만유인력의 법칙을 정립하게 하였다.

A 타원궤도의 법칙이라고 알려진 Kepler의 제1법칙은 태양을 공전하는 행성이 지나가는 길이 원보다는 타원의 모양에 가깝다는 것을 나타낸다. B 원들이 하나의 중심점으로부터 모든 지점간의 거리가 일정한데 반해, 타원은 두 개의 중심점을 가진다. C 이 법칙은 다른 공전하는 천체들에 적용시켜도 입증되어 왔다. D

일반적으로 면적 속도 일정의 법칙이라고 알려진 제2법칙은 가상의 선을 태양의 중심에서 공전하는 행성의 중심으로 연결했을 때, 그것이 동일한 시간에 동일한 공간을 지나면서 이동한다는 것이다. 행성이 태양 주위를 자체의 궤도에서 공전할 때 변화무쌍한 속도로 이동하기 때문에 이 사실은 매우 중요하다. 각 행성과 태양 간의 거리가 짧을수록 속도는 더 빨라진다.

마지막으로, 조화의 법칙이라고 알려진 Kepler의 제3법칙이 있다. 제1법칙과 제2법칙이 발표된 지 약 10년 후인 1619년에 발표된 이 법칙은, 주어진 두 행성의 공전 주기의 제곱은 태양의 평균 거리의 세제곱과 같다는 것이다.

이 법칙들 배후에 있는 Kepler의 추론이 더 이상 타당하다고 여겨지지는 않지만, 이 법칙들 자체는 정확하고 또한 대단히 중요하다. Newton의 차후 이론들과 더불어 Kepler의 세 법칙은 현대 천문학과 현대 물리학 기초의 핵심일 뿐 아니라, 17세기 과학 혁명의 기폭제로 여겨지기도 한다.

Glossary ellipse 타원 focal point 중심점

25. 지문에서 단어 his가 가리키는 것은
    (A) Tycho Brahe
    (B) Johannes Kepler
    (C) Isaac Newton
    (D) 황제

    > Kepler는 Tycho Brahe의 사망 후 왕립 수학자로서의 그의 역할을 승계 받았다고 했으므로, his는 Tycho Brahe를 나타낸다.

26. 2단락에 따르면
    (A) Newton은 처음에는 Kepler의 생각에 동의하지 않았다.
    (B) Brahe의 연구는 Kepler의 세 법칙의 기초가 되었다.
    (C) Kepler는 Brahe의 사망 후에 수학을 그만두었다.
    (D) 신성 로마 제국은 Kepler를 Newton에게 소개했다.

    > 2단락에서는 Tycho Brahe가 사망한 후 그가 남긴 연구 자료와 관측 자료를 이용해 Kepler가 행성 이동에 관한 세 개의 법칙을 세웠다고 밝히고 있다. 따라서 (B)가 답이 된다.

27. Johannes Kepler에 대해 사실이 아닌 것은 무엇인가?
    (A) 그는 Tycho Brahe를 위해 일했다.
    (B) 그는 왕실 수학자로 일했다.
    (C) 그는 중력의 법칙을 제시했다.
    (D) 그는 행성의 운동을 연구했다.

    > 중력의 법칙을 발견한 것은 Kepler가 아니라 Isaac Newton이므로 (C)는 사실이 아니다.

28. Isaac Newton에 대해 추론할 수 있는 것은 무엇인가?
    (A) 그는 Kepler의 법칙 중 하나가 정확하지 않다는 것을 입증했다.
    (B) 그는 Johannes Kepler의 작업을 연구했다.
    (C) 그는 한때 Tycho Brahe의 멘토였다.
    (D) 그는 Johannes Kepler와 라이벌이었다.

    ● 행성의 이동에 대한 Kepler의 법칙이 Newton의 만유인력의 법칙 발견에 영향을 주었다고 했으므로, Newton은 Kepler의 작업을 충분히 연구했음을 추론할 수 있다.

29. 왜 작가는 circles 를 언급하는가?
    (A) 대부분의 행성의 모양을 묘사하기 위해서
    (B) 햇빛이 곡선 이동하는 이유를 설명하기 위해서
    (C) 태양계가 어떻게 팽창했는지를 보여주기 위해서
    (D) 타원과 그 모양을 비교하기 위해서

    ● Kepler의 제1법칙에서 행성들은 태양 주위를 타원 궤도로 공전한다고 했는데, 타원은 원과 달리 중심점이 하나가 아닌 두 개인 차이가 있으므로, 타원의 특징을 원과 대조하여 설명하고자 원을 언급했다고 할 수 있다.

30. 주어진 문장이 3단락에 들어갈 수 있는 곳을 가리키는 네 개의 네모 [■]를 보시오.
    행성의 공전 궤도에서 이 두 지점 중 하나는 필수적으로 태양이 될 것이다.
    이 문장이 어디에 가장 적절한가?

    ● 주어진 문장에서는 두 지점 중의 하나가 태양이라고 했으므로 두 지점이 무엇을 의미하는지가 그 앞에 나와야 한다. C 앞 문장에서 타원이 두 중심점을 가진다고 했으므로, 주어진 문장은 C 자리에 들어가는 것이 가장 자연스럽다.

31. 지문에서 it 이 가리키는 것은
    (A) 선   (B) 중심
    (C) 태양   (D) 행성

    ● 문장에서 it은 행성이 이동할 때 동일 시간에 동일 공간을 통과한다고 했으므로, 이것은 주절 문장에서 언급한 태양의 중심에서 공전하는 행성의 중심으로 그어지는 가상의 선임을 알 수 있다.

32. 지문에서 fluctuating 을 대체하기에 가장 적합한 것은
    (A) 다양한   (B) 줄어드는
    (C) 놀라운   (D) 가속하는

    ● fluctuating은 '변화무쌍한, 다른'이라는 뜻으로 '다양한'이라는 의미의 varying으로 대체할 수 있다.

33. 아래 문장 중 지문에서 음영 처리된 문장의 핵심 정보를 가장 잘 나타낸 것은 어느 것인가? 잘못된 보기들은 중요한 의미를 바꾸거나 핵심 정보를 생략한다.
    (A) 그의 법칙이 틀리다고 입증되었지만, Kepler는 아직도 존경받고 있다.
    (B) Kepler의 법칙이 잊혀진 이유는 그것들이 타당하지 않기 때문이다.
    (C) Kepler의 법칙은 여전히 정확하다고 여겨지지만, 그의 추론은 그렇지 않다.
    (D) Kepler는 보다 더 정확한 개념을 위해 그의 법칙들을 포기했다.

    ● Kepler의 법칙이 그 자체로는 정확하고 과학적으로도 중요하지만, Kepler가 그 법칙을 발견하기 위해 배후에서 추론한 것들은 타당하지 않다고 했으므로, (C)의 내용이 해당 문장의 핵심 정보라 할 수 있다.

34. 지문에서 단어 catalyst 와 가장 비슷한 의미는
    (A) 과학자   (B) 카타르시스
    (C) 도화선   (D) 남은 것

    ● catalyst는 '기폭제'라는 뜻으로 (C) trigger가 가장 비슷한 의미를 지니고 있다.

35. 6단락에서 작가의 주요 목적은
    (A) Kepler 연구의 중요성을 강조하는 것이다.
    (B) Kepler의 추론이 왜 틀렸는지를 설명하는 것이다.
    (C) Kepler와 Newton의 유산을 대조하는 것이다.
    (D) Kepler가 오해 받아왔다는 것을 제시하는 것이다.

    ● 6단락에서는 Kepler의 법칙이 현대 천문학과 현대 물리학의 기초가 되었을 뿐 아니라, 17세기 과학 혁명의 기폭제가 되기까지 했다고 언급하고 있으므로, 6단락의 목적은 Kepler 연구의 중요성을 강조하기 위함이라고 말할 수 있다.

36. 지문의 간단한 요약을 위해 도입 문장이 아래에 주어진다. 지문에서 가장 중요한 내용을 표현하는 세 개의 보기를 선택하여 요약문을 완성하라.
    Johannes Kepler는 영향력이 높은 독일 수학자이다.

    보기
    (A) Kepler의 연구는 과학 혁명에서 중요한 역할을 했으며, 현대 천문학과 현대 물리학에 영향을 주었다.
    (B) 면적 속도 일정의 법칙은 행성이 다른 속도로 태양을 공전한다는 것이다.
    (C) Kepler는 처음 두 개의 법칙 이후 10년 만에 세 번째 법칙을 냈다.
    (D) Tycho Brahe는 Kepler의 멘토가 되었으며, 그는 (Tycho Brahe의) 뒤를 이어 왕실 수학자가 되었다.
    (E) Kepler와 Newton은 가까이 함께 일했으며 서로에게 영향을 주었다.
    (F) Kepler는 행성 운동의 세 법칙을 고안해냈는데, 그것들은 타원 궤도의 법칙, 면적 속도 일정의 법칙, 조화의 법칙이다.

    ● 지문에서는 Kepler가 영향력 있는 독일의 위대한 수학자로 Tycho Brahe의 조수로 일하면서, Brahe 사후 왕실 수학자로서의 자리를 승계 받아 그의 연구를 밑바탕으로, 과학사에 중요한 자리를 차지하고 있는 세 개의 법칙을 발견했다고 말하고 있다. 타원 궤도의 법칙, 면적 속도 일정의 법칙, 조화의 법칙이라고 알려진 Kepler의 세 개 법칙은 과학 혁명에서 하나의 기폭제가 되었으며, 현대 천문학과 현대 물리학의 기초가 되었다. 이와 같은 내용을 바탕으로 해당 문장을 순서대로 고른다.

TOEFL iBT® Codebreaker
Reading Basic